The Fundamentals of Ethics

The Fundamentals of Ethics

Sixth Edition

RUSS SHAFER-LANDAU
University of Wisconsin-Madison

OXFORD
UNIVERSITY PRESS

OXFORD
UNIVERSITY PRESS

Oxford University Press is a department of the University of Oxford.
It furthers the University's objective of excellence in research, scholarship,
and education by publishing worldwide. Oxford is a registered trade mark
of Oxford University Press in the UK and in certain other countries.

Published in the United States of America by Oxford University Press
198 Madison Avenue, New York, NY 10016, United States of America.

Library of Congress Cataloging-in-Publication Data

Names: Shafer-Landau, Russ, author.
Title: Fundamentals of ethics / Russ Shafer-Landau, University of
    Wisconsin-Madison.
Identifiers: LCCN 2023013831 (print) | LCCN 2023013832 (ebook) | ISBN
    9780197697474 (paperback) | ISBN 9780197697498 (epub)
Subjects: LCSH: Ethics.
Classification: LCC BJ1012 .S43 2024 (print) | LCC BJ1012 (ebook) | DDC
    170—dc23/eng/20230508
LC record available at https://lccn.loc.gov/2023013831
LC ebook record available at https://lccn.loc.gov/2023013832

Printed by Quad/Graphics, Inc., Mexico

A father's greatest pleasure:

Pride in his children's character
Joy in their company

To my darlings

Max and Sophie

CONTENTS

.... ❧ ....

PART TWO

Normative Ethics: Doing the Right Thing

PART THREE

Metaethics: The Status of Morality

PREFACE

············ ❧ ············

This book is divided into three parts—one on the Good Life, another on Doing the Right Thing, and the last on the Status of Morality. You can read these parts in any order. Many will want to begin at the end, for instance, with a discussion of whether morality is a human invention, or is in some way objective. Some will prefer to start in the middle, asking about the supreme principle of morality (and whether there is any such thing). And others may want to begin at the beginning, by thinking about human well-being and the quality of life. Each part can be understood independently of the others, though there are of course many points of connection across the three main branches of moral philosophy. No matter where you begin, there are footnotes in most chapters that provide cross-references to relevant discussions elsewhere in the book.

When beginning a new area of study, you're bound to encounter some unfamiliar jargon. I've tried to keep this to a minimum, and I suppose that you can be thankful that we're doing ethics here, rather than physics or anatomy. I define each technical term when I first use it, and have also put together a glossary, which appears at the end of the book. Each specialized term that appears in **boldface** has an entry there.

You may be interested enough in what you read here that you'll want to continue your studies in moral philosophy. There is a natural place to begin—the companion volume to this book, *The Ethical Life*, described later in this preface. I have also compiled a list of Suggestions for Further

Reading for each chapter or pair of chapters. This list appears at the end of the book, just before the index. I have selected the readings with an eye to what might be accessible and interesting to those just beginning their study of moral philosophy.

There is so much that is fascinating about ethics. This tempts a textbook author to go on and on. And yet there are page limits that must be respected. Deciding what to keep and what to leave on the editing floor has been a real challenge. Perhaps you think that the balance hasn't always been well struck. Perhaps you find certain discussions unclear or boring. I'd like to know about this. The best way to get in touch is by e-mail: Russ-Shaferlandau@gmail.com.

New to the Sixth Edition

I'm very pleased that students and instructors have found this book useful enough to warrant a new edition. I have made numerous small changes in the hopes of improving clarity and accuracy. Substantive improvements have been made to many sections, including:

- What Is Morality? in the Introduction
- Opening of chapter 3
- The Appeal to Self-Evidence in chapter 16
- Self-Evidence and the Testing of Moral Theories in chapter 16
- Two Kinds of Ethical Relativism in chapter 19
- Error Theory: The Theory and Its Attractions in chapter 20
- Expressivism: The Theory and Its Attractions in chapter 20
- Hume's Argument in chapter 22

I have also introduced four new sections:

- Moral Conduct Is Rational Only If God Exists in chapter 5
- A new opening section of chapter 15
- Two Assumptions in chapter 16
- Ethical Objectivism: The Theory and Its Attractions in chapter 21

The comprehensive **Oxford Learning Link** associated with this book has been updated, as has its **Instructor's Manual**. These resources contain loads of helpful material—so much so that they deserve a brief summary all their own.

Digital Resources and Oxford Learning Link

Oxford University Press offers a variety of digital solutions that:

- Engage your students in the required reading
- Make assigned content available on the first day of class
- Provide the required resources available at the lowest cost possible

Inclusive Access

Your institution may already have an Inclusive Access (IA) program in place in which students pay for their course materials through their course registration. https://pages.oup.com/he/us/oup-inclusiveaccess.

Through IA, rather than relying on individual student purchases, digital products are delivered directly to an entire class of students through their LMS (Learning Management System) at the most affordable price, increasing the use of our products.

Our partnerships with major higher education bookstore retailers and e-learning delivery leaders make it possible for students to easily and quickly access affordable content on the first day of class.

With Inclusive Access, you can:

- Provide students with course material on **Day One**
- Make course material **more affordable**—students **save as much as 70%**
- **Increase engagement** with immersive, engaging digital content
- **Enjoy academic freedom**—virtually any content can be adopted for use in Inclusive Access
- **Improve student success and retention** with analytical tools and insights

How Does It Work?

All students are given access to digital course materials on day one of classes through your school's Learning Management System. For more information, please visit https://pages.oup.com/he/us/oup-inclusiveaccess.

Direct to Student purchasing:

Now available! Students can purchase their course materials directly from OUP at the lowest retail price available. Please visit https://global.oup.com/ushe/?cc=us&lang=en. Search for the book in use by author name or book title.

E-book solutions for students:

OUP partners with the largest e-book providers so that students have access to course content anytime, anywhere.

Oxford University Press philosophy titles are available through major publishing e-book vendors:

Perusall

Perusall is a collaborative reading and learning platform that prepares students for class. The platform incorporates a unique e-book reader with social annotation tools that motivate students to actively participate in their learning, come to class prepared, and become more engaged with the course content you assign. For instructors, Perusall will help you teach more effectively, understand student misconceptions prior to class, introduce active learning strategies, and save time. Find out more at perusall.com.

RedShelf

As one of the nation's leading edtech companies, RedShelf has helped thousands of colleges, businesses, and publishers transition effortlessly from traditional print to more affordable, efficient digital textbooks and learning content.

Offering a vast catalog of titles on our award-winning eReader, plus an end-to-end Content Delivery System to streamline every step in the distribution process, RedShelf is a premier e-book partner.

Award-Winning eReader

All of the digital books are delivered on the award-winning RedShelf eReader, packed with built-in study tools including highlighting, definitions, text-to-speech, flashcards, note-sharing, and more. Please visit https://www.about.redshelf.com/home.

VitalSource

VitalSource is a leading authority in digital course materials, e-Textbooks, and student savings. Bookshelf® by VitalSource is the world's leading eReader, preferred by thousands of institutions and millions of students in 240+ countries and territories for reading, studying and succeeding.

Partnering with publishers and institutions since 1994, VitalSource has the most extensive academic digital content catalog available and are at the forefront in setting privacy and security standards to protect learners around the world.

Features include: online/offline access, text to speech tool, study tools (such as highlighting, flashcard creation, notes, etc.). Please go to https://www.vitalsource.com/.

Oxford Learning Link

Oxford Learning Link delivers a wealth of engaging digital learning tools and resources to help both instructors and students get the most of their Oxford University Press title. Students can access self-study resources and instructors can view instructor resources at **https://learninglink.oup.com/access/shafer-landau-fundamentals6e**.

Enhanced E-book

Included in Oxford Learning Link, Oxford's Enhanced e-books combine high-quality text content with a rich assortment of integrated multimedia and practice questions to deliver a more engaging and interactive learning experience.

The Enhanced e-book version of *The Ethical Life* is available via RedShelf, VitalSource, Perusall, and other leading higher education e-book vendors.

Oxford Learning Link for *The Ethical Life* includes the following resources.

Instructor Resources

- **Test Bank**—over 150 test questions in multiple choice, short answer, and essay formats
- **Instructor's Manual**—includes learning objectives, chapter outlines, lecture suggestions, class activity suggestions, issues for discussion, video resources, and Internet resources
- **Lecture PowerPoints**—presentations for course instruction, enabling instructors and/or lecturers to spend less time preparing class materials and more time with students

Student Resources

- **Enhanced E-book**—contains section-level practice quizzes, topical videos, and chapter summaries
- **Chapter Quizzes**—assignable multiple-choice questions to evaluate chapter comprehension

- **Video Quizzes**—short assessments capturing students' understanding and application of key concepts
- **Learning Objectives and Key Concepts**—to guide study and reinforce reading comprehension
- **Web Activities**—for thematic chapters and country profiles, suggested activities to familiarize students with today's major comparative politics sources and databases

A Note on the Companion Volume

There are two kinds of introductory books. One is the sort that you have in your hands right now. It's one person's take on the subject, and your fate, dear reader, depends on how reliable and engaging that author happens to be. I have tried to be both, but you will have to be the judge of that. There are benefits to a single-authored book. At its best, you'll get a coherent narrative that draws connections between various discussions. You'll be handed the important highlights, be introduced to the really big ideas, and get an accurate map of the relevant terrain.

But there is another approach, equally valid. And that is to hear what the major figures in the area have to say, to familiarize yourself with the original voices in the field. For those with an interest in going this route, I have put together a companion volume, *The Ethical Life: Fundamental Readings in Ethics and Moral Problems*, which allows you to do just that.

The Ethical Life gathers together readings from more than forty authors on the main subjects that are covered here. There are many entries on the good life, on the central ethical theories, and on the status of morality. There are also about thirty additional readings on pressing moral problems, such as the death penalty, terrorism, abortion, racism, animal rights, and other urgent matters. There are many resources that can help readers through that book—introductions to each reading, study questions, suggestions for further reading, and a website with sample quizzes, essay questions, and lots of extra materials.

The fullest introduction to ethics would include both of these approaches. *The Ethical Life* will give you lots of primary sources, and *Fundamentals* can help you to place them in context, clearly setting out their ideas and providing some critical evaluation of their strengths and weaknesses. For those who are content to take my word for it, *Fundamentals* will be enough. For those who want to see what other philosophers have to say about these important matters, *The Ethical Life* might be a good place to start. And for those of you attracted by both approaches, working through each in tandem with the other can provide a well-rounded picture of what moral philosophy is all about.

Acknowledgments

I wrote this book because my editor at the time, Robert Miller, asked me to. Well, not really. He asked, and I refused. He did it again, and I refused. Obviously, I did finally give in. I want to thank Robert for his persistence, but much more importantly for his unflagging enthusiasm and his uncommon good sense.

One of Robert's many kindnesses was to solicit feedback from so many talented philosophers. I hope that the following folks will accept my gratitude for having provided very helpful comments on drafts and previous editions of this book: Paul Abela, Luke Amentas, Martin Andersson, Kristopher Arca, Thomas Avery, Ralph Baergen, Olivia Bailey, Stacy Bautista, Chad Bogosian, Jeffrey Brand-Ballard, Tim Cannon, Don Carrell, Tom Carson, Michael Cholbi, Janice Daurio, Janelle Derstine, David Detmer, Josh DiPaolo, Howard M. Ducharme, Adam English, Matthew Eshleman, Daan Evers, Bud Fairlamb, Steve Finlay, Robert Fischer, Matthew Flummer, Galen Forseman, Sheron Fraser-Burgess, Brett Gaul, Deke Gould, Christopher Grau, Clifton F. Guthrie, Craig Hanks, Michael Hannen, Dan Hausman, Richard Haynes, Clevis Headley, Kelly Heuer, Darren Hibbs, Ryan Hickerson, Richard Hine, John Huss, Clark Hutton, Scott James, Julian Katz, Erin Kealey, Jacquelyn Ann Kegley, Monica Link Kim, Dan Kofman, Avery Kolers, Keith Allen Korcz, Jacob Krch, Robert Lane, Hoon Lee, Patrick Linden, Jessica Logue, Andres Luco, Eugene Marshall, Michael McKenna, William Darryl Mehring, Brian Merrill, John G. Messerly, Richard Mohline, Jay Newhard, Nathan Nobis, Kristian Olsen, Aleksandr Pjevalica, Philip Robbins, Barbara R. Russo, Jesse Steinberg, Glenn Tiller, Rebecca Weaver, James Woolever, and Ruigand Xu. Robert M. Farley has consistently provided extremely smart and unusually helpful advice. And a superstar trio—Tyler Doggett, Christian Miller, and David Sobel—deserve special mention for having devoted an extraordinary amount of serious attention to the initial draft of this book. Finally, the work for previous editions' ancillary materials was undertaken by my stellar research assistants Justin Horn, Ben Schwan, and Emma Prendergast. The ancillary materials for this edition were done by Stephanie Hoffmann and Lukas Myers. I am very grateful for their dedicated efforts in making these first-rate resources.

R.S.L.

Madison, Wisconsin

Summer 2023

The Lay of the Land

There is so much to know about our world. And for those who are the least bit curious, we have more resources than ever to give us the insights we seek. We can turn to a variety of scientists, doctors, economists, historians, and journalists to help us better understand ourselves, our world, and our place within it.

But there is a set of vital questions that such experts will never answer. These are questions about how we ought to live. Sure, financial advisors can tell us how we ought to invest our money. Personal trainers can advise us on getting in shape. Career counselors can steer us in one direction or another. But if we are interested instead in what our guiding ideals should be, in what sort of life is worth living, in how we should treat one another, then we must turn to philosophy. *Ethics*—also known as *moral philosophy*—is the branch of knowledge concerned with answering such questions.

The field of ethics is vast, and—bad news first—there is no chance of covering all of its interesting and important issues within these pages. In selecting the topics for treatment, I have chosen those that seem to me most central. These can be grouped under three headings, each representing a core area of moral philosophy:

1. **Value theory:**[1] What is the good life? What is worth pursuing for its own sake? How do we improve our lot in life?

---

1. All technical terms and phrases that appear in **boldface** are defined in the glossary at the end of the book.

2. **Normative ethics**: What are our fundamental moral duties? Which character traits count as virtues, which as vices, and why? Who should our role models be? Do the ends always justify the means, or are there certain types of action that should never be done under any circumstances?
3. **Metaethics**: What is the status of moral claims and advice? Can ethical theories, moral principles, or specific moral verdicts be true? If so, what makes them true? Can we gain moral wisdom? If so, how? Do we always have good reason to do our moral duty?

The structure of this book mirrors this threefold division. The first part is focused on the good life, with an emphasis on explaining the nature and sources of well-being. We ask, for instance, about whether happiness is the be-all and end-all of a good life, the only thing desirable for its own sake. And, naturally, we'll consider views that deny this, including the theory that tells us that getting what we want—whatever we want—is the key to the good life.

Then it's off to normative ethics, which is devoted to examining our moral relations with one another. Who counts—are animals, ecosystems, or fetuses morally important in their own right? Is there a fundamental moral rule, such as the **golden rule**, that can justify all of our specific moral duties? What role do virtue, self-interest, and justice play in morality? Are we ever allowed to break the moral rules? If so, when and why? These are among the most important questions taken up in normative ethics.

Finally, to metaethics. This part of moral philosophy asks questions about the other two. Specifically, it asks about the status of ethical claims, rather than about their content. We all have views about what is right and good. Are these just matters of taste? Is moral authority based on personal approval? Social customs? God's commands? None of the above? Is morality in more or less good working order, or is it just a convenient fiction that keeps us in our place? These are the questions that we will take up in the last section of the book.

There is no shortage of folks offering advice about these questions. The self-help industry has its gurus, motivational speakers, and best sellers, each aimed at guiding us on the path to a good life. Political pundits, religious leaders, and editorial writers are more than happy to offer us their blueprints for righteous living. They don't always agree, of course. It would be nice to have a way to sort out the decent advice from the rest.

Those of you turning to philosophical ethics for the first time are likely to be hoping for something that I can't provide, namely, a simple recipe for doing the sorting. It is perfectly natural to want a clear method for distinguishing correct from incorrect answers about the good life and our moral duty. Indeed, when I first went to college, I enrolled in a philosophy course hoping for just such a thing. My failure to find it left me deeply disappointed. I abandoned philosophy for a few years, and even dropped out of college for a while. After I returned, I went looking for it again. I've finally realized that in this area of life, while there is plenty of good advice, it can't be summed up in one snappy formula, captured in a neat slogan that can be inscribed in a fortune cookie or on a bumper sticker.

Ethics is hard. It needn't be weakness or fuzzy thinking that stands in the way of knowing the right thing to do, or the proper goals to strive for. We are right to be puzzled by the moral complexity we find in our lives. While we might yearn for clarity and simplicity, this wish for easy answers is bound to be repeatedly frustrated.

Doubts about Ethics

When people learn of the difficulties that face each important attempt to solve ethical puzzles, they often become pessimistic about making any progress in ethical thinking. The major temptation is to regard the entire enterprise as bankrupt, or to judge that all ethical views are equally plausible.

Doubts about morality are plentiful, and it would be silly to ignore them in a book that is so focused on trying to improve our moral understanding. The last four chapters of this book are entirely devoted to such doubts; those who feel them acutely might do best to start with that material, and then work your way to the other parts of the book that are focused on the good life and normative ethics.

For now, let me say just a few things to the doubters. Perhaps the most important is this: among those who have thought longest and hardest about ethics, the view that morality is all make-believe, or that all moral standards are correct only relative to individuals or societies, is deeply controversial. There are *lots* of problems with such views. Some of these problems may be devastating.

As a result, it would be a serious mistake just to assume that morality is a fiction, or that personal or cultural opinion is the ultimate measure of what is right and wrong, or that moral knowledge is permanently out of reach. We must follow the arguments where they lead. They may indeed lead us ultimately to embrace such positions. But they might not. And we can't know one way or the other until we've actually done the hard work.

Since I really love this part of ethics—the metaethical part—I can't resist saying just a bit more here. In my experience, most of those who harbor serious doubts about morality base those doubts on one or more of the following considerations:

(A) Individuals constantly disagree about what's right and wrong, and societies do, too. If there were some objective truth in ethics, then we should expect all really smart people to agree on it. They don't. So there is no objective truth in ethics.

(B) There are universally correct moral standards only if God exists. But God doesn't exist, so ethics is just a "human construct."

(C) Science tells us the truth about the world, and science says nothing about what's right and wrong. And that's because nothing really is right or wrong.

(D) If there were a universal ethic, then that would make it okay for some people to impose their own views on others. But that's not okay at all. Therefore there is no universal ethic.

(E) If there were objective moral rules, then it would always be wrong to break them. But every rule admits of exceptions; no moral rule is absolute. That shows that we do make up the moral rules after all.

This is going to sound like cheating, but here goes: every single one of these arguments is problematic. I'm not going to defend that claim right now—that's what the last four chapters of this book are for. So I don't expect you to believe me (yet). Still, there is a lesson here: until these (or other) arguments are laid out with care and successfully defended, we are in no position to assume that they are more than superficially plausible.

I think you'll soon see that we can make a lot of progress in our moral thinking. And even if morality *is* in some way a human invention, there is still lots to learn, and there are many ways to make mistakes when thinking about what is good and right. It's important to avoid these errors. Doing moral philosophy can help with this.

Look at it this way. Lots of people believe that when it comes to art, beauty is in the eye of the beholder—there are no objective, universal standards of good taste. Suppose that's true. And suppose that morality is just like art in this respect. Still, our tastes can be educated and improved. Many people are much wiser than I am about music and painting, for instance. Even if there are no universal standards of good taste, it would be silly of me to pass up a chance to talk with people who have thought long and hard about artistic matters. Why should I dismiss their opinions and refuse to hear them out? I'm no genius. Maybe I could learn a thing or two.

That's *exactly* the right attitude to take about ethics. Especially when so much is at stake—the very quality of our life and our relations with others—it would be terrible to close our minds to new and challenging ideas. Those who have thought so hard about the central questions of existence may well have something to teach us.

I encourage you to resist the diagnosis that in ethics, anything goes. As you work your way through this book, I hope you come to agree that good moral thinking is disciplined thinking. There are many ways that we can go wrong in our moral reflections, and failure here can have the most disastrous results. Though it is sometimes hard to know when we have got it right in ethics, it is often very easy to know when we (or others) have made a mistake. There are clear cases of people ruining their lives, or doing morally horrific things. We should keep that in mind before siding too quickly with those who say that every moral view is as good as every other.

Ethical Starting Points

One of the puzzles about moral thinking is knowing where to begin. Some critics of morality deny that there are any proper starting points for ethical reflection. They believe that moral reasoning is simply a way of rationalizing our biases and gut feelings. This outlook encourages us to be lax in moral argument and, worse, supports an attitude that no moral views are any better than others. While this sort of pessimistic view might be true, we shouldn't regard it as the default view of ethics. We should accept it only as a last resort.

In the meantime, let's consider some fairly plausible ethical assumptions, claims that can get us started in our moral thinking. The point of the exercise is to soften you up to the idea that we are not just spinning our wheels when thinking morally. There are reasonable constraints that can guide us when thinking about how to live. Here are some of them:

- *Neither the law nor tradition is immune from moral criticism.* The law does not have the final word on what is right and wrong. Neither does tradition. Actions that are legal, or customary, are sometimes morally mistaken.

- *Everyone is morally fallible.* Everyone has some mistaken ethical views, and no human being is wholly wise when it comes to moral matters.
- *Friendship is valuable.* Having friends is a good thing. Friendships add value to your life. You are better off when there are people you care deeply about, and who care deeply about you.
- *We are not obligated to do the impossible.* Morality can demand only so much of us. Moral standards that are impossible to meet are illegitimate. Morality must respect our limitations.
- *Children bear less moral responsibility than adults.* Moral responsibility assumes an ability on our part to understand options, to make decisions in an informed way, and to let our decisions guide our behavior. The fewer of these abilities you have, the less blameworthy you are for any harm you might cause.
- *Justice is a very important moral good.* Any moral theory that treats justice as irrelevant is deeply suspect. It is important that we get what we deserve, and that we are treated fairly.
- *Deliberately hurting other people requires justification.* The default position in ethics is this: do no harm. It is sometimes morally acceptable to harm others, but there must be an excellent reason for doing so or else the harmful behavior is unjustified.
- *Equals ought to be treated equally.* People who are alike in all relevant respects should get similar treatment. When this fails to happen—when racist or sexist policies are enacted, for instance—then something has gone wrong.
- *Self-interest isn't the only ethical consideration.* How well-off we are is important. But it isn't the only thing of moral importance. Morality sometimes calls on us to set aside our own interests for the sake of others.
- *Agony is bad.* Excruciating physical or emotional pain is bad. It may sometimes be appropriate to cause such extreme suffering, but doing so requires a very powerful justification.
- *Might doesn't make right.* People in power can get away with lots of things that the rest of us can't. That doesn't justify what they do. That a person can escape punishment is one thing—whether his actions are morally acceptable is another.
- *Free and informed requests prevent rights violations.* If, with eyes wide open and no one twisting your arm, you ask someone to do something for you, and she does it, then your rights have not been violated—even if you end up hurt as a result.

There are a number of points to make about these claims.

First, this short list isn't meant to be exhaustive. It could be made much longer.

Second, I am not claiming that the items on this list are beyond criticism. I am saying only that each one is very plausible. Hard thinking might weaken our confidence in some cases. The point, though, is that without such scrutiny, it is perfectly reasonable to begin our moral thinking with the items on this list.

Third, many of these claims require interpretation in order to apply them in a satisfying way. When we say, for instance, that equals ought to be treated equally, we leave all of the interesting questions open. (What makes people equals? Can we treat people equally without treating them in precisely the same way? Etc.)

Not only do we have a variety of plausible starting points for our ethical investigations, we also have a number of obviously poor beginnings for moral thinking. A morality that celebrates genocide, torture, treachery, sadism, hostility, and slavery is, depending on how you look at it, either no morality at all or a deeply failed one. Any morality worth the name will place *some* importance on justice, fairness, kindness, and reasonableness. Just how much importance, and how to balance things in cases of conflict—that is where the real philosophy gets done.

What Is Morality?

A lot of people ask me: Is morality different from ethics? Good question. While people sometimes distinguish the two—speaking, for instance, as if ethics is always a matter of group behavior, while morality applies only to individuals—I will largely treat "ethics" and "morality" as synonyms. When considering a corporation's or a politician's ethical lapses, we might as well describe them as moral failings. When talking of the moral virtue of those who inspire us, we could just as easily put the point in terms of their ethical goodness. For the most part, "ethical" and "moral" are just different ways of saying the same thing.

That said, philosophers often distinguish ethics from morality in the following way: ethics is the philosophical study of morality. That's the way I use the word in the title of this book. In this sense, ethics is the same thing as moral philosophy. According to this usage, ethics is *about* morality—morality is the subject matter of ethics, which is a branch of philosophical study.

If ethics is the study of morality, another question naturally arises: What is morality? Though there is no widely agreed-on definition of morality, we know that it is centrally concerned with protecting people's well-being, with fairness, justice, respect for others, virtue, responsibility, rights, liberties, social cooperation, praise, and blame. But the precise nature of such concern is highly disputed, as we'll soon see.

As just indicated, the absence of a definition does not leave us entirely in the dark. (After all, no one has yet been able to offer informative definitions of *literature*, or *life*, or *art*, and yet we know a great deal about those things.) We can get a better sense of our subject matter by considering the questions that are distinctive of ethics—namely, those that structure this book, the ones focused on the good life, our duties to others, the nature of virtue, etc. We can supplement this by considering the starting points listed above, and many others that we could easily identify.

We can also better understand morality by contrasting it with other systems of guidance, such as the law, etiquette, self-interest, and tradition. Each of these represents a set of standards for how we ought to behave, ideals to aim for, rules that we should not break. But the fact that a law tells us to do something does not settle the question of whether morality gives its stamp of approval. Some immoral acts (like cheating on a spouse) are not illegal. And some illegal acts (like voicing criticism of a dictator) are not immoral. Certainly, many laws require what morality requires and forbid what morality forbids. But the fit is hardly perfect, and that shows that morality is something different from the law. That a legislature passed a bill is not enough to show that the bill is morally acceptable.

We see the same imperfect fit when it comes to standards of etiquette. Forks are supposed to be set to the left of a plate, but it isn't immoral to set them on the right. Good manners are not the same thing as morally good conduct. Morality sometimes requires us *not* to be polite or gracious, as when someone threatens your children or happily tells you a racist joke. So the standards of etiquette can depart from those of morality.

The same is true when it comes to the standards of self-interest. I've just been watching the entire run of *The Shield*, a police drama set in a crime-ridden district of Los Angeles. Early in the series, the main character, Vic Mackey, murders a fellow police officer who was set to reveal Mackey's corruption. Mackey successfully frames a criminal for the murder: a classic case of protecting one's own interests by acting immorally. Though the relation between self-interest and morality is contested, it is a plausible starting point to assume that morality can sometimes require us to sacrifice our well-being, and that we can sometimes improve our lot in life by acting unethically. So the standards of morality are not the very same as those of self-interest. (We will see a challenge to this view when considering *ethical egoism* in chapter 8.)

Finally, morality is also distinct from tradition. That a practice has been around a long time does not automatically make it moral. Morality sometimes requires a break with the past, as it did when people called for the abolition of slavery or for allowing women to vote.

True, people do sometimes speak of *conventional morality*, which is the set of traditional principles that are widely shared within a culture or society. These principles, like those of the law and etiquette, are the result of human decisions, agreements, and practices. Conventional morality can differ from society to society. At least some of its principles can be traced to common misunderstandings, irrationality, bias, or superstition.

When I write about morality in this book, I am *not* referring to conventional morality. I am assuming that some social standards—even those that are long-standing and very popular—can be morally mistaken. (We'll examine this assumption at length in chapter 19.) So when I talk about morality from this point on, I will be referring to moral standards that are not rooted in widespread endorsement, but rather are independent of conventional morality and can be used to critically evaluate its merits.

It's possible, of course, that conventional morality is all there is. But this would be a very surprising discovery. Most of us assume, as I will do, that the popularity of a moral view is not a guarantee of its truth. We could be wrong on this point, but until we have a chance to consider the matter in detail, I think it best to assume that conventional morality can sometimes be mistaken. If so, then there may be some independent, "critical" morality that (i) does not have its origin in social agreements, (ii) is untainted by mistaken beliefs, irrationality, or popular prejudices, and (iii) can serve as the true standard for determining when conventional morality has got it right and when it has fallen into error. That is the morality whose nature we are seeking to explore in this book.

Moral Philosophy and Moral Theories

Moral philosophy is primarily a matter of thinking about the attractions of various ethical *theories*. When we develop and test these theories, we are bound to look beyond the details of specific cases. We are trying to find the deepest truths about our subject matter—how to live. Such truths are wide-ranging and apply to countless cases. That's why moral philosophers so often look beyond the details of specific cases and focus instead on very general principles.

Moral theorizing is the result of a perfectly natural process of thinking. We are questioning beings, interested in seeking out ever deeper explanations of things. And we are uneasy if there is no chance of a unifying explanation, an account that can coherently organize the various aspects of our thinking and experience. This is clear in psychology, for instance, where researchers have always been drawn to unifying views of human motivation. For many psychologists, it all comes down to self-interest (egoists), or to how we have been conditioned (behaviorists), or our sexual impulses (Freudians), etc. This process is evident in physics, too, where the dream is one day to discover the unified theory—a single master principle that will explain *all* of the workings of the physical world, from the movements of subatomic particles to the behavior of the largest stars and galaxies.

The same desire for unification is also present in ethics. We might begin a conversation by insisting on the immorality of some specific action—say, revealing a patient's confidential information. But someone might challenge our view, and in reply, we would cite a moral rule to back it up: revealing such information is wrong because it betrays a trust. But why is it wrong to betray a trust? Because (we might say) such actions fail to show respect for the person who has been betrayed. But why is it wrong to fail to show respect? And is it always wrong to do such a thing, or are there exceptions? If there are exceptions, what explains *them*? This is a perfectly natural way of going on. We are searching for increasingly general moral principles with the power to explain more and more cases. The hope is eventually to land on just a single principle, one that will do all of the explaining we need in the moral realm.

Suppose that we think really carefully about our moral beliefs, and find that we ultimately justify them by means of four principles:

- Don't impose unnecessary harm.
- Be nice to others.
- Act justly.
- Tell the truth.

Is there a next step? Of course! Aren't you curious to know whether there is a yet more general rule, one that can explain why these four principles are justified? Like researchers in most areas, moral philosophers remain dissatisfied unless they can offer a truly comprehensive theory that will unify and impose order on our thoughts. Physicists want this. Psychologists want this. So do philosophers.

That's why our focus will mostly be on these very general ethical theories. They represent the natural outgrowth of some extremely compelling ethical ideas—ones that you surely have relied on when trying to justify your own moral views. There is something important in taking our core ethical beliefs and seeing where they lead. They lead to ethical theories; doing moral philosophy is the process of tracing the lines that connect our basic moral views to these more developed theories, and then testing them to see how well they can hold up against our curiosity and critical intelligence.

Moral Reasoning

Moral reasoning, like all reasoning, involves at least two things: a set of reasons, and a conclusion that these reasons are meant to support. When you put these two things together, you have what philosophers call an **argument**. This isn't a matter of bickering or angrily exchanging words. An argument is simply any chain of thought in which reasons (philosophers call these **premises**) are offered in support of a particular conclusion.

Not all arguments are equally good. This is as true in ethics as it is in science, mathematics, or politics. It is easy to mistake one's way when it comes to ethical thinking. We can land at the wrong conclusion (by endorsing child abuse, for instance). We can also arrive at the right one by means of terrible reasoning. We must do our best to avoid both of these mistakes.

In other words, our moral thinking should have two complementary goals—getting it right, and being able to back up our views with flawless reasoning. We want the truth, both in the starting assumptions we bring to an issue and in the conclusions we eventually arrive at. But we also want to make sure that our views are supported by excellent reasons. And this provides two tests for good moral reasoning: (1) we must avoid false beliefs, and (2) the logic of our moral thinking must be rigorous and error-free.

The first test is pretty easy to understand. Consider the following quote, written in 1833, by the pro-slavery author Richard Colfax:

[T]he mind will be great in proportion to the size and figure of the brain: it is equally reasonable to suppose, that the acknowledged meanness of the negroe's intellect, only coincides with the shape of his head; or in other words, that his want [i.e., lack] of capability to receive a complicated education renders it improper and impolitic, that he should be allowed the privileges of citizenship in an enlightened country.[2]

And here is William John Grayson, antebellum congressman and senator from South Carolina, on the same subject:

Slavery is the negro system of labor. He is lazy and improvident. . . . What more can be required of Slavery, in reference to the negro, than has been done? It has made him, from a savage, an orderly and efficient labourer. It supports him in comfort and peace. It restrains his vices. It improves his mind, morals and manners.[3]

There are false beliefs galore in these (and other) defenses of American chattel slavery. Africans, and those of African descent, are not inherently lazy or unfit for a complicated education; they do not have heads with different shapes than anyone else; head shape is not correlated with intelligence; slavery was anything but comfortable. When one starts with false assumptions, the entire chain of reasoning becomes suspect. Good reasoning, in ethics as elsewhere, must avoid false beliefs if we are to have any confidence in its conclusions.

But it is possible to develop moral arguments that fail, even though every single one of their premises is true. The failure is of the second sort mentioned above: a failure of logic.

Consider this argument:

1. Heroin is a drug.
2. Selling heroin is illegal.
3. Therefore, heroin use is immoral.

This is a moral argument. It is a set of reasons designed to support a moral conclusion. Both of the premises are true. But they do not adequately support the conclusion, since one can accept them while consistently rejecting this conclusion. Perhaps the use of illegal drugs such as heroin really

---

2. Richard H. Colfax, *Evidence against the Views of the Abolitionists, Consisting of Physical and Moral Proofs, of the Natural Inferiority of the Negroes* (New York: James T. M. Bleakley, 1833), p. 25.

3. William John Grayson, *The Hireling and the Slave* (Charleston, S.C.: John Russell, 1855), p. vii.

is immoral. But we need a further reason to think so—we would need, for instance, the additional claim that all drug use is immoral.

The argument in its present form is a poor one. But not because it relies on false claims. Rather, the argument's logical structure is to blame. The logic of an argument is a matter of how its premises are related to its conclusion. In the best arguments, the truth of the premises guarantees the truth of the conclusion. When an argument has this feature, it is **logically valid**.

The heroin argument is invalid. The truth of its premises does not guarantee the truth of its conclusion—indeed, the conclusion may be false.

Since the best arguments are logically valid, we will want to make sure that our own arguments meet this condition. But how can we do that? How can we tell a valid from an invalid argument, one that is logically perfect from one that is logically shaky?

There is a simple, three-part test:

1. Identify all of an argument's premises.
2. Imagine that all of them are true (even if you know that some are false).
3. Then ask yourself this question: supposing that all of the premises were true, could the conclusion be false? *If yes*, the argument is invalid. The premises do not guarantee the conclusion. *If no*, the argument is valid. The premises offer perfect logical support for the conclusion.

Validity is a matter of how well an argument's premises support its conclusion. To test for this, we must assume that all of an argument's premises are true. We then ask whether the conclusion must therefore be true. If so, the argument is valid. If not, not.

Note that an argument's validity is a matter of the argument's structure. It has nothing to do with the *actual* truth or falsity of an argument's premises or conclusion. Indeed, *valid arguments may contain false premises and false conclusions*.

To help clarify the idea, consider the following argument. Suppose you are a bit shaky on your U.S. history, and I am trying to convince you that John Quincy Adams was the ninth president of the United States. I offer you the following line of reasoning:

1. John Quincy Adams was either the eighth or the ninth U.S. president.
2. John Quincy Adams was not the eighth U.S. president.
3. Therefore, John Quincy Adams was the ninth U.S. president.

In one way, this reasoning is impeccable. It is logically flawless. This is a valid argument. If all premises of this argument were true, then the conclusion would have to be true. It is impossible for 1 and 2 to be true and 3 to be false. It passes our test for logical validity with flying colors.

But the argument is still a bad one—not because of any logical error, but because it has a false premise (number 1; John Quincy Adams was the sixth U.S. president) and a false conclusion. The truth of an argument's premises is one thing; its logical status is another.

The lesson here is that truth isn't everything; neither is logic. We need them both. What we want in philosophy, as in all other areas of inquiry, are arguments that have two features: (1) they are logically watertight (valid), and (2) all of their premises are true. These arguments are known as **sound** arguments.

Sound arguments are the gold standard of good reasoning. And it's easy to see why. They are logically valid. So if all of their premises are true, their conclusion must be true as well. And by definition, sound arguments contain only true premises. So their conclusions are true. If you can tell that an argument is valid, and also know that each premise is correct, then you can also know that the conclusion is true. That is what we are after.

I started this section by claiming that not all moral arguments are equally good. We're now in a position to see why. Some arguments rely on false premises. Others rely on invalid reasoning. Still others—the worst of the lot—commit both kinds of error.

To reinforce these points, consider one more moral argument. Some people say that killing animals and eating meat is morally okay, because animals kill other animals, and there is nothing immoral about that. Is this a sound line of reasoning?

Not as it stands. To see this, let's reconstruct the argument by stating it in premise-conclusion form. This is something that I'm going to do for dozens of arguments over the coming pages. For those of you who want to improve your philosophy skills, there's no better way to do so than to take a line of reasoning in ordinary English and try to set it out step by step. That makes it easier to tell just what is being claimed, and so easier to determine the logical structure of the argument and the truth of the premises.

Here is my take on this popular *Argument for Meat Eating*:

1. It is morally acceptable for nonhuman animals to kill and eat other animals.
2. Therefore, it is morally acceptable for human beings to kill and eat nonhuman animals.

As stated, there is only one premise to this argument. And it is true. So if the argument is problematic, it's not because it contains any false premises. Rather, it has to be because of its logic.

And that is indeed its flaw. The argument is invalid; the premise does not adequately support the conclusion. We can assume that the premise is true (indeed, we *should* accept it), but the conclusion might still be false. The truth of the premise is not enough to guarantee the truth of the conclusion, since what is morally acceptable for nonhuman animals may not be morally acceptable for us. We would need a further premise, to the effect that we are allowed to do anything that such animals do, in order to make this argument valid.

So as it stands, the Argument for Meat Eating is invalid. Therefore it is unsound. Does that mean that its conclusion is false?

No. And here is another important lesson about reasoning: bad arguments may contain true conclusions. After all, even true claims can be supported by poor reasoning. The fact that the Argument for Meat Eating is invalid does not show that its conclusion is false. It shows only that this particular way of defending that conclusion is no good. For all we know, there might be other, better arguments that can do the trick.

The Argument for Meat Eating, like many other invalid arguments, can be modified so that it takes on a logically perfect form. Indeed, a charitable reading of the argument would show that there is an underlying assumption that, if brought out into the open, would allow us to transform the argument into a valid one. With a little tweaking, for instance, we get the following:

1. If it is morally acceptable for nonhuman animals to kill and eat one another, then it is morally acceptable for humans to kill and eat nonhuman animals. (This is the underlying assumption.)
2. It is morally acceptable for nonhuman animals to kill and eat one another.
3. Therefore, it is morally acceptable for humans to kill and eat nonhuman animals.

And this argument is logically perfect. If premises 1 and 2 are true, then the conclusion, 3, has to be true.

But even this version is unsound. Not because it is invalid, but because it now contains a false premise. Premise 2 is true. But premise 1 is not. Four reasons explain this.

First, animals that eat other animals have no choice in the matter. We do.

Second, a carnivore's survival depends on its eating other animals. Ours does not. With rare exceptions, human beings can survive perfectly well without eating animal flesh. There are hundreds of millions of vegetarians leading healthy lives.

Third, none of the animals we routinely eat (chickens, cows, pigs, sheep, ducks, rabbits) are carnivores. They *don't* eat other animals. So if their behavior is supposed to guide our own, then we should eat only plants.

Fourth, it is implausible to look to nonhuman animals for moral guidance. They are not **moral agents**—they can't control their behavior through moral reasoning. That explains why they have no moral duties, and why they are immune from moral criticism. But we, obviously, are moral agents, and we can guide our behavior by the moral decisions we make.

Again, this analysis does not prove that the argument's conclusion is false. It just shows that this version of the argument, like the original, is unsound. Meat eating may be perfectly morally acceptable. But this argument fails to show that.

I have spent some time on this argument, not because I want to defend a view about whether vegetarianism is morally required, but because I want to illustrate the possibility of real moral argumentation. We started with a version of the argument that has convinced a lot of people. But when we laid it out clearly, we could see that it was invalid. So we modified it, making an underlying assumption explicit, and doing so in a way that gave us a logically perfect argument. But even this improved version is unsound, because its first premise is false.

Can I be absolutely sure that the premise is false? No. I will be the first to admit that further argument might reveal the error of my thinking. What's more, there is no foolproof method that can perfectly sort true claims from false ones. We may offer excellent reasons and arguments on behalf of our moral views, but at the end of the day, it's possible that not everyone will be convinced.

But this is no different from any other area of inquiry. There is no litmus test that can distinguish all true biological claims from false ones, accurate economic forecasts from the inaccurate, correct chemistry hypotheses from incorrect ones. There is potential for disagreement in all areas of thinking.

The absence of a perfectly reliable test for truth does not mean that all claims are equally true, or that truth is in the eye of the beholder. The earth is not a cube. Six is less than ten. Queen Victoria is dead. Chromosomes contain DNA. These claims are each true. Their opposites are false. And our say-so has nothing to do with it. These claims would be true even if we were not around to make them. They aren't true because we think they are; we think they are true because they are.

Perhaps things are this way in ethics, too. We will spend a lot of time considering whether that is so, when we discuss metaethics in the last part of the book. For right now, the important thing to note is that we must rely on our good sense and good judgment in all areas of investigation, not just in ethics. The lack of a precision test for truth does not spell the defeat of moral inquiry, since other areas of investigation get along just fine without one.

Moral reasoning is just what its name implies—offering and evaluating reasons that are meant to support moral conclusions. It is not merely a matter of doing a gut check and venting one's feelings. Not every reason is a good one. Some reasons fail to support their conclusions. Others represent false beliefs. And while it is sometimes hard to separate fact from fiction, this needn't hobble us. Many claims are clearly true, many clearly false. For the others, there is evidence and argument that we can bring in to try to settle the matter. This won't always yield decisive results. But that's the nature of our situation. We can't always be sure of things, in ethics or elsewhere. That shouldn't prevent us from trying to get it right, and backing up our moral views with the best possible arguments.

Looking Ahead

In the pages to come, I present and evaluate a lot of arguments. These are the ones at the very heart of morality, the ones on behalf of theories that try to answer the deepest questions of ethics. As we will see, no theory—about the good life, our moral duties, or the status of morality—has earned anything like unanimous support among philosophers.

I say this not to dash your hopes, but to give you a realistic take on what to expect. There is a very broad consensus on a number of points in ethics. Consider, for instance, the twelve starting points mentioned earlier in this introduction, a sampling that could easily have been expanded. The moral issues that tend to capture our attention are those that are hotly disputed. What often goes unnoticed is the substantial amount of moral agreement, even across time and place.

Still, when it comes to devising a theory that can offer a comprehensive account of morality, things become much trickier. And then a natural, despairing thought: greater minds than ours have spent lifetimes trying to solve the core questions of ethics, and none of their theories has gained universal support. So what's the use?

It's a fair question. But there is a good answer. We are thinking about how to live; what could be more important than that? We can make a lot of progress in our own thinking by studying the thoughts and arguments of those who have devoted so much effort to this vital task. We may realize that our own "philosophy of life" is marred in ways that we hadn't foreseen. Or we might come to appreciate certain benefits of our views that had escaped our notice. Those of you who work your way through this book will certainly be in a much better position to critically assess your own moral views, and to improve your thinking about how to live your life.

What ethicists across the ages have done is to take a common insight—say, that happiness is the key to a good life, that we must treat everyone fairly, that we must prevent harm—and see how far we can get by consistently applying this insight. Consistency is not to be sneezed at. It's not the hobgoblin of little minds, but a minimum test of a theory's plausibility. Inconsistent, contradictory views cannot be true, which is why philosophers try so hard to avoid them.

Suppose that you are involved in a moral debate, or are thinking about how to improve your own life. If you go deep enough, you'll probably land on a view that you can no longer defend. Perhaps it's one of the twelve mentioned earlier. Perhaps it's something else. Whatever it is, the truth of that view is important. And unsurprisingly, philosophers across the ages will have examined that view very carefully. We can learn from their work. We can find out what is attractive about these starting points. And we can also discover how they might be vulnerable.

That's not everything. Agreed. You won't find, by the end of the book, a recipe for the best life, or a simple step-by-step guide for doing your duty. This book does not belong on the self-help shelves. You probably already figured that out, since such manuals are a lot chattier and far easier to read than this one. But those books never get to the deepest issues—most of them assume, for instance, that happiness is what we should be trying for, or that getting what you want is what life is all about. Philosophers subject such thoughts to intense scrutiny. And it isn't clear whether they survive.

Let's start our work together by having a look at these views, ones that focus on the good life for human beings. There are a lot of surprises in store.

Discussion Questions

1. What are the three main areas of moral philosophy? How might answering questions in one area inform the way we think about the other areas?

2. What are some reasons for doubting that moral truth or moral progress are possible? Do you think such doubts are correct? Why or why not?

3. Do you find the "ethical starting points" presented here to be plausible? Do you think we can prove that such starting points are correct? Do we need to?

4. How do moral standards differ from those of the law, etiquette, or tradition?

5. What are the two ways that a moral argument can fail? Can an argument with either of these failings still have a true conclusion? Why or why not?

6. Is it possible for a valid argument to be unsound? What about for a sound argument to be invalid? For each, either give an example of such an argument or explain why it is impossible.

7. What is the point of trying to develop a moral theory? Do you think that there might be a single, ultimate moral principle that can explain the truth of all other moral principles?

PART ONE

The Good Life

CHAPTER 1

············ ❧ ············

Hedonism

Its Powerful Appeal

1.1 Happiness and Intrinsic Value

If you are like me, and like everyone else I know, you've spent a fair bit of time thinking about how your life can go better. You may be doing pretty well already, or may be very badly off, or somewhere in between. But there is always room for improvement.

To know how our lives can be better, we first need to know how they can be good. In other words, we need a standard that will tell us when our lives are going well for us. That standard will help us determine our level of *well-being*, or *welfare*.

Many things can improve our well-being: chocolate, sturdy shoes, vaccinations, a reasonable amount of money. These things pave the way to a better life—they help to make it possible, and may, in some cases, even be indispensable to it. Philosophers call such things **instrumental goods**,[1] things that are valuable because of the good things they bring about.

If there are instrumental goods, then there must be something they are good *for*, something whose value does not depend on being a means to anything else that is good. Such a thing is worth pursuing for its own sake; it is valuable in its own right, even if it brings nothing else in its wake. Philosophers call such things **intrinsically valuable**. Instrumental values are things that are good precisely because they help to bring about things that are intrinsically valuable.

---

1. All terms and phrases that appear in **boldface** are defined in a glossary at the end of the book.

When asking about what makes a life go better for us, we will of course want to know which things are instrumentally valuable, so we can get our hands on them. But when we take a philosophical step back and ask *why* (for instance) going to the dentist, or making money, makes us better off, we will need to have some grasp of what is intrinsically good for us—something whose presence, *all by itself*, makes us better off.

A natural way to start thinking about this is to consider some clearly good lives, ones that definitely qualify as being good for the people who live them. My top ten wouldn't include those of anyone you'd ever heard of. Instead, I'd pick the lives of certain of my friends and acquaintances, people who are deeply invested in their exciting work, secure in their love for others, physically healthy and active, and possessed of modest but real self-esteem and self-respect. But there is no need to be limited by my choices. Think about your own top candidates, and then ask yourself this question: What makes each of those lives so good? Is there a single feature that each of them shares, something that explains why they are as good as they are? If so, what is it?

The most popular answer is just what you'd expect: happiness. On this view, a good life is a happy life. This means something pretty specific. It means that happiness is necessary for a good life; a life without happiness cannot be a good life. It also means that happiness is sufficient for a good life: When you are happy, your life is going well. The happier you are, the better your life is going for you. And the unhappier you are, the worse off you are.

On this view, there is only a single thing that is intrinsically good for us: happiness. Everything else improves our lives only to the extent that it makes us happy. Likewise, there is just one thing that is intrinsically bad for us: unhappiness. Unhappiness is the only thing that directly reduces our quality of life.

But what is happiness? There are many answers to this question. Within philosophical circles, however, one of them has arguably attracted the most attention. This is the view known as **hedonism**. The name comes from the Greek word *hédoné*, which means "pleasure." According to hedonists, happiness is the combination of pleasure and the absence of pain. So, for hedonists, a life is good to the extent that it is filled with pleasure and is free of pain.

Before we can assess hedonism, we have to recognize that there are two fundamental kinds of pleasure: physical pleasure and attitudinal pleasure (enjoyment). The first kind is the sort we experience when we taste a delicious fall apple, or when we let the jets from a hot tub dissolve the tension in our backs. These very different kinds of pleasurable feelings usually make us happy, at least for the moment. But such feelings are not the same thing as happiness.

As the hedonist understands it, happiness is attitudinal pleasure: the positive attitude of enjoyment. It can range in intensity from mild contentment to elation. Being happy does not necessarily feel like anything; there is no special sensation or physical quality associated with happiness. I can enjoy a home-team victory or a beautiful painting without experiencing any physical pleasure.

In order to be at all plausible, hedonism must be understood as the view that enjoyment, rather than physical pleasure, is the key to the good life. This may come as a surprise, since we nowadays think of hedonists as those who are always pursuing sensual pleasures. But we must abandon that picture, and fix our sights instead on the view that identifies the good life as one that is full of sustained enjoyment, containing only minimal sadness and misery. That is the hedonist's model of the best life for human beings.

Happiness, understood from now on as enjoyment, is indeed a good candidate for an intrinsic value.[2] It's not like a vaccination or a chocolate bar. If such things generate no benefits—if, say, the vaccination fails to protect you from disease, or if you hate chocolate (I've heard of such strange people)—then there is nothing valuable about them. They are good, when they are, only because of the benefits they bring about. Thus they are only instrumentally good. Happiness isn't like that. It is worth pursuing for its own sake. It is valuable in its own right.

1.2 The Attractions of Hedonism

Hedonism can trace its origins in the West to the ancient Greeks. Epicurus (341–270 BCE), the first great hedonist, argued that pleasure was the only thing worth pursuing. Yet he was not calling on us to pursue carnal

---

2. Many who reject hedonism still believe that happiness is the key to a good life. The disagreement is about what happiness really is. Hedonists insist that it is a kind of experience we have—the experience of enjoyment. Others, such as Aristotle, claim that happiness is much more than this; it is, in particular, a combination of enjoyment, intelligence, virtue, and activity. The sort of happiness that we discuss in this chapter and the next is the one that hedonists have in mind—namely, enjoyment.

pleasures. Epicurus argued that the most pleasant condition is one of inner peace. The ideal state of tranquility comes largely from two sources: moderation in all physical matters, and intellectual clarity about what is truly important.

Philosophy is the path to such clarity. Philosophy can reveal the false beliefs that cause so much unhappiness—specifically, as Epicurus saw it, our beliefs that death is bad for us, that the gods are mean-spirited and easily angered, and that sex and money are key ingredients in the good life. Philosophy can help explain the error of such popular ways of thinking, and thereby ease us along the path to happiness.

Skip ahead a couple thousand years, and consider the view of English philosopher John Stuart Mill (1806–1873), perhaps the most famous hedonist since Epicurus. Mill's critics claimed that hedonism was a "doctrine of the swine," because it advised us to live like animals, gaining as much brute pleasure as possible. Mill argued that pleasures come in different levels of quality, and that the best pleasures for human beings were those that come only through hard work—especially the work of the mind. Intellectual and artistic pleasures topped his list; physical pleasures were at the bottom. Mill thought that people who have enjoyed both physical and intellectual pursuits always prefer the intellectual pleasures. That was good enough for him, since he also thought that the true test of something's value was the approval of those with knowledge and experience.

As you might expect from a view whose popularity spans thousands of years, there is a great deal to be said on behalf of hedonism. Here are the most important reasons that have won it so many fans.

There Are Many Models of a Good Life

There are a variety of ways to live a good life, and hedonism explains why this is so: there are many paths to happiness. Can woodcutters, professional athletes, or musicians live very good lives? Not according to Plato (427–347 BCE) and Aristotle (384–322 BCE), who thought that philosophical contemplation was essential to a truly good life. Nowadays we are likely to reject such views as narrow-minded and elitist. We think that people from all walks of life have the potential to be well-off. This democratic view about the prospects for the good life fits comfortably with the hedonistic outlook. Because the sources of happiness vary quite widely, and happiness is the key to a good life, there are many ways to live a good life.

Hedonism offers us a kind of flexibility that some of its competitors lack. Many of these competitors identify a kind of activity, such as doing philosophy, as the greatest good. They then say that those who don't pursue it, or who pursue it badly, are unable to lead a good life. Hedonism rejects all such approaches. The best activity for human beings is the one that brings us the greatest happiness. But what makes me happy needn't make you happy. So my recipe for the good life may legitimately be very different from yours.

Personal Authority and Well-Being

This diversity of good lives has an interesting implication: hedonists provide each of us with a substantial say in what the good life looks like. And that seems a plus. Much of what makes us happy is a matter of personal choice. As a result, we each get plenty of input into what makes our lives go well.

So long as we really do know what will make us happy, hedonism supports the resistance we feel when others try to tell us how to live our lives. And when others counsel us, *for our own good*, to give up happiness and to pursue a less enjoyable way of life, hedonism assures us that such advice is deeply mistaken.

In one sense, however, hedonism does not allow us to have the final say about what is good for us. If hedonism is true, then happiness improves our lives, whether we think so or not. According to hedonists, those who deny that happiness is the sole thing that is intrinsically good for us are wrong, no matter how sincere their denial. In this way, hedonism follows a middle path between approaches to the good life that dictate a one-size-fits-all model and those that allow each person to decide for herself exactly what is valuable.

Misery Clearly Hampers a Good Life; Happiness Clearly Improves It

Hedonists tell us that misery takes away from a good life, and this is hard to deny. To test this claim, imagine a life full of sadness, with no compensating enjoyments. Surely this life is bad for the person who leads it. It may be good in other respects—the very sad person might, for instance, be a brilliant artist or a mathematical genius. But we are not asking whether the life is good in any way at all. Rather, we are asking about whether the life is going well for the person living it. Specifically, we are asking whether a really miserable person can have a high level of well-being. This is hard to accept, and hedonism explains why that is.

Hedonists also claim that happiness improves one's welfare. To test this, again imagine two people leading identical lives, with only one difference: the first person enjoys his life, and the second doesn't. Surely the first person is better off. If we were to choose between these lives solely on the basis of what would be best for us, we'd select the first, without question. That is precisely what hedonism would recommend.

The Limits of Explanation

The claim that happiness is intrinsically beneficial seems about as obvious as anything in ethics. And the value of everything else seems easily explained by showing how it leads to happiness.

If hedonism is true, then happiness directly improves one's welfare, and sadness directly undermines it. Just about everyone believes that. Indeed, how could we even argue for something as basic as this? This is where thinking in this area *starts*. Perhaps no claim about well-being is more fundamental than the one that insists on the importance of experiencing happiness and avoiding misery.

When we undertake something that is painful or difficult, it makes sense to ask why we'd do such a thing. Suppose, for instance, that you spot me red-faced, huffing and puffing, as I make my way around a track. Why am I willing to suffer so? To get in shape. Why is that important? To be healthy. Why is that important? Because it makes me happy. That's where all such lines of questioning seem to end. If being healthy only made me miserable—not easy to imagine, but possible—then what good would it do me? True, it might make me more attractive, or allow me to live longer, or make me a better athlete. But if *those* things didn't make me happy, it is hard to see how being healthy would make me better off.

It is perfectly sensible for us to ask about how we'd be better off by studying hard, playing by the rules, dieting, or telling the truth. We can defend the value of such things if we can show that they make us happier. But that shows only that they are instrumental goods. By contrast, we don't need to show that happiness leads to anything else in order to show that it is valuable. We recognize that to be happy is already to be in a desirable state. This supports the hedonist's claim that happiness is intrinsically valuable.

Rules of the Good Life—and Their Exceptions

Hedonism can justify the many rules for living a good life, while at the same time explaining why there are exceptions to these rules.

Almost all of us are better off if we manage to be free of manipulation, crippling illness, enslavement, constant worry, unwanted attention, treachery, and physical brutality. Remove these burdens, and you immediately improve the quality of life. The hedonist's explanation is simple and plausible: in almost every case, eliminating these things reduces our misery.

On the positive side, we can improve our lives by making sure that they contain interesting work and hobbies, trustworthy friends, a giving and understanding romantic partner, and a commitment to causes we strongly believe in. Why? Because such things usually add enjoyment to our lives.

These lists are not complete, and I'm not concerned to argue for any specific item on either one. The lists are meant to reflect common sense. And the point is that hedonism can explain why common sense says what it does. Certain things reliably damage our welfare, because they almost always bring misery in their wake; other things just as reliably improve our quality of life, because they are a source of enjoyment.

Hedonism can also explain why there are exceptions to these rules. Some people enjoy being humiliated or manipulated. For them, we must put these experiences on the positive side of the ledger. Others, such as certain masochists, delight in experiencing various kinds of physical pain. So such pain *adds* to their quality of life, while diminishing it for the rest of us.

Hedonism thus explains why it is so hard to come up with universal, iron-clad rules for improving our lives. Such rules hold only for the most part, because increasing our welfare is a matter of becoming happier, and some people find happiness in extremely unusual ways. Hedonism honors both the standard and the uncommon sources of happiness; no matter how you come by it, happiness (and only happiness) directly makes you better off.

Happiness Is What We Want for Our Loved Ones

I have two children, Max and Sophie. I love them very much. I have a very strong desire that they be happy, and an even stronger desire that their lives contain as little misery as possible. This makes perfect sense if hedonism is true.

That's because parents who deeply care for their children want what is best for them. I, like so many other parents, want my children to be happy. That shows that happiness is what is best for them. Right?

Not necessarily. Consider the words of Philippa Foot (1920–2010), a philosopher who rejected hedonism:

> I recall a talk by a doctor who described a patient of his (who had perhaps had a prefrontal lobotomy) as "perfectly happy all day long

picking up leaves." This impressed me because I thought, "Well, most of us are not happy all day long doing the things we do," and realized how strange it would be to think that the very kindest of fathers would arrange such an operation for his (perfectly normal) child.[3]

What Foot is suggesting here is that parents who really care about their children would want things for them *other than* their happiness. If happiness is of paramount importance, and if a lobotomized person experiences more happiness than the rest of us, then why shouldn't a loving parent sign up her child for such an operation? But the thought is absurd. And the reason, apparently, is that happiness is not the only thing that improves the quality of life. In Foot's example, parents quite reasonably give greater priority to their children's ability to develop their talents, and to pursue worthwhile activities—even those that bring them less happiness.

I think that there is definitely something to Foot's observation. But it is possible to make a common mistake when thinking about it. The error lies in assuming that the following is a surefire test for becoming better off:

> (T) If someone knows you very well, loves you, and for your own sake wants you to have X, then X makes you better off.

Most parents know their children very well, love them, and, for their sake, want them to be happy. If (T) is correct, this shows that happiness makes them better off.

But (T) is not correct, because even the dearest friend or parent can be mistaken about what will increase another person's welfare. Consider a father who loves his daughter and wants what is best for her. Yet he truly believes that a woman's welfare is a matter of how well she serves her husband. Suppose that his daughter has married someone who is physically and emotionally abusive. Such a father might advise his daughter to remain with her abuser, *for her own good.* Or consider parents whose son has told them that he is gay. They are appalled. They may really love him, and want him, for his own sake, to marry a nice young woman. But marrying a woman is not going to make this man better off. The cares of those who love you are not always a reliable indicator of where your self-interest lies.

---

3. Philippa Foot, *Natural Goodness* (New York: Oxford University Press, 2001), p. 85.

Hedonism can explain why this test (T), which initially sounded so plausible, fails in the end. If hedonism is true, then there is a different, and perfectly reliable, test of when well-being is improved:

(H) If something makes you happier, then it promotes your well-being; if something fails to make you happier, then it fails to promote your well-being.

The hedonist's test will sometimes conflict with (T). Staying with an abusive husband will not promote a daughter's happiness; marrying a woman will not promote a gay son's happiness. Therefore (H) tells us that such actions will not improve their well-being. And that is correct. (T) gives us the wrong results in these cases. (H) gives us the right ones.

But there is a nagging suspicion that more needs to be said. Although (H) provides the right answers in these cases, it does seem to get things wrong in the specific case that Philippa Foot described. After all, we don't want our children lobotomized, even if they'd be happier as a result! That seems to show that happiness is not the be-all and end-all of a good life. Let's now see whether that's so.

1.3 Discussion Questions

1. What is the difference between intrinsic value and instrumental value?
2. What is the difference between physical pleasure and attitudinal pleasure? Which kind of pleasure do hedonists claim is always intrinsically valuable? Why do you think that hedonists make this distinction, rather than claiming that all pleasure is intrinsically valuable?
3. In what sense does hedonism "give us a say" in what the good life looks like? Do you think that this is an attractive feature of hedonism? If so, why? If not, why not?
4. Can you think of any case in which experiencing pleasure fails to contribute to a person's well-being? If so, consider what a hedonist might say in order to undermine such a case.
5. Imagine someone who chooses to sacrifice his or her own happiness in order to help others, and claims that this is the best sort of life to live. Would the existence of such a person be a problem for hedonism? Why or why not?
6. What is the point of Foot's comments about lobotomies? How do you think a hedonist might respond to Foot's challenge?
7. Given the arguments of this chapter, do you think hedonism is correct? Why or why not?

.... ❧ ....

CHAPTER 2

Is Happiness All That Matters?

You probably already knew this, but just in case you didn't: no philosophical theory worth its salt is free of difficulties. As a result, you aren't going to get, in this chapter or any of the others, a decisive, knockdown argument for one theory or another. Brilliant minds have developed the theories we consider in this book. And equally brilliant minds have failed to climb on board.

So it should come as no surprise that hedonism, a perennial contender for "Best Theory of Human Welfare," should also have its critics. They have been busy. Here are the major concerns that they have identified.

2.1 The Paradox of Hedonism

> Mankind does not strive for happiness; only the Englishman does that.
> —*Friedrich Nietzsche,* Twilight of the Idols

Hedonism had become entrenched in certain philosophical circles in mid-nineteenth-century England, and Nietzsche was never shy about poking fun at his philosophical contemporaries. He despised hedonism, but this quote does not, by itself, express a critique of the view. After all, Englishmen (and other hedonists!) might well reply that even if many people don't in fact strive for happiness, they *should* do so, and *would* do so if they knew what was good for them. If something always makes us better off, then it seems reasonable to try very hard to acquire it, doesn't it?

Recall that hedonists view happiness as attitudinal pleasure—enjoyment—rather than physical pleasure. And when it comes to enjoyment, the strategy just mentioned completely backfires—those who are constantly trying to maximize their own enjoyment almost never succeed. Philosophers call this the *paradox of hedonism*.

The paradox reminds me of an embarrassing poster I had hanging on my bedroom wall as a child. It showed a butterfly and, not far away, a man sitting in a meadow. The caption read: "Happiness is like a butterfly—the more you pursue it, the more it eludes you. Be still and let it come to you."

We can use this distressing vignette to develop an argument against hedonism. Let's call it the *Paradox of Hedonism Argument*:

1. If happiness is the only thing that directly makes us better off, then it is rational to directly pursue it.
2. It isn't rational to do that.
3. Therefore, happiness isn't the only thing that directly makes us better off.

This argument is valid.[1] Its logic is perfect: *if* both premises are true, then the conclusion must be true. But we also need to know whether both premises really are true. If they are, then hedonism is sunk.

I think the second premise is pretty plausible. The icky sentiment on my childhood poster is correct. Those who seek only happiness, and fixate on acquiring it, are bound to be disappointed. Aiming directly for happiness is not the best way to get it. You'd do far better to seek a partner you love and respect, to develop an exciting hobby, or to find a career you can be proud of. Doing any of these things is a much surer route to happiness.

So the second premise looks good. And the first premise also seems plausible. If happiness is really the only thing that is valuable in its own right, then you should go for it.

But this premise is suspect, precisely because the direct pursuit of good things sometimes prevents us from getting them. Think of the professional golfer in the midst of a slump. She desperately wants to regain her swing. But the more she focuses on this, the harder it becomes. Or consider the immature student who wants more than anything to be well liked, and so tries, way too eagerly and very annoyingly, to be pals with his classmates. Such behavior is self-defeating. He'd be much better off trying less hard.

---

1. See the discussion "Moral Reasoning" in the Introduction.

The bottom line is that even if happiness is our greatest good, it may be irrational to aim for it directly. And if that is so, then premise 1 is false. As a result, the paradox we've just considered, while surprising, does not pose a serious threat to hedonism. It doesn't challenge the idea that happiness is the only thing of intrinsic value. It just tells us that aiming directly for happiness is not a smart way to get it.

2.2 Evil Pleasures

Some people take great delight in doing the most awful things. Think of supposed friends who tempt others into addiction, or a powerful boss who betrays a vulnerable employee. These tawdry people may really be enjoying themselves. But when such enjoyment comes at someone else's expense, it hardly seems a good thing, much less the best thing.

We can build another anti-hedonist argument around this point. Call it the *Argument from Evil Pleasures*:

1. If hedonism is true, then happiness that comes from evil deeds is as good as happiness that comes from kind and decent actions.
2. Happiness that comes from evil deeds is *not* as good as happiness that comes from kind and decent actions.
3. Therefore, hedonism is false.

This argument fails, and it's instructive to see why. There is a confusion contained within it, and it's one that is easy to make.

When we say that happiness that comes from one source is as good as happiness from any other source, we might mean that each is *morally equivalent* to the other. When we read premise 2 and nod our heads approvingly, this is probably what we have in mind.

But this is not what hedonists have in mind. They don't think that each episode of happiness is as morally good as every other. Rather, they think that the same amount of happiness, no matter its source, is *equally beneficial*. According to hedonism, happiness gained from evil deeds can improve our lives just as much as happiness that comes from virtue. In this sense, happiness derived from evil deeds *is* as good as happiness that comes from virtue—each can contribute to our well-being just as much as the other. Hedonists therefore reject premise 2.

And aren't they right to do so? Think about why the happiness of the wicked is so upsetting. Isn't it precisely because happiness benefits them, and we hate to see the wicked prosper? If happiness doesn't make us better off, why is it so awful when the wicked enjoy the harms they cause? And for those who share my vengeful streak: Why is it gratifying to see the wicked suffer? Because misery always cuts into our well-being, and we think it right that the wicked pay for their crimes. Hedonism makes perfect sense of these feelings.

2.3 False Happiness

Imagine a woman who is happy in her marriage, partly because she trusts her husband and believes that he has been completely faithful. Suppose her belief is true. Now imagine another woman who is as happy as the first, and for the same reasons. But in this case, her belief is false—her husband has been cheating on her without her knowledge. It seems that the first woman's life is going better for her. And yet these two women are equally happy.

This story provides us with the basis of an *Argument from False Happiness*:

1. If hedonism is true, then our lives go well to the extent that we are happy.
2. It's not the case that our lives go well to the extent that we are happy; those whose happiness is based on false beliefs have worse lives than those whose happiness is based on true beliefs, even if both lives are equally happy.
3. Therefore, hedonism is false.

This is in one way like the Argument from Evil Pleasures, since both claim that the *source* of happiness determines how beneficial that happiness is. Critics say that if happiness comes from immoral action, or false belief, then it makes us less well-off than otherwise.

Hedonists deny this. Happiness is happiness, regardless of its source. Hedonists accept the first premise. So they must reject the second.

But it is harder to do so here, when it comes to false beliefs. The late Harvard philosopher Robert Nozick (1938–2002) tried to show this, in a thought experiment involving an "experience machine."[2] Imagine that there is an amazing virtual reality machine that lets you simulate any experience you like. Suppose you program it for a lifetime of the very best

---

2. The example, and Nozick's discussion of it, can be found in his book *Anarchy, State, and Utopia* (New York: Basic Books, 1974), pp. 42–45.

experiences. Once you plug in, you think you're in the real world, and have no memory of life outside the machine. Your entire life from then on is lived in the machine, and you are as happy as can be, believing yourself to be doing all of the things you truly enjoy.

Compare this with a case in which someone actually does the things and enjoys the experiences that the plugged-in person only dreams of. It seems clear that the second life—the real one—is more desirable. Yet both lives contain the same amount of happiness.

This is meant to show that happiness is not the sole element of well-being. A good life is one that is happy, yes, but not only that. Our happiness must be based in reality. A pleasant life of illusion is less good for you than an equally pleasant life based on real achievement and true beliefs.

2.4 The Importance of Autonomy

One of the other things we want from life is to make our own choices about it. We resent it when other people manipulate us, even if they mean well. Sometimes we even prefer the definite prospect of sadness to a more pleasant life that is forced upon us without our consent. In short, we want **autonomy**—the power to guide our life through our own free choices—even if it sometimes costs us our happiness.

Not only do we want autonomy, but we also think that a life without it cannot be fully good. Consider the inhabitants of Aldous Huxley's *Brave New World*. Huxley created a fictional society in which war, poverty, and emotional distress have all disappeared. How have such things been achieved? The rulers have introduced a pacifying drug, called *soma*, which all citizens must take. Books and shows that may upset people have been banned. Close relationships are forbidden, so as to prevent the heartache that comes from the loss of a friendship or a loved one. Better to have loved and lost than never to have loved at all? Not in this society.

The citizens of this brave new world have become complacent animals, obedient to the political masters who are intent on manipulating them. Though this society might well be a happier one than ours, it seems clear that something valuable is missing. That something is autonomy.

We don't need to seek out imaginary tales to appreciate the importance of autonomy to a good life. When we go to the doctor's office, we don't want to be lied to—even if we would be happier were we deceived. Many dying patients turn down the offer of pain medication, because it can interfere with their ability to make rational decisions. Such patients prefer to face their end in a clear-eyed way, even if it means that they are more miserable as a result.

Autonomous choices don't always lead to happiness. Things go wrong. We make free choices that lead to damaged relationships, financial disaster, missed opportunities. Still, we need only imagine a life without autonomy to see what a tragedy it would be. Read the reports of Soviet psychiatrists who systematically drugged and tortured critics of the regime.[3] Many of these critics went insane; others were reduced to bowing and scraping before their white-coated masters.

These doctors caused appalling unhappiness. But that is not the only harm they did to their victims, and in some cases it is not the worst of the damage done. Even if drugs had kept the dissidents happy, the actions of these doctors would still have been a horrendous crime, because of the way in which they tried to crush the independence of their victims.

A searing picture of how the loss of autonomy undermines well-being can be found at the conclusion of Ken Kesey's *One Flew over the Cuckoo's Nest*. Its hero, R. P. McMurphy, is a free spirit with contempt for rules and for the authorities who enforce them. McMurphy is committed to a mental institution and slowly broken, eventually being forced to submit to a lobotomy that leaves him an empty shell. (Recall Foot's anecdote of the previous chapter.) That this is all supposedly done for his own good only makes the tragedy greater. At the end, he may be happier, having at this point only a childlike capacity to understand the world. But it hardly seems that he is better off as a result. And the explanation is simple: preserving our autonomy is vitally important, even if it doesn't always make us happier.

It's a good thing to be able to exercise autonomous choice, and this explains what is objectionable about **paternalism**—someone's limiting your liberty against your will, but for your own good. Some people might be better off if they were forbidden from gambling, Alpine climbing, or riding a motorcycle without a helmet. But even if that is so, there is something regrettable about no longer having the choice to do such things. We lose the opportunity to take chances, to risk our happiness, to exercise real freedom. Manipulation and paternalism, even when done in a way that gains us happiness, are still objectionable to some extent. And that is

---

3. A couple of accessible places to start are Harvey Fireside, *Soviet Psychoprisons* (New York: W. W. Norton, 1982), and Peter Reddaway and Sidney Bloch, *Soviet Psychiatric Abuse: The Shadow over World Psychiatry* (Boulder, Colo.: Westview Press, 1984).

because they sacrifice something of intrinsic value: autonomy. Happiness is not the only thing that is important in its own right. Autonomy is, too.

Here we have the makings of another argument against hedonism. Call this the *Argument from Autonomy*:

1. If hedonism is true, then autonomy contributes to a good life only insofar as it makes us happy.
2. Autonomy sometimes directly contributes to a good life, even when it fails to make us happy.
3. Therefore, hedonism is false.

The first premise is clearly true. The central claim of hedonism is that happiness is the only thing, in itself, that makes us better off. All other things (e.g., autonomy, virtue, knowledge) improve our lives only to the extent that they make us happier.

So everything hinges on the second premise. It seems plausible. When we consider the lives of those who have been deprived of their autonomy, we see the absence of a great value, something that, by itself, appears to make a life a better one. Given a choice between drug-induced contentment and plotting our own risky course through life, we prefer the latter path. We want our lives to be authentic, to reflect our own values, rather than those imposed on us from the outside—even if we are not always happier as a result. Hedonism cannot account for that.

2.5 Life's Trajectory

If hedonism is true, then those whose lives contain the same amount of happiness and unhappiness must be equally well-off. But this seems false.

Consider the sad case of Delmore Schwartz, a brilliant writer and conversationalist, who served as the basis of the title character in Saul Bellow's novel *Humboldt's Gift*. Schwartz earned many awards early in his career, and taught at Princeton and Harvard for several years. But his last decade was spent in increasing frustration and isolation. Addicted to alcohol and drugs, and experiencing increasingly severe paranoia and mental illness, he died alone in a seedy hotel in Times Square, the promise of his early years left unfulfilled.

It is impossible to say just how much happiness and sadness filled Schwartz's life. But imagine a person whose early life was largely heartache and hardship—Oprah Winfrey, for instance, or Mary Karr, whose terrific memoir *The Liars' Club* portrays a childhood about as miserable as can be.

In such lives, the suffering eventually yields to happiness, and many years of satisfaction and pleasure.

When we compare lives with such different trajectories, it is hard to resist the thought that a life that begins badly but continually improves is better than a life that starts out with a bang and goes slowly, steadily downhill—even if there is no difference in the total amounts of happiness contained in each life. We can fashion this thought into the *Trajectory Argument*:

1. If hedonism is true, then the overall quality of a life depends entirely on the amount of happiness and unhappiness it contains.
2. The overall quality of life depends on at least one other factor: whether one's life reflects an "upward" or "downward" trajectory.
3. Therefore, hedonism is false.

To make this criticism stick, we need to be sure that we are not sneaking in extra happiness on the part of the fortunate person whose life ends better than it began. The total happiness and unhappiness within the lives being compared must be the same. The only difference must be in the timing of the happiness and misery. If we take care to respect this requirement, I think we still feel that equal amounts of happiness and misery may not yield lives of equal well-being. If that is so, then something other than happiness and misery determines how good a life is. In this case, it is not autonomy, but rather the "shape" of a life. Continual improvement makes for a better life than one that has long been sliding downhill, even if both lives contain the same amounts of happiness and misery.

2.6 Unhappiness as a Symptom of Harm

Consider an Olympic marathon runner who is poised to bring home gold. She has trained for years for this event. Suppose that she pulls a hamstring the day before the race, and is unable to compete. All that work, to no end. She's devastated.

Why does this reaction make sense? It seems well explained if we assume that the development of our talents is important in its own right. This athlete sees that something terrible has happened, and *that* is why she is unhappy. What's most regrettable in her case isn't her unhappiness. It's the destruction of her talents. (After all, would everything be fine if someone slipped her a soma pill?)

When is it rational to feel miserable about how your life is going? Simple: when something really bad happens to you. On the face of it, this can include a huge number of things—losing a leg in a car accident, being jilted by someone you love, missing the opportunity of a lifetime, etc. Each of these rightly causes great sadness. If hedonism is correct, however, this short list, and the much longer one we could undoubtedly put together, are basically mistaken, for there is only one truly bad thing that can happen to you, and that is to experience sadness. Things can harm you only if they cause you to be unhappy.

If hedonism is true, then as long as we remain alive and greet each day happily, our lives cannot go badly. A stiff upper lip—or a soma pill, or genuine indifference—is enough to protect against harm.

So, for those who want to be immune from harm, here is the recipe: you must become either emotionally blank or permanently upbeat. Those who are never sad are never harmed. Talents might go to waste; limbs might atrophy; senses deaden, friendships break, curiosity dim—if hedonism is correct, none of this will undermine well-being, so long as you are not saddened by it.

Perhaps unhappiness always makes us worse off. But other things might do so as well. Consider how reasonable it is to be saddened, say, at a failed chance at love, or at the death of a dear friend. Such things diminish our happiness. But they do so only because our happiness, in these and so many other cases, depends on our appreciating what has value in its own right. If loving relationships didn't by themselves make us better off, it wouldn't be so clear that their loss is our loss. We mourn because we have been deprived of someone whose presence has directly made our lives richer.

Hedonism runs into trouble when trying to account for this. Here is an argument that shows how. Call it the *Argument from Multiple Harms*:

1. If hedonism is true, then you can be harmed by something only because it saddens you.
2. You can be harmed in other ways.
3. Therefore, hedonism is false.

The first premise is clearly true. And the second also seems plausible. Tragedies don't disappear just because their victims are reconciled to them. The unhappiness we experience is bad for us. But it can also be a *symptom* of the loss of something that, all by itself, matters to our well-being. Our misery in such situations is evidence that things other than happiness can directly make a difference to our well-being. If that is so, then hedonism is mistaken.

2.7 Conclusion

Hedonism has always had its fans. And, as we have seen, there are many good reasons for its popularity. It explains why there are many paths to a good life. It strikes a balance between a view that imposes just one blueprint of a good life and a view that allows anything to be valuable so long as you think it is. It provides a ready explanation for why misery so clearly damages a life and why happiness so clearly improves it. Hedonism offers a natural stopping point for explaining what is intrinsically valuable. It accounts for why the rules of a good life allow for exceptions. And happiness is what we want for our loved ones—what better evidence that happiness truly contributes to a good life?

And yet hedonism is not problem-free. I think that hedonists have good replies to the paradox of hedonism and the worry about evil pleasures. But things become trickier when we consider the value of a happiness that is based on false beliefs. Further, hedonists cannot allow for the intrinsic value of autonomy. They can't make sense of the idea that, of two lives containing the same amount of happiness, the one that continually shows improvement is better than the one that has gone steadily downhill. Hedonists also fail to appreciate that unhappiness is often a symptom that something intrinsically valuable—something other than happiness—has been lost.

Perhaps happiness is not, after all, the key to our well-being. Let's now consider an alternative approach—one that tells us that getting what you want is the measure of a good life.

2.8 Discussion Questions

1. What is the paradox of hedonism? Do you think the paradox gives us good reason to reject hedonism? Why or why not?
2. If you had a chance to get into the "experience machine" for the rest of your life, would you do it? Why might the idea of the experience machine pose a challenge for hedonism?
3. What are "evil pleasures," and why do they seem to be a problem for hedonism?

4. What is autonomy? Can hedonism account for the value of autonomy? Defend your answer.

5. What is false happiness? Construct a case of your own that provides an example of such happiness, and then assess its impact on the plausibility of hedonism.

6. What does it mean to talk about the "shape of a life"? Are some lives better than others simply in virtue of their "shape"?

7. Of all of the objections to hedonism presented here, which do you think is the strongest? Do you think that the hedonist has a convincing reply? Why or why not?

CHAPTER 3

.... ❧ ....

Getting What You Want

S uppose that you're unsure about what it takes to live a good life. So you visit your nearest philosophy department, plunk yourself down in the ethicist's office, and ask her directly. And suppose she gives you the following advice:

1. Love the one you're with.
2. Get in shape.
3. Dance.
4. Study philosophy.
5. Build things.

That strikes me as a pretty good list. It's not the whole of a good life, agreed, but it's not a bad start.

But what if you disagree? What if you're a terrible dancer? What if you don't care about the benefits of getting in shape? Maybe you're a klutz, like me, and can't build anything more complicated than a paper airplane.

Come to think of it, what could possibly qualify this professor to give advice about the good life? Surely, you might think, *you* get to decide for yourself what's going to make your life better off. Dancing and building things may work wonders for her, but that doesn't mean that her recipe for success has any universal authority. No recipe does. It all depends on what you care about.

The **desire satisfaction theory** of human welfare takes this sort of criticism very seriously. The theory tells us that your life goes well for you to the extent that you get what you want. At the other end of the spectrum, your life goes badly just when your desires are frustrated. More precisely, something is intrinsically good for you *if* it satisfies your desires, *only if* it satisfies your desires, and *because* it satisfies your desires. Something is instrumentally good for you if, only if, and because it helps you to fulfill your desires.

You might think that this view is no different from hedonism—after all, isn't happiness just a matter of getting what you want? Importantly, the answer is *no*. It's possible to get what you want and be no happier as a result. It's also possible to be happy even when you don't get what you want. While the desire satisfaction theory shares some of hedonism's attractive features, these two views are importantly different, as we'll see.

One way to bring out the difference between the two theories is by clarifying the notion of satisfaction here. A desire is satisfied just in case the object of the desire—what the desire is for—comes about. If you want a hearty dinner, then your desire is satisfied just in case you get one. If you want to be loved, then your desire is satisfied just so long as others really do love you. And so on. Importantly, talk of desire satisfaction can mislead us into thinking that desires are satisfied only if we get a *feeling* of satisfaction. That's not what's going on with this theory. Unlike hedonism, which makes the experience of enjoyment the key to a good life, the desire satisfaction theory denies that well-being is measured by experiences or feelings (of satisfaction, fulfillment, enjoyment, or anything else).

There is a lot to like about the desire satisfaction theory. Here are some of its main selling points.

3.1 A Variety of Good Lives

The desire satisfaction theory explains why there are many models of a good life, rather than just a single one. What makes my life good may be very different from what does the trick for you, because you and I may not want the same things. Our deepest desires determine what counts as life's improvements or failures. On this line of thinking, *nothing*—not health, love, knowledge, or virtue—is an essential ingredient in making everyone's life better off. Whether our lives have been improved depends entirely on whether our desires have been fulfilled.

It seems possible to have a good life that consists in wholehearted devotion to religious causes, to philosophy, music, travel, social justice, *Star Trek* conventions, or a favorite sports team. A good life focused on none of these, or a combination of these, also seems possible.

This makes perfect sense if we assume that our individual desires hold the key to a good life. I prefer chocolate to vanilla, and you don't? Then chocolate makes me better off, and vanilla does the same for you. You really, really want to collect igneous rocks? Splendid. Then you'd better get your hands on some. But my life will go perfectly well without any. The desire satisfaction theory easily accounts for this: your life goes well to the extent that your desires are satisfied. Since people desire very different things, there is a wide variety of good lives.

3.2 Personal Authority

Against the previous point, many people would argue that the good life must be focused on a single kind of pursuit—religious devotion, inner harmony, creativity, or philosophy, to name just a few prominent candidates. But there is something worrying about such single-mindedness. For each of these candidates, there are many who feel excluded and even angered at the suggestion that their life doesn't fit the favored model. After all, if you love excitement and hate tranquility, can inner harmony really be the key to your well-being?

If the desire satisfaction theory is correct, then each of us has the final say on what makes our life go well, because it's our own desires that determine how well we are faring. Further, no one gets to dictate which basic desires we should have. That is a personal matter. There is no universal standard for appropriate desires: to each his own. This view gives us a huge amount of freedom to choose our own vision of the good life. The only limitation here is that the good life must consist of satisfied desires. But what these desires are *for*—that is entirely up to you.

3.3 Avoiding Objective Values

A popular approach says that the good life consists of a handful of activities and experiences: gaining knowledge, experiencing love, appreciating art and music, being virtuous, and taking enjoyment in all of these things. This is an example of an **objective theory of human welfare**. It is objective in the sense that what directly contributes to a good life is fixed independently of your desires and your opinions about what is important.

There are lots of objective theories of welfare. Some theories, for instance, insist that the more knowledge you have, the better your life is going for you—even if you don't care very much about obtaining knowledge.

(I'm skeptical of such a view: is your life really better now that you know I have a cat named Oscar?) Other theories insist that virtue is required for a good life, no matter how you feel about virtue's importance. Hedonists claim that happiness is intrinsically valuable—even if, very unusually, you don't care about being happy.

Desire satisfaction theorists reject *all* objective theories of welfare. In doing so, they spare themselves the huge controversies that surround the defense of objective values. It is really difficult to argue for such values. That's because, for any contender, we can always ask a simple question: how can something make my life better if I don't want it, and don't want what it can get me? Sure, *if* you want to be a star athlete or a world-class musician, then daily practice will improve your life. But if you have no such dreams, and don't care about anything that such practice can get you, then *how could* it be good for you? That's a very hard question. Desire satisfaction theorists never have to answer it.

3.4 Motivation

Many people think that something can be good for us only if we can be motivated to pursue it. This thought is what underlies many of the suspicions about objective theories. Some people are left completely cold when they imagine (say) a life of wealth or power. We suspect that if this is true, then such things really don't make them better off. These doubts can be expressed in the *First Motivation Argument*:

1. If X is truly good for you, then you will be motivated to get X—so long as you know about X and know how to get it.
2. Many people who know about WEALTH and know how to get it aren't motivated to become wealthy.
3. Therefore, WEALTH will not improve the lives of such people.

We can repeat this argument for anything that is said to be an objective good—virtue, religious observance, fame, health, and so on. Regardless of which good you put forward (i.e., no matter how you fill in the blank in the argument above), there will always be some intelligent people who don't care about it. The upshot is that this argument threatens all objective theories of well-being.

Objective theories of well-being have a difficult time explaining the connection between what's good for us and our motivations. On the desire satisfaction theory, explaining this is a piece of cake. To see this, consider the *Second Motivation Argument*:

1. If something is intrinsically good for you, then it will satisfy your desires.
2. If something will satisfy your desires, then you will be motivated (at least to some extent) to get it—so long as you know what you want and know how to get it.
3. Therefore, if something is intrinsically good for you, then you will be motivated (at least to some extent) to get it—so long as you know what you want and know how to get it.

The first premise states a central claim of the desire satisfaction theory. The second premise seems clearly true, once we understand that desires motivate us to do things. And the argument is valid, so if both premises are true, then the conclusion must be true. Indeed, many theorists regard this conclusion as an important truth, and think that it is a major strike against objective theories that they cannot allow for it.

3.5 Justifying the Pursuit of Self-Interest

What is the point of trying to improve your life? Some regard this as a rhetorical question. Desire satisfaction theorists don't. They have an answer.

I think that there is always some reason to do what is best for yourself. Almost everyone thinks so. But what if someone challenged this claim? Is there anything that we can say on its behalf?

Desire satisfaction theorists have something to say. And this is a big plus, since it is always best to be able to justify a claim, rather than have to insist on its truth without being able to back it up. We can offer the following argument to support the view that there is always good reason to look out for ourselves. Let's call this the *Argument for Self-Interest*:

1. If something makes us better off, then it satisfies our desires.
2. If something satisfies our desires, then we have reason to obtain it.
3. Therefore, if something makes us better off, then we have reason to obtain it.

Premise 1 states an essential claim of the desire satisfaction theory. And premise 2 seems pretty plausible. Our wanting something gives us a reason to get it. If you want to lose weight, then you have reason to exercise and watch your calories. If you want to ace that exam, you have reason to study hard. If you want to complete your collection of Romanian postage stamps, then it's a good idea to track down the missing ones and buy them.

In short, if there is always reason to get what you want, and if (as the desire satisfaction theory says) getting what you want always makes you better off, then there is always reason to make yourself better off.

Contrast this with an objective theory of well-being. Suppose, for instance, that an objectivist claims that inner peace is good for you, whether you know it or not. But suppose that inner peace is not your cup of tea. You embrace risk, you hate to be bored, and you enjoy a life of turmoil and excitement. If you don't care about inner peace, and it gets you nothing you do care about, then it is hard to see why there is any reason for you to seek it. The same goes for any other supposed objective good.

Desire satisfaction theorists easily handle this problem. If they are right, you have reason to promote your self-interest because you have reason to get what you want, and getting what you want is the key to self-interest.

3.6   Knowledge of the Good

If the desire satisfaction theory is correct, then we have a straightforward answer to one of life's eternal questions: how can I know what is good for me? The answer is simple: be clear about what you want. Then make sure you know how to get it.

This isn't always easy in practice. I may really want to get someone to fall in love with me, but finding the best method to do this could be (to put it mildly) quite tricky.

Difficulties can also arise if I want conflicting things—and don't we all? In such cases, you should fulfill the desire that you care about more. Again, it isn't always easy in practice to tell which one this is. Sometimes we realize only too late that we made a mistake and pursued a goal that mattered less to us than the one we passed up. In that case, we chose badly—we may have gained some good, but we would have gained even more had we satisfied our deeper desire.

These are not difficulties with the desire satisfaction theory. After all, at times it really is very hard to know how to make our lives better. A plausible theory of well-being should explain why we are puzzled, when we are. It should also give us clear advice in many cases. The desire satisfaction theory does both. It tells us why it is sometimes so difficult to know what is best for us—because we don't know how to get what we want, or we aren't sure about what we want most. And it also explains the easy cases—these are precisely those where we do know what we want, and know how to get it.

Compare this picture to the one offered by objectivists. If personal opinion or preference does not determine what is best for us, then how can we know what to aim for? Objectivists insist that (say) knowledge, virtue, and inner peace are intrinsically good for us. But how can they defend such claims if we consistently deny them? What if—as is really the case—different objectivists disagree among themselves about what is intrinsically beneficial? Are we just supposed to "intuit" the truth here? What happens if I intuit the importance of virtue and you don't? How do we resolve the dispute between those who are sure that virtue is the key to a good life and those who insist that fame and fortune are what it's all about?

Desire satisfaction theorists avoid all such difficult questions. They deny that there are any objective goods. They are thereby spared the task of explaining how we could have knowledge of such things. You want to know how to make yourself better off? Get clear about what you really care about. Then find out how to get it. It isn't always easy. But it isn't a deep mystery, either.

3.7 Discussion Questions

1. Many people think that there is just one path to the good life. Do you agree? If so, what argument(s) can you give to someone who thinks otherwise?

2. Many people find the desire satisfaction theory attractive on the grounds that it leaves what counts as a good life "up to us." To what extent are our desires "up to us"? Can we really choose whether we want something or not?

3. What is an objective theory of human welfare, and why isn't the desire satisfaction theory an objective theory? Is the denial of objective values an attractive or an unattractive feature of a theory of well-being?

4. The desire satisfaction theory tells us that our lives go better so long as we get what we want—no matter what we want. Can you think of any examples where this isn't so?

5. Why is it difficult for objective theories to explain the connection between well-being and motivation? How does the desire satisfaction theory solve this problem?
6. According to the Argument for Self-Interest, we always have reason to pursue what we want. Does this assumption seem true to you? Can you think of any counterexamples?
7. Look back at the objections to hedonism presented in chapter 2. Does the desire satisfaction theory do a good job handling all of the concerns raised there? Defend your answer.

.... ~ ....

CHAPTER 4

Problems for the Desire
Satisfaction Theory

The previous chapter offers a very nice laundry list of attractions of the desire satisfaction theory. These attractions help to explain why it is so popular. But (you guessed it) there are also a number of difficulties that this theory faces, and some of them are serious enough to force us to revise the view, and possibly even to reject it.

To appreciate these worries, let's remind ourselves of the two central claims of the desire satisfaction theory:

(A) If something is intrinsically good for us, then it fulfills our desires; if something is instrumentally good for us, then it helps us to fulfill our desires.

(B) If something fulfills our desires, then it is intrinsically good for us; if something helps to fulfill our desires, then it is instrumentally good for us.

(A) tells us that something must (help to) satisfy our desires in order to be beneficial; desire satisfaction is *necessary* for becoming better off. (B) tells us that satisfying our desires is enough to make us better off; desire satisfaction is *sufficient* for becoming better off. Let's begin by considering (A), and then move to a discussion of (B).

4.1 Getting What You Want May Not Be Necessary for Promoting Your Good

We can test (A) by seeing whether we can come up with an example in which something benefits us, even though it doesn't satisfy or help to satisfy any of our desires. If there are any such examples, then (A) is false.

There do seem to be such examples. Three spring to mind.

The first is that of pleasant surprises. These are cases in which you are getting a benefit that you didn't want or hope for. Imagine something that never appeared on your radar screen—say, a windfall tax rebate, an unexpectedly kind remark, or the flattering interest of a charming stranger. It makes sense to say that you're a bit better off as a result of such things, even though they didn't satisfy any of your desires. Of course, now that you've experienced such things, you may well want more of them. But that's because they have made your life better already. And they did that without answering to any of your pre-existing desires.

The second case is that of small children. We can benefit children in a number of ways, even though we don't give them what they want and don't help them get what they want. A parent benefits her five-year-old by teaching him to read, for instance, even though the child doesn't want to read and doesn't know enough about the benefits of literacy to find them appealing.

The third case is suicide prevention. Those who are deeply sad or depressed may decide that they would be better off dead. They are often wrong about that. Suppose we prevent them from doing away with themselves. This may only frustrate their deepest wishes. And yet they may be better off as a result. (We will return to this example later.)

In each of these cases, we can improve the lives of people without getting them what they want or helping them to do so. They may, later on, approve of our actions and be pleased that we acted as we did. But this after-the-fact approval is something very different from desire satisfaction. Indeed, it seems that the later approval is evidence that we benefited them, even though we did not do anything that served their desires at the time. And that is evidence that (A) is mistaken.

4.2 Getting What You Want May Not Be Sufficient for Promoting Your Good

If (B) is true, then we are better off whenever our desires are satisfied; desire satisfaction is sufficient for (i.e., a guarantee that) improvement in our quality of life. There are many reasons to doubt this.

Desires Based on False Beliefs

Sometimes we want something for its own sake, but our desire is based on a false belief. When we make mistakes like this, it is hard to see that getting what we want really improves our lives. Suppose you want to hurt someone for having insulted you, when he did no such thing. You aren't any better off if you mistreat the poor guy. Or perhaps you desperately want to be popular with a certain group of people, but only because you think that they are glamorous and happy. Once you get to know them better, you come to realize how shallow and miserable they are. As the old saying goes: beware of what you wish for—it may come true.

From now on, then, we should understand the desire satisfaction theory to insist that it is only *informed* desires whose satisfaction will improve our lives. Fulfilling desires based on false beliefs may not improve our welfare. So the real thesis under consideration will be:

(C) If something fulfills our *informed* desires (i.e., those not based on false beliefs), then that thing is intrinsically good for us; if it helps us to fulfill our informed desires, then it is instrumentally good for us.

Disinterested and Other-Regarding Desires

All of us want some things that seem entirely unrelated to us. Our desires are directed, say, at the interests of strangers, or at no interests at all. (Perhaps I want there to be an even number of planets, and now that Pluto has been banned from the club, I've finally gotten my wish.) In such cases, we can get what we want, even though it is hard to see how our lives are improved as a result.

A few years ago I read about a whale that had beached itself on a New England coast. I remember wanting that whale to survive, to be eased back into the ocean without being harmed. And it was. It's easy to see that the whale was better off as a result of the rescue operation. But it's not so easy to see that my life got any better.

There is a natural reply to such examples. My life was indeed mildly improved, because I was pleased to get what I wanted. And that may be true. The problem with this reply, however, is that it is not available to desire satisfaction theorists, since they *do not assign any intrinsic value to pleasure*. If those theorists are correct, then your life goes better just so long as more of your desires are satisfied—regardless of how much pleasure this yields. A more pleasant life is not necessarily better for those who live it. After all, some people may despise pleasure. Though only a handful of people may feel this way, still, for those who do, the desire satisfaction theory tells us that added pleasure does not amount to a personal benefit.

Disappointment

Recall the important distinction, from last chapter, between a desire's *being satisfied* and a person's *feeling satisfied* that she got what she wanted. These can come apart. And that appears to spell trouble for the desire satisfaction theory.

Consider a young musician who has staked his hopes on becoming famous some day. And that day comes—but all he feels is disappointment. He got what he wanted. He knows it. And he hates how it feels.

Getting what you really want can sometimes be a huge letdown. All that buildup, and then, rather than any feeling of joy, just a blank sort of sadness—or worse. You've invested yourself in some project, have brought it to a successful end, and then find yourself filled with emptiness, boredom, or depression.

I was reminded of these points when reading the following passage from the autobiography of tennis legend John McEnroe:

> I was playing great tennis, and I destroyed [Ivan] Lendl to win the '84 Masters. . . . I'd finally taken my game to what felt like a notch above all my opponents'. It should have been great. I wish it had been. But it wasn't.
>
> It still felt hollow—I'd thought it would help straighten me out . . . but it wasn't doing a thing for me inside. It reminded me of the story of King Midas: My success wasn't translating into happiness.[1]

If seeing your desires come true only makes you miserable, then how could this mark an improvement in your life? The desire satisfaction theory commits us to saying that you are better off in such a case. This is very difficult to accept.

We could, of course, modify the desire satisfaction theory once again:

(D) If something has fulfilled our informed desires, and we are pleased as a result of this, then that thing is intrinsically good for us.

(D) might be true. But that should be small comfort, for it now seems that *pleasure* is what is making our lives better off, rather than desire satisfaction per se. That of course is something that hedonists will defend, but it's bad news for desire satisfaction theorists. After all, if getting what you want only makes you miserable, it is hard to see how you are any better off as a result.

---

1. John McEnroe with James Kaplan, *You Cannot Be Serious* (New York: Berkeley Books, 2002), p. 172.

Ignorance of Desire Satisfaction

Consider a case in which my informed desires are satisfied. I get what I'd hoped for. But I don't realize this. I never know that my goal has been met. It doesn't seem that I am any better off in such a situation.

Imagine a person deeply committed to finding a cure for a terrible disease. After years of hard work, she succeeds. But she goes to her grave never realizing this. She thinks her efforts have been wasted. Her success does not, by itself, seem to mark any improvement in her life.

Or think of a man who very much wants to be a father. He has a series of relationships, one of which leads to a pregnancy and then to a child. But the mother never informs him of this, and he never finds out through other channels. His desire is satisfied, but it's hard to see that his quality of life has improved.

As in the cases of disappointment, what we have here are examples in which our informed desires are satisfied, but we don't seem to be any better off as a result. That spells trouble for the desire satisfaction theory.

Impoverished Desires

The theory we've been considering says that having a good life is essentially a matter of fulfilling your desires. Our desires, however, are often shaped by the way we have been raised. The expectations that we have been taught to have are especially important influences. And this creates a problem.

Some parents have raised their children to believe themselves unworthy of love, or incapable of real accomplishment. Some societies continue to treat the women among them as second-class citizens (if citizens at all). Women in such societies are told from the earliest age that any political or professional hopes are unnatural and beyond their reach.

It's easy to take such messages to heart. If you are told from the cradle that your greatest ambition should be to serve your master, then you may well end up with no desire any stronger than that. If desire fulfillment is the measure of a good life, then such lives can be very good indeed.

That doesn't seem right. For instance, it is tempting to think that a slave cannot live a very good life, regardless of whether her desires are fulfilled. And that is because she is unfree. But desire theorists reject the idea that there is anything intrinsically valuable about freedom. Nothing is important in its own right—not intellectual or artistic achievement, not freedom, not pleasure. If it has been drilled into your head that it is foolish to seek freedom, or that education is unnecessary for "your kind," then a reasonable response may well be to abandon hope for any such things. Better to have goals you can achieve than to set yourself up for constant disappointment.

And yet what kind of life is that? The desire satisfaction theorist seems forced to say that it may be among the best. The lower your expectations, the easier they are to satisfy. As a result, those who set their sights very low may have a greater number of satisfied desires than those with more challenging goals. But this hardly seems to make for a better life.

The Paradox of Self-Harm and Self-Sacrifice

If the desire satisfaction theory is correct, then getting what you want makes you better off. But what if people want to harm themselves? This needn't be irrational. For instance, people may feel remorse for wrongs they have done, and want to do penance. Others may despise themselves, full of self-loathing, convinced that they deserve only harm, rather than good. No matter their ultimate motive, they deeply want to harm themselves.

In other cases, people want to sacrifice their self-interest in order to promote the good of someone they care about, or some cause that is more important to them than their own welfare.

It seems possible for such people to succeed. People can willingly harm themselves, and they can sacrifice their well-being to causes that matter to them. But the desire satisfaction theory denies this: if such people satisfy their self-destructive or self-sacrificing desires, then the theory says that they are better off! So long as they get what they really want, then they must be benefited as a result. And yet their fondest wish is to harm or to sacrifice themselves. So the theory generates a paradox: wanting to harm or sacrifice yourself makes it impossible to do so. Since it does seem possible both to want such things and to succeed, the desire satisfaction theory is suspect.

The Fallibility of Our Deepest Desires

Most of us don't intentionally set out to harm ourselves. But there are other cases in the neighborhood that pose problems for the desire satisfaction theorist. I am thinking here of suicide, where the would-be suicide is regarding her death *not* as a harm, but rather as a benefit. She is not trying to make herself worse off. Rather, she is trying to improve her life—by ending it. True, this also has an air of paradox about it. Let's see what a desire satisfaction theorist can say about such cases.

There are many different kinds of suicides. The one that poses the sharpest problem is that of a person whose life, by our lights, has terrific promise and is definitely worth living. Yet the suicidal person does not share our view. Suppose, in a common example, that a young man's lover has broken up with him and left, never to return. He is stricken with grief and decides to kill himself. This becomes his obsession; he most wants to die. If the desire satisfaction theory is true, then the deeper the desire, the better off its fulfillment will make you. Thus in his case, dying is his best option. Nothing else will make him as well off.

It is hard to accept that. And desire satisfaction theorists may have an out. After all, their best view is that the satisfaction of *informed* desires is what contributes to your well-being. And the suicide's desire to end his life might be based on a false belief. But which belief would this be? He may be well aware of all of the facts of his life, and look at them with only pain and anxiety. In that case, it is tempting to think that his false belief is this: *my life is going very badly, and isn't likely to get any better.*

The problem is that desire satisfaction theorists may have to regard this belief as *true*. On their view, your desires determine how well your life is going. If this person is clear-eyed, and sees that he is getting very little of what he wants, then his life really is going poorly. Further, he may be quite self-aware about what he is likely to want in the future—a relationship with his former lover—and realize that this desire is bound to be frustrated. If so, then his life is *not* going to improve.

What we want to tell such a person is this: change your desires! Stop wanting her so much. (Not that this is easy. Not that it can happen overnight.) But suppose that he won't, and that he knows this. We tell him to change his desires, because his current obsession is only causing him misery and preventing him from taking an interest in other things that really matter. Yet from the desire satisfaction theorist's perspective, such advice is fundamentally mistaken. Things matter only to the extent that you care about them. If, at bottom, you really want to die, then you are better off dead.

This is one of many possible examples of basic desires that can appear to be fundamentally off base. Consider the following cases, offered by philosopher Joel Feinberg (1926–2004). The first is that of an exhibitionist who exposes himself in public, not to solicit or threaten others, but just because he wants, as Feinberg puts it, "exposure for exposure's sake." Or a kleptomaniac—in Feinberg's example, a high school student who was otherwise as normal as you or I, but who was caught in possession of twenty-one shirt buttons, seven pairs of clippers, nine bike wrenches, five pocket mirrors, and a variety of oil cans, violin strings, and combs. He didn't intend to use these things for any purpose at all. He just wanted them in their own right. Feinberg's last example invites us to consider "a well-off man who shoplifts only one kind of item, women's brassieres. He could easily afford to pay for these items. . . . He does not enjoy stealing them and suffers great anxiety in worrying about being found out. . . . If you ask him for an explanation of his bizarre conduct, he will confess himself as puzzled by it as any observer."[2]

Such cases allow us to see how one of the main attractions of the desire satisfaction theory—its reluctance to criticize our desires, to hold them up to any objective standard of value—is also a weakness. It isn't that hard to satisfy these unusual desires. So if the theory is correct, the good life is easily within the grasp of such people. But the thought that any of them is living a good life is very hard to accept.

4.3 Conclusion

There are a number of reasons to think that the good life consists in our getting what we want. But there are some serious problems with this view. Most of the problems boil down to this: the desire satisfaction theorist cannot recognize that any desires are intrinsically better than any others. If your heart is set on repeatedly counting to nine, or on saying the word *putty* until you die, then (on this view) succeeding in such tasks yields a life as good as can be for you.

But a promising youth may have a death wish; an oppressed slave may want only to serve her master; a decent but self-loathing man may most want to be publicly humiliated. We can imagine these desires fulfilled, and yet the resulting lives appear to be impoverished, rather than enviable. Indeed, we regard such people as unfortunate precisely because of what they want—their desires are not fit to be satisfied, because they fail to aim for worthy ends.

To say such a thing, however, is to side with the objectivist, and to reject an essential element of the theory we're considering. For the desire satisfaction theorist, nothing but satisfied desires make us better off, and

---

2. Joel Feinberg, "What Is So Special about Mental Illness?" in Feinberg, *Doing and Deserving* (Princeton, N.J.: Princeton University Press, 1970), pp. 272–292. The examples and quotes are taken from p. 281.

there are no objective standards that elevate some basic desires over others. On this view, value is in the eye of the beholder, and so those who prefer to publicly expose themselves or to steal worthless trinkets may really be living the best life a human being can live.

Compare two lives. The first is that of a successful professional musician who takes great enjoyment in seeing new cities, cooking gourmet meals for her beloved family, taking fine nature photos, and running marathons. The second is that of a partially lobotomized adult who has enough cognitive powers to have informed desires, though not very many, and none of great complexity. If you were deciding between them, solely on the basis of self-interest, wouldn't you choose to have the musician's life—even if you knew that it contained fewer satisfied desires?

Some adults have the mental powers of an infant or a very small child. I am not claiming that such people have nothing to live for, or that their lives cannot be good ones. I am assuming, however, that such lives are not the very best ones that human beings can lead. And yet they may contain the greatest number of satisfied desires, especially if the relevant desires are very easy to fulfill. If the desire satisfaction theory is true, the quality of life in such a case is unsurpassed. That, too, is very difficult to accept.

Further, suppose that *all* of your deepest desires have been satisfied, but that this leaves you only completely miserable. The desire satisfaction theorist must regard this as the best sort of life, whereas most of us would think it horrible to be in such a situation.

I think that the challenges recorded here are serious enough to cast doubt on the desire satisfaction theory. Getting what we want is not, it seems, an essential part of the good life. It is neither a guarantee of it, nor a requirement.

What, then, holds the key to the good life? Happiness is surely a part of it; it can't be good for a person to go through life without any enjoyment at all. But as earlier discussions have shown, there is more to the good life than happiness. The conclusion we are forced to is that the good life depends on objective values, things that are valuable even if we fail to value them. Happiness is one objective value. Autonomy is another. There are doubtless others. These are things worth wanting, things that we ought to obtain or achieve if we seek the best life for ourselves. Want the complete list? The only way to get it is by doing (a lot) more philosophy.

4.4 Discussion Questions

1. Can something be good for you, even if you don't want it?
2. What does it mean for a desire to be "informed"? Why might the satisfaction of uninformed desires fail to contribute to our well-being?
3. Suppose that one of your desires is fulfilled, but that you never discover this, and so derive no feeling of satisfaction from this. Are you any better off as a result of your desire having been fulfilled?
4. Why is the phenomenon of feeling disappointed at getting what you want a problem for desire satisfaction theorists? How might they try to defend their theory against such cases?
5. Recall the examples of those who are slaves, potential suicides, or kleptomaniacs. Do you think that they are better off if their desires are satisfied? If not, what is the strongest reply that a desire satisfaction theorist can make to such examples?
6. Is it possible to be "brainwashed" into desiring something that isn't really in your interest? If so, what sort of pressure does this put on the desire satisfaction theory?
7. Do you agree that the good life depends on objective values? If so, what items (if any) would appear on your list of things that have objective value?

4.5 Cases for Critical Reflection

Social Media

Essena O'Neill seemed like she had the perfect life. In 2015, the eighteen-year-old Australian model and vegan advocate had over a half million followers on the social media platform Instagram. O'Neill found that she was able to make an income by marketing products to her social media followers, sometimes earning as much as $2,000 for a single post. O'Neill was young and beautiful, and many of her Instagram posts featured images of her smiling.

In October 2015, O'Neill publicly disavowed her Instagram persona. She explained that she had spent her teenage years addicted to social media and seeking social approval: "I spent hours watching perfect girls online, wishing I was them. Then I was 'one of them.' I still wasn't happy, content or at peace with myself."[1] O'Neill revealed the lengths she would go through to get the right pose for her next Instagram photo, sometimes sucking in her stomach to appear extremely thin. She would obsessively check the number of "likes" she got on her photos. O'Neill described the insecurity behind her Instagram persona: "I just want young girls to know this isn't candid life, or cool or inspirational. It's contrived perfection made to get attention."[2]

There is a growing body of research looking at whether social media is making us unhappy. A recent study found that the more you use Facebook over time, "the more likely you are to experience negative physical health, negative mental health and negative life satisfaction." A 2017 study of eighteen- to twenty-two-year-olds found an association between time spent on social media and "anxiety symptoms and the greater likelihood of an anxiety disorder." Social media can be addicting, and some use it compulsively, but some people believe that quitting social media might improve your mood.[3]

Questions

1. Does social media give us a distorted view of what constitutes a good life or what it looks like for someone's life to go well?
2. Would a hedonist think there is anything wrong with extensively using social media? Why or why not?
3. According to the desire satisfaction theory, is there anything wrong with extensively using social media? Why or why not?

The Ascetic Life

Asceticism is a lifestyle characterized by the pursuit of spiritual goals and abstinence from pleasure. The term *ascetic* comes from the Greek *áskesis,* meaning "athletic discipline." Ascetic practices have been observed in many religious traditions. Early Christian ascetics disciplined themselves through observances such as sexual renunciation and

---

1. http://time.com/4096988/teen-instagram-star-essena-oneill-quitting-social-media/.

2. https://www.theguardian.com/media/2015/nov/03/instagram-star-essena-oneill-quits-2d-life-to-reveal-true-story-behind-images.

3. http://time.com/collection/guide-to-happiness/4882372/social-media-facebook-instagram-unhappy/.

fasting. Contemporary ascetic hermits, nuns, and monks leave behind the civilized world in order to seek God in solitude.[1] In India, ascetic Jain nuns sleep on concrete floors and spend long hours in meditation. They practice nonviolence to the point that they refuse even to kill insects. Sadika Sansiddhi, a young ascetic nun living in New Delhi, explains: "You have to restrict your wants and desires to reach a higher spiritual level."[2]

In an extreme form of asceticism, some Buddhist monks in the eleventh through twentieth centuries practiced a ritual of self-mummification. They believed that having a body with delayed composition increased a monk's holiness. It took years to complete the ritual, which involved starvation and dehydration. During the first few years, ascetic monks would increase their physical activity and severely decrease their caloric intake, eating only nuts, seeds, and berries. Toward the end of the ritual, the monks would drink tea that helped prevent decomposition, eating only bark, roots, and sometimes stones. When a monk felt he was close to death, he would enter a tomb or coffin. The dying monk would spend his final hours chanting and occasionally ringing a bell.[3]

Questions

1. Do you think practicing asceticism is necessary for the good life? Sufficient? Why or why not?
2. According to hedonism, do ascetics lead good lives? Why or why not?
3. According to desire satisfaction theory, do ascetics lead good lives? Why or why not?

Competitive Eating

On July 4, 2018, at the annual Nathan's Famous Hot Dog Eating Contest on Coney Island in Brooklyn, New York, renowned competitive eater Joey "Jaws" Chestnut set a world record. He consumed seventy-four hot dogs

---

1. https://www.huffingtonpost.com/norris-j-chumley-phd/the-value-of-asceticism-t_b_806700.html.

2. http://articles.latimes.com/2005/sep/11/news/adfg-nun11.

3. https://strangeremains.com/2015/01/30/read-about-self-mummification-an-extreme-way-of-saving-money-on-embalming/.

in ten minutes, claiming his eleventh victory in the competition. Chestnut took home the coveted Mustard Belt and a $10,000 prize.[1]

In preparation for competition, Chestnut adheres to a strict diet and training process. During this time, his diet consists of hot dogs, protein supplements, and water. He fasts for a few days leading up to a practice day, when he'll consume between thirty-five and seventy hot dogs in a sitting. Describing the athletic component of his process, Chestnut says, "I think the whole practice and recovery, it's similar to marathon runners when they're slowly ramping up, they hit it and hit it again. . . . They hit the muscle group, and they let it recover, they hit it again."[2]

Competitive eaters use special swallowing techniques and learn to relax and stretch their stomachs to accommodate more food. The competitors often appear to be relatively thin and healthy, but not much research has been done to understand the health effects of competitive eating on the body. Side effects of competitive eating include nausea, vomiting, and diarrhea. In rare cases, competitive eaters may suffer choking, inflammation, and stomach rupture.[3]

Competitive eating spectators may find themselves feeling queasy, but we often admire great athletes, seeing their accomplishments—competitions won, records set—as the pinnacle of human flourishing. Sport challenges competitors physically and mentally. As Joey Chestnut remarked at the 2012 Hot Dog Eating Contest, "This sport isn't about eating. It's about drive and dedication, and at the end of the day hot dog eating challenges both my body and my mind."[4]

Questions

1. Do you think participation in athletic sport is an important part of the good life? Why or why not?
2. Would a proponent of hedonism see competitive eating as part of the good life? Why or why not?
3. Would a proponent of desire satisfaction theory see competitive eating as part of the good life? Why or why not?

---

1. https://www.nbcnews.com/news/us-news/joey-chestnut-downs-record-74-hot-dogs-nathan-s-famous-n888876.
2. https://www.gq.com/story/joey-chestnut-nathans-interview.
3. https://www.cbsnews.com/news/how-competitive-eating-affects-the-body/.
4. https://www.medicaldaily.com/joey-chestnut-winner-nathans-famous-hot-dog-eating-contest-consumes-more-25000-calories-quest-247410.

PART TWO

Normative Ethics: Doing the Right Thing

CHAPTER 5

Morality and Religion

Religion has always been the most popular source of morality. In times of need and moral perplexity, religious believers consult priests, rabbis, imams; they avidly read their sacred texts; they look to long-standing religious traditions for guidance. Since hundreds of millions of people view morality through the lens of one religion or another, it is important that we examine this relationship carefully.

We aren't going to try to determine here whether God exists. Nor are we going to explore specific doctrines that separate one religion from another. Instead, I want to take a step back and examine four central assumptions that underlie the widespread view that morality depends on religion:

1. Religious belief is needed to motivate us to do our duty.
2. Acting morally is rational only if God exists.
3. Morality must be created by someone, and God is by far the best candidate for the job.
4. Religious wisdom is the key to providing us with moral guidance.

Let's examine these assumptions in order.

5.1 First Assumption: Religious Belief Is Needed for Moral Motivation

A popular argument in favor of the religious life states that **atheism**[1] (the view that God[2] does not exist) prevents us from seeing why we should be moral. And if we are blinded to our reasons to be good, then we will probably be bad. Without belief in God, people are more likely to stray from the path of virtue. It will be harder for them to sacrifice self-interest when duty calls. But once God is in the picture, our will is strengthened. Religious people are going to be more *conscientious*—more firmly committed to living up to their own ethical ideals—than atheists or **agnostics** (those who are unsure whether God exists or not).

This may be true. If it is, what would explain it?

The most popular answer cites our fear of God and our desire for a happy afterlife. The thought of spending eternity in flames, or divorced from God's love, is a pretty powerful check on our immoral impulses. If God exists, justice will eventually be done—and woe, then, to the sinner. Good deeds will be rewarded, if not here on earth, then in an otherworldly paradise. So believers have a very strong incentive to be moral. Nonbelievers don't have such incentives. They will therefore fall more easily into temptation.

Suppose this is correct. Still, this wouldn't show that religious people are more likely to do good. It would show only that they are more likely to be conscientious. But being conscientious doesn't always translate into doing good. Some of the leaders of the Inquisition were very conscientious. Their conscience led them to torture their victims in an intensely cruel way. Religious conviction may strengthen our commitments. But religion has sometimes asked its followers to wage war, not peace; to take the land and wealth of others; and to destroy the cultures

---

1. All terms and phrases that appear in **boldface** are defined in the glossary at the end of the book.

2. The God discussed in this chapter is the one endorsed by traditional monotheistic religions: a perfect being who is omniscient (all-knowing), omnipotent (all-powerful), and morally flawless. For simplicity's sake, I also rely on traditional usage and refer to God as a male, though nothing that follows hangs on this usage. I recognize that there are important religious views that reject monotheism, as well as this specific conception of God. Most of the discussion in this chapter applies even to these views, but in some cases the focus must be narrower. At those points, I thought it made sense to address the views likeliest to be shared by my readers.

of nonbelievers. Religion doesn't always help us to become better people. It all depends on whether the religious principles we believe in are morally good in the first place.

But let's imagine a best-case scenario, one in which our religious views *are* morally attractive. And suppose that religious believers really are more likely than nonbelievers to be conscientious. What would this show? It would *not* show that God exists. Nor would it show that morality depends in any way upon God. Rather, it is an argument for the practical benefits of certain religious beliefs. It says that believers with morally good views are more likely than nonbelievers to do the right thing.

Yet the benefits of holding a belief are one thing, its truth another. For all that this reasoning shows, religious beliefs may simply be useful fictions, false beliefs that do a lot of good.

I am not saying that this is so. In fact, let us grant, for argument's sake, that some set of religious beliefs is correct. Still, this account of how religious belief strengthens our moral motivations is problematic. The reason is simple. If hope for heavenly reward or fear of God's anger is what prompts us to do good, then we may well do the right thing—but for the wrong reasons.

To see this, imagine a person who does her duty, but only because she thinks that God punishes those who misbehave and rewards those who act morally. Such a person is not well motivated. She is doing her duty not because she loves God, but rather because she sees God as threatening the worst punishments or offering the best bribes. Such a person is unreliably moral, for if she came to believe that God really didn't offer the expected rewards and punishments, then she would see no reason to be moral.

Fear of God has been a traditional way to get people to do their duty. But when it is effective, it undermines moral character, rather than supports it. People who deserve our praise and admiration are those who do their duty for its own sake. Rather than acting from ulterior, self-interested motives, they do what is right because it is right. Agnostics and atheists have just as much reason to adopt this attitude as **theists** (those who believe in God's existence) do.

Even if fear of God is the most effective way to get people to do what they should, this would not show that God exists. It would not show that religious beliefs are correct. Nor would it show that atheists or agnostics are unable or unlikely to behave in morally admirable ways. Being well motivated requires a love and respect for the morally important things in life. Religion has often fostered such an outlook—religious believers can indeed be well motivated, basing their actions not on fear or self-interest but rather, say, on a love of God, or a gratitude for His kindness. But religion isn't required for admirable moral motivation, and it can, when accompanied by mistaken moral beliefs, actually prevent believers from fulfilling their moral duties.

5.2 Second Assumption: Moral Conduct Is Rational Only If God Exists

Is it rational to do what morality tells you to do? That depends on whether there is good reason to follow the moral path. You're rational to the extent that you act on good reasons. So: are there good reasons to do your duty? In some cases, the answer is an easy *yes*. Among these are cases where there is no conflict between morality and self-interest. Many theists believe there is *never* any such conflict: it's always in our interest to do what God wants, God always wants us to do what's right, so it's always in our interest to do what's right. If there is always good reason to protect your self-interest, then there is always good reason to do what morality tells you to do.

This line of reasoning supports the following conclusion: *if* God exists, then it is rational to do your duty. This claim tells us that God's existence is sufficient to show that acting morally is rational. But is it necessary? That is what is affirmed by Assumption 2: it is rational to act morally *only if* God exists. The thought here is that if God doesn't exist, then we no longer have good reason to do as morality instructs. Why believe that?

Here's the usual explanation: if God doesn't exist, then morality and self-interest will sometimes conflict. That's because there is no all-powerful being to guarantee that good deeds are rewarded and bad deeds are punished. Indeed, if there is no God, then those who always act morally are playing a losing game, since they will sometimes have to take a hit by acting morally. But there's no good reason to act that way—it's irrational to knowingly sacrifice your self-interest. Instead, if atheism is true, then the rational thing is to amp up your quality of life, even if that means acting immorally along the way. The upshot is that it is rational to act morally, but only if God exists (since God will ensure that doing your duty serves your interests). That is just what Assumption 2 says.

Here's the crucial claim in this line of reasoning: you have good reason to do something only if acting that way will serve your interests. But that claim is problematic. Assumption 2 inherits these problems.

Let's focus on a pair of them. The first is that theists should deny that good reasons for action are limited to acts that benefit yourself. For instance, they should allow that there is a good reason—indeed, the best possible reason—to do whatever God wants you to do, *even if* God wants you to sacrifice your self-interest. You might think that God would never want that. Maybe. There are loads of controversial assumptions packed into *that* thought.

Rather than take them up, let me briefly introduce the other problem, which is that there seem to be many cases where we have good reasons to act that are not rooted in self-interest. Among these are reasons that stem from the well-being of others. You're important. But so are other people. Imagine you are traveling through a town you'll never return to, where you know no one. You see someone leave a backpack under a bench at a crowded playground. You investigate and discover that there's a bomb inside, with a timer set for sixty minutes. Your bus is set to leave town in twenty minutes. You'll be miles away when the bomb detonates. You could notify someone and save all of those innocents. Or you could just walk away. Isn't there good reason to take the first option—even if there's no reward in store for you? The reason doesn't come from your own self-interest. It comes from the needs and interests of others.

If that is correct—a matter discussed at greater length elsewhere in the book[3]—then Assumption 2 rests on a mistake. The mistake is thinking that the only good reason to do something is a self-interested reason. That view is incompatible with most religious traditions, and is also in conflict with intuitive examples designed to show that the concerns of others can also supply good reasons for action. Sometimes these reasons are very strong, as when we can easily save the lives of others at little cost to ourselves. In those cases, and likely in many others, it is rational to do the moral thing, even if God is not there to ensure that we benefit thereby. That is directly contrary to the second assumption.

5.3 Third Assumption: God Is the Creator of Morality

If God is dead, then everything is permitted.

Many people feel the force of this thought, recorded by one of Dostoevsky's characters in his novel *The Brothers Karamazov*. On this view, atheism spells the doom of morality.

---

3. See chapter 8, "The Best Argument for Ethical Egoism," chapter 11, "Morality and Rationality," and chapter 14, "Why Be Moral?"

The underlying idea seems to be this: because morality is a set of **norms** (i.e., standards that we ought to live up to), there must be someone with the authority to create them. Without God, there is no one but we human beings to make up the moral law. And we lack the needed authority to do the work. Our say-so doesn't make things right; our disapproval cannot make things wrong. We are limited in understanding and bound to make mistakes. A morality built upon our imperfections would lack credibility.

But a morality created by God—that is a different story entirely. After all, God is wholly perfect. What better credentials could there be for drafting a moral code?

Add to these credentials the following vision. Imagine a godless universe, lacking any divine purpose. Where would moral norms come from? If we are wholly material beings, governed by physical laws, then there are many ways that we *will* behave. But there seems to be no way that we *ought to* behave. If we are just very complex bundles of matter, without any externally imposed aims or purposes to live up to, then it is difficult to see how there can be moral duties at all. To get moral requirements into the picture, we must have someone with the authority to impose those duties on us. Only God could possibly qualify.

This vision of God's role in morality—as its ultimate author, the one who makes up the moral code—rests on a crucial assumption: that morality must be created by someone. This assumption serves as the first premise of a popular *Argument for God's Creation of Morality*:

1. Every law requires a lawmaker.
2. Therefore, the moral law requires a lawmaker.
3. Humans cannot be the author of the moral law (since we are imperfect in so many ways).
4. If humans cannot be the author of the moral law, then God is its author.
5. Therefore, God is the author of the moral law.[4]

This line of thinking leads directly to the following view, known to philosophers as the **divine command theory**:

An act is morally required just because it is commanded by God, and immoral just because God forbids it.

---

4. A variation on this argument, which seeks to show that moral rules *are objective* only if God exists, is considered in the section "Atheism Undermines Moral Objectivity" in chapter 21. That discussion focuses primarily on the claim that laws require lawmakers.

This view first received an airing in Western philosophy in a short dialogue by Plato called the *Euthyphro*, where Socrates interrogates the title character and asks the following question: *"Do the gods love actions because they are pious, or are actions pious because the gods love them?"*

With a few substitutions, we can get a newer version of Socrates's question that is more relevant to our topic: *"Does God command us to do actions because they are morally right, or are actions morally right because God commands them?"* The divine command theory answers our new question by affirming the second option. Actions are morally right just because God insists that we perform them. Prior to God's commands, nothing was right or wrong. Morality simply did not exist.

I think that this is the natural, default view for a religious believer when thinking of God's relation to morality. But it is not without its problems.

There are two of them. One is obvious. The divine command theory makes morality depend on God's commands. But God may not exist. Or, as **deists** believe, God may exist, but may not command us to do anything. Deists claim that God set creation in motion, and then retired to survey His universe, refusing to involve Himself in human affairs. If the divine command theory is true, and if either atheism or deism is correct, then nothing is right or wrong. Morality would be a complete sham.

But let's assume that God does exist, and does care enough about us to tell us what to do. To appreciate the second problem, imagine the point at which God is choosing a morality for us. God contemplates the nature of rape, torture, and treachery. What does He see? Being **omniscient** (all-knowing), God sees such actions for what they are. Crucially, He sees nothing wrong with them. They are, at this point, morally neutral. Nothing, as yet, is right or wrong.

But God did, at some point, make a decision. He forbade rape, theft, and most kinds of killing. If the divine command theory is correct, then He didn't forbid them because they were immoral. So why *did* God forbid them?

It may be presumptuous of us to try to answer that question. But we can ask a slightly different question: did God have reasons for His decisions, or not?

If the divine command theory is true, then there is trouble either way. (This is the second problem I mentioned.) If God lacks reasons for His commands—if there is no solid basis supporting His decisions to prohibit certain things and require others—then God's decisions are arbitrary.

It would be as if God were creating morality by a coin toss. But that is surely implausible. That sort of God would be arbitrary, and thus imperfect.

So a perfect God must have had excellent reasons for laying down the moral law as He did. *But then these reasons, and not God's commands, are what makes actions right or wrong.* Actions are not right *because* God commands them. Whatever reasons support God's choices also explain why actions have the moral status they do.

Suppose, for instance, that God really did forbid us from torturing others, and that God had very good reasons for doing so. Although we can't presume to know God's thoughts, let's just assume for now that God based His decision on the fact that torture is extremely painful, humiliating, and an attack on a defenseless person. Assuming that these are the relevant reasons, then these reasons, *and not God's say-so*, are what makes torture immoral. These reasons can fully explain why torture is wrong. Torture is wrong *because* it is extremely painful, humiliating, and so on.

God's condemnation does not turn a morally neutral action into an immoral one. Rather, God recognizes what is already bad about torture. There is something in the very nature of torture that makes it morally suspect. Since God knows everything, God knows what is detestable about torture. Since God wants us to be good, God orders us not to attempt such actions. God commands us to refrain from torture because torture is immoral.

The *Euthyphro Argument* summarizes this line of thinking:

1. Either God has reasons that support His commands, or God lacks reasons for His commands.
2. If God lacks reasons for His commands, then God's commands are arbitrary—and that renders God imperfect, undermining His moral authority.
3. If God has reasons that support His commands, then these reasons, rather than the divine commands, are what make actions right or wrong—thereby refuting the divine command theory.
4. Therefore, either God is imperfect, or the divine command theory is false.
5. God is not imperfect.
6. Therefore, the divine command theory is false.

To avoid portraying God as arbitrary, we must assume that He issues commands based on the best possible reasons. And here are the best possible reasons: God sees that an action such as torture is immoral, sees, with perfect understanding, that such things as kindness and compassion are good, and then issues the divine commands on the basis of this flawless insight. This picture preserves God's omniscience and integrity. But it comes at the expense of the divine command theory, and God's authorship of the moral law.

And after all, what is the alternative? If there is nothing intrinsically wrong with rape or theft, then God could just as well have required that we do such things. He could have forbidden that we be generous or thoughtful. But this makes a mockery of morality, and of our view of God as morally perfect.

The *Divine Perfection Argument* expresses this point:

1. If the divine command theory is true, then a morally perfect God could have created a flawless morality that required us to rape, steal, and kill, and forbade us from any acts of kindness or generosity.
2. A morally perfect God could not have issued such commands—anyone who did so would be morally imperfect.
3. Therefore, the divine command theory is false.

The first premise is certainly true. The divine command theory says that God's choices wholly determine morality, and that nothing determines God's choices. If God's choices were fixed in advance, the only plausible explanation would be that certain kinds of actions were already right and others already wrong, and that God, in His infinite wisdom, knew this and issued His commands accordingly. But that is to deny the central idea of the divine command theory.

The second premise is highly plausible. A moral code that required such horrific acts, and forbade such good ones, could not be authored by someone worthy of love and worship, someone fit to serve as a model of moral perfection.

In my experience, many religious people still feel suspicious about rejecting the divine command theory. They worry that the theory is needed to preserve God's perfection. If God doesn't create the moral law, then how can He be perfect?

True, abandoning the divine command theory does mean giving up the view that God is the author of morality. But this is actually needed in order to *preserve* God's perfection. It allows us to say that God is perfectly wise, perfectly moral, and perfect in His love for us. Being infinitely wise, He knows all that is good and evil. Being morally perfect, he flawlessly measures up to the highest moral ideals. Caring for His human creatures,

He passes along some of that wisdom to us, to better guide our lives. Further, if we reject the divine command theory, then this allows us to say that God bases His commands on the best possible reasons. There is no room in this picture for the sort of arbitrariness that would undermine divine perfection.

If this is all on the right track, then we can see that the pessimism of Dostoevsky's thought is misguided. The absence of God does not mean the absence of morality. God is not needed to create the moral law; indeed, a perfect God is one who fully understands, embraces, and adheres to a moral law not of His own making.

A perfect God cannot create morality through His whims. If God cannot be morally mistaken, it is because His understanding is perfect. But when it comes to morality, it is the understanding of one who does not author the moral law, but rather completely knows that law, and the reasons that support it.

5.4   Fourth Assumption: Religion Is an Essential Source of Moral Guidance

Theists are often reluctant to reject the divine command theory because they think that rejecting it leaves God entirely out of the moral picture. But it doesn't.

Suppose that God exists, but is *not* the author of the moral law. God could still play a crucial role in morality—not by being its inventor, but by being its infallible reporter, and our expert guide. God knows everything—including every single detail of the moral law. And if God is all-loving, then God will want to share some of that wisdom with us. How will He do it? By means of revelation, either personal and direct (say, by talking to you or giving you signs of certain kinds), or by indirect means (say, by inspiring the authors of a bible).

Importantly, religious believers who reject the divine command theory could easily accept the following claim:

> An act is morally required if God commands it, and is immoral if God forbids it.

This looks like the divine command theory, but it is importantly different. This view does not claim that acts are right and wrong *because* of God's commands. God's commands don't *make* actions right (or wrong). But if God exists, then His verdict is nonetheless morally decisive. God will never make a mistake. If God commands you to do something, then, morally speaking, the matter is settled.

God doesn't have to be the author of morality in order to play a vital role in teaching us how to live. We can see this by considering an analogy. Imagine a perfectly accurate thermometer. If we wanted to know the temperature, we'd look to this device. But the thermometer is not creating the temperature. It is recording it in an error-free way. If we reject the divine command theory, then God is playing a similar role regarding morality. He is not creating the moral law. He is telling us what it is, in a way that is never mistaken.

There are some worries, of course. Here are some worth mentioning:

- Those who are not religious will need to look elsewhere for moral guidance.
- And they may be right to do so, because God may not exist.
- Further, God may exist—and yet not offer any advice to us.

This is the God of the deists. To rightly trust religious texts or religious authority, you must first have more reason to believe that God exists and relays moral wisdom to us than the reverse.

Even if God exists, and offers us moral advice, there are still two serious problems for those who seek divine guidance:

- We must select a source of religious wisdom from among many choices.
- We must know how to interpret that source.

These two problems can be illustrated by working through a popular *Argument from Religious Authority*:

1. If the Bible prohibits abortion, then abortion is immoral.
2. The Bible prohibits abortion.
3. Therefore, abortion is immoral.

The first premise asserts the moral authority of the Bible. But which bible? Different religions offer us different sacred texts, whose details sometimes contradict one another. So we must choose. There is presumably one right choice and many wrong ones. The odds are stacked against us.

Premise 1 is plausible only if God has authored the Bible, or dictated its terms. Religious believers therefore have to make a case that this is so. They must justify the claims that God exists, that God has communicated with humanity, and that their favorite sacred scripture is the one that contains God's wisdom. It won't be easy to do this.

If God is all-powerful, then He could provide some extremely clear, undeniable evidence to settle these matters, evidence that would convince agnostics, atheists, and members of competing religions. But God has thus far chosen not to do this. That makes defense of premise 1 especially tricky.

And the challenges don't end there. Even if theists can adequately defend the first premise, and so justify the selection of their preferred sacred text, there is the further matter of how to interpret that text. Neither the Hebrew nor the Christian scriptures, for instance, ever explicitly *mentions* abortion, much less prohibits it. Thus, even if you wanted to adopt a literal reading of those scriptures, problems will arise. There will be many important topics (such as abortion) that are never mentioned in the crucial text. Those that are mentioned may receive contradictory treatments (consider, as an early example, the literally incompatible creation stories of Genesis chapters 1 and 2). There may also be morally troubling advice on offer (think of the passages in Leviticus that permit slavery and the subordination of women, or those that require killing adulterers and disrespectful children).

Yet if we move away from a literal reading, we are faced with countless possibilities for interpreting religious texts. Believers must choose among them, and justify their choice in the face of a wide number of conflicting approaches. A defense of premise 2 is, therefore, no easy matter.

A final difficulty comes when having to balance the demands of a sacred text with the layers of tradition that form a crucial part of any living religion.

When your interpretation of a religious document conflicts with long-standing religious practice, or the advice of generations of religious authorities, which should win out? Consider as an example the famous eye-for-an-eye principle, which seems to be clearly required by God in the Hebrew scriptures (Exodus 21:23; Leviticus 24:20; Deuteronomy 19:21). Yet Jewish communities and their religious leaders have, for at least two millennia, read the decree in an imaginative, nonliteral way, softening its implications for wrongdoers and extending the principle to apply to cases where it cannot be taken literally. Does the text take priority over traditional practice and religious authority? Or is it the other way around? Believers must have a plausible view about how to settle such conflicts. Without one, their take on what God really wants for us may be very wide of the mark.

To summarize: those who seek divine guidance in trying to lead a moral life may succeed. But several conditions must be met. It must be the case that (1) God exists, and that (2) we can be justified in believing this. (3) God must offer us moral advice, and (4) we must be able to defend the claim that He does so. Further, (5) theists must be justified in selecting a particular source of religious and moral wisdom, such as the Koran, the Book of Mormon, or the Christian scriptures. Theists must also (6) defend specific interpretations of those sources. Finally, when an interpretation conflicts with tradition, religious believers must (7) successfully argue for the priority of one over the other.

This is a daunting list. Yet philosophy is full of such lists, and the difficulty of a project is not, by itself, proof of its failure. Religious believers have their work cut out for them, no doubt of it. But then so does everyone else.

5.5 Conclusion

There is a great deal to think about when discussing the relation between morality and religion. I have narrowed the focus to four major assumptions, because these seem to lie at the heart of most debates about God's role in morality.

Is God needed to ensure that we are morally motivated? No. Morally admirable behavior comes when we do our duty for its own sake, rather than from self-interest. Fear of God, or desire for heavenly reward, do not necessarily tarnish our character. But they are no substitute for a direct love of morality, which can be displayed as much by atheists as by religious believers.

Must God exist in order for moral action to be rational? It might seem so, since it may strike you that if God is not around to ensure that good deeds are rewarded and bad deeds punished, then moral action is irrational. But this thought is based on the idea that the only good reason to do anything is because it will enhance your self-interest. Yet nearly all religions reject that thought. Further, the needs and interests of others seem to be good reasons to act on their behalf, even if it means sacrificing yourself in the bargain. If that is so, then moral action can be rational, even if God does not exist.

Does God create morality? No. Rather, God (if He exists) understands everything, and so knows precisely what is wrong with such things as rape and torture, and right about such things as compassion and kindness. He issues commands on the basis of this perfect understanding, out of love for His creatures. A God who issues commands for good reasons will rely on the very best reasons—and those can explain, all by themselves, what is right and wrong.

Does religion offer reliable moral guidance? Possibly. That depends on many things—whether God exists and speaks to us, whether we can know which texts are divinely written or inspired, whether we can defend our favored interpretations against the competition, and whether we can balance these interpretations against the importance of religious tradition and authority in cases of conflict.

In the rest of the book, I do not make use of specifically religious claims. There are two reasons for this. First, we have seen the many challenges to the assumption that morality is based on religion, and it is worthwhile seeing how far we can get without having to rely on that assumption. Second, there is important precedent among religious philosophers for thinking that God gave us reason and understanding in order to make the fundamental truths of morality available to everyone. After all, a caring God would want even nonbelievers to understand the immorality of rape and genocide, and to appreciate the goodness of generosity and loving kindness.

Let us proceed, then, to consider the views of those who, in most cases, were religious themselves, but who sought secular foundations for the moral theories they developed.

5.6 Discussion Questions

1. How might religion motivate people to behave morally? Why is this kind of motivation sometimes thought to be morally problematic?
2. Does the existence of a law imply the existence of a lawmaker? Defend your answer.
3. "Since God created everything, God created morality. Therefore, the divine command theory is true." Assess this line of reasoning.
4. Describe the two possible relationships between God's commands and morality suggested by Socrates. Which account do you find more attractive and why?
5. There are many different religious texts offering us moral guidance, and some of them give conflicting advice. Is there a reliable way of deciding which text (if any) is correct?
6. All things considered, do you think religion is a good source of moral guidance? Why or why not?

.... 🐦 ....

CHAPTER 6

Natural Law

6.1 The Theory and Its Attractions

You are an animal.

I'm not trying to insult you. Just stating a fact. I am an animal, too. And so is everyone else we know. The basic needs of animals—food, water, security, companionship, freedom from pain—are the basic needs of human beings. All humans, like every other animal, share the same fundamental plight: certain one day to die, and vulnerable to harm in the meantime. Perhaps the key to morality lies in understanding our place in the natural order of things. Many have thought so.

In trying to discover what makes for a good human life, we might take a cue from the rest of the animal kingdom and ask about why their lives go well, when they do. It seems that there is a common answer: animals live good lives when their nature is fulfilled, and bad lives when it isn't. A racehorse, by nature, is built for speed. English pointers are meant to aid in the hunt. Chameleons naturally blend in with their background. When fillies break a leg, or chameleons cannot camouflage themselves, their lives go poorly. A good pointer will be able to track and give chase; a bad one will sit lazily and ignore nearby prey.

In each of these cases, nature is dictating the terms of appraisal. The things *in* nature *have* a nature. Such things are bad when they are unnatural, and good to the extent that they fulfill their nature. Perhaps we can say the same thing about human beings.

That is the guiding thought of the **natural law theory**. By its lights, good human beings are those who fulfill their true nature; bad human beings are those who don't. The moral law is the natural law—the law that requires us to act in accordance with our nature. (As we'll see, this is a different kind of natural law from the one that physicists use to describe the workings of molecules or galaxies.) At its most basic, natural law theory tells us that *actions are right just because they are natural, and wrong just because they are unnatural. And people are good or bad to the extent that they fulfill their true nature—the more they fulfill their true nature, the better they are.*

The natural law theory promises to solve some very serious problems in ethics. Four of these are especially important.

1. *Natural law theory promises to explain how morality could possibly be objective, that is, how moral standards depend on something other than human opinion.*

According to this theory, human nature can serve as the objective standard of morality. We do right when our acts express human nature, and do wrong when they violate it. Since individuals and entire societies can be mistaken about what our true nature is, they can be badly off target about what morality asks of us.

Many natural law theorists are theists, who claim that our nature was given to us by God. Indeed, the most brilliant and influential exponent of natural law theory, St. Thomas Aquinas (1225–1275), melded Aristotelian and Christian views to argue that we are morally bound to fulfill our nature precisely because God endowed us with it. But that is not an essential element of the theory. What is crucial is that human nature is meant to serve as the ultimate moral standard, regardless of whether our nature has arisen from divine origins or in some other way. If this theory is correct, then so long as there is such a thing as human nature, there is an objective source of morality.

2. *Natural law theory easily explains why morality is specially suited for human beings, and not for anything else in the natural world.*

Almost everyone agrees that a distinctive human feature is our sophisticated reasoning abilities. A few other animals may be able to reason in basic ways, but no species on earth can approach our ability to assess various ways of life, critically analyze the merits of actions and policies, and then govern our behavior on the basis of our reflections. This capacity for rational thought also seems to be the cornerstone of morality. **Moral agents**—those who bear responsibility for their actions, and who are fit for praise or blame—are those who can control their behavior through reasoning. That's why we don't hold animals (or trees or automobiles) morally responsible for the harms they sometimes cause. Only human beings have the sort of nature that enables them to be moral agents. Natural law theory can thus explain why moral duties apply only to human beings (or, if there are any, to other life forms who share our rational powers).

> 3. *Natural law theory has a clear account of the origins of morality.*

The theory tells us that morality is only as old as humanity itself, that morality dates to the earliest days of humankind. But that isn't because morality depends on human opinion, as so many people believe. Rather, it is because morality depends on human nature. No humans, no human nature. No human nature, no morality.

> 4. *Natural law theory may solve one of the hardest problems in ethics: how to gain moral knowledge.*

Natural law theory provides a straightforward recipe for acquiring moral knowledge: first, determine what our human nature is; second, figure out whether various actions fulfill it. As we'll soon see, there are a variety of views of what human nature consists in. But once we settle on one of those views, then it is, in theory at least, a straightforward matter to determine whether a given action fulfills our nature. If it does, then we can know that it is right; if it runs counter to our nature, then we can know that it is wrong.

6.2 Three Conceptions of Human Nature

We often approve of actions by declaring them to be perfectly natural, or excuse someone's harmful conduct by saying that it was the natural thing to do under the circumstances. We also condemn certain actions as unnatural or say of an especially awful act that it was a crime against nature. This all makes excellent sense, on the assumption that natural law theory is true.

In order to apply the natural law theory to real moral problems, we need a sharp understanding of human nature, for it is human nature that, on this theory, will determine the standards of morality. Human nature is what makes us human. It is the set of features that is essential to being human; if we were to lose these features, we would also lose our humanity. Natural law theorists are committed to the idea that there is a human essence, a set of traits that define us as human beings.

What is the nature of human nature? Here are three familiar—and problematic—answers.

Human Nature as Animal Nature

On one understanding, we are animals by nature, and so to act according to our nature is just to behave as other animals do. Other animals need protection against predators and enough food to eat, and this explains why it is morally acceptable for us to defend ourselves against attackers and to grow food and feed ourselves. That certainly sounds plausible. But looking to other animals for moral guidance is actually quite a poor idea.

We've already seen a brief discussion of this in the Introduction ("Moral Reasoning"), where I criticized an argument for meat-eating that tried to justify that practice by claiming that animals eat other animals. Leave aside the fact that most animals we eat do not eat other animals. Even when it comes to true carnivores, the fact that an animal kills and eats another animal does not give us moral license to do the same. After all, some animals kill their own young; others brutalize the weaker members of their own species. That doesn't make it right for us to do these things.

So the fact that we share many traits, needs, and interests with other animals is not going to unlock the puzzle of determining our human nature—at least if that nature is supposed to also provide moral standards that we must live by. We need to look elsewhere for an understanding of human nature that might be morally relevant.

Human Nature Is What Is Innate

Innate traits are ones we have from birth. They are natural in the sense of being inborn, natural as opposed to being learned or acquired from parents and society. On this line of thinking, our true nature is the one we are born with; traits we acquire through socialization are artificial, and stain the purity of our earliest days.

If Jean-Jacques Rousseau (1712–1778) was right, we are innately angelic. Before society corrupts us, our noble nature shines through. We are by nature pleasant, cooperative, and considerate. If our nature holds the key to morality, then morality is largely as we think it is. It requires us to be kind, cooperative, and attentive to the needs of others.

That would be a comfort. But what if Thomas Hobbes (1588–1679) had it right? He thought that we are innately selfish, competitive, and distrustful. We are born that way and, for the most part, stay that way. If the natural is the innate, and if we are required to act on our true nature, then the Hobbesian view is going to force us to abandon many of our conventional ethical beliefs.

The view that the natural is what is innate is widely held. This explains why so many people think that studies focused on infants will unlock the key to human nature. The thought is that society is bound to change our natural state, and so we gain the deepest insight into human nature by discovering what we are like before society changes us in so many ways.

Yet if natural law theory is correct, and if the natural is the very same thing as the innate, then we need to resolve the nature/nurture debate before we can know what is right and wrong. And that seems mistaken. We are *very* confident that morality is not a counsel of selfishness, mistrust, and competition, even if we are uncertain about whether such traits are innate. We can be very sure that killing people because of their skin color is immoral, even if we aren't sure whether we have an innate tendency to harm people who don't look like us.

This raises a general point: *the ultimate origins of our impulses are irrelevant to the morality of our actions.* Rape and robbery are immoral, no matter whether the impulse to commit these crimes is innate or acquired. Cheerfully comforting the sick is a good thing, even if we weren't born with a desire to offer such help. Since the morality of our actions and our character traits does not depend on whether they are innate or acquired, natural law theorists must look elsewhere for an understanding of human nature.

Human Nature Is What All Humans Have in Common

Many people think that our nature is whatever traits we all share. These universal human features would make up the essence of humanity. Such a view lets us scientifically determine our human nature. The data wouldn't always be easy to come by. But with a lot of effort, we could discover our human nature just by observing the features that all humans have in common.

There are two problems with such a view. First, there may be no universal human traits. And second, even if there are, they may not provide good moral guidance.

It may seem silly to deny that there are any universal human traits. Doesn't everyone want to have enough food and water to remain alive? Don't all adults have a sex drive? Aren't we all capable, to one degree or another, of complex thinking about our future? Yet some people want to die, not to live; others are indifferent to the attractions of sex; still others are so mentally impaired as to be unable to think at all about their future. For just about any trait (perhaps every trait) that is said to be part of human nature, we can find exceptions that undermine the rule.

Natural law theorists have a reply to this, which is best appreciated by considering an example. Return to the case of nonhuman animals and think about their nature. For instance, it is part of a buck's nature to be alert to predators, to have four legs, to grow antlers, and to be fawn-colored. Still, there are bucks with only three legs. A few fail to grow antlers; others are deaf to predators; still others are albinos. We might say of such specimens that they aren't really bucks, not fully bucks, or not all that a buck should be.

If that sounds right, then we might adopt the following strategy. Perhaps human nature, like that of nonhuman animals, is determined not by what *every* member of the species shares, but only by what *most* members share. Bucks can have a nature, even if some bucks fail to perfectly live up to it. The same goes for human beings.

This strategy won't work. There is the difficult problem of setting a threshold. Just how many humans need to have a trait before it qualifies as part of human nature? But leave that aside. The real problem is this: the fact that most humans have a certain trait is morally irrelevant.

Suppose, for instance, that most of us are selfish and mean. On this line of thinking, being selfish and mean would then be part of human nature. That would make such behavior morally right, on the natural law view. But that's awfully difficult to accept.

Even if everyone, or most of us, were cruel and malicious, that would not make cruelty and malice morally good. Even if people were usually or typically nasty and petty, these traits would still be vices, not virtues. The fact that many, most, or all people behave a certain way or have certain character traits is not enough to show that such behaviors and traits are morally good.

6.3 Natural Purposes

If human nature is not a matter of the (innate) traits that all or most of us have, then what is it? The answer given by most natural law theorists is this: human nature is what we are designed to be and to do. It is some function of ours, some purpose that we are meant to serve, some end that we were designed for.

It may seem that this conception of human nature places us squarely outside the realm of science, and in the domain of religion. How could science tell us what our purpose is? Doesn't talk of our being designed for something imply the existence of an Intelligent Designer?

Many natural law theorists, following Thomas Aquinas's lead, have made just these assumptions, and have developed their views within the context of one religious tradition or another. On these views, God is our Intelligent Designer. When God created us, He assigned us a specific set of purposes. These are what make up our human nature. Since God is all-good, frustrating God's purpose is immoral. That's what we do when we act unnaturally. That's why it is wrong to act unnaturally.

There is a lot to say about such a view, but most of it has already been said in the previous chapter. On the present account, we must act naturally because that is the way we respect God's plans for us, which are at the heart of morality. Though this isn't quite the same thing as making God's *commands* the basis of morality, it is close enough to have inherited most of the strengths and weaknesses of the divine command theory. Rather than revisit that topic, let's consider a secular interpretation of natural purposes.

The challenge is to make sense of the idea that we have been designed to serve some purpose, without having to invoke an Intelligent Designer. Strictly speaking, of course, nature has no designs for us. Nature is not an intelligent being with intentions and plans. Still, it *can* make sense to speak of something's natural function or purpose. The mechanisms of evolution and natural selection, rather than God, can serve as the source of our natural purposes.

For instance, nature designed our brains to enable us to think, our liver to detoxify our blood, and our pancreas to regulate glucose levels. We can say what mitochondria are for, what the heart and kidneys are meant to do. In each case, there is a purpose that these organs serve, even if no one assigned them this purpose.

But that sort of talk doesn't easily translate to human lives. What is a human being *for*? Does the question even make sense?

To answer this question, we need to understand the idea of a natural purpose. Two secular accounts might offer some insight. Call the first account the *Efficiency Model*, and the second the *Fitness Model*.

Consider the Efficiency Model. Sticking with the example of a heart, we can say that pumping blood is its natural purpose, because nothing pumps blood as well as a heart. Hearts have a certain structure that enables them to pump blood more efficiently than anything else in the body. That is why the purpose of a heart is to pump blood.

Human beings can have a function or a purpose, then, if we are more efficient than anything else when it comes to certain tasks. Well, we are. Yet there are so many of them. For instance, we are better than anything else at designing puzzles and writing essays. But on this model, natural law theory cannot be correct, given its claim that unnatural action is immoral, for that would mean that we act immorally whenever we are bad at puzzle design or essay writing. We are also far better than any other animal at building weapons, and far more talented at using instruments of torture. But if acting naturally is always morally acceptable, then these actions, if they really are among our natural purposes, are beyond reproach. Something has gone wrong.

If the Efficiency Model is correct—if human nature is given by our natural purposes, and these purposes are whatever we are most efficiently able to accomplish—then natural law theory must fail. There are too many such purposes, and many have nothing moral about them. Perhaps the Fitness Model will do better.

On this account, our organs have the purposes they do because it is extremely *adaptive* for them to serve these roles. The natural purpose of the heart, brain, liver, and lungs is to do what enhances **fitness**: roughly, our success at survival and reproduction. We are able to survive, and pass on our genes to our offspring, only because these organs function as well as they do. Nature has designed hearts and kidneys and brains (etc.) to improve our chances of survival. This is their natural purpose; it is ours, too. We are meant to survive and to transmit our genes to the next generation. That is what a human life is *for*. In a godless world, that is all the purpose our lives can have.

Since our natural purposes are survival and procreation, we can see why so many natural law theorists have thought suicide immoral and have condemned birth control and homosexual sex. We also have a ready explanation of why courage, endurance, and fortitude are true virtues—those who possess them are (in the relevant sense) fitter than those who don't.

Suppose that the natural law theory is true. And suppose that we fulfill our human nature just when we fulfill our natural purposes. Two things follow:

1. Acting naturally—fulfilling our natural purposes—is always moral.
2. Acting unnaturally—frustrating our natural purposes—is always immoral.

But if the Fitness Model is correct, then both claims are false.

To see why claim 1 is false, recall that natural actions are those in which we use our mind and body to satisfy the purposes they were designed for. In the Fitness Model, these purposes are survival and reproduction. So natural actions are those that increase the chances of our survival and reproduction. But men can increase the chances of passing on their genes by raping as many women as they can. That is about as immoral as anything I can think of. And survival? Consider the words of Primo Levi, an Auschwitz prisoner: "The worst—that is, the fittest—survived. The best all died."[1] Sometimes those best schooled in violence and treachery are the ones likeliest to live another day. If we understand natural purposes as the Fitness Model advises, then claim 1 is false.

Claim 2 is also false. Suppose that our natural purposes are survival and procreation. A woman whose doctor has told her that becoming pregnant will threaten her life is not acting immorally if she has a tubal ligation—even though doing so will undermine her ability to procreate. A soldier who sacrifices his life to spare his endangered comrades is acting nobly, rather than immorally—even though he has thereby undermined the natural purpose of self-preservation. Not every act that frustrates a natural purpose is immoral, even if it is God, and not nature alone, that has endowed us with these various purposes.

What this shows is that the Fitness Model is as vulnerable as the Efficiency Model. Neither gives us a solid understanding of what human nature is that supports the natural law view that acting naturally is moral and that acting unnaturally is immoral. Until we are given a better method for determining our nature, the natural law theory is in trouble.

The weakness of the various understandings of human nature allows us to see why a classic moral argument fails. That argument—call it the *Natural Law Argument*—goes like this:

1. If an act is unnatural, then it is immoral.
2. Suicide, contraception, and homosexual sex are unnatural.
3. Therefore suicide, contraception, and homosexual sex are immoral.

The first premise is false on all of the interpretations we have so far considered. Whether unnatural actions spring from acquired traits rather than

---

1. Primo Levi, *The Drowned and the Saved* (New York: Knopf, 1986), p. 82.

innate ones; whether they are rare or unusual rather than typical or even universal; whether they frustrate nature's purposes rather than conform to them; still, such actions can be morally acceptable.

This does not prove that suicide, contraception, and homosexual sex are morally okay. What it shows, however, is that this popular argument is highly suspect, and will certainly fail unless we have a better understanding of human nature to rely on.

6.4 The Argument from Humanity

This may be a good time to consider another famous argument of the natural law tradition: the *Argument from Humanity*. This is perhaps the most widely heard anti-abortion argument in public debates on the subject. The argument is straightforward:

1. It is always wrong to deliberately kill an innocent human being.
2. A fetus is an innocent human being.
3. Therefore, it is always wrong to deliberately kill a fetus.

A great deal could be said about that first premise, but let's leave it aside for the moment and focus on the second. It seems clearly true to a great many people. And it seems just as clearly false to many others. What is going on here?

The explanation, I think, is that the term *human being* is **ambiguous**—it has more than one meaning. There are at least two senses of the term used in these debates, and members of each camp tend to use their preferred meaning. The result is that a lot of the discussions about the morality of abortion end up going nowhere.

For our purposes, the important question is whether a fetus is an innocent human being. And that depends on how we define humanity. What is the essence of humanity? It is tempting, of course, to look to science for an answer. It tells us that being a member of the species *Homo sapiens* is the essence of humanity. On this biological account, premise 2 is clearly true, since fetuses of our species are certainly innocent of any wrongdoing.

But if we give a purely scientific definition of humanity, then premise 1 **begs the question** against pro-choice opponents. In ordinary English, it's perfectly fine to beg a question—where this simply means to raise or invite a question. But in philosophy-speak, begging the question means something different, and is serious flaw. When philosophers accuse an argument of begging the question, this means that one of its premises already assumes the truth of the conclusion it is meant to support. That's just what premise 1 does here. It does not provide an independent reason for rejecting the pro-choice position. Those who advance premise 1 without any supporting argument for it are preaching to the choir, since *only those who already oppose abortion will accept this first premise*. If humanity is defined in purely biological terms, then the first premise needs a lot of defense—indeed, as much defense as the argument's conclusion.

Alternatively, we might think of humanity not as a biological category, but rather as a moral one. On such a view, to be human is to have a certain moral status. It is to be entitled to a broad set of moral rights, including the right to life. On this reading, premise 1 may well be true, though some critics will argue that even this moral rule has some exceptions. (We consider the matter in some detail in chapter 15.) Still, even if premise 1 turns out to be true, the second premise, the one that grants fetuses a wide range of basic rights, just as clearly begs the question. It needs as much defense as the conclusion it is meant to support.

So the term *humanity* (like the term *natural*) is ambiguous. This isn't any kind of problem, so long as we are very clear about which meaning we are relying on. But once we *are* clear about its different meanings, and make sure that the same meaning is being used in both premises, we can see that the argument is bound to beg the question. What this shows is that the argument cannot stand alone. Depending on which meaning of *human* we use, opponents of abortion will have to provide a strong supplemental argument to defend premise 1, premise 2, or both.

There is a basic philosophical point here: you can't solve complex moral problems with definitions alone. You can't solve the abortion debate just by defining a human being in terms of species membership. Nor can you solve it if you define *human being* as a person possessed of basic moral rights. We can define *humanity* in any way we like—by reference to species, genetic code, moral rights, rationality, self-awareness, linguistic ability, or in any of a dozen other ways. But no matter what definition we come up with, there is no shortcut through a lot of further complicated moral argumentation. Definitions alone will never spare us the hard philosophical work it takes to solve complex moral problems.

There is no better contemporary illustration of this point than the *Marriage Argument*, given by many natural law theorists and other opponents of same-sex marriage:

1. Marriage is defined as a relation between a man and a woman.
2. Homosexual relations are between a man and a man, or a woman and a woman.
3. Therefore, homosexual relations can never qualify as a marriage.

The search for a definition is the search for an essence. For instance, defining bachelors as unmarried adult males is supplying the essence, the central nature, of being a bachelor. Is marriage essentially a relation between those of opposite sexes, as defenders of the argument claim? Or is its essence the expression of mutual love, honor, and commitment, as supporters of same-sex marriage assert? Or something else entirely?

I won't try to settle this debate here. But the point raised earlier applies to this argument as well. The real question behind debates about same-sex marriage is whether the state is morally required to give the same legal rights to homosexual couples that it gives to heterosexuals. *That* question cannot be settled by setting forth a definition, especially one that will appeal only to those on one side of the debate. It can be settled only by examining the ultimate point of marriage, the morality of homosexuality, the proper role of the state, and other difficult matters.

Definitions are tools for thinking clearly. They clarify the subject matter and tell everyone precisely what the focus of discussion is. But having a subject firmly in mind is one thing; determining its moral status is quite another. Definitions alone will never solve a moral problem.

While this does not undermine the natural law theory, it must make us very careful of how we employ it. Even if we agree on a definition of human nature, and so on what is essential to being human, there is a great deal to do—indeed, there is almost everything yet to do—before we can draw important moral lessons about how to live our lives.

6.5 Conclusion

The deep appeal of the natural law theory is its promise to base morality on something clear and unmysterious: nature and its workings. Moral laws, on this account, are just natural laws, though ones that regulate human beings rather than planets, molecules, or gravitational forces. But as we have seen, it is difficult to try to read off recommendations for how we ought to act from descriptions of how nature actually operates.

And that shouldn't be too surprising. Natural laws describe and predict how things will behave. They summarize the actual behavior of things, and, unless they are statistical laws (of the sort that assign a probability to outcomes, rather than a certainty), they cannot be broken.

Moral laws are different in every respect. They can be broken, and often are. They are not meant to describe how we actually behave, but rather to serve as ideals that we ought to aim for. Nor are they designed to predict our actions, since we so often fall short of meeting the standards they set.

Nature can define the limit of our possibilities. Our nature does not allow us to know everything there is to know or to hold our breath for hours at a time. On the assumption that morality does not demand the impossible of us, nature can, in this way, set the outer bounds of what morality can require. But it can do no more. It cannot, in particular, tell us what we *are* required to do. Nor can it tell us what we are forbidden from trying to achieve. Nature has, at best, only a limited role to play in moral theory.

6.6 Discussion Questions

1. Many people think of *human nature* as consisting of innate traits that all humans share. Is this conception of human nature a suitable basis for morality? Why or why not?
2. Suppose that most animals behaved in a certain way. Would that provide evidence that it is natural for us to follow their lead? If so, what implications would this have for natural law theory?
3. Do human lives have a purpose? Does knowing the purpose of human lives help us to determine what is morally required?
4. Is there a single correct definition of *human nature*? If not, is this a problem for the natural law theory?
5. What roles can definitions play in resolving important moral disputes? Provide an answer in the context of a discussion of the Argument from Humanity.
6. How are moral laws different from the laws of physics or chemistry? Do these differences undermine the natural law theory?

6.7 Cases for Critical Reflection

Psychopath? You're Hired!

Radio Relations, a London-based media agency, once advertised a job opening for a "Psychopathic New Business Media Sales Executive Superstar!" The job advertisement read: "You didn't expect to see a job for a psychopath did you but this is no ordinary role. We're not looking for a psycho but for someone with some of the positive qualities that psychopaths have."[1] The word *psychopath* is often associated with violent behavior and heinous crimes. However, studies on psychopaths have claimed that people with psychopathic traits can thrive in business and other industries, including journalism, law, and politics. Top sales professionals and corporate executives often display psychopathic behaviors, including narcissism, superficial charm, and lack of empathy or concern for other people. Some think that as many as one in five corporate bosses are psychopaths, which is similar to the proportion among those in prison.

There isn't yet scientific consensus regarding whether psychopathy is an innate quality in some people or if it's caused by environmental factors—or a combination of the two—but researchers have found that there are certain genes associated with psychopathic traits. Some scientists have even reached the conclusion that psychopaths have an evolutionary advantage, finding a genetic correlation between psychopathic traits and reproductive outcomes.[2]

Questions

1. If psychopathic behaviors are innate qualities in some people, does that make these qualities good or desirable? What would a natural law theorist say?
2. If psychopathic behaviors contribute to evolutionary fitness, does that make them morally good? If not, does that pose a challenge to the natural law theory? Why or why not?
3. Someone could argue that if psychopathy is an innate quality, then psychopaths shouldn't be held responsible for their bad behaviors, because they couldn't help behaving that way. Should psychopaths be held to be morally responsible for bad actions? Are psychopaths moral agents?

---

1. https://www.independent.co.uk/news/business/news/psychopath-job-advert-radio-relations-sales-executive-listing-a7369471.html.
2. https://tonic.vice.com/en_us/article/kzkajv/psychopaths-may-have-an-evolutionary-advantage.

Terror-Bombing

They say that war is hell. Military leaders in war are faced with agonizing decisions, and some theorists think that ethical behavior isn't even possible in the context of war. Among controversial wartime decisions in history is that of Winston Churchill and British leaders to bomb German cities during World War II. In war, civilians are sometimes killed unintentionally in attacks on military targets or weapons factories. However, the British attacks on Germany in World War II often specifically targeted cities full of civilians. As a result of the policy of terror-bombing, around 300,000 Germans were killed and 780,000 were injured. Most of these individuals were civilians. The policy had further consequences, setting a precedent for Harry Truman's decision to drop the atom bomb on Hiroshima and Nagasaki.

Many historians believe that the purpose of the bombing was to destroy civilian morale in Germany. In a radio broadcast on the bombings, Churchill said, "The German people taste and gulp each month a sharper dose of the miseries they have showered upon mankind." Some British officials opposed the policy of terror-bombing, maintaining that the deaths of civilians were justified only as "a by-product of the primary intention to hit a military target."[1]

Questions

1. There is widespread disagreement about whether human beings are innately aggressive and violent, and human history has a long track record of nations and peoples going to war with each other. Do you think war and violence are natural? Why or why not?
2. If violence is natural behavior for human beings, then does that make it moral? Why or why not?
3. Would a natural law theorist endorse the decision to terror-bomb German cities? Why or why not?

Dr. Death

Dr. Jack Kevorkian was a medical pathologist who famously—or infamously—helped approximately 130 sick patients end their lives during the 1990s. Kevorkian advocated for the right to euthanasia (the assisted death of a patient) and was nicknamed "Dr. Death." In most cases,

---

1. Michael Walzer, *Just and Unjust Wars: A Moral Argument with Historical Illustrations*, 4th ed. (New York: Basic Books, 2006).

Kevorkian would hook his patients up to a machine that administered a sedative and a lethal drug dose. Kevorkian took steps to ensure the comfort and consent of his patients. He required that they express a clear wish to die and gave them at least a month to consider the decision before agreeing to assist. Kevorkian once publicly released a videotape of himself giving a lethal injection to a patient suffering from Lou Gehrig's disease, and in 1999 he was found guilty of second-degree murder.[1]

Dr. Kevorkian's actions drew controversy. Some supported his efforts to help suffering and terminal patients die on their own terms, but others believed that he needed to be stopped. Most medical doctors abide by the Hippocratic oath, a pledge of medical ethical conduct requiring physicians to "first do no harm." The oath further states, "I will not give a lethal drug to anyone if I am asked," which is often interpreted as a prohibition on euthanasia.

Euthanasia is most commonly sought by terminal patients, though Dr. Kevorkian argued that patients should have a right to assisted suicide even if they aren't terminal: "What difference does it make if someone is terminal? We are all terminal."[2] Some instances of euthanasia involve intentionally administering a lethal drug to bring about the patient's death. Other cases involve merely withdrawing treatment for a terminal patient—for example, by switching off a machine that had been keeping the patient alive. In still other cases, doctors will administer *potentially* lethal doses of painkilling drugs to relieve the painful suffering of a patient while not directly intending to kill the patient.[3]

Questions

1. Do you think it is ever morally permissible for a doctor to assist in the death of a patient? Why or why not?
2. According to natural law theory, is it ever morally permissible for a doctor to assist in the death of a patient? Why or why not?
3. In some cases, euthanasia leads to the death of a patient prior to when her death would have naturally occurred. Would a natural law theorist find this to be morally acceptable? Why or why not?

1. https://www.nytimes.com/2011/06/04/us/04kevorkian.html.
2. http://www.cnn.com/2010/HEALTH/06/14/kevorkian.gupta/index.html.
3. http://www.bbc.co.uk/ethics/introduction/doubleeffect.shtml.

CHAPTER 7

.... ❧ ....

Psychological Egoism

7.1 Egoism and Altruism

Early in his masterpiece the *Republic*, Plato recounts a story that was well known to his readers. This is the tale of Gyges the shepherd. While feeding his flock one day, a great earthquake shook the land and created an opening deep in the ground. Gyges descended and beheld many wonders, including a large bronze horse. It was hollow, with doors that Gyges managed to open. Inside he found the corpse of a giant, naked except for one thing: a golden ring encircling one of his fingers. Gyges slipped the ring off, tried it on for size, and discovered that it made him invisible. After testing it a few times to make sure of its powers, Gyges went into town, killed the king, captured the throne, and married the queen. He was able to satisfy his every want. And did just that.

The lesson many have taken from this story is that we are all, deep down, just like Gyges. We are always looking out for Number One. If we had the power to do as we liked, we would always seek out our own best interests, no matter the harms we caused. The only thing that keeps us in check here in the real world, where no such ring exists, is a worry that we'd be punished in one way or another if we did whatever we wanted to do.

This is the view of **psychological egoism**, which tells us that there is only one thing that *ultimately* motivates human beings: self-interest. Psychological egoism allows that we needn't always be motivated by thoughts of self-interest—we can be motivated, say, by a desire to please others, or to meet a deadline, or to help a co-worker out of a jam. We can have a wide variety of motivations. But psychological egoism says that all such motivations arise because of a deeper desire to benefit ourselves, where such benefit amounts to gaining something good or preventing something bad from happening to us. When we want to please others or help them out of a jam, we do so ultimately because we think that this will help us in some way. If this theory is true, then **altruism**—the direct desire to benefit others for their own sake, without any ulterior motive—does not exist.

In certain moods—especially when we are feeling doubts about whether people are as virtuous as they think or say they are—it is easy to believe that psychological egoism is true, and that altruism is just a comforting myth.

But sometimes it's very hard to accept such a dark view of ourselves. Just ask U.S. Army sergeants Cedric Thomas, Ian Newland, and Lyle Buehler. On December 4, 2007, they were patrolling the streets of Adhamiya, Iraq, crouched in a Humvee with their buddy Ross McGinnis, a nineteen-year-old army private. McGinnis had earned a reputation as the company prankster, a lean kid who was always asking difficult questions and making jokes. The crew was on the streets in an effort to identify a good location for a new generator that would provide electricity for the locals in the neighborhood. They stopped for a moment outside of a two-story building.

Kelly Kennedy, whose book *They Fought for Each Other*[1] tells the story of these men and the army battalion they were embedded with, describes what happened next:

> McGinnis yelled over the Humvee's intercom system: "Grenade!"
>
> The insurgents had lobbed so many grenades at the team that the guys reacted calmly, looking around for the offending weapon.
>
> "Where?" Thomas shouted.
>
> McGinnis yelled again: "The grenade is in the truck!"
>
> Then Newland could hear it ricocheting around the turret, a heavy metallic drum. McGinnis tried to grab it so he could toss it back out before it blew, but he missed. He stood as if he were going to leap out of the top of the Humvee, but instead he dropped down from his fighting position into the truck. Newland thought McGinnis was trying to escape the grenade. But he wasn't. McGinnis realized that his teammates hadn't spotted it, and so he was chasing it. Newland couldn't move quickly enough to get out of the truck with its combat-locked doors, and none of the guys quite understood what was going on because McGinnis hadn't dived out.

---

1. The excerpt that follows is taken from pp. 108–109 of Kennedy's book, published by St. Martin's Press, New York, 2010.

Then Newland saw it, a fist-sized black bullet of metal. He heard McGinnis say, "It's right here!" And it was. Right on the radio mount in front of the Humvee between driver Sergeant Lyle Buehler and truck commander Thomas. Newland froze as his brain processed this information. It was there. It was live. It was going to blow.

Then he watched as McGinnis threw his back against the radio mount, against the grenade. McGinnis wasn't going to bail. He knew his friends didn't have time. Newland could see the determination in his friend's face.

Seconds later, the grenade exploded. McGinnis was killed instantly.

We can't ask Ross McGinnis why he acted as he did. Nor can we pose that question of so many others who have made the ultimate sacrifice. Many such accounts are recorded at the fascinating website http://carnegiehero.org, which details the stories of everyday people who have made life-saving rescues at extreme personal risk. There are many reports of people jumping into freezing waters or blazing automobiles in order to save complete strangers. A number of the rescuers died in their efforts.

Why would people do such things? There seem to be many reasons. Some tried only to help a victim in need. Some felt called by duty to offer help. Others may have had mixed motives, of compassion and care on the one hand, and perhaps a small desire for praise and popularity on the other.

If psychological egoism is true, then these explanations are all wrong. None of these people was a true hero, since every one of them was driven by self-interest to save the lives of others. It is important to see how strong a claim this is. Psychological egoists are not saying that people usually act out of self-interest, or that altruism is rarer than it seems. Rather, their claim is that actions are *never* done from altruistic motives.

True, people often do help one another. But egoists will explain this in self-interested terms. Suppose, for instance, that my boss asks me at the last minute to babysit his bratty children. I am miserable, but smile anyway and quickly agree. Though I benefit my boss, the only reason I do so is because I expect to get something from it. If I didn't—if I knew, for instance, that he was soon retiring, and was powerless to advance my career or get me a raise—then I wouldn't agree to help. Psychological egoists are well aware that people help one another in many ways. But that doesn't show that they do so from altruistic motives.

As its name implies, psychological egoism is a psychological view, rather than an ethical theory. It aims to *describe* the facts and limits of human motivation, rather than *prescribe* the standards that we ought to live up to. If it is true, every single action—mine and yours and everyone else's—is done from the hope of personal gain.

Those who prefer a more flattering picture of humanity, one that allows us our altruistic motives, will want to debunk the theory. It isn't easy.

We can't refute this kind of egoism just by pointing to examples, such as smoking, in which people know that they are jeopardizing their health or their life. That is because those who smoke presumably gain some satisfaction from doing so. They are moved by a desire for pleasure, even if it lasts only the three or four minutes that their cigarette does.

Nor can we refute egoism by pointing to examples of people accepting extreme pain—say, the sort that comes from a root canal. When people sit still in a dentist's chair, they do so with their future in mind. They want to prevent something really bad from happening to them down the road—gum disease, rotting teeth, and so on. It's hard to imagine why people would accept such pain if they thought there was nothing to be gained by it.

So the egoist's claim must be understood as follows: *all human actions are ultimately aimed at avoiding some personal loss or gaining some personal benefit (or both), either in the short run or in the long term (or both).*

Many actions fail to achieve any of these aims. This doesn't undermine egoism, though, since the theory is not about the results of our actions but about their motivations. An action can be done with the thought that it will gain you millions, even if it leaves you penniless. Such a case is no threat to psychological egoism.

It is true that certain kinds of behavior, such as sneezing or snoring, are not motivated by self-interest. Egoists can handle this sort of case as well. The egoist thesis is one about actions that result from a person's intention to do something. Suppose that an epileptic suffers a seizure. Her arm shoots out and hits someone. The egoist needn't say that she was somehow trying to benefit herself. She wasn't intending to do anything at all. In order to refute psychological egoism, you must provide examples in which a person intends to do something, even though she wasn't trying to benefit herself.

7.2 Does It Matter Whether Psychological Egoism Is True?

Since psychological egoism is not an ethical theory, what bearing could it have on our ethical concerns?

As it happens, quite a bit. The *Implications of Egoism Argument* spells this out pretty clearly:

1. If psychological egoism is true, then we can't be altruistic.
2. If we can't be altruistic, then it can't be our duty to be altruistic.
3. Therefore, if psychological egoism is true, then it can't be our duty to be altruistic.
4. Psychological egoism is true.
5. Therefore, it can't be our duty to be altruistic.

Premise 1 is true by definition. No matter whether you like or hate psychological egoism, you should accept this premise. Premise 2 is also very plausible. If we can't be altruistic, then it can't be our duty to be altruistic. Why? Because we are not required to do the impossible—morality might be pretty demanding at times, but it can't be *that* demanding. The initial conclusion, 3, follows logically from 1 and 2, so if they are true, as they certainly seem to be, then 3 must be true as well.

That leaves only premise 4, which asserts the truth of psychological egoism. Suppose that it is true, and that altruism is a myth. Then we have no duty to be compassionate, considerate, kind, or generous. We would have to radically change our moral ideals, ridding them of altruistic elements. The resulting morality would be largely unrecognizable. Most of what we take for granted about the ethical life would turn out to be mistaken.

It may sound overdramatic to put it this way, but the fate of morality as we know it depends on whether psychological egoism is true. Let's see whether it is.

7.3 The Argument from Our Strongest Desires

There are two central arguments that seek to establish the truth of psychological egoism. The first of them is the *Argument from Our Strongest Desires*. The argument begins by claiming that every action you perform is based on your strongest desire. But if your strongest desires are what's moving you, then you are pursuing self-interest. So, whenever you act, you are pursuing self-interest. That is just what the psychological egoist claims:

1. Whenever you do something, you are motivated by your strongest desire.
2. Whenever you are motivated by your strongest desire, you are pursuing your self-interest.
3. Therefore, whenever you do something, you are pursuing your self-interest.

Consider the argument's initial claim: our actions are always caused by our strongest desires. Apparent counterexamples spring to mind: visiting a nagging relative, enduring a tedious commute, handing over your wallet to a gunman. Does anyone really want to do these things? Probably not. But that doesn't show that this first premise is false. We can explain such actions by pointing to *other* things that people want—to sustain family harmony, to keep one's job, to stay alive.

The case of **strictly conscientious action** is more difficult for the egoist to handle. Such action occurs when you do what you think is required of you, even in the face of great temptation. Your desires all push one way, and duty calls in another. People sometimes follow the latter path.

Of course, we could say that even here, people are acting on their strongest desire. It's just that in cases where people knuckle down and resist temptation, their strongest desire is to do their duty.

This move could save premise 1. But that should be cold comfort to egoists, for if they relied on this move, then they would have to admit that premise 2 is false. They would have to say that our deepest desire is not always to benefit ourselves. Sometimes we most want to do our duty, even when it comes at a personal cost.

When we put it this way, it becomes clear that egoists must deny the existence of strictly conscientious action. Of course, people do help others, and people sometimes speak of themselves as acting just for the sake of duty. But egoists do not take such talk at face value. They insist that those who help others, despite what they might say, are really just looking out for themselves. People sometimes lie to others to impress them. And people sometimes lie to themselves, deceiving themselves with self-flattery.

These points are undeniable, but they fail to show that conscientious action never occurs. We can all think of apparent cases of such action, and even if some of the evidence is tainted by lies and self-deception, we have no reason (as yet) to think that *all* of it is suspect. Until we are given such a reason, the case of conscientious action presents a real problem for the egoist's argument.

There is another way to put this worry. Let us grant for the moment that premise 1 of the argument is true. So we always do what we most want to do. But *that doesn't yet show that our strongest desires are always for personal gain.* That is precisely what has to be proven.

Have a look at premise 2 again. It states that our strongest desires are always for our own personal gain. But those who believe in altruism will not accept that. Indeed, if we sign on to premise 1, then premise 2 begs the question—it assumes the truth of the conclusion that it is meant to support. It is preaching to the converted. It is not a neutral thesis that can appeal to both fans and opponents of psychological egoism. Only those who already reject the existence of altruism will accept such a premise. Everyone else will think that our strongest desires may sometimes be for something other than self-interest. Premise 2 assumes that just because a desire is mine, it must have a certain object—me. Or, more specifically: my self-interest. But *whose* desire it is, and *what* the desire is for—these seem to be completely separate issues. The egoist says that just because a desire is mine, then it has to be aimed at my self-interest. But why couldn't it be aimed at your welfare? Or the well-being of a friend, or my country, or even a stranger?

The egoist might respond: if you are doing what you really want, aren't you thereby self-interested? It is important to see that the answer may well be *no*. For all we know, some of us deeply want to help other people. When we manage to offer such help, we are doing what we really want to do. Yet what we really want to do is to benefit someone else, not ourselves.

Now, if people get what they really want, they may be better off as a result. (But they might not: think of the anorexic or the drug addict. Or think of the cases of disappointment discussed in chapter 4.) Yet the fact that a person gains from her action does not prove that her motives were egoistic. The person who really wants to help the homeless, and volunteers at a soup kitchen or shelter, may certainly derive pleasure from her efforts. As a general matter, when you discover that your deepest desires have been satisfied, you often feel quite pleased. But that does not mean that your ultimate aim is to get such pleasure. That's what needs to be shown; we can't just assume it in trying to figure out whether our motives are always self-interested.

In short, even if this argument's first premise is true, its second premise begs the question. We don't yet have reason to doubt the possibility of altruistic motivation.

7.4 The Argument from Expected Benefit

So let us consider another argument, the *Argument from Expected Benefit*. This argument claims that people always expect their actions to leave them at least a bit better off. And if they do, then their constant aim is to gain from their actions. So whenever people act, they are trying to get some personal benefit. That is just what psychological egoism predicts:

1. Whenever you do something, you expect to be better off as a result.
2. If you expect to be better off as a result of your actions, then you are aiming to promote your self-interest.
3. Therefore, whenever you do something, you are aiming to promote your self-interest.

I have my doubts about this argument. Premise 1 seems to ignore the existence of pessimists. And even optimists sometimes expect to suffer for their actions. Consider a person who thinks she can get away with a convenient lie but admits the truth anyway, knowing the grief that's in store for her as a result. Or imagine an employee late for an important appointment who increases his delay by helping a stranger cross a dangerous street. He doesn't anticipate any reward for his good deed, and knows that this delay is only going to stoke his boss's anger. Both cases seem to be counterexamples to the claim that our actions are always accompanied by an expectation of personal benefit.

These examples, and the many others like them that we could imagine, are bound to be controversial. Egoists may insist that people always *do* expect to gain from their actions, even if it sometimes appears that they don't. After all, appearances can be misleading. It may look as if we sometimes expect only the worst. But deep down, we may always believe that our actions will make us better off.

I am not convinced, but for now, let's assume that my doubts are mistaken and that premise 1 is secure. Even so, the second premise—the one that says that if you expect a benefit, then that is your aim—is very implausible.

The problem is that it looks like the egoist is begging the question again. Return to those who enjoy volunteer work. Such people may well expect to gain something from their activities. Volunteers often report feelings of deep satisfaction from their efforts. But this doesn't show that their motives are self-interested. A volunteer, with all sincerity, may claim that her aim is to help others, rather than to help herself. The enjoyment she experiences from her volunteer activities is nice, no question about it. But it is a side effect, a foreseen benefit, and not the motive of her actions.

Again, the egoist will insist that we can't be sure of her sincerity. And even if she is sincere, she may not realize the true motives that get her to the shelter every week. She may just be looking for the approval of her fellow volunteers, or for her efforts to be publicized in a way that will boost her career. We can't be sure that this isn't what's going on.

That is true: we can never be absolutely certain of our own motives, much less those of others. But that is not enough to show that the egoist is correct. After all, if we can't be certain of our motives, then we can't certain that they are egoistic, rather than altruistic. The egoist's claim—that whenever we expect some benefit, our aim is to get it—is controversial. It *seems* that there are counterexamples, though we can't be sure there really are. Given evidence that appears to undermine premise 2, the egoist needs to defend it.

And a defense is not far to seek. The best way to support this premise is by citing a more general principle that supports it. And this is the natural candidate:

(G) Whenever you expect your action to result in X, then your aim is to get X.

If (G) is true, then whenever I expect to get money, glory, or approval from my actions, that is my aim. Generally, if I expect some personal gain, then my goal is to obtain it. That is just what the argument's second premise says.

The problem is that (G) is false. Whenever I lecture to a large audience, I expect some people to fall asleep. Believe me, that is not my goal. If I ever had the chance to play against a professional tennis player, I'd expect to lose. But it wouldn't be my aim to do so. My goal would be to enjoy the experience and to learn a thing or two. If a student fails to prepare for an exam, she may expect to receive a poor grade. It hardly follows that she is trying for one.

So expecting something doesn't always mean aiming for it. And that poses a direct challenge to premise 2 of the Argument from Expected Benefit. It might be true, but we have seen no good reason to think so.

Indeed, the best reason to accept premise 2—namely, principle (G)—is false. If we are to have any confidence in this argument, the egoist needs to furnish us with much better support for both of its premises.

7.5 Two Egoistic Strategies

Things aren't looking that promising for egoists. But there are still two strategies that they can use to try to show that the evidence of altruism is overrated.

Appealing to the Guilty Conscience

Consider people who have taken great risks to oppose oppressive regimes. Many of these people claim that their conscience wouldn't let them do otherwise—had they taken the safe path, they wouldn't be able to live with themselves. In their eyes, to give in to evil is to tarnish oneself. Many people speak of the terrible guilt they'd feel if they did nothing to fight against injustice.

Egoists insist that even these people are wholly self-interested. They are opposing injustice in order to make sure that they can sleep well at night, that they can be free of crippling guilt. Having a clean conscience is a benefit. And so such people are acting from self-interested motives after all.

It is important to see why this sort of reasoning does not work. If a person is truly good, she will certainly be troubled at the thought of doing wrong. But that does not prove that her actions are motivated by a desire for a guilt-free conscience. Indeed, if she did not care about others, then she wouldn't lose a wink of sleep at the thought of their misery. Those who suffer pangs of guilt from having harmed others, or having missed a chance to help them, are precisely those who care about other people.

There is a basic difference between those who are deeply upset over the damage they cause and those who aren't. On the one hand, it is reported that the Nazi war criminal Adolf Eichmann slept like a baby, despite having engineered the deaths of hundreds of thousands in the concentration camps. On the other, we all know those who are beside themselves at the very thought of having done a serious wrong. Egoists lump both kinds of people together and, in doing so, fail to appreciate that those who are subject to guilt must have altruistic concerns. If they didn't, then they wouldn't feel so bad when their actions end up harming others.

Expanding the Realm of Self-Interest

There appear to be many people who are altruistically motivated, and who show this by their expressions of care for those they love. Consider the mother who gives away the last of her food to save her only child. This seems like the essence of altruism. And yet the egoist might say that the mother is really looking out for herself, by trying to avoid a terrible personal loss, for she would be devastated at witnessing the death of her child. Further, since the mother cares deeply about her child, the mother's well-being rests in large part on how well her child is faring. By helping her child, the mother is thereby helping herself.

Much of what was just said is true. But this cannot be good news for the egoist, since the details of this little story imply that egoism is false. For most parents, their own well-being crucially depends on that of their children. And so, when parents tend to the needs of their children, they are usually helping themselves in the bargain. But this doesn't show that parents are motivated by self-interest when they offer such help. As we've seen, even if people expect to gain by helping others, that doesn't prove that their aim is to acquire such benefit. Further, if a parent suffers at the thought of her child's misery, then that is evidence of altruism, not egoism. Those who care only for themselves do not suffer when thinking of the misery of others.

The second egoist strategy is thus confused. When we present difficult cases for egoism—that of Ross McGinnis smothering a live grenade in his Humvee, or that of a mother giving her last bit of nourishment to her child—the egoist cannot sensibly reply that such people are motivated only by self-interest. For such people, what really matters is living honorably, or seeing their children flourish. Their concerns are directed at something other than their own gain. That is not something that the egoist can make sense of.

7.6 Letting the Evidence Decide

People often benefit one another. Just think of the good that aid workers, nurses, teachers, and parents do. Sometimes their motives are clearly self-interested. But not always. In many cases, people report that their primary motivation is to help someone else, even when such action is known to come at a personal cost. As we have seen, the egoist must view all such reports as misleading, based on either self-deception or the intended deception of others.

This puts the egoist's thesis in jeopardy. We can see the danger by constructing a dilemma: either we do or we don't allow the evidence to settle the question of whether altruism exists. There is trouble either way.

To appreciate the difficulties, consider this cautionary tale. As I write this, my hair, once dark black, now has a substantial amount of gray in it. Suppose a friend of mine starts teasing me about this. I tell him that I can't help it. "Yes, you can," he replies. "Grecian Formula will do the trick." "Oh, I doubt that," I say. "Those elves won't let anything stand in their way."

What elves? Why, the invisible ones. The ones who have turned my black hair gray. Each night they cover a strand or two with permanent gray paint, and over time, I've become more gray than black. And worse, there's nothing I can do about it, since I can't catch them and put a stop to the madness. After all, they are invisible. And very clever.

My friend, who thought I was joking, now becomes alarmed. "You know, don't you, that invisible elves don't exist. And hair color is a matter of genetics." He tracks down the latest data to make his point. Naturally, I dismiss this as the product of a conspiracy planted by the geneticists. No matter what sort of evidence my friend provides, I stick to my guns—it's the elves who are behind it all.

This unshakable conviction is not the mark of a rational mind, but rather the crazy faith of someone seriously out of touch with reality. In refusing to allow that I may be mistaken, I am being stubborn and dogmatic. If the evidence fails to support my beliefs, then I fault the evidence, rather than change my beliefs.

Some people are utterly convinced that the earth is flat; others, that space aliens built the Egyptian pyramids; yet others, that George W. Bush ordered the destruction of the World Trade Center. Many of these people feel certain of their views. No amount of evidence is going to get them to change their mind.

But these beliefs, like mine in the invisible elves, are not rational. They are not supported by the evidence. And the worry is that a belief in psychological egoism is no better than the ones I've just described. If psychological egoists stubbornly deny all contrary evidence, and routinely dismiss the many cases of apparent altruism, then their view is similar to the invisible elf hypothesis. If I refuse in advance to allow the chance that my pet theory is mistaken, and refuse even to admit the possibility that evidence might cast doubt on it, then I am irrationally clinging to a prejudice.

For all I have said, psychological egoism may yet be true. And invisible elves may really exist. But it wouldn't be rational to think so.

So let us opt for the other half of the dilemma. We should keep an open mind and let the evidence decide whether altruism exists. But if we go this route, and subject psychological egoism to serious testing, then egoism fails the relevant tests.

One way to see this is to point to the vast literature in academic psychology, which confirms the existence of what C. Daniel Batson, the foremost researcher in the area, calls the "**empathy-altruism hypothesis**." This hypothesis states that empathy can prompt altruistic motivation. Empathy is the ability to imaginatively place oneself in another's shoes, to see things as through her own eyes, and to feel what she is feeling. Through a long series of experiments, Batson and a variety of collaborators have amassed a great deal of evidence in favor of the empathy-altruism hypothesis.[2]

These experiments are quite varied, and this is certainly not the place to undertake a thorough review. But many of the most important experiments have a common structure. First, Batson and his collaborators sorted test subjects into two randomized groups, and then used a device for creating greater empathy in one group than in another. Then they asked members of each group whether they were willing to help someone in need. Their hypothesis was that the more empathic subjects would be more likely to offer such assistance, even when it was made clear that they would not be rewarded for doing so or penalized for refusing to help. This hypothesis has been vindicated in study after study.

To make this more concrete, consider the details of one prominent experiment.[3] Batson and a collaborator had several dozen students in a psychology class listen to an interview with someone who was identified as a fellow student who had broken both legs in an accident, and was requesting help to review class notes. One group of students was instructed to focus entirely on the objective details of the situation and not to concern themselves with how this fellow student felt about her situation. Students in the second group were told, instead, to take the perspective of the person being interviewed, and not to concern themselves with focusing on all of the information presented. As a result, it was determined that students in the second group felt much more empathy than those in the

---

2. This evidence is summarized in C. Daniel Batson, *The Altruism Question: Toward a Social-Psychological Answer* (Hillsdale, N.J: Erlbaum Publishers) 1991, and Batson's *Altruism in Humans* (New York: Oxford University Press), 2011.

3. This is described in detail in Miho Toi and C. Daniel Batson, "More Evidence that Empathy Is a Source of Altruistic Motivation," *Journal of Personality and Social Psychology* (43), pp. 281–292.

first group for the accident victim. Further, students in the second group were more than twice as likely as those in the first to actually volunteer to help this student—over 70 percent did so. Because students were promised confidentiality in their answers, and were given other guarantees that they would in no way be called out or stigmatized if they declined to volunteer, the results appear to constitute honest responses that reveal genuine motivations of altruism—ones that increase in a way that corresponds to increased empathy.

Batson himself has emphasized that one experiment cannot substantiate the existence of altruism. Nor can two or three. But he and his colleagues, and many other researchers, have conducted hundreds of such experiments, and the accumulated results strongly confirm the empathy-altruism hypothesis. They do not *prove* it, if by "proof" one means a demonstration whose conclusion is absolutely certain. But science does not deliver such proofs—all scientific findings are subject to revision in light of further evidence and theorizing. It's also true that one could doubt whether the test subjects in these experiments are really delivering their honest views, or whether their honest views are cloaking some deep, hidden egoistic impulses. But to discredit all of this experimental evidence on the basis of such doubts is once again to make psychological egoism untestable, and so to deny in advance that there is any evidence that could possibly undermine one's confidence in egoism. That makes belief in egoism an article of faith, rather than a well-confirmed hypothesis.

Egoism is a theory about human motivation. And there are two sorts of evidence we can rely on when it comes to determining people's motives: testimony and behavior. People can tell us what moves them, and we can see for ourselves how they behave. Neither kind of evidence is perfect. We can misinterpret behavior. And people can be deceptive about their true motives. Still, testimony and behavior are the only sources of evidence we have.[4] And they both point strongly to the existence of altruism. To discredit all such testimony, and to reinterpret all such behavior, is to

---

4. What about sophisticated fMRI or other brain-scanning techniques? They may someday provide evidence, but any such evidence really depends on the evidence of testimony and behavior. That is because we can tell whether a certain synapse firing indicates altruistic motivation only if we can correlate such firing with what subjects say and do. We must see, for instance, that certain synapse firings reliably correlate with action that helps others, or with people telling us of their altruistic motivation. Without evidence of that connection, brain scans could never tell us whether their subjects were motivated by self-interest or altruism.

render egoism as unreasonable as my invisible elf hypothesis. If we are prepared to let evidence decide the matter, we must decide that psychological egoism is false.

7.7 Conclusion

The truth of psychological egoism would spell the defeat of morality as we know it. If altruism is impossible, then morality cannot reasonably ask us to sacrifice self-interest for the sake of others. The central moral virtues of benevolence, kindness, and compassion would have no place in morality. If all we *can* do is look out for Number One, then there is little point in demanding that we do otherwise.

So the stakes are high. And psychological egoism can seem the only clear-eyed, unsentimental view of human nature. We're all familiar with cases in which we gave ourselves credit for being altruistic, only to realize, later on, that we were really just looking out for ourselves.

But when we examine the arguments and evidence, there is reason to take a more charitable view. Few of us are saints. But few of us are wholly self-absorbed, either. And this opens up the possibility that we may become better than we are, more altruistic and more generous, shifting our attention away from our own needs and onto the needs of others.

A plausible philosophical principle, first offered by Aristotle, is instructive in this context. The principle tells us to *follow the appearances*. It directs us to think that things are really as they seem, that appearances match reality—until we have excellent reason for doubt. It *appears* that there is plenty of altruistic motivation. People often speak of how much they care about others. And there are many cases in which people have actually offered help to others, strangers and loved ones alike. All of this evidence might be highly misleading. But the arguments that egoists provide, and the strategies they offer to handle counterexamples, are unconvincing. They fail to give us excellent reason to doubt the appearances of altruism. Until better arguments and strategies come along, we should trust the appearances and regard psychological egoism with great suspicion.

7.8 Discussion Questions

1. Psychological egoism is not an ethical theory, but a descriptive view about human behavior. Given this, how might the truth of psychological egoism have implications for ethics?

2. How do psychological egoists explain extreme acts of self-sacrifice, such as falling on a grenade for one's fellow soldiers? Do you find their explanation of such phenomena compelling?

3. Many people think that whenever people act voluntarily, they are acting on the basis of their desires. If this is true, does this mean that all voluntary action is self-interested?

4. Suppose that people always do what they most want to do. Is that enough to show that psychological egoism is true? Why or why not?

5. If someone expects to benefit from an action, does that show that she is trying to advance her self-interest? Why or why not?

6. Is there any possible observation that could disprove psychological egoism? If so, what would it be? If not, is this a good or a bad feature of the theory?

7. All things considered, do you agree with the psychological egoist's claim that all human behavior is fundamentally self-interested? Defend your answer.

CHAPTER 8

.... ❧ ....

Ethical Egoism

Psychological egoism is a theory about human motivation: it tells us that all of our actions are ultimately motivated exclusively by self-interest. This is not an ethical view, because it says nothing about what is good or bad, right or wrong.

But as we have seen, if psychological egoism is true, then there is little point in fashioning a morality that demands self-sacrifice. Morality does not demand the impossible. If psychological egoism were true, then all morality could possibly do is to ask that we look out for ourselves.

This is precisely the advice of **ethical egoism**. Unlike the psychological version, ethical egoism really is a moral theory. It tells us about what we are morally required and forbidden to do. Specifically, it says that there is one ultimate moral duty—to improve your own well-being as best you can. Whenever you fail to achieve this goal, you are behaving immorally.

Many ethical egoists have been psychological egoists as well. But this isn't required. You might reject psychological egoism, and so think that we *can* be altruistic, while denying that we *should be* directly concerned with the well-being of others. Ethical egoism gains strength from psychological egoism, but this is not its only source of support. As we will see, there are several arguments for thinking that (surprisingly) ethics is all about getting ahead in the world and making ourselves as well-off as we can be.

8.1 Why Be Moral?

Imagine that you are a stockbroker with inside information about an upcoming corporate takeover. Once the takeover is announced, the company's stock will soar. If you were to purchase a large amount of that stock right now, you'd stand to make millions. Should you do it?

Suppose that you are seriously thinking about this. You've carefully calculated the chances of getting caught, and have determined that the risk is small. Further, even if you are caught, the penalty is slight enough as to make the risk worth taking. Still, you are sure that such behavior is immoral. Brokers are able to gain privileged information only on the condition that they not take unfair advantage of it. You'd be doing just that. Yet since the potential gain is so great, why let morality stand in the way?

There are countless situations that pose the same problem. Imagine cheating on an exam to increase the chances of landing an excellent job. Or lying to an investigator to avoid prosecution. Or doing some creative bookkeeping to minimize a tax burden. Or spreading nasty rumors in order to hurt a competitor.

In a perfect world, virtue would always be rewarded and vice would never flourish. But what should we do, here in our imperfect world, when immorality promises great rewards? What to do when moral behavior is met with ridicule, a prison term, or a bullet? It is easy when morality and self-interest give the same advice. But what if they don't?

If ethical egoism is true, there are no such cases. This sort of egoism claims that *actions are morally right just because they best promote one's self-interest.* On this view, conflicts between self-interest and morality are impossible, because our fundamental moral duty is to maximize self-interest. If, among all of the options available to you, there is one that will serve you best, then that is the option that morality requires.

It may seem that there is nothing "ethical" at all about such a theory. Consider this: if people can best improve their lot in life by secretly killing political opponents, stealing from the weak, or humiliating their employees, then ethical egoism imposes a moral duty to do such things. But how could a plausible ethical theory do that?

Indeed, it seems that we can use such examples to create a decisive anti-egoist argument—call it the *Argument from Paradigm Cases*:

1. If an ethical theory requires killing, rape, or theft, just because such actions maximize self-interest, then that theory cannot be true.
2. Ethical egoism sometimes requires such actions, just because they sometimes do maximize self-interest.
3. Therefore, ethical egoism cannot be true.

A paradigm is a model, a very clear example. Some of the examples used in this argument are the clearest cases of immorality we can think of. The underlying thought here is that any ethical theory ought to classify these actions as immoral, and explain why they are so obviously wrong. Ethical egoism fails to do that.

Ethical egoists (henceforth, just *egoists*) can offer two replies to this argument. They can reject its first premise. Or they can reject the second.

To reject the second premise, egoists must claim that killers, rapists, and thieves *can never best advance their own interests by perpetrating such crimes*. This claim could be true if there is a God who punishes these actions with eternal damnation. It could also be true if such acts deserve suffering, and a doctrine of karma guaranteed that you eventually get what you deserve. But suppose that you don't find such accounts convincing. Are there other ways to defend the idea that those who kill, rape, and steal are never better off as a result?

Plato thought he could do it. He tried to show that those who are unjust are always harmed because of their injustice. He spent a good part of the *Republic* arguing that all-powerful tyrants, though able to control and acquire so much in this world, are still doomed to terrible lives. Even as they tell themselves how much fun they are having, they are inwardly miserable, constantly fearful and insecure, leading lives filled with anxiety and suspicion. Once we see what an immoral life is really like, we will realize that we are far better off being moral.

Plato's argument depends heavily on his claims about the inner lives of immoral people. I think it fair to say that his case is not fully persuasive. Certainly, many immoral people are deeply troubled and unhappy. But others are able to sleep well at night, take pride in a job well done (assassination, theft, betrayal), and find friends within a network of like-minded associates. The bad guys sometimes get away with it, have a lot of fun in the meantime, and never regret the harm they have caused.

Much more, of course, needs to be said about what is truly beneficial for us. Chapters 1–4 cover these issues, but they are hardly the final word on the matter. And since we don't have space here to discuss religious views of the afterlife, we have to admit that the jury is still out on the truth of premise 2. Perhaps it is false—perhaps there is some very powerful argument that can show that wrongdoing will *never* maximize the self-interest of anyone. If that argument can be given, then we can strike down premise 2. And that, of course, would be great news for the egoist, since the fall of premise 2 would spell the defeat of the entire Argument from Paradigm Cases.

But let's assume for the moment that premise 2 is true, and that, as it seems, some immoral actions really do best promote the interests of those who commit them. If that is so, then egoists must take aim at premise 1 of the argument. And that, in fact, is precisely what they will do.

Suppose that we will not always do best for ourselves by following the familiar laundry list of moral rules. Then conventional morality and self-interest will sometimes clash. When that is so, the egoist is forced to reject conventional morality. And since the first premise of the argument is just an expression of conventional morality, the argument begs the question against the egoist.

Think about it this way. Only those who already dislike egoism would accept the first premise. Premise 1 is not a neutral claim. Rather, it assumes that egoism is mistaken. It assumes, specifically, that self-interest cannot morally justify actions such as rape and theft. True, such actions do seem to be paradigm cases of immorality, and so any moral theory that encouraged such actions would be suspect. But an egoist who accepts premise 2 will claim that our paradigms are mistaken. And they might be. We can't absolutely rule out such a possibility.

Still, we can recall Aristotle's advice, recorded at the end of the previous chapter. We have reason to stick with the appearances, and to take things at face value, until we are given excellent reason for doubt. It *seems* that killing, rape, and theft are very clear cases of immorality, especially when they are done to serve self-interest. That is just what premise 1 says. Given how appealing that premise is, we are right to insist that egoists provide a compelling counterargument, one that can reveal the error of our popular ways of thinking. Let's now consider two prominent attempts to do just that.

8.2 Two Popular Arguments for Ethical Egoism

As we have just seen, ethical egoism can clash very radically with our deepest moral beliefs. This happens in three ways.

First, egoism may *require* some actions that seem highly immoral. If promoting self-interest requires a knifing in the back, the betrayal of a friendship, or the illegal use of insider information, egoism insists that we do these things.

Second, egoism may *forbid* us from doing some actions that seem clearly morally good. Egoists think that any action that involves a genuine self-sacrifice is immoral. Egoism insists that it is wrong to be kind, keep your promises, or care for your children, if you pass up a chance at personal gain by doing so.

Third, egoism may *permit* us to escape some very important moral duties. It seems, for instance, that we each have a duty of easy rescue. If saving someone comes at little or no cost to ourselves, then we must do what we can to help. Yet if your interests are best served by ignoring such victims, then egoism frees you of any duty to help. Indeed, as a general matter, egoism requires that we help others only when we help ourselves in the bargain.

The Self-Reliance Argument

These claims require defense. Here is one that offered by Ayn Rand (1905–1982), whose writings on behalf of ethical egoism have been very influential in contemporary culture.[1] Call it the *Self-Reliance Argument*:

1. The most effective way of making everyone better off is for each person to mind his own business, and tend only to his own needs.
2. We ought to take the most effective path to making everyone better off.
3. Therefore, we each ought to mind our own business and tend only to our own needs.

There are two problems with this argument. Its first premise is false. And its second premise is one that egoists cannot accept.

The first premise is false because those who are in need of help would not be better off if others were to neglect them. If you are suffering a heart attack and I know CPR and am the only one able to help, then you are definitely *worse* off, not better, if I decide to leave you alone and go on my way.

Nor is complete self-reliance even a good general policy. It might be better if everyone were self-reliant than if everyone were constantly sticking their nose into other people's business. But these are surely not our only two options. There is a middle path that allows a lot of room for self-interest but also demands a degree of self-sacrifice, especially when we can offer great help to others at very little cost to ourselves. Everyone would be better off if people helped others to some extent, rather than if people offered help only when doing so served self-interest.

Further, the argument's emphasis (in premise 2) on our doing what will improve everyone's well-being is not something that the egoist can

---

1. Her novels *The Fountainhead* (1943) and *Atlas Shrugged* (1957) have sold millions; for a more explicit presentation of her philosophical views, one might try *The Virtue of Selfishness* (1964).

accept. For ethical egoists, the ultimate moral duty is to maximize personal benefit. There is no moral requirement to make everyone better off. The egoist allows people to help others, or to have a care for the general good, but only when doing so will maximize their own self-interest. And not otherwise.

The Libertarian Argument

There is another popular argument for severely limiting our duties to others, one that also receives expression at a variety of places in Rand's writings. Call this the *Libertarian Argument*. Libertarians claim that our moral duties to help other people have only two sources: consent and reparation. In other words, any duty to aid another person stems either from our voluntarily agreeing to accept that duty (i.e., our consent), or from our having violated someone's rights, and so owing a duty to repair the wrong we have done. But if I do not consent to help other people, and have done them no wrong, then I have no duty to help them.

This is a fascinating argument. There is little controversy that our duties can originate as the libertarian suggests. The real question is whether there are sources of duties *other than* consent and reparation. In the example of offering easy rescue, for instance, it seems that the victim's needs, together with my ability to help at little cost, are enough to generate a duty that I help. Consent did not enter the picture—I was morally required to help even if I didn't agree to do so. And I had done the victim no wrong, so reparation was not an issue. The libertarian will deny that someone else's needs, plus one's own ability to help, are enough to generate a moral duty of offering assistance. After all, if I need $10,000 for knee surgery, and you are a millionaire who could easily afford to pay for it, you are not automatically required to hand me the money.

There is a lot one might say about the Libertarian Argument. Indeed, I think that it poses one of the most fundamental challenges in political philosophy. Yet we can avoid a look into its details, because even if the argument is sound, it cannot support ethical egoism.

The basic explanation for this is that egoists cannot accept the argument's central claim. Egoists deny that there are two ultimate sources of moral duty (consent and reparation). In fact, egoists deny that *either* of these is a source of moral duty. For them, self-interest is the only source of our moral duties. We must fulfill our voluntary agreements, or repair the damage we've done, only when doing so is in our best interest. *When it is not, we have no moral duty.*

The Libertarian Argument tells us, for instance, that if we promise to volunteer at a local hospital, or consent to the details of a home sale, then we should follow through. However, if doing so fails to make us better off, then egoism says that we have no duty to stick to our agreements. Indeed, egoism *forbids* us from holding up our end of the deal. Libertarians would require that we keep our word. Since egoism and libertarianism often give such conflicting advice, egoism cannot gain support from libertarianism.

8.3 The Best Argument for Ethical Egoism

Despite their popularity, the Self-Reliance and Libertarian Arguments fail to support ethical egoism. To locate a stronger foundation for the view, I think that we need to focus on one of the perennial questions in ethics, and see how well the egoist can answer it. It is here that egoism finds its strongest support.

The perennial question is the one we began with: why be moral? Ethical egoism has a watertight answer to this question. We should always be moral because morality always serves self-interest. We all agree that there is good reason to look after ourselves. Since that is so, and since morality (as the egoist sees it) always advises us to protect our interests, there is always good reason to do as morality requires.

We can mold this line of thought into a very powerful argument— call this the *Best Argument for Ethical Egoism*. It starts with the common thought that every moral duty provides an excellent reason to obey it. And it then says that we have reason to do things only if there is something in it for us. It would be irrational, for instance, to sacrifice your own well-being if you got nothing in return for such sacrifice. When you put these two thoughts together, you arrive at the conclusion that whenever we are morally required to do something, doing it must promote self-interest. This is just what ethical egoists believe.

Here is the argument in a nutshell:

1. If you are morally required to do something, then there is good reason for you to do it.
2. If there is good reason for you to do something, then doing it must make you better off.
3. Therefore, if you are morally required to do something, then doing it must make you better off.

The argument is logically valid. Its two premises are each widely accepted. And on the face of it, they are each highly plausible. Consider the first premise. If I am duty-bound to do something, don't I have some good reason to follow through? Perhaps this good reason isn't always decisive—there might sometimes be even better reasons that count against doing my duty. But at the very least, being morally required to (say) keep a promise, or tell the truth, indicates at least some reason to do such things.

Now consider the second premise. It is hard to doubt that there are compelling reasons to protect your own interests. If some action promises me no gain, but only loss, then what reason is there for me to do it? I'd be irrational to sacrifice my interests without the promise of some compensating benefit. It might be heroic to give up one's life for a stranger or to forfeit one's last chance at happiness so that others may enjoy life. But reason can't require such sacrifice.

My own view is that the Best Argument for Ethical Egoism is ultimately unpersuasive. I think that the first premise is true, but have come to doubt the second premise. Once we examine this theory of reasons with a little more care, it may be less plausible than a first look would suggest.

We can begin to see this by considering two superficially similar claims:

(A) If an action makes you better off, then there is good reason for you to do it.

(B) If there is good reason for you to do an action, then doing it must make you better off.

Claim (A) looks pretty good. It tells us that self-interest is always a good reason for doing something. It doesn't say that this is the only reason for acting. And it doesn't say that it is always the best reason.

Though (A) is an extremely attractive claim, it is difficult to explain its plausibility. It seems to me just one of those rock-bottom assumptions we make about the kinds of reasons we have. If someone were to deny it, for instance, it isn't clear what we could say on its behalf. That doesn't show it to be implausible. Not everything can be explained. It may be that (A) is more basic than any other claim we might use to defend it.

This isn't the case for (B), which should look familiar. It is the same claim as the Best Argument's premise 2. And it seems that there are many counterexamples to it. Cases of easy rescue provide the most compelling ones. If I see a terrible traffic accident occur, and have a cell phone with me, I have a reason to dial 911. I have that reason even if making the call will gain me nothing. If I see a window washer high up on a ladder and notice that my walking companion is about to accidentally bump into it, I have a reason to warn my friend and make sure that she avoids the ladder. I have that reason even if there is no benefit to me of doing so.

Defenders of premise 2 cannot accept this, and that seems a strike against their view. We can allow that promoting self-interest is a good reason for doing things. But why is it the *only* good reason? I don't know of any compelling answer to this question.

In the absence of such an answer, we have some basis for thinking that premise 2 is false. And if it is false, then the Best Argument for Ethical Egoism is unsound, since that argument relies on it. This does not by itself show that ethical egoism is false. But if we can combine the absence of a strong argument for ethical egoism with the presence of strong reasons to oppose it, then this does leave us with a powerful case against ethical egoism.

8.4 Three Problems for Ethical Egoism

The three most serious problems for ethical egoism are (1) that it violates some of the deepest and most central moral beliefs we have, (2) that it cannot allow for the existence of moral rights; and (3) that it arbitrarily assigns self-interest complete priority over the interests of others.

Egoism Violates Core Moral Beliefs

We have already mentioned the first criticism, and have allowed that it can't refute egoism all by itself. Still, if a theory deeply violates common sense, and if there is no compelling argument for that theory, then we are justified in rejecting it. Egoism does run strongly counter to common sense, since it imposes a moral duty to kill, rape, torture, or humiliate whenever doing so best serves self-interest. It allows us to ignore the vital interests of others, even if we can promote them at no cost to ourselves. And we have not seen a compelling argument for ethical egoism. Until we do, we are therefore right to trust our core moral beliefs, and so reject egoism.

Egoism Cannot Allow for the Existence of Moral Rights

It isn't clear that egoism can make sense of moral rights. These are moral claims that give a person control over certain aspects of her life, even if it is to another person's advantage to ignore such moral claims. If I have a right to be free of physical attack, for instance, then it is wrong of anyone else to beat me to a pulp, even if doing so somehow makes them better off. Egoists can offer no one a guarantee against this (or any other) sort of personal violation.

Suppose that it is in your best interest to kill me, or to deny me freedom of speech, or to take what I own. If egoism is true, then you are morally permitted—indeed, morally required—to do these things. And if you are morally allowed to do them, then it is hard to see how I could have a right that you not do such things. My right to life or to free speech is worthless if other people are allowed to kill me or shut me up whenever it serves their interests to do so.

Egoists can reply that they grant each person the right to pursue self-interest. This is true, in a way. But not in a way that offers us any protection. To see this, consider two things we might mean when we say that everyone has a right to pursue self-interest:

(A) All people are allowed to pursue self-interest.
(B) Each person is entitled to a certain sphere of personal freedom that imposes a duty of non-interference on everyone else.

Egoists accept (A). They can't accept (B). Yet (B) is the only version that offers us protection against the actions of others.

(A) is toothless. To see this, imagine a plot device that became familiar to me as a child. A surprising number of 1970s TV episodes imagined a warped villain who had some hapless victim at his mercy. The villain says to him, "You are perfectly free to run. I'm not stopping you. So run!" The victim is allowed to run. In this sense, he has a right to flee. But there is a catch. The villain is also allowed to hunt his victim and kill him if he can. The victim's right to run is basically worthless in such a situation. It offers him no protection at all.

Now, back in the real world, suppose that your self-interest conflicts with mine. If egoism is true, then I have a duty to harm you, since that will benefit me. And you have a duty to harm me for the same reason. Even though we are each allowed to pursue our self-interest, egoism can't forbid other people from harming us if it is in their interest to do so. It grants us a right of the sort described in (A). But that offers us no moral protection against interference from others, where such interference can be terrible indeed. It can even amount to killing, if killing is what would maximize someone else's interests.

If egoism is correct, then our basic moral duty is to make ourselves as well-off as possible. We may have to hurt others in order to fulfill that duty. And that means that morality will not protect them from such harm. Nor will it protect us, if the tables are turned. So the best that egoism can do here is to tell us that we are each free to pursue self-interest. It cannot offer us the sort of moral rights we really want—those that protect us from unwanted interference by others.

Egoism Arbitrarily Makes My Interests All-Important

Now we arrive at the deepest threat to ethical egoism. This theory tells us that we should give complete priority to the interests of a single person (oneself) over the interests of everyone else. If that were really so, then there would have to be some relevant difference that could justify this different treatment. But what could that be? My basic needs—for food, shelter, physical security, good health, and so on—are shared by nearly every human being. I am unique, of course, but then so is everyone else. I have my special talents, but again, so does everyone else.

Ethical egoists need to explain why we are allowed to entirely discount the basic needs of others, even though these needs may be identical to our own. I think that egoists can, in fact, make a partial reply here.

Suppose that my leg has been wounded in a hunting accident. I can still drive to the hospital and get it cared for. I know that doing so is going to cost me almost all of the money I have. Once I arrive at the hospital, I see another victim of a hunting accident, with an injury very like my own. He is obviously poor, needs the surgery as badly as I do, but lacks the money to pay for it. Most of us agree that it would be acceptable if I used my money to pay for my own surgery, rather than forgo it and pay for his. But why?

To make the case harder, assume that this other accident victim is as nice a guy as I am, is just as smart and community-minded as I am, and so on. Still, I am allowed to give myself preferential treatment here. Our cases appear alike, and yet common sense allows me to give myself priority over another person who is my equal in every relevant respect.

Perhaps common sense is just mistaken in allowing people to give some priority to their own needs over those of others. If it is, then ethical egoism is certainly false. But suppose that common sense has it right, so that in the hunting example, for instance, I am allowed to spend the money on myself rather than on a stranger. If so, then morality does grant individuals some extra consideration when determining their own fate. When things are equal, we are allowed to tip the scales in our own favor.

I do not know how to explain this. Like the claim that we have some reason to promote self-interest, this principle seems to be a basic axiom of any plausible ethical view. Yet even if we accept that people are morally allowed to give themselves some priority, that does not mean that they are allowed to give themselves *complete* priority over others. Ethical egoism claims that the interests of others, considered in themselves, *count for nothing*. We are to treat our own interests as the only thing of intrinsic moral importance.

Ethical egoism tells us that even when the stakes are very high for others, and very small for ourselves, we are entitled to ignore the needs, wants, and interests of those who are our equals in all relevant ways. Egoism completely denies the moral importance of other people or other things (such as the environment), except insofar as they can help us to benefit ourselves. That is a kind of deep bias that requires substantial defense. It isn't clear what that defense could be.

8.5 Conclusion

Ethical egoism tells us that morality is all about making myself (whoever I happen to be) better off. If egoism is true, then we have only one basic moral duty: to maximize self-interest, even if doing so means killing others, stealing from them, or framing them for crimes that we committed. If egoism is true, we have no direct duties to help others in need, even if offering such help costs us nothing. It is clear that for these reasons, egoism violates a number of our core moral beliefs. As such, egoists must offer really compelling arguments to get us to abandon those beliefs and switch to the new ones that egoists prefer. Yet even the best argument for ethical egoism is not good enough. Until we are presented with a new argument for ethical egoism, we are right to be highly skeptical of its claims.

If doubts about ethical egoism are on target, then morality does indeed place some intrinsic value on the interests of others. But how far should this be taken? Must we sacrifice *everything* for others—even for strangers? Or is there some middle ground, a principled way to balance our own needs with everyone else's?

The next theory we consider, utilitarianism, will begin the process of shifting the moral focus away from ourselves. As we'll see, utilitarians don't deny the value of self-interest. They just deny that your interests are any more valuable than anyone else's. This move to impartiality is very important in moral thinking. Let's see how far it can take us.

8.6 Discussion Questions

1. What is the difference between psychological egoism and ethical egoism? Does the truth of one of these theories imply the truth of the other?
2. Is it ever in one's self-interest to commit murder or theft? If so, does this affect the plausibility of ethical egoism?
3. Would everyone be better off if each of us just pursued our own self-interest? If so, is this a strong consideration in favor of ethical egoism?
4. Are consent and reparation the only sources of our moral duties? If there are other sources, what are they? If there aren't any other sources, does that show that ethical egoism is true?
5. Is it ever rational to act contrary to one's self-interest? If so, under what circumstances? If not, does this show that ethical egoism is true?
6. How do you think that an ethical egoist might try to argue for the existence of moral rights? Can such an argument succeed?
7. Most people agree that discrimination on the basis of morally irrelevant traits (such as race or gender) is immoral. Does ethical egoism endorse such discrimination by promoting one's own interests over the interests of everyone else? Why or why not?

8.7 Cases for Critical Reflection

Kidneys

In the United States, around 100,000 people are waiting for a kidney transplant. Many who are waiting must undergo dialysis treatment to survive. In 2014, 4,761 patients died waiting, and 3,668 became too sick to receive a transplant.[1] Often, transplant kidneys come from deceased organ donors or living donors who are a relative or friend of a patient. In some cases, a patient receives a kidney from someone who voluntarily donates without any personal knowledge of the patient. Almost all of us can be healthy with just one kidney, and kidney donation does not change the donor's life expectancy or risk of developing kidney disease. As with any surgery, there are risks including bleeding and infection. Death resulting from giving a kidney is extremely rare.[2]

---

1. https://www.kidney.org/news/newsroom/factsheets/Organ-Donation-and-Transplantation-Stats.

2. https://weillcornell.org/services/kidney-and-pancreas-transplantation/living-donor-kidney-center/about-the-program/risks-and-benefits-of-living-donation.

In 2006, Paul Wagner donated a kidney to a total stranger. He had learned about a website called MatchingDonors.com, which helps match people in need of a kidney transplant with altruistic donors. The website includes photos and messages from patients seeking donors. It was there that Wagner found Gail Tomas Willis, a music teacher and mother of two, whose message read, "Desperately need your help to live." Wagner felt immediately compelled to help her: "This was a real human being who had a family and whose family wanted to keep their mother. And I just couldn't turn my back on that."[3] Donating a kidney to a stranger seems immensely self-sacrificing, but many donors don't think so. One donor, Kimberly Brown-Whale, thinks everyone should consider it:

> We can do more than we think we can. If you're sitting around with a good kidney you're not using, why can't someone else have it? For a couple of days of discomfort, someone else is going to be freed from dialysis and be able to live a full life. Gosh, I've had flus that made me feel worse.[4]

Questions

1. How could a psychological egoist explain the actions of these kidney donors, who seem to be motivated by something other than self-interest?
2. Is anyone is ever morally obligated to donate a kidney to someone? Why or why not?
3. According to ethical egoism, is anyone ever morally obligated to donate a kidney to a stranger, or even a close family member? Why or why not?

Cannibalism

In 1972, the Uruguayan Air Force Flight 571 crashed in the remote Andes Mountains. There were forty-five people on board, including nineteen members of a rugby team and some of their family, friends, and supporters. After the initial crash, twenty-eight survived, but soon faced the possibility of death by starvation. The survivors reluctantly turned to cannibalism, sustaining themselves on the flesh of the dead until they were

---

3. https://www.cbsnews.com/news/the-ultimate-gift-found-online/.
4. https://www.newyorker.com/magazine/2009/07/27/the-kindest-cut.

finally rescued. One survivor, Roberto Cannessa, described the agony of this decision:

> The bodies of our friends and team-mates, preserved outside in the snow and ice, contained vital, life-giving protein that could help us survive. But could we do it? For a long time we agonised. I went out in the snow and prayed to God for guidance. Without His consent, I felt I would be violating the memory of my friends; that I would be stealing their souls. We wondered whether we were going mad even to contemplate such a thing. Had we turned into brute savages? Or was this the only sane thing to do? Truly, we were pushing the limits of our fear.[1]

Cannibalism is considered by many to be morally wrong, and we balk at the thought of dining on the flesh of a deceased loved one. While cannibalism may strike us as taboo, the practice of consuming human flesh is historically and globally widespread. Cannibalistic practices have been documented in many places in the world, including North and South America, Africa, and the Pacific Islands. In some cultures, cannibalism is considered sacred, and in ancient Egypt, pharaohs believed that eating human flesh guaranteed an eternal afterlife.[2]

Questions

1. Do you think cannibalism is ordinarily morally wrong? Why or why not? Is it wrong in extreme circumstances, like those experienced by the survivors of Flight 571?
2. The survivors of Flight 571 were reluctant to cannibalize their dead loved ones, even though it was plausibly in each of their self-interest to do so. What could a defender of psychological egoism say about this case? How plausible is their view?
3. What would a defender of ethical egoism say about this case? Is their reply plausible? Why or why not?

---

1. https://www.independent.co.uk/news/world/americas/cannibalism-andes-plane-crash-1972-survivors-terrible-decision-stay-alive-a6895781.html.
2. https://aeon.co/ideas/eating-people-is-wrong-but-its-also-widespread-and-sacred.

CHAPTER 9

.... ❧ ....

Consequentialism

Its Nature and Attractions

....

Do all the good you can, by all the means you can, in all the ways you can, in all the places you can, at all the times you can, to all the people you can, as long as ever you can.

....

This philosophy of life has long been attributed to John Wesley (1703–1791), English religious thinker and founder of the Methodist Church. Our business here on earth is to do good—as much and as often as we can. Our efforts must extend beyond ourselves, to all whom we might help. Benevolence should be our guiding aim, and a life of altruism and good works should be the record we leave behind.

This advice can be summarized quite simply, in the motto that defines the **consequentialist** outlook: do as much good as you can. It is a very attractive picture of the moral life—so appealing, in fact, that some very fine philosophers have thought it impossible to reject this view. G. E. Moore (1873–1958), an English thinker famous in his day for his rigorous thought, declared it plain that what is right is whatever produces the most good. If you have a choice between two options, and the first is less good than the second, choosing the first can't possibly be right. *Acts are morally right just because they maximize the amount of goodness in the world.* Moore thought that those who failed to accept this simply didn't know what they were talking about.[1]

---

1. G. E. Moore, *Principia Ethica* (Cambridge: Cambridge University Press, 1903).

Certainly, any plausible moral theory will insist on the central importance of doing good. We commonly justify our actions by pointing to the good they did, and criticize actions by showing that they caused unnecessary harm. That makes perfect sense if consequentialism is correct.

Before we get to the details of the consequentialist picture, let's briefly consider a contemporary puzzle—the morality of capital punishment—that can illuminate the basic nature of this ethical outlook. There are many views about the morality of the death penalty, but most of them can be sorted into two large groups. In the first, consequentialist camp, people insist that such punishment is justified only if it improves our lives. It will have to decrease crime, increase security, and expand respect for human life. If capital punishment is to be justified, we must show that we will be better off with it than without it. We must look to the future, and ask three things: What are the benefits of executing criminals? What are the drawbacks? Which policy would yield the greatest cost-benefit ratio? Survey all of the available options. Whichever policy is **optimific** (i.e., such as to yield the greatest balance of benefits over drawbacks) is the one that morality requires.

A second group asks not about what the future will hold, but rather about what the past requires of us. Specifically, the focus is on whether certain people deserve to be killed for the crimes they have committed. On this line of thinking, even if the death penalty is extremely costly, fails to prevent crime, and perhaps even increases the crime rate by making the population more hard-hearted, we should still impose it if we can show that criminals deserve to be executed. Before we consider making people happy, or reducing their misery, we must first do justice. If giving out just deserts happens to reduce crime, so much the better. But if it doesn't, we should still execute the murderers among us if they deserve it.

My aim here isn't to try to resolve this thorny issue, but rather to reveal what is distinctive about the consequentialist approach to ethics. Consequentialists are those who encourage us not to cry over spilt milk. They direct our attention to the future, not the past. They ask us to look at the *consequences* of our actions or policies—hence the name of their theory. For them, the ends justify the means, so long as the ends are good enough. When we want to know whether our plans are in line with morality, we will ask about results. Did my action achieve better results than any other I could have done? If so, then my action was morally required. If not, then it wasn't.

9. 1 The Nature of Consequentialism

Its Structure

Consequentialism says that *an action is morally required just because it produces the best overall results* (i.e., is optimific). But how can we determine whether an act is optimific? It won't always be an easy thing to do in practice. But in theory, it's pretty straightforward. There are five steps to this process:

1. First, identify what is intrinsically good—valuable in and of itself, and worth having for its own sake.[2] Familiar candidates include happiness, autonomy, knowledge, and virtue.
2. Next, identify what is intrinsically bad (i.e., bad all by itself). Examples might include physical pain, mental anguish, sadistic impulses, and the betrayal of innocents.
3. Then determine all of your options. Which actions are open to you at the moment?
4. For each option, determine the value of its results. How much of what is intrinsically good will each action bring about? How much of what is intrinsically bad?
5. Finally, pick the action that yields the greatest net balance of good over bad. That is the optimific choice. That is your moral duty. Doing anything else is immoral.

We can develop dozens of different versions of consequentialism, depending on which things we regard as intrinsically valuable. Indeed, though I didn't say so at the time, ethical egoism, the view we considered in the last chapter, is a form of consequentialism. It identifies just one thing—one's own self-interest—as intrinsically good, and tells us that morally right actions are those that maximize this value. The many consequentialist alternatives include, for instance, views that state that acts are right just in case they yield the greatest improvement in environmental health, or best advance the cause of world peace, or do more than any other action to increase the amount of knowledge in the world. Each of these is a version of consequentialism.

Thus consequentialism isn't just a single theory, but is rather a family of theories, united by their agreement that results are what matter in ethics.

---

2. For more on intrinsic value, see the discussion "Happiness and Intrinsic Value" in chapter 1.

We can't discuss every member of the family here, so I will restrict my attention, for the most part, to its most prominent version—**act utilitarianism**.

According to act utilitarianism, well-being is the only thing that is intrinsically valuable. And faring poorly is the only thing that is intrinsically bad. Thus this view states that *an action is morally required just because it does more to improve overall well-being than any other action you could have done in the circumstances.* Philosophers call this ultimate moral standard the **principle of utility**.

Some utilitarians have been hedonists; others, desire satisfaction theorists; still others have defended the idea that there are a variety of things that directly contribute to our welfare. At present, we don't need to take a stand on this matter.[3] The important point is that, according to act utilitarianism, acts are right just because they maximize the overall amount of well-being in the world.

When there are attractions and difficulties that are specific to act utilitarianism as opposed to other versions of consequentialism, I note them. But for the most part, we can get a good sense of the consequentialist ethic just by focusing on act utilitarianism.

Maximizing Goodness

If act utilitarianism (henceforth, just *utilitarianism*) is correct, then we are duty-bound to maximize well-being. But what, exactly, does this mean? John Stuart Mill (1806–1873), one of the greatest utilitarians, famously summarized the utilitarian outlook by saying that it required us to create *the greatest good for the greatest number.* But this popular slogan overlooks an important nuance, one that Mill was well aware of.

Mill was a hedonist, who believed that only happiness was intrinsically valuable and only unhappiness was intrinsically bad. Let's just assume the truth of hedonism for the moment, to better appreciate what maximizing goodness requires. If we combine utilitarianism and hedonism, we get this ultimate moral principle: produce the greatest *overall balance* of happiness over misery. There are two common misunderstandings of this principle. Let's clear them out of the way first, so that we can see what Mill really had in mind.

First misunderstanding: *in choosing among acts that benefit people, we must benefit the greatest number of people.* Mill rejects this.

---

3. For more detailed discussion of theories of well-being, see chapters 1–4.

Suppose we have to choose between an act that benefits more people, and one that benefits fewer. Mill's principle does *not* say that we automatically have to pick the first option. That's because the benefit to the majority may be very small, whereas the benefit to the minority may be very large.

Imagine that the legislature has a surplus this year. They could spend that money giving 90 percent of the citizens a $50 gas coupon. Or they could spend that money trying to prevent homelessness and starvation among the poorest 10 percent. In a variety of plausible scenarios, giving the money to the poor will yield more good, even though that benefits fewer people. If that is so, then the money must be directed to combat poverty.

Second misunderstanding: *we must always choose that action that creates the greatest amount of happiness.* Mill also rejects this.

Suppose we have to choose between two plans. The first creates more happiness than the second. Mill's principle does *not* say that we automatically have to favor the first plan.

That's because the first plan may also create a huge amount of misery, while the second plan creates very little. Imagine a Roman emperor who wanted to please his public. His choice: offer gladiator contests, or a series of grand athletic competitions. Suppose that watching the gladiators would create more happiness. But imagine, reasonably, that this would also create much more misery than the athletic games would do. It might be that the athletic games would produce the greatest *net balance* of happiness over misery, even though more *total* happiness would have been created by offering a chance to see men killing one another.

The correct interpretation: utilitarians tell us to do what brings about the best overall situation, by choosing the act that creates the greatest net balance of happiness over unhappiness. So out with the gladiators and in with the athletes.

Moral Knowledge

Utilitarians make the rightness of an action depend on all of its results, no matter how long after the action they occur. There is no statute of limitations on counting consequences. Sometimes the results of one's actions do not last more than a moment. In other cases, they may continue for decades or centuries. (Just think of Lincoln's assassination or Jesus's crucifixion.)

This raises an immediate worry. If the rightness of an action depends on all of its results, and these haven't yet occurred, then how can we know whether an action is the right one to do? Utilitarians are split on how best to answer this question. The first group thinks that the morality of actions depends on their *actual* results; the second group thinks that it depends instead on their *expected* results. This makes a big difference in the utilitarian account of how we gain moral knowledge.

The standard view is the first one. Right actions are those that actually bring about the best possible results. But since these are still in the future when the action is performed, we can never be completely sure that what we are about to do is the right thing.

Yet every moral theory has to allow for some degree of moral ignorance—cases where we don't know what is right or wrong. We are not morally infallible. Many utilitarians explain this by saying that since we don't have a crystal ball, and can't perfectly predict the future, we can never be certain in advance that our actions are morally right.

Still, there is a huge amount of past experience that we can call upon. For instance, we can be reasonably sure that if we were to pick up a gun and shoot a perfect stranger at point-blank range, then the results would not be optimific. True, we can't be absolutely certain of this—that stranger could be the next Stalin or bin Laden, for instance. But we should not expect certainty when it comes to moral questions.

Other utilitarians are uncomfortable with this. They want to make moral knowledge easier to get. As they see it, we should be able to know the morality of our acts when we perform them, rather than having to wait until all of the results are in. After all, if we had to wait for those results, we might *never* know the morality of some of our actions, since they could have unexpected outcomes that occur even after our deaths.

For utilitarians in this second camp, the solution to this worry is to make the rightness of actions depend not on their actual results, but on their expected results. On this view, acts are morally required just because they are *reasonably expected* to be optimific. Since we are often in a position to make reasonable predictions about the results of our actions, we can often know, prior to performing them, whether they are morally right or wrong.

Actual Versus Expected Results

Suppose that, with the best possible motives, I take an aged stranger's arm and help him across the street. As we cross, a reckless driver crashes into my companion, killing him. Had I not tried to be kind, he would still be at the curb, a bit delayed, but unharmed. If the morality of an act depends on its actual results, then, from a utilitarian perspective, I did something immoral. A different option (refusing to help the man across the street) would have had better results.

If that sounds harsh, there is an easy remedy. If we evaluate actions based on their *expected* results, then, morally speaking, I am in the clear. That's because anyone in my shoes could reasonably expect that helping the man across the street would have excellent results.

Interestingly, most utilitarians reject the view that makes rightness a matter of expected, rather than actual, results. The expected-results version makes it easier to get moral knowledge, and does not condemn actions that are reasonably expected to be optimific. But it has two problems that have lost it most of its supporters.

First, it will sometimes *require* actions that turn out to have disastrous results, when other options would have produced much better outcomes. Some acts that we expect to turn out well end up doing great harm, and when that is so, this proposal would still regard the disastrous actions as morally right.

Suppose, for instance, that I am a member of a parole board and have excellent evidence that a criminal has had a change of heart. I authorize his release and later read that he went on a killing spree just days afterward. Most utilitarians find it extremely difficult to morally prefer an act that resulted in many innocent deaths over one that would have resulted in none. They would say that my action was the wrong one, though (as we'll shortly see) I am not to be blamed for it, since I had intended to bring about good results.

Second, some actions are expected to turn out badly, but end up with surprisingly good results. I remember a time as a kid when I got up my courage and confronted a bully, even though I thought that this would only make him nastier to me and his other victims. Instead, he unexpectedly backed down and stopped his harassment.

If utilitarians make rightness a matter of expected results, then they must judge my action to be immoral. But condemning an act with excellent results is too much for most utilitarians to stomach.

Assessing Actions and Intentions

If we stick to the classic version of utilitarianism, one that judges actions on the basis of their actual results, what should we say about cases where good intentions yield awful results, or bad intentions yield pleasant surprises? Here utilitarians will insist on separating the issues. They will have one standard for evaluating actions, and another for judging intentions.

Actions are right provided they are optimific. But intentions are morally good provided that they are reasonably expected to yield good results. So, in the case of my helping the pedestrian, these utilitarians would judge my action wrong, while praising my intentions. On this view, we cannot immediately say that I am to blame just because I did something immoral. Nor can we say that I am to be praised just because I did something right. Imagine a case in which I am jealous of someone, my jealousy and malice lead me to try to hurt him, but I bungle my attempt and he emerges unharmed. I am blameworthy, even if my action turns out, very surprisingly, to have been optimific. (Suppose, for instance, that my failed attempt leads me to scrutinize my emotional shortcomings, seek to better myself, and to reconcile with my former enemy.)

According to utilitarianism, *there is no essential connection between the morality of an action and the morality of the intentions behind it.* If you are trying to do harm, when you had the chance to do good, then you are to blame—even if your action somehow manages to maximize well-being. If you intend a kindness, then you are to be praised, even if, through no fault of your own, your action backfires and only misery results.

Here is the picture thus far. Consequentialists say that our fundamental moral duty is to make the world the best place it can be. Utilitarians in particular understand this to mean that we must contribute as much to the improvement of well-being as we can. Though theorists differ, most claim that whether an action is optimific depends only on its actual (and not expected) results. All results count, not just those that occur in the short term. When we fail to maximize good results, we act wrongly, even if we had the best intentions. Though good intentions may earn us praise, they are irrelevant to an action's morality. When we pass up a chance to do an action that would have had better results, we are doing something wrong. Always.

9.2 The Attractions of Utilitarianism

Impartiality

Utilitarianism is a doctrine of impartiality, and this is one of its great strengths. It tells us that the welfare of each person is equally morally valuable. No matter your social position, economic status, religion, ethnic background, or gender, your well-being is just as important as anyone else's. In the gladiator example, for instance, we didn't have to ask whether the happiness went to wealthy nobles or impoverished slaves. It didn't matter. Everyone's well-being counts, and everyone's well-being counts equally.

We nowadays take such equality for granted. But the idea, when advanced by the earliest utilitarians, was quite a radical one. Indeed, utilitarians have a long history of challenging conventional moral wisdom. Jeremy Bentham, whose *Introduction to the Principles of Morals and Legislation* (1781) gave the first really sophisticated defense of utilitarianism, was a dedicated abolitionist. Bentham's godson, John Stuart Mill, wrote one of the earliest and greatest works on behalf of female equality, *On the Subjection of Women* (1869). Peter Singer, perhaps the most famous living philosopher, continues the utilitarian tradition of seeking to expand our moral concerns with his influential work on behalf of ethical vegetarianism and against animal experimentation.

According to utilitarians, we develop a truly moral outlook only when we broaden our concerns so that we are focused not just on ourselves, or on our friends, family, or fellow citizens. The moral point of view is nothing less than an impartial concern for everyone whose well-being may be affected by our actions.

The Ability to Justify Conventional Moral Wisdom

As the examples of abolitionism, gender equality, and animal welfare show, utilitarians are not afraid of controversy. They know that their recommendations will sometimes conflict with popular opinion. But they don't regard that as a strike against their theory. Rather, they see it as a strike against popular opinion.

That said, utilitarians think that most of our deeply held moral beliefs are correct. There is a special reason for this, one that utilitarians regard as a great advantage of their view. As they see it, utilitarianism does a better job than any competing moral theory in justifying most of our basic moral beliefs.

Consider the things we regard, deep down, as seriously immoral: slavery, rape, humiliating defenseless people, killing innocent victims. Each of these clearly tends to do more harm than good. Utilitarianism condemns such acts. So do we.

Now consider the things we strongly believe to be morally right: helping the poor, keeping promises, telling the truth, bravely facing danger. Such actions are highly beneficial. Utilitarianism commends them. So do we.

Utilitarianism can also explain our shared views about virtues and vices. According to utilitarianism, a character trait is a virtue just because it tends to cause us to act in highly beneficial ways. Compassion, kindness, and benevolence appear on almost anyone's list of central moral virtues. Utilitarianism has a natural account of this. Such character traits tend to promote our flourishing and to reduce misery.

Greed, malice, ingratitude—these are bound to make most people's top ten list of moral vices. Utilitarianism easily explains this. When people are motivated by such things, they tend to harm others. Utilitarians thus condemn such traits as vices. So do we.

Our core moral beliefs could be mistaken. But until we see an excellent argument for such skepticism, we are right to decide among competing moral theories by selecting one that justifies our deepest beliefs, and clashes with only a few of them. No moral theory manages to do this perfectly—as we'll see, each of the major views captures some fundamental moral beliefs, at the expense of some others. Still, utilitarianism earns pretty high marks in this department.

Conflict Resolution

One of the most important things that an ethical theory can do is to provide advice about how to resolve moral conflicts. Utilitarianism delivers. Because it has just a single ultimate rule—maximize well-being—it can offer concrete guidance where it is most needed.

Consider this familiar moral puzzle. I overhear some nasty gossip about my friend. She later asks me whether people have been spreading rumors about her. I know that she is extremely sensitive, and that if I answer honestly, it will send her into a downward spiral for several days. I also know that the source of this gossip is someone who actually likes my friend, and was speaking impulsively and out of character. He's probably feeling bad about it already, and probably won't repeat this unkindness.

Of course we need to know a lot more about the situation before we can be confident about a recommendation, but if we just stick with the details given here, the utilitarian will advise me not to reveal what I have heard. Honesty may be the best *policy*, but that doesn't mean that full disclosure is always called for. When we consider our options, utilitarians tell us to pick the one that increases overall well-being. Telling the truth won't always do that.

Utilitarianism thus gives us a clear method for resolving moral conflict. We can apply the principle of utility to determine which choice to make in difficult cases.

John Stuart Mill saw this clearly. In a fascinating discussion at the end of his *Utilitarianism* (1861), Mill touts the superiority of the utilitarian view of justice over its competitors. He does this, in part, through a discussion of taxation. We can all agree that our system of taxation must be just, but that doesn't get us very far. We can make a case that charging everyone an identical amount of money is just, since we are thereby treating everyone alike. Or we can insist that everyone pay the same percentage of his income—again, a form of treating everyone alike. Or we can require a graduated tax, taking a higher percentage from those who can most easily afford it. Which should we do?

Fans of each of these ideas (and others) will offer many arguments on behalf of their position. Sorting it all out could be excruciating, and that is because we have no clear way of applying the test that tells us to adopt just policies. Utilitarianism cuts through the conflicting claims and offers direct advice: maximize well-being. Of course it's not always easy to know which tax policy will do this, but at least we have a clear direction for pursuing our question.

Whenever we are faced with conflicting moral advice, utilitarianism can greatly simplify matters. It tells us to focus on just one question: which option will maximize well-being? Coming up with an answer will sometimes be hard. But at least we know where to look. That is half the battle won.

Moral Flexibility

During the winter of 1846–1847, members of the Donner party, traveling by horse and coach in search of a pass through California's Sierra Nevada range, found themselves buried in heavy mountain snows. It wasn't long before their supplies of food and fuel ran out. Almost half of the eighty-seven members of their party died that winter. Some of those who survived faced a terrible choice. They could starve to death, or remain alive by eating the remains of their fellow travelers.[4]

In the choice faced by members of the Donner party, one might regard the prohibition on eating human flesh as **absolute**—not to be violated under any conditions. Even though honoring the rule means losing one's life, some rules are never to be broken.

Utilitarians would disagree. And their disagreement is based not on specific views about cannibalism, but on very general grounds. For utilitarians, no moral rule (other than the principle of utility) is absolute.

---

4. Compare the plight of the Uruguayan rugby team described in the last chapter's Cases for Critical Reflection.

It is morally okay to violate any rule—even one that prohibits cannibalism, or torture, or the killing of innocents—if doing so will raise overall well-being.

Utilitarians think that it is an excellent thing that so many of us are unwilling even to contemplate such actions. Our reluctance is almost always beneficial. But in unusual situations, we are right to violate taboos or break familiar, deeply held moral rules if we maximize well-being in doing so.

Utilitarianism is thus a doctrine of moral flexibility. Most of us think that moral rules must allow some exceptions. But where to draw the line? How do we know whether to follow a moral rule or to break it? Utilitarianism gives us an answer. Morality is not a free-for-all. It is not a case of "anything goes." We ordinarily do best when we obey the familiar moral rules (don't steal, lie, kill, etc.). But there are times when we must stray from the conventional path in order to improve overall welfare. When we do this, we do right—even if it means breaking the traditional moral rules.

9.3 The Scope of the Moral Community

In the winter of 2007, two high school boys from Reading, Ohio, decided to have some fun. They sprayed Lysol into a cat's face, crushed its spine, popped its eyes out, impaled it with a stake, and dismembered it. Then they bragged to their classmates about what they had done.

What these boys did was very wrong, and utilitarians have a ready explanation of this. Most competing moral theories do not.

Utilitarians argue that animals are members of the **moral community**. To be a member of the moral community is to be important in your own right. It is to be owed a certain amount of respect. Membership in the moral community imposes a duty on everyone else to take one's needs seriously, for one's own sake.

Every moral theory needs to have a way to determine who gains entry to the moral community. The utilitarian test is recorded in a famous slogan by Jeremy Bentham: "The question is not, Can they *reason*? nor, Can they *talk*? but Can they *suffer*?"[5]

Tables and chairs are not members of the moral community. Neither are cars. We owe them nothing. They are important, when they are, only

---

5. Jeremy Bentham, *Introduction to the Principles of Morals and Legislation* (1781), ch. 17.

because we care about them. If we had no interest in them at all, then there would be nothing wrong with having them destroyed. Utilitarianism easily explains their second-class status: such things can't suffer, and so they have no independent moral importance.

But animals are a different matter. They *are* members of the moral community. They are important in their own right. Their importance does not depend on whether we happen to care about them. And the utilitarian explanation of this is very plausible: animals count because they can suffer. Those teenagers from Ohio caused excruciating, pointless suffering. That's why their actions were so terrible.

Just to be clear, utilitarians allow that it is sometimes okay to harm members of the moral community. There are many cases in which maximizing overall well-being comes at a price. For instance, it may be acceptable to conduct certain intensely painful animal experiments, provided that they bring about very beneficial results. The point here is that, from the utilitarian perspective, we are not allowed to ignore the suffering of others. It doesn't matter whether the victims are human beings or not.

Indeed, utilitarians have argued that species membership is, in itself, completely morally irrelevant. What counts is whether you can suffer, and nonhumans can certainly do that. If an animal suffers to the same extent as a human, that is an equal misfortune. Harming a human is not, *in and of itself*, any worse than causing the same harm to a (nonhuman) animal.

A number of utilitarians have advanced a powerful argument that relies on this controversial position. It is called *The Argument from Marginal Cases*:

1. If it is immoral to kill and eat "marginal" human beings, and to painfully experiment on them, then it is immoral to treat nonhuman animals this way.
2. It is almost always immoral to kill and eat "marginal" human beings, and to painfully experiment on them.
3. Therefore, it is almost always immoral to kill and eat animals, and to painfully experiment on them.

I dislike the name of this argument, because I think it distasteful to refer to any human being as "marginal." But its name is so familiar in philosophical circles that we will stick with it here.

"Marginal" human beings are those whose mental lives are no more developed than those of the nonhuman animals we routinely eat and experiment on. There are many causes of such developmental limitations: severe brain trauma, extreme birth defects, and so on. The basic idea behind the Argument from Marginal Cases is that such human beings are no more morally important than the animals we harm in our labs or factory farms. Since they are of equal importance, we must treat them equally. If we are not prepared to eat or experiment upon such human beings, then we shouldn't be willing to treat animals that way, either.

Many people find the Argument from Marginal Cases repugnant. They recoil at giving animal interests the same weight as those of human beings. Utilitarians push back: everyone counts, and everyone counts equally. *Everyone* means every member of the moral community. Animals are members. So their interests count for just as much as those of human beings.

Almost no one rejects premise 2 of the Argument from Marginal Cases. You've got to be awfully hard-hearted to be willing to subject marginal human beings to the sort of treatment we apply to animals in our labs and farms. True, there might be rare exceptions where such treatment is acceptable—that's the point of saying that it is *almost* always wrong to do such things to human beings. But these would have to be extremely unusual cases.

So the real action occurs in premise 1. Its defenders support it in this way. They say that marginal human beings, and farm and lab animals, are moral equals. They are moral equals because (as utilitarians see it) they can equally suffer. And, as moral equals, anything that is wrong to do to one of them should be wrong to do to the others.

The obvious place to attack this reasoning is with the claim that animals and marginal humans are moral equals. If you don't like that claim, then it is up to you to find a better test for inclusion in the moral community. Familiar examples are problematic.

Perhaps the ability to reason is the relevant test. As we know, Bentham rejected this test, but even if he was wrong to do so, this isn't going to help. That's because the reasoning powers of marginal humans are no better than those of animals. In fact, some animals—such as pigs and primates— are very smart, and no doubt smarter than some human beings.

There are many other tests of independent moral importance that philosophers have advanced. Here are some of the most popular ones: the ability (1) to communicate, (2) to have emotions, (3) to elicit sympathy from others, (4) to be self-aware, (5) to be self-governing, (6) to assert claims on one's behalf, or (7) to think about and plan for one's future.

Utilitarians insist that the capacity to suffer is a better test of membership in the moral community than any of these seven alternatives. But even if you have doubts about that—and many do—utilitarians will argue that animals and marginal humans fare equally well on each of these tests. Many animals possess these traits or abilities to the same degree as marginal human beings.

In my experience, most people at this point try to argue in one of two ways. Some say that every human is more important than any animal, because God created each of us as an exalted being whose life has more value than that of any animal. Well, that's a possibility, but defending it is a task for theologians, as the defense will ultimately rest on claims about God's existence and His purposes and intentions. So we are going to leave this aside.

Another thing that people often say in this context is that marginal human beings, *just because they are human*, are more important than animals. On this view, the test of whether you are a member of the moral community is whether you are human. No matter how "marginal," a human is still a human, and so more important than any animal.

But this is a bad argument. It clearly begs the question against the utilitarian. You're not going to accept this line of reasoning unless you already accept the view that all marginal humans are more important than all nonhuman animals.

Further, we should ask why species membership is the all-important test of moral status. Your genetic code, or the species of your parents, doesn't seem to be what establishes your moral importance. To see this, imagine a time, perhaps not so far in the future, in which we encounter (or create) beings who are like us in every way—except that they are made of silicon. They think like us. They feel emotions as we do. They are self-aware. They feel pain. They look exactly like us. The *only* difference between them and us is which species we belong to.

I don't know how to argue for this, and perhaps you disagree, but it seems to me that this difference doesn't justify treating these beings as second-class citizens. In fact, it seems that they are just as morally important as we are—after all, without cutting them open, we couldn't tell them apart from a human being, because they are identical to us in every way except the internal circuitry.

If you share my view about this case, then you should reject the idea that species membership is, in itself, a morally important trait. And if that is so, then we can't resist the Argument from Marginal Cases by claiming that marginal human beings, just by virtue of their humanity, are more important than animals.

Thus if you do think that every marginal human being is more important than every nonhuman animal, then the ball is in your court. You have to identify a litmus test of moral importance that is better than the utilitarian one, and one that gives humans an edge, no matter how mentally developed they happen to be. It won't be easy to do this. Many think it can't be done. Exercise: see for yourself.

Utilitarianism makes it pretty easy to gain entry into the moral community. Infants, toddlers, the severely mentally disabled, the extremely mentally ill, and almost all nonhuman animals are members. It certainly seems that these people and animals are important in their own right. They are not mere playthings to be used for our own purposes. We owe them respect. Utilitarianism easily explains why this is so.

9.4 Slippery Slope Arguments

Utilitarian reasoning is widespread in moral and political arguments. One very popular form that such reasoning can take is that of a **slippery slope argument**. These arguments are designed to criticize certain social innovations on the grounds that allowing them will lead to terrible results in the long run. Though such arguments have been given by people from all parts of the political spectrum, a slippery slope argument is always morally conservative, in that it offers moral reasons for preserving the status quo. The metaphor works like this: imagine that we are positioned at the top of a very steep hill. At the bottom of the hill lies disaster. Once we take even a tiny step from our safe perch, we are destined to tumble all the way down—the slope is slippery precisely because we can't stop ourselves from the inevitable crash.

In current debates about genetically modifying food, decriminalizing drug use, or allowing state scrutiny of personal emails and letters, some of the most powerful critical voices come from those who offer slippery slope arguments. Such critics sometimes concede that these practices are highly beneficial in the short run. But these opponents caution that the long-term harms that are likely to arise from these practices will far outweigh the benefits. There are two essential elements to any such argument. The first is a prediction that serious, avoidable harm will result if some new policy or practice is allowed. The argument combines this prediction with the utilitarian requirement to choose options that will minimize harm or maximize happiness. If, for instance, allowing the production and sale of genetically modified food will cause way more suffering and far less benefit than prohibiting it, then we should ban its manufacture and use. According to this argument, doing anything else would be both short-sighted and immoral.

Let's unpack the metaphor of a slippery slope by considering a classic example of such an argument, one that opposes voluntary active eutha-nasia—deliberately killing a terminally ill patient who has competently requested assistance to end her life. Most opponents of this type of eutha-nasia concede that it can sometimes be more merciful than letting nature take its course, since hastening a patient's death can minimize his suffer-ing while also respecting his desire to end his life on his own terms. But that's not the end of the story.

Opponents of voluntary active euthanasia often argue as follows: if we allow this practice, then we will be authorizing doctors and nurses to sometimes kill their patients. And once medical professionals are making decisions about whose life is worth living and whose life is not, then, over time—not next week, next year, or even five years from now, but perhaps in a generation or two—our commitment to protecting innocent life will inevitably weaken. Down the road, we will become so morally corrupted that we won't even recognize it as corruption. Medical professionals will be killing elderly patients who want to live, but whose care is extremely expensive. They will be killing infants born with various illnesses and deformities. Perhaps, in a move reminiscent of the Nazi "euthanasia" pro-grams (which were simply disguised campaigns to murder patients in mental hospitals), we will allow the killing of the mentally ill and the men-tally disabled, justifying such practices with the claim that we are really doing these people a favor.

Such an outcome rightly strikes us as horrific. And we might think that there is no way that allowing a merciful end to patients' lives will land us in such a morally compromised position. But proponents of this slip-pery slope argument claim that once we take the fateful step of letting doctors kill their patients, then centuries of moral inhibitions will begin to be erased. To use a different metaphor, we will have opened Pando-ra's box, and once it is open, there is no way of preventing the dreadful consequences.

Here is another example, with lower stakes. From the early 1930s to the mid-1960s, the Hollywood production code prohibited the use of profanity, the realistic depiction of serious violence, and any hint of even partial nudity or sexually suggestive scenes. When the code was challenged by directors and studio bosses, its defenders employed straightforward slippery slope reasoning. They argued that any move away from the status quo would eventually bring us to a point where directors felt free to have their actors use the "F" word, to graphically depict scenes of brutal torture and killing, and to show full nudity and simulated sex in their movies—a scenario that, sixty years ago, seemed so morally outrageous and far-fetched as to be impossible. Clearly, it wasn't.

We can undermine a slippery slope argument by showing that the dire forecast at its core is not as plausible as it may seem. The editorial pages of many Southern newspapers in the 1950s and 1960s were filled with slippery slope arguments that foretold the doom that would come if long-standing segregationist laws were lifted. Similar arguments were frequently heard decades earlier in debates about allowing women to vote—changing the centuries-old prohibition was bound to lead to chaos within families and across society. These predictions were mistaken, and the arguments that incorporated them failed as a result.

It is sometimes easy to determine when a prediction of disaster is unreasonable. The slippery slope defenses of Jim Crow laws, for example, were based on unwarranted fears, long-standing prejudice, and deep-seated ignorance. But sometimes it's quite difficult to know whether a prediction at the heart of a slippery slope argument is plausible. This is often the case with truly radical social reforms, ones that have rarely (if ever) been tested. Only a very small number of places have allowed voluntary active euthanasia, for instance, and even where it is permitted, it has been legal only for a relatively short time. Without a substantial track record to rely on, it might be unclear whether allowing it will have the disastrous results that opponents predict. In that case, we need further arguments to tell us how to respond to such uncertainty.

Opponents of voluntary active euthanasia will argue that we should allow it only if we have clear evidence that it won't lead to disaster. Since we lack such evidence, we should continue to forbid it. Supporters will argue that such a rule would prevent all sorts of morally important social innovations; after all, we can't prove that they will be beneficial if we are never permitted to test them in the first place. Those who favor allowing active euthanasia will further argue that the status quo results in needless suffering, that it undermines a patient's right to self-determination, and that a doctor's primary moral duty is to benefit her patients—and that, in unusual cases, assisting in a patient's death is the best way to benefit him.

The arguments here are complicated, and there is no shortcut to developing an informed opinion about this specific issue. The point here, however, isn't to try to settle the matter one way or the other. Indeed, this argument, like all slippery slope arguments, can be evaluated only after taking two steps. We must first evaluate the prediction that lies at the heart of the argument. Will legalizing active euthanasia really have the terrible results that its opponents expect? Will continuing to forbid it have yet worse results? Answers to such questions can be harder or easier to come by, depending on the specific issue that is the focus of a slippery slope argument. Still, even in cases where we can come to some reasonable conclusion about the relevant prediction, a slippery slope argument is secure only if its second element—utilitarianism—is also plausible. Is it? Read on.

9.5 Discussion Questions

1. How does act utilitarianism differ from ethical egoism? Which do you think is more plausible and why?
2. What is it for an action to be *optimific*? How might an action bring about more happiness than any other alternative, but still fail to be optimific?
3. Most utilitarians think that sometimes people are not to blame for performing actions that are wrong, and that sometimes people should not be praised for doing the right thing. Why do they think this? Do you agree?
4. How do utilitarians account for cases in which we lack moral knowledge? Do you find such an account plausible?
5. Utilitarians reject the existence of absolute moral rules (other than the principle of utility). Do you think that there are any absolute moral rules? If so, what are they, and how can their absolute status be defended against the utilitarian view that the ends justify the means?
6. Utilitarians think that some humans are morally equal to some animals. What exactly do they mean by this, and how do they argue for it? Do you agree with them? Why or why not?
7. Provide your own example of a slippery slope argument and explain how it can best be defended (or critiqued).

❧

CHAPTER 10

Consequentialism
Its Difficulties

10.1 Measuring Well-Being

According to utilitarianism, we must do what is optimific. We must maximize overall well-being. Thus, to know whether an action is morally required, we need to do four things: (1) add up all of the benefits it produces, (2) add up all of the harm it causes, (3) determine the balance, and then (4) see whether the balance is greater than that of any other available action.

There are many complex cases where it is impossible in practice to follow these steps. There is simply too much information to be gotten, and no one is smart enough or has time enough to gather it all. This explains the extent of our moral ignorance, according to utilitarians. But if it is impossible *in principle* to follow these steps, then utilitarianism is sunk.

Some people do think it impossible. They think that there is no way to undertake step 1 or step 2. Since the problems are the same for either one, let's just focus on step 1.

In order to add up all of the good produced by an action, I would need some way to measure it. Well-being would have to come in quantities, so that I could measure the amount of one person's welfare, measure another's, and another's, and add them all together. But that seems completely implausible.

This problem might be solved if well-being were simply a matter of the degree to which our desires were satisfied. We could then determine how well off someone was by noting what percentage of his desires were fulfilled. But even aside from the difficulties with this view that we encountered in chapter 4, there is the further worry about whether all desires should have the same status in determining one's well-being. To appreciate this worry, imagine that I have 1,000 desires. (This is obviously artificial, but it will help make the relevant point.) Suppose that 900 of these desires are, by my own lights, pretty superficial—they don't help define who I truly am, they are fleeting, their frustration doesn't leave me in a really bad mood, and so on. Now suppose that all 900 of these desires are satisfied. But also suppose that the remaining 100, which are ones that I am deeply invested in, ones that *do* help to structure my character and personality, remain unfulfilled.

How well off am I? It seems to me that I'm actually in quite a bad state, even though a whopping 90 percent of my desires are fulfilled. This shows that we can't measure well-being just by focusing on the percentage of desires that are satisfied. Things get even more complicated if I am trying to compare my level of welfare with that of someone else whose overall percentage of satisfied desires is lower, but many of whose deeper desires *are* satisfied.

Things are even more difficult if we shift focus from a desire satisfaction theory to a pluralistic view of well-being. Such a view claims that there are many sources of personal welfare. The list differs from philosopher to philosopher, but familiar candidates include knowledge, virtue, love, happiness, and friendship. The idea is that the more you have of these things, the better your life is going for you.

This sort of view creates really hard problems of measurement. How are we to measure degrees of friendship? Of love? Of virtue? And then combine them into some overall measure of personal welfare?

Pluralism raises hard problems even if we think that there are only two components of well-being rather than many. Suppose, for instance, that happiness and autonomy are the only things that intrinsically contribute to a good life. If utilitarianism is right, then we must maximize both of these values.

The problem is that it is not always possible to do this. Sometimes we have to choose between happiness and autonomy. Suppose that a patient is dying but doesn't know it. His family begs his doctors to keep this a secret, knowing that he will sink into a terrible depression if he learns the truth about his illness. Still, keeping that information from the patient undercuts his autonomy. In such a case, doctors may either respect the patient's autonomy or allow him some happiness. They can't do both.

There are many cases like this. Should parents allow their teenage daughter to date an older man they know to be abusive? Should families intervene to prevent a relative from joining a cult? Should a superpower undermine the results of a foreign democratic election, if the newly elected government is set on oppressing its citizens and waging war against innocent neighbors? Answering such questions of course requires a great deal of information. But once we have it, we may still face a choice between respecting autonomy and reducing misery. When that is so, which should we do?

Utilitarianism has no way of answering this question, once we allow that both autonomy and happiness are intrinsically valuable. If happiness were all-important, then we could always give the nod to it. If autonomy were the supreme value, we could insist on honoring it, even at the cost of unhappiness. But if the two are both of ultimate importance, then it is very hard to know what to do if they conflict.

John Stuart Mill himself encountered something like this problem, even though he thought that happiness is the only thing that is intrinsically valuable. He wanted to protect utilitarianism from the objection that it was a "doctrine of the swine," attractive only to those who preferred a life of easy pleasure to the more challenging intellectual pleasures. To Bentham's motto "Pushpin is as good as poetry" (pushpin is a simple tavern game), Mill replied that "it is better to be Socrates dissatisfied than a fool satisfied." Bentham urged us to maximize pleasure, no matter its quality. Mill couldn't stand that. He insisted that we maximize the *quality* of our pleasures, as well as their quantity.

Leave aside Mill's elitism here, his view that some pleasures are "higher" than others. The deepest problem lies in his demand that we maximize two things (quantity and quality of pleasures), not one. But what if we can't do both? A big bag of potato chips, a six-pack, and the TV clicker may bring loads of low-level fun. Or I could spend the same five hours trying to reconstruct a difficult philosophical argument. Little pleasure, but very high quality. There is no principled advice that the utilitarian can offer here, so long as both the quantity and the quality of pleasure are of ultimate importance.

You might think the solution to this problem is obvious: get rid of the idea that there is more than one thing that is intrinsically valuable, and, having done that, abandon Mill's suggestion that there is more than one relevant dimension of importance of that single remaining intrinsic value. But even this is problematic, as we can see if we assume that quantity of happiness alone is the correct measure of well-being. After all, happiness comes in many flavors. There is the happiness of momentary elation, of steady contentment, of physical excitement, of mental challenge, of exhausted gratitude. And that is only a small portion of the catalogue. Given these different kinds of happiness, it would be very surprising if there were some common measure of happiness that applied to each person.

These problems can be summarized in the *Argument from Value Measurement*:

1. Utilitarianism is true only if there is a precise unit of measurement that can determine the value of an action's results.
2. There is no such unit of measurement.
3. Therefore, utilitarianism is false.

I think that utilitarians should admit that premise 2 is true. There is no precise unit that can measure happiness or, more generally, well-being.

So utilitarians must resist premise 1. But how? After all, utilitarians are asking us to compare different actions on the basis of which one maximizes well-being. When we make other comparisons, and ask (for instance) about which person is tallest, or fastest, or wealthiest, we can do this just because there are precise units of measurement to rely on: height can be parceled out in millimeters, speed in fractions of a second, wealth in terms of dollars and cents. These precise units of measurement enable us to determine when the relevant "value" (height, speed, wealth, etc.) is maximized. Such examples make premise 1 look very appealing.

Still, I think utilitarians are right to reject it. There are clear cases where some actions create more overall benefit than others, even though there is no precise way to quantify these benefits. Consider the good produced by a kindly grandmother who takes in her wandering, orphaned grandchildren, and compare that to the benefits of a couple enjoying a friendly game of cards. The first case is obviously more beneficial than the second. So long as there are clear cases such as this one, there must be some way to measure benefits, even if it is imprecise.

And we can, of course, say the same thing about harms. There is certainly a harm when a husband curses his wife in front of their children. But there is far more harm when a cholera outbreak hits a refugee camp. We can't say precisely how much more harm there is, but it is clear that there is a greater amount in one case than another. That is enough, I think, to cast doubt on premise 1 of the argument.

I think that these examples are also enough to show that we can—at least sometimes—fulfill steps 1 and 2 of the utilitarian calculus. We can survey our options and determine which is most beneficial, and which is most (or least) harmful.

Still, there is trouble when it comes to steps 3 and 4. Step 3 asks us to balance the harms and benefits of a given action and then, in step 4, to compare that balance with the ones generated by all alternative actions. If we could figure out the third step, the fourth would probably be unproblematic. But given that benefits and harms are such different things, how can we really strike a balance among them?

What we can say, on behalf of utilitarianism, is that there will be easy cases, cases where the morality of the action is clear. If, among all of one's choices, there is an act that produces both the most benefit and the least harm, then that is your moral duty. If, among all of your choices, there is no chance of improving well-being, then you must choose the act that will cause the least amount of harm. And if, among all of your choices, none will cause any harm, then you are required to do the one that produces the most good. Of course, since we aren't able to precisely quantify harm or benefit, it may be unclear which choice produces the most benefit, or the least harm. But when it is clear, these guidelines give straightforward moral advice that the utilitarian will endorse.

The problem is that many situations we face in the real world do not fit any of these three patterns. Whether one act is optimific can be quite unclear—not because we are ignorant of all of its results (though we often are), and not even because there is no way to be precise about the amount of benefit and harm it causes, but rather because it is not clear how to strike a balance between benefits and harms. When two or more acts each promise to produce some benefit, at the cost of some harm, there may be no real answer to the question of which action is optimific. And this is where we stand in *most* cases. If that is so, then utilitarianism will have lost one of its primary advantages—namely, its ability to give concrete advice about what to do in morally complex situations.

10.2 Utilitarianism Is Very Demanding

There are three areas in which utilitarianism seems to demand too much of us mere mortals: deliberation, motivation, and action. Let's consider these in turn.

Deliberation

It might seem that in order to think about how to act, we must first have a huge amount of information. We must know all of the options we face, and their likely results. Then we must determine the overall value of each of our options. And then compare these values to see which yields the optimific outcome—sometimes in a matter of seconds.

But that's just impossible. We're not computers. We can't gain that kind of knowledge in advance of every action. Utilitarianism simply demands too much information, and calculating skills that no one could possibly possess.

Mill had a ready reply to this objection. Christians can usually know perfectly well what their religion requires of them, without having to reread the entire Bible prior to each action. They rarely need to do fancy calculations to determine their religious duty, because there are centuries of accumulated wisdom that they can rely on in a pinch. So, too, with utilitarianism. We don't need to spend a lot of time thinking about it to know that assaulting or killing someone will cause more harm than good. In most situations, we can rely on common wisdom, based on thousands of previous cases, to know what is going to be beneficial or harmful.

Of course there are exceptional circumstances, ones where we do have to stop and carefully puzzle out the pros and cons of a given action. But that's not a problem for utilitarianism—all moral theories allow for such cases.

Furthermore, it simply defeats the purpose of doing good if you spend so much time deliberating. The person likeliest to fulfill the utilitarian goal of improving the world is the one who knows when to stop and think about her choices, and when not to. Too much time pondering one's options can freeze a person, and result in too many wasted opportunities. Ordinarily, it is far better to act spontaneously; we can make time for careful calculation in those rare cases where it is truly needed.

Motivation

Still, doesn't utilitarianism require us to be saints, always on the lookout for chances to do good? Must we *always* try do what is optimific?

A plausible moral theory is one that most of us can live by. But asking us to be constantly benevolent, never taking more than a moment or two for ourselves—how many of us can be so altruistic? If no one but a saint can meet its standards, then utilitarianism is in deep trouble.

Utilitarians would agree with this. They do *not* believe that we must always be strategizing about how to improve the world. The reason is simple. People motivated in this way usually fail to achieve their goal.

The idea is that those who are always trying to get the best outcome are often bound to miss it. This isn't as strange as it sounds. Think of people whose sole purpose in life is to be as happy as they can be. Such people are rarely very happy. Constantly striving for this goal only makes it more elusive.[1]

So, too, with pursuing global happiness. Those who aim only for this tend to be busybodies, cranks, obsessives. (Go read Nick Hornby's *How to Be Good*, a novel whose central character, David Carr, has committed himself to doing as much good as he can. Result: he brings only misery to family and friends.) Having just a single motive—producing the greatest good for the greatest number—would almost certainly backfire. If that is so, then utilitarians are off the hook. Their theory would not require that we always have benevolence in mind.

There is another way to think about these criticisms regarding deliberation and motivation. To understand this new take on the subject, we need to distinguish between a **decision procedure** and a **standard of rightness**. A decision procedure is just what it sounds like—a method for reliably guiding our decisions, so that when we use it well, we make decisions as we ought to. A standard of rightness tells us the conditions that are necessary and sufficient for actions to be morally right.

Consequentialism is, above all, a standard of rightness. It says that an action is right just because it is optimific. This standard is meant to explain precisely why actions are right, when they are.

Importantly, a standard of rightness need not be a good decision procedure. Indeed, most consequentialists think that their standard of rightness—the principle of utility—fails as a decision procedure. Unless we find ourselves in very unusual circumstances, we should *not* be asking ourselves whether the act we are about to do is optimific.

The reasons given earlier explain this. Using the principle of utility as a decision procedure would probably *decrease* the amount of good we do in the world. That's because we would probably spend too much time deliberating or second-guessing our motivations, thereby reducing our chances of doing good. Whenever that is so, utilitarians require that we

---

1. Recall the discussion of this point as it relates to the paradox of hedonism in chapter 2.

use something other than the principle of utility to guide our deliberations and motivations.

Action

The last area in which utilitarianism is said to be too demanding is that of action. Even if we needn't always deliberate with an eye to doing what is optimific, and even if we needn't always have a saint's motivations, we really must act so as achieve optimific results. Whenever we fail, we are behaving immorally. That is bound to strike most people as excessive.

Recall John Wesley's motto: Do all the good you can, by all the means you can, etc. Such a life would be one of great and constant self-sacrifice. Anytime you can do more good for others than you can for yourself, you are required to do so. If you are like most readers of this book—in no danger of starvation, able to afford a night out, a new pair of jeans, a vacation every so often—then utilitarianism calls on you to do a great deal more for others than you are probably doing.

Consider the extraordinary Dr. Paul Farmer, profiled in Tracy Kidder's book *Mountains Beyond Mountains*. Before his death in 2022, Farmer was a professor at Harvard who cofounded *Partners in Health*, a nonprofit group designed to provide free treatment to many of the world's poorest people. Before moving with his family to Rwanda a few years ago, Farmer spent most of the year apart from his wife and young daughter, to maximize the time he could spend treating critically ill patients in rural Haiti. He lived like a pauper and donated his Harvard salary to Partners in Health. He didn't take vacations—if he did, some patients would die whose lives he could have saved. He tried (but failed) to love his wife and daughter no more than anyone else. He insisted that everyone—no matter how poor, how socially disadvantaged, how distant from us—was deserving of an equal chance to live a decent life. He didn't cite utilitarianism as the basis of his work. But he came as close as anyone I've heard of to living up to the strenuous demands that utilitarianism imposes.

Now you might be thinking that Farmer is an exception. You're not a doctor; you are in no position to save lives. Utilitarianism demanded so much of Farmer because of his special expertise. When it comes to the average person, though, utilitarianism doesn't require much self-sacrifice at all.

But think again. If I have a choice between spending $1,000 on a beach vacation and sending that money to UNICEF (the United Nations Children's Fund), it's an easy call. UNICEF literature claims that $1,000 can provide 100 families with a basic water kit for use during emergencies, immunize 1,000 children against polio, or provide enough woolen blankets to cover 250 children during winter-weather emergencies. I'd be unhappy if I had to give up my vacation. But my unhappiness pales in comparison to the suffering of those whose lives could be saved if I spent my money on them, rather than myself. If utilitarianism is correct, then no more vacations for me (or you, probably).

There is an important lesson here: utilitarianism cannot make room for **supererogation**—action that is "above and beyond the call of duty." Such behavior is admirable and praiseworthy, but is not required. A classic case of supererogation is that of a bystander dashing into a burning building in order to rescue strangers trapped inside. Utilitarians must deny that even this is a case of supererogation, because they deny that *any* actions are above and beyond the call of duty. Our moral duty is to do the very best we can do. If, among all of the options available to you at the time, dashing into the building is going to minimize harm, then this is what you must do. Attempting the rescue isn't optional. It is your duty.

Utilitarians know that this isn't going to go down very easily, but they reply that morality can indeed be quite demanding. Most of us believe, for instance, that morality can sometimes require us to give up our great enjoyments, and occasionally our lives. So the real issue isn't whether morality can be extremely demanding—it can. The issue is how often morality will ask us to sacrifice our own interests for those of others.

Our views about how much sacrifice morality requires are shaped by how we have been raised. Most of you have been brought up in relatively wealthy societies, where citizens are used to tax rates that leave them a lot of discretionary income. Suppose, instead, that you were raised in a society that celebrated an ethic of giving, one that made it a real priority to benefit the poor. In that case, you'd probably think it criminal to give only a small fraction of your money to relieve poverty.

Utilitarians must agree that their view can demand great sacrifices of those who have a lot to give, and frequent and substantial sacrifices from the rest of us. That the implications of a moral theory are burdensome, however, is not a decisive strike against it. That it threatens the status quo and challenges the comforts of the well-off may be a mark of its truth, rather than its falsity.

10.3 Impartiality

The impartiality required by utilitarianism really is a substantial benefit of the theory. The happiness of a celebrity or a billionaire is no more important than that of a homeless person or a refugee. From the moral point of view, everyone counts equally; no one's interests are more important than anyone else's.

Yet there is also something worrying about impartiality, since morality sometimes seems to recommend *partiality*. It seems right, for instance, that I care about my children more than your children, that I care more for friends than strangers, more for my fellow citizens than those living halfway around the world. And it also seems right to translate my care into action. If I have saved a bit of money, and it could either pay for my son's minor surgery or relieve the greater suffering of famine victims, most of us will think it at least permissible to pay the surgeon. But to do that is to be partial to the interests of my son. Utilitarianism does not allow that. It rejects the idea that a person, just because he is my son, my dear friend, or my fellow citizen, is more deserving of my help and attention.

Utilitarians can argue that there are many situations in which we should give preference to our near and dear—not because they deserve it or are more important than strangers, but because that is what is most beneficial. They could argue, for instance, that the results of sending my money overseas would actually be worse than relieving my son's suffering. Utilitarians will remind us that we must consider all consequences, not just short-term ones. If I were to sacrifice my son's interests so readily, he would feel hurt, and less secure in my love for him. These feelings are bad in themselves and would probably cause further harm in the long run. By contrast, famine victims who don't even know me won't feel slighted by my passing them over so that I can care for my son's needs. So if we take a sufficiently broad view of things, we can see that being partial to the interests of family and friends is usually optimific after all.

This sort of reasoning is sometimes correct. When all is said and done, we often get better results when focusing on family, friends, and fellow citizens. But not always. After all, in the tale just told, the long-term result of my not sending famine aid is that some people actually die, whereas my son, though in pain and perhaps resentful of my sending the money abroad, would still be very much alive. From an impartial point of view, the death of famine victims is surely worse than my son's medical problems. When minimizing harm means giving one's time or money to strangers, utilitarianism requires that we do so—even if that means sacrificing the important needs of friends and family.

This emphasis on impartiality leads to another concern. We are to count everyone's well-being equally. But suppose that nearly everyone in a society has a deep-seated prejudice against a small minority group.

And suppose, further, that they use this prejudice to defend a policy of enslavement. Depending on the circumstances, it could be that utilitarianism *requires* slavery in this society.

When deciding the matter, we must take all of the harms to the slaves into account. But we must also consider the benefits to their oppressors. Everyone's interests count equally. Rich or poor, white or Black, male or female. So far, so good. But also: ignorant or wise, just or unjust, kind or malicious—everyone's interests count, equally. If enough people are sufficiently mean and ignorant, then utilitarianism can permit them to impose such suffering. Though such cases are not likely to occur that frequently, they can. And when they do, utilitarianism sides with the oppressors. That is a serious problem for any moral theory.[2]

10.4 No Intrinsic Wrongness (or Rightness)

When considering the sort of case just described, it is tempting to fall back on the following view. Certain types of action—think of torture, rape, enslavement—are intrinsically wrong (i.e., wrong by their very nature). We don't need to check the results of such behavior in order to know that they are immoral. All we need to know is what such actions are truly like. Armed with this knowledge, we can see that they shouldn't be done.

Utilitarians cannot accept this. For them, the morality of an action always depends on its results. This feature of the theory is precisely what supports its moral flexibility: any sort of action can be morally right, so long as its outcome is optimific. Even actions that cause only terrible suffering can be morally right, provided that they manage to prevent even greater suffering. Utilitarianism's moral flexibility comes from its refusal to absolutely prohibit any kind of action.

Suppose that utilitarianism is correct and there is nothing wrong, in and of itself, with killing innocent people. Usually, of course, such killings

---

2. Consider this passage from the memoirs of writer Alexander Waugh, who recounts the terrors of corporal punishment at his boarding school: "The monks enjoyed whipping the boys as a release from the constraints of their celibacy, and my father, throughout his life, always claimed that to be beaten was a small sacrifice for a boy and a great treat for a monk." (This is from Waugh's book *Fathers and Sons* [New York: Doubleday, 2007].) This remark, no doubt issued tongue in cheek, nevertheless illustrates a weakness of utilitarian reasoning. Whether the oppressors are abusive teachers, corrupt politicians, soldiers rampaging through civilian areas, or slave owners, the utilitarian counts their welfare as equal to that of their victims. If no other action would produce as much overall benefit, then the abuse is, by the utilitarian's lights, morally justified.

will not be optimific. But imagine a person who is really badly off and whose future is grim. He wants to live, and enjoys some small pleasures every now and then. But most of his life is quite bad, and that's not going to change. The world would contain less misery if he were to die. And so we must kill him—provided, of course, that we avoid causing even greater harm by doing so. If we were caught, then we would be sent to jail, our own families would suffer, other vulnerable people would become much more afraid, and so on. But if we can kill this man without being caught, while convincing everyone that he died of natural causes, then utilitarianism tells us that we *must* do so. This is no murder. It is justifiable homicide. That's because this man's life was lowering the overall level of well-being in the world. With him out of the picture, that level rises.

Utilitarians reject any absolute ban on killing innocents (or torturing them, or stealing from them, etc.). This has a very important implication: any kind of harmful action, no matter how awful, is permitted, provided it is necessary to prevent an even worse outcome.

This utilitarian rationale is the one that many truly vicious political leaders have relied on to defend their record. In a candid moment, they might admit to having tortured their opponents, crushed civil rights, allowed their cronies to enrich themselves at the expense of the country. The story is always the same: we are not perfect, but toppling us and allowing our opposition to take over would be even worse. So you must support us.

This is usually nothing other than a lame effort to dignify the ruthless pursuit of self-interest. But sometimes these people are (also) telling the truth. Though their regime is terrible, no viable alternative would be any better. If utilitarianism is correct, then supporting such a government would be morally right. Trying to overthrow it would be immoral.

You might recoil at this. You might think that we should never dirty our hands by supporting evil. Utilitarianism denies this. Life does not always present us with happy choices. We may have to choose between collaborating with evil, or refusing to do so, thereby allowing an even worse outcome to occur. In such cases we must always collaborate, since our ultimate moral duty is to minimize harm. If utilitarianism is correct, no kind of action is always morally beyond the pale.

Utilitarians deny that any type of action is intrinsically wrong. And as they see it, no kind of action is intrinsically right, either. One might think, for instance, that there is something right, in and of itself, about keeping a promise, telling the truth, or helping the needy. But utilitarians deny this. On their view, the merit of an action depends entirely on its results. Any instance of promise keeping, truth telling, or kindness that fails to be optimific is *immoral.*

10.5 The Problem of Injustice

Perhaps the greatest problem for utilitarianism can be simply put: we must maximize well-being, but sometimes we can do this only by committing some serious injustice. Moral theories should not permit, much less require, that we act unjustly. Therefore, there is something deeply wrong about utilitarianism.

To do justice is to respect rights; to commit injustice is to violate rights. If it is ever optimific to violate rights, then utilitarianism requires us to do so.

Consider two examples from wartime: **vicarious punishment** and **exemplary punishment**. Vicarious punishment targets innocent people as a way to deter the guilty. Such a tactic often backfires. But it can sometimes be extremely effective. You might stop terrorists from their dirty work by abducting their relatives and threatening to torture them. You might prevent guerilla attacks by killing the residents of the villages that shelter them. Though the torture and deliberate killing of innocent civilians certainly infringes their rights, the utilitarian will require that it be done if it prevents even greater harm.

Exemplary punishment is punishment that "makes an example" of someone. I recently came across a good instance of this in E. L. Doctorow's book *The March*, a fictionalized account of Sherman's 1864 march to the sea. At one point in his campaign, Southern guerrillas captured, tortured, and killed some of Sherman's soldiers while his army was encamped. How to prevent such attacks in future? Sherman had the Southern prisoners of war in his camp brought before him. He selected one at random. Then he had the man publicly shot, and announced that he'd repeat the exercise in the case of future guerrilla attacks. The attacks stopped immediately.

Sherman's command likely saved more lives than it cost, and so, by utilitarian standards, it was the right thing to do. But it came at the expense of the prisoner's moral rights. Shooting that prisoner stopped the guerrilla attacks. But that doesn't mean that the prisoner deserved to die.

Cases of vicarious and exemplary punishment are cases in which people do not deserve to be harmed. There are also many examples in which people do deserve some sort of penalty or punishment, but it is not optimific to give them their just deserts. Think of situations in which a student rightly receives a failing grade and appeals for a better one. Sometimes it really would be most beneficial to give the student the grade he wants, rather than the grade he has earned. Perhaps a job or a scholarship is on the line. If the benefits outweigh the costs, utilitarianism requires that the professor change the grade.

There are more serious cases. After World War II, U.S. officials determined that it was beneficial to allow many Nazi scientists to escape punishment, so long as they agreed to share their weapons intelligence. Prosecutors sometimes let acknowledged murderers go free, if the killers testify against the crime bosses who once hired them. Political leaders with blood on their hands are often allowed to retire peacefully, so as to avoid the civil strife that would result were they prosecuted for their crimes. If utilitarianism is correct, then we must minimize harm—even if doing so means letting the guilty escape justice.

It is true that when rights are violated, victims are usually harmed. So utilitarianism usually condemns injustice. But not always. A bank manager may embezzle millions, and doctor the records to ensure that his theft is never discovered. He and his family may live like kings, and no one be the worse for it. A thief may steal a valuable jewel that its owner has come to hate. Suppose the owner had secretly wanted to be rid of it. The owner's rights have surely been violated, but neither he nor anyone else is the worse for it. In such cases there is only benefit, and little or no harm. Utilitarianism thus approves of such thefts. And yet they were undertaken entirely for selfish reasons, and achieved only selfish gains. These examples, and others offered earlier, should give us pause. A plausible moral theory has to give justice the importance it deserves. It's not clear that utilitarianism can do this.

10.6 Potential Solutions to the Problem of Injustice

For as long as utilitarianism has been around, its fans have had to deal with the objection that it shortchanges justice. They have had ample time to develop replies. Let's consider these replies by framing each of them as a response to the *Argument from Injustice*:

1. The correct moral theory will never require us to commit serious injustices.
2. Utilitarianism sometimes requires us to commit serious injustices.
3. Therefore utilitarianism is not the correct moral theory.

There are four replies that are especially important. We'll consider three of them here, and then devote the next section to the fourth.

Justice Is Also Intrinsically Valuable

This might sound puzzling, but the first reply accepts this argument in every respect. Utilitarianism cannot allow for the independent importance of justice, and that disqualifies it from being a good moral theory. Strictly speaking, then, utilitarianism is false. But if we make a small change to the doctrine, then all will be well.

A defining feature of utilitarianism is its view that well-being is the only thing that is intrinsically valuable. Suppose we amend that, and say that justice is also important in its own right. So we should maximize well-being *and* maximize justice in the world. That will solve the difficulty.

Or will it? It seems, instead, that we just open ourselves up to the problem aired earlier, in which consequentialism loses its ability to give guidance when promoting one value comes at the expense of another. If we are to maximize happiness and justice, what happens when we can't do both? Which should we give priority to?

We could say: always give priority to justice. But this isn't very plausible. Suppose that there has been gridlock in the state legislature. For months, lawmakers have been unable to pass a spending bill. Finally, a compromise package comes to the floor. If it doesn't get passed, there is no telling when another spending package will be voted on. In the meantime, government will shut down, tens of thousands of people will not receive paychecks, medical assistance, or welfare support. Furthermore, the spending bill looks *terrific*. It solves a great number of the state's problems, gives aid to the neediest, and sponsors projects that will do genuine good for most communities. There is only one problem: it includes a clause that unfairly denies a small community the agricultural subsidies that the governor had promised it. Still, given the alternatives, a legislator should definitely vote for the spending bill, even though this means a minor injustice. As a general matter, if the stakes are extremely high, and the injustice very small, then it *may* be right to perpetrate injustice.

Rather than always giving priority to justice, we might instead always give priority to well-being. But then we are right back to the original theory, and so have made no progress in solving the problem of injustice.

What seems right to say is this: sometimes it's best to prefer well-being to justice, and sometimes not. But without any principle to sort this out, we don't really have a coherent theory at all.

Injustice Is Never Optimific

In the face of this problem, some utilitarians deny premise 2, and so deny that their theory ever requires us to commit injustice. They say that if we carefully consider all of the results of unfair actions, we will see that those actions aren't really optimific. A policy of vicarious punishment, for instance, may work in the short run. But it will cause such anger among the target population that an even greater number of them will join with the opposition. And that will mean more innocent bloodshed over time.

Such a calculation is certainly true in many cases. But it is unwarranted optimism to suppose that things will always work out so fortunately. Sometimes, for instance, terror movements do lose support when the surrounding civilian population is forced to take the hit. And there are times when exemplary executions decrease violence over the long run. Injustice can sometimes prevent great harm. It can, on occasion, also produce great benefits and little or no harm. Utilitarianism must approve of such actions.

Justice Must Sometimes Be Sacrificed

A third utilitarian strategy allows that well-being and justice sometimes conflict. But when they do, it is justice, and not well-being, that must take a backseat. Justice is only a part, not the whole, of morality. Of course it is important to respect people's rights, but that is because doing so is usually optimific. When it isn't, rights must be sacrificed. So premise 1 of the Argument from Injustice is false.

Utilitarians who defend this strategy know that their recommendations will sometimes clash with conventional wisdom. But as we have seen, this is not a fatal flaw. Received opinion is not the final word in ethics. Utilitarianism began its life as a radical doctrine. That legacy remains.

Utilitarians can claim that our deepest moral convictions, including those that require us to do justice, reflect a utilitarian framework. We are socialized to tell the truth, protect the weak, keep our promises, and so on, *because doing so tends to be optimific*. But when it is not, utilitarians ask us to look at morality's ultimate standard, and to set aside our ordinary scruples in favor of the principle of utility.

It is a good thing, from a utilitarian point of view, that we are so reluctant to approve of injustice. But as we saw in the previous chapter (in the section "Actual Versus Expected Results"), virtuous motivation can sometimes lead to poor results. When it does, utilitarianism condemns the action as immoral. If, for instance, Sherman's qualms about injustice had prevented his execution of the prisoner, many more innocent lives would have been lost. If innocent lives are so important, then surely (say utilitarians) we ought to save as many as possible. That sometimes requires us to act unjustly.

Most of us agree that justice can sometimes be outweighed by other moral concerns. If, in a previous example, a legislator must authorize a minor injustice in order to pass an immensely beneficial spending bill, then morality gives the go-ahead. If you can administer CPR to a stricken passerby, and so save his life, then it is worth committing a minor injustice to do so. So justice may sometimes be sacrificed. But when? Utilitarians have an answer: whenever the results of doing so are optimific. If you don't like that answer, you need to supply a better principle that tells us when injustice is, and is not, permitted.

10.7 Rule Consequentialism

There is a moral theory that deserves special mention here, because it promises to handle a number of objections to utilitarianism, while keeping much of its spirit. This is **rule consequentialism**—the view that *an action is morally right just because it is required by an **optimific social rule**.*

An optimific social rule is a rule that meets the following condition: if (nearly) everyone in a society were to accept it, then the results would be optimific.

The basic idea is this. Rather than determine an action's morality by asking about its results, we ask instead about whether the action conforms to a moral rule. This is a familiar model in ethics. Most moral theories operate this way. What distinguishes them from one another is their different claims about what makes something a moral rule. Rule consequentialists have a specific view about this. The moral rules are the optimific social rules.

To know whether a rule is an optimific social rule, follow these three steps:

1. Carefully describe the rule.
2. Imagine what a society would be like if just about everyone in it endorsed the rule.
3. Then ask this question: will that society be better off with this rule than with any competing rule?

If the answer to this question is *yes*, then this rule is an optimific social rule. If the answer is *no*, then it isn't an optimific social rule, and so is not a genuine moral rule.

Let's make this concrete. Return again to the example in which General Sherman orders a captive to be shot. Is that a morally acceptable thing to do? According to rule consequentialism, we answer this question by figuring out the moral rules that govern the treatment of prisoners of war. One of these rules might be: do not execute prisoners of war without a fair trial. Another might be: execute prisoners of war if you think that doing so will be highly beneficial. And of course there are many other candidates. But let's just stick with these two.

The rule consequentialist will ask us to imagine societies that are governed by each of these competing rules. Which society would be better off?

That depends, of course, on what makes societies and their citizens better off. Rule consequentialists differ on this question. Some are hedonists; others are desire satisfaction theorists; still others defend different lists of objective goods.

The most prominent contemporary version of rule consequentialism, that offered by the philosopher Brad Hooker,[3] says that there are two, and only two, things of intrinsic value—happiness and justice. Optimific social rules will be ones that both increase happiness and respect rights.

So, which of the two rules regarding captured prisoners will, over the long run, maximize both happiness and justice? It is very probably the first rule, which requires captors to try their prisoners fairly. A society governed by the second rule would give too much discretion to commanders, who might make serious mistakes about the benefits of killing their captives without due process. There may be isolated cases in which ordering such a killing is optimific. But *as a general policy*, it is probably optimific to forbid such behavior.

If that is so, then rule consequentialists will condemn Sherman's order. And that is surely what justice requires. Rule consequentialism will probably also instruct professors to give their students the grades they deserve, rather than those they would like to have. It will condemn the actions of thieves, even if they don't get caught and their victims suffer in only minor ways.

---

3. See Brad Hooker, *Ideal Code, Real World* (New York: Oxford University Press, 2000).

You see where this is going. When we focus on what is optimific as a general policy, we repeatedly get advice that agrees with our notions of justice. Even rule consequentialists who reject the intrinsic value of justice, and insist that well-being is the only thing of ultimate value, will almost always defend policies that are just. That's because in the long run, and as a general matter, just *policies* maximize well-being, even if, in isolated cases, just *actions* do not.

Rule consequentialism also solves other problems with act utilitarianism. It supports our belief that morality permits a certain degree of partiality, because policies that allow us to give preference to friends, loved ones, and fellow citizens will very often be highly beneficial.

Rule consequentialism makes it much easier for us to know the right thing to do. Rather than trying to predict the benefits and harms of each available action, and then trying to balance them against one another, we are instructed to follow relatively simple rules. The complex calculations associated with act utilitarianism are replaced by fairly straightforward rules.

Rule consequentialism can also say that certain actions are simply forbidden, even if they will sometimes achieve very good results. For instance, even if it would be optimific here and now to torture a prisoner, there may well be an optimific rule that forbids political torture. In most cases and over the long run, societies that ban torture may be much better off, in terms of both happiness and justice, than those that allow their officials to torture prisoners. If that is so, then torture is immoral—even if, in unusual cases, it yields real benefits.

So rule consequentialism has a lot going for it. And it has been fairly influential—many professional codes of conduct have been formulated with rule consequentialism in mind. Yet rule consequentialism is not without its critics. Perhaps unsurprisingly, the criticism that has attracted the most attention comes from act utilitarians, and can be expressed quite simply. Rule consequentialists demand that we obey moral rules, *even when we know that breaking them would yield better results*. But that is irrational, since in these cases, rule consequentialists know in advance that their ultimate goal (making the world the best place you can make it) will not be fulfilled. It is irrational to knowingly defeat your own goals. Rule consequentialists do this whenever they issue a recommendation that differs from act utilitarianism.

Act utilitarianism demands that we always do what is optimific. So, by definition, whenever rule consequentialists give us different advice, we are required to act in a way that fails to yield the best results. Rule consequentialists would deny military commanders a license to execute the innocent, would forbid torture and embezzlement and vicarious punishment—even when specific instances of such action would be most beneficial. The charge is that this is self-defeating, since a consequentialist's ultimate aim is to produce the best possible results.

No matter what your ultimate goal is, the rules that *generally* achieve that goal will sometimes fail to do so. If you know that you are in one of those exceptional situations, then why follow the rule? Suppose that justice, not happiness, is the ultimate value. Suppose, too, that justice would be best served if everyone were to follow a certain rule, such as one that prohibits tampering with evidence. But why follow that rule if you know that this time, unusually, breaking the rule will yield the most justice? This is a hard question. But as we've seen, and as we will continue to see, every moral theory faces hard questions.

10.8 Conclusion

Consequentialism is a perennial favorite with moral philosophers. Its emphasis on equality and impartiality, its moral flexibility, its inclusion of animals and less-than-fully autonomous human beings within the moral community, its orientation to the future, and its emphasis on results have great appeal for many ethical thinkers.

But we have also seen that there are worries for consequentialism, and these are not easily solved. We usually admire impartiality, but sometimes think that partiality is what morality demands. The consequentialist promise of being able to offer concrete advice to solve moral conflicts may be unfulfilled. Consequentialism can require a degree of self-sacrifice that strikes many people as extreme. It sometimes demands that we perform truly awful actions, so long as they are needed to prevent even greater horrors. And it sometimes calls on us to commit injustice. We considered four solutions to this last problem, none of which seemed wholly satisfying.

It is fitting, then, that we now turn to a competing view that gives pride of place to justice: the theory of Immanuel Kant.

10.9 Discussion Questions

1. Is there any way of measuring how much happiness is brought about by an action? Do we have any method for comparing the happiness of two different people? If the answer to these questions is *no*, is this a problem for utilitarianism?

2. Critics claim that utilitarianism demands that we be saintly in our motivations. Explain this criticism and then discuss why you find it (im)plausible.

3. If utilitarianism is correct, then we may be morally required to undertake substantial sacrifice for others. What limits on such sacrifice does the utilitarian favor? Are these limits acceptable?

4. Utilitarianism requires us to be impartial. What does this amount to? In what sense does utilitarianism require that we treat all people equally? Is this a positive or a negative feature of the theory?

5. How do utilitarians reply to the thought that certain kinds of action are intrinsically immoral? Do you find their replies convincing?

6. Which utilitarian reply to the Argument from Injustice do you think is the most promising? Do you think that this reply is ultimately successful? Defend your answer.

7. What is rule consequentialism? How does the theory deal with the problem of injustice that threatens act utilitarianism? Do you find rule consequentialism to be a plausible ethical theory?

10.10 Cases for Critical Reflection

The Ford Pinto

During the 1970s, Ford Motor Company manufactured the Ford Pinto, a subcompact car. Lee Iacocca, then the president of Ford, envisioned the Pinto as an inexpensive American alternative to popular Japanese and German imports. However, the car was plagued by defects. Notably, the Pinto's design required that the gas tank be located behind the rear axle, placing it next to the rear bumper. This left the car vulnerable to catching fire in the event of rear-end collisions, which caused a number of fatalities.

The publication *Mother Jones* reported on the Ford Pinto safety issue, and the public became outraged upon learning that high-level employees at Ford had been aware of the design flaw all along.[1] It was revealed that a cost-benefit analysis, a method that businesses use to evaluate the strengths and weaknesses of alternatives, determined that reinforcing the rear end of the car would be more costly than the potential payout to victims. It would have cost $11 per car to make a design improvement that would have prevented an estimated 180 fire deaths each year. In the cost-benefit analysis, Ford priced the loss of an individual human life at

---

1. https://www.motherjones.com/politics/1977/09/pinto-madness/.

$200,725, ultimately determining that the design improvement would be costlier than the potential losses. While the story of the Ford Pinto caused serious moral controversy, some have argued that the Pinto was no less safe than other cars at the time, noting that Pinto fatality rates were in the middle range of fatality rates for cars of its type.[2]

Questions

1. According to act utilitarianism, did Ford Motor Company do something morally wrong by selling the Ford Pinto to consumers without fixing the rear-end design flaw? Why or why not?
2. According to act utilitarianism, should Ford Motor Company have informed the public about the design flaw? Why or why not?
3. According to rule consequentialism, should Ford Motor Company have informed the public about the design flaw? Why or why not?

Torture

In 2003, the United States military became embroiled in an armed conflict in Iraq following President George W. Bush's declaration of a war on terrorism, a response to the September 11, 2001, terrorist attacks. In 2004, photographs documenting human rights violations and the abuse of detainees in the Iraq Abu Ghraib prison were released. Members of the U.S. Army and the Central Intelligence Agency had been using enhanced interrogation techniques, such as sleep deprivation, which is widely regarded as a form of torture. Abuses of the detainees included physical abuse, sexual abuse, and murder. The public was shocked by the graphic photos depicting these rights violations, and the abuses were widely condemned.[1]

Torture and prisoner abuse are serious offenses. However, some would argue that torture is not always wrong. Consider the ticking time bomb thought experiment. The authorities have captured a terrorist who has planted a ticking time bomb, but he refuses to disclose its location. Unless stopped, the attack will result in the death of thousands of innocent people. The authorities believe that the only way to extract the information necessary to stop the attack is to torture the terrorist.

---

2. https://daily.jstor.org/what-made-the-pinto-such-a-controversial-car/.
1. https://www.nytimes.com/2004/05/23/magazine/regarding-the-torture-of-others.html.

Questions

1. Is torture always morally wrong? Why or why not?
2. Is it morally permissible to torture the terrorist in the ticking time bomb scenario? Why or why not?
3. According to act utilitarianism, should the authorities torture the terrorist in the ticking time bomb scenario? Why or why not?
4. According to rule consequentialism, should the authorities torture the terrorist in the ticking time bomb scenario? Why or why not?

Effective Altruism

Effective altruism is a growing social movement aimed at doing the most good possible. Effective altruists engage in research to identify the most effective charities, and they donate money as generously as possible to those organizations. The Against Malaria Foundation, for example, is popular among effective altruists. The organization provides inexpensive insecticide-treated nets to prevent malaria, one of the leading killers of children in Africa.[1] The goal of effective altruism is to alleviate as much suffering and death as possible with one's work and charitable donations.

One effective altruism organization, 80,000 Hours, advises people on choosing careers that will maximize their impact on the world.[2] For many, this could mean taking the highest paying job and donating large chunks of the salary. One effective altruist, Toby Ord, founded an organization called Giving What We Can, which asks members to sign a pledge to donate at least 10 percent of their yearly income.[3] Some effective altruists commit to giving away far more. For example, Julia Wise, a social worker, and her husband, Jeff Kaufman, live on just 6 percent of their income so they can give $100,000 a year to charity.[4] This sounds like an enormous sacrifice, though at least one wide-ranging psychological study found a positive connection between giving to charity and subjective well-being.[5]

---

1. https://www.givewell.org/charities/top-charities.
2. https://www.economist.com/international/2018/05/31/to-help-save-the-world-become-a-banker-not-a-doctor.
3. https://www.bbc.com/news/magazine-11950843.
4. https://qz.com/515655/this-couple-lives-on-6-of-their-income-so-they-can-give-100000-a-year-to-charity/.
5. https://www.apa.org/pubs/journals/releases/psp-104-4-635.pdf.

Questions

1. According to act utilitarianism, are effective altruists doing the morally right thing? Why or why not?
2. Do you think you are morally obligated to give a significant portion of your income to charity? If so, how much do you think you should give? If not, why not?
3. Do you think it is important to choose a career that will allow you to do the most good in the world? Why or why not?
4. Do you think the actions of effective altruists like Julia and Jeff are supererogatory? Why or why not?

CHAPTER 11

···· ❧ ····

The Kantian Perspective

Fairness and Justice

Imagine a person who reasons as follows: I should keep my money rather than pay it out in taxes, because if I keep it, I'll be able to afford a wonderful vacation for myself and my family. And no one is actually going to suffer if I pocket the money, since it's only a few thousand dollars that we're talking about. There's no way that money could bring as much happiness in the government's hands as it could in mine.

Suppose he is right about that. He spends the money on his vacation. He and his family have a terrific time. He is never caught.

Still, he has done something wrong. So has the person who cheats on her exams and gets away with it. So has the person who gleefully speeds down the emergency lane and escapes the traffic jam that the rest of us are stuck in. So has the person whose campaign of dirty tricks has gotten him securely into office.

Despite any good results that may come from their actions, these people did wrong—or so we think. And the explanation of their immorality is simple. What they did was unfair. They took advantage of the system. They broke the rules that work to everyone's benefit. They violated the rights of others. No matter how much personal gain such actions bring, they are still wrong, because they are unfair and unjust.

Immanuel Kant (1724–1804) thought this way, and was very likely the most brilliant philosopher ever to have done so. He remains perhaps the most important voice of opposition to utilitarianism, and to its claim that the ultimate point of morality is to improve well-being rather than do justice.

11.1 Consistency and Fairness

There is a natural way to understand what is wrong with the actions in the examples just given. In each case, people are making exceptions of themselves. Their success depends on violating rules that most other people are following. This is a kind of inconsistency—of playing by one set of rules while insisting that others obey a different set.

People are inconsistent to the extent that they treat similar cases differently. Tax cheats or dirty politicians are in the same boat as the rest of us. There's nothing special about them, or their situation, that exempts them from the rules that everyone must follow. That you can get away with making an exception of yourself doesn't mean that it is right to do so.

Our deep opposition to unfairness, and the resulting importance we attach to consistency, are revealed in two very popular tests of morality. Each takes the form of a question:

1. What if everyone did that?
2. How would you like it if I did that to you?

When we ask such questions—in the face of a bully, a liar, or a double-crosser—we are trying to get the person to see that he is acting unfairly, making an exception of himself, living by a set of rules that work only because others are not doing what he is doing. These basic moral challenges are designed to point out the inconsistency, and so the immorality, of that person's behavior.

Consider the first question: what if everyone did that? This question is really shorthand for the following test: *if disastrous results would occur if everyone did X, then X is immoral.* If everyone used the emergency lanes in traffic jams, then ambulances and fire trucks would often fail to provide needed help, leaving many to die. If everyone cheated on their taxes, society would crumble. If every candidate resorted to dirty tricks, then the entire political system would become corrupted. The test works easily and well for these cases.

But the test fails for other cases, and so it cannot serve as a reliable way to learn the morality of actions. Consider a common argument against homosexual sex: if everyone did that, disaster would soon follow, for the human race would quickly die out. Even if this were true, that wouldn't show that homosexual sex is immoral. Why not? Well, consider those who have decided to remain celibate—perhaps they are priests, or committed lifelong singles who believe that one shouldn't have sex without being married. What if everyone did *that*—in other words, refrained from having sex? The same results would follow. But that doesn't show that celibacy is immoral.

The real problem for this test, apart from the fact that it sometimes delivers mistaken verdicts, is that it makes the morality of an action depend on how it is described. Suppose the sexual relations of a gay couple were described as their having consensual, enjoyable sex. In that case, their actions would pass the test. But that undermines the test, because it shows that the test yields contradictory results. The very same action is said to be both morally wrong and morally acceptable, depending only on how it is described. Without any independent guidance on how to select one description over another, this test cannot do the job it was supposed to do—namely, identify which acts are immoral.

What about the other test, the one that asks, how would you like it if I did that to you? This is a direct application of the **golden rule**, which tells you to treat others as you would like to be treated. The golden rule is the classic test of morality. Clearly, it is meant to be a test of consistency. If you wouldn't want to be slandered or exploited, then don't do such things to others. If you do them anyway, you are acting inconsistently, hence unfairly, and therefore immorally.

Getting people to imagine what it would be like to switch places with their intended victims is often a very effective way to convey a moral message. That is why films and literature are often such powerful tools of moral education. But imaginatively filling someone else's shoes, and asking yourself whether you'd accept being treated in a certain way, is actually an unreliable test of morality. The golden rule cannot be correct.

Kant himself identified the basic reason for this. The golden rule makes morality depend on a person's desires. Most of us don't like to be hit. And so the golden rule forbids us from hitting others. Good. But what about masochists who enjoy being hit? The golden rule allows them to go around hitting others. That's bad. The morality of hitting people shouldn't depend on whether you like to take a beating every now and then.

Consider a related problem, that of the fanatic. Fanatics are principled people. It's just that their principles are ones that we find frightening and revolting. Some fanatics are so wedded to their cause, so strong-willed and self-disciplined, that they would accept the suffering that they want to impose on their victims, were the role of victim and persecutor reversed. True, few Nazis, for instance, would really accept a march to the gas chamber were they to discover their Jewish ancestry. Most Nazis, like most fanatics generally, are opportunists of bad faith, ones with very limited empathy and only a feeble ability to imagine themselves in someone else's place. If roles really were reversed, they'd much more likely beg for mercy and abandon their genocidal principles. But some would not. There are true believers out there who are willing to suffer any harm in the name of their chosen cause. The golden rule licenses their extremism because it makes the morality of an action depend entirely on what you want and what you are willing to put up with.

The golden rule also fails to give us guidance on **self-regarding actions** (i.e., those that concern only oneself). That's not a problem for most people these days, since it's now unusual to think that we owe moral duties to ourselves. But in Kant's time, self-regarding duties were widely endorsed, and many people still think, for instance, that there is something immoral about suicide or about letting one's talents go to waste, even if no one else is harmed in the process.

Because the golden rule sometimes gives the wrong answer to moral questions, it cannot be the ultimate test of morality. Something else must explain why it works, when it does. Kant thought he had the answer.

11.2 The Principle of Universalizability

Kant, like most of us, felt the appeal of the two tests just discussed. He agreed that common sense is deeply committed to the importance of fairness and consistency, something that these two tests were trying, but not quite succeeding, in capturing. His aim was to identify the ultimate principle of morality, one that would explain the attraction of the two tests while correcting for their shortcomings.

He thought he had found it in the following standard, the **principle of universalizability**:

> An act is morally acceptable if, and only if, its maxim is universalizable.

To understand what this means, we need to understand two things: what a **maxim** is, and what it is for a maxim to be **universalizable**.

A maxim is simply the principle of action you give yourself when you are about to do something. For instance, if you send a regular check to Oxfam, your maxim might be: contribute $50 per month to Oxfam to help reduce hunger. A maxim has two parts. It states what you are about to do, and why you are about to do it. You dictate your own maxims. These are the rules you live by.

Kant thought that every action has a maxim. Of course we don't always formulate these maxims clearly to ourselves prior to acting, but at some level, whenever we act, we intend to do something, and we have a reason for doing it. A maxim is nothing but a record of that intention and its underlying reason. Maxims are what we cite when we try to explain to others why we act as we do.

If we lack a maxim, then we aren't really acting at all. We could be moving our bodies, as we do when we sneeze or roll across the bed in our sleep. But the absence of a maxim in these cases shows that these are mere bodily movements, rather than genuine actions.

Kant thought that an action's rightness depends on its maxim. And this leads directly to a very important point. For Kant, the morality of our actions has nothing to do with results. It has everything to do with our intentions and reasons for action, those that are contained in the principles we live by. This is a clear break with consequentialism.

Indeed, we can imagine two people doing the same thing, but for different reasons. That means that they will have different maxims. And even if their actions bring about identical results, one of the actions may be right and the other wrong, since only one of the maxims may be morally acceptable. This is something that act consequentialists cannot accept.

It might be, for instance, that I keep my promises to you because I think it's right to do so. But I might instead keep my promises because I want you to like me so much that you leave your fortune to me in your will. Assume that these different reasons don't change the results of keeping my promises. Then the utilitarian thinks that each case of promise keeping is equally good. But since my maxim is different in these cases, Kant thinks that the morality of these actions might be different. It all depends, as we'll shortly see, on whether their maxims are universalizable.

Many people agree with Kant's view that the morality of our actions depends not on their results, but on our maxims. This supports our thought that those who set out to do evil are acting immorally, even if, through sheer chance, they manage to bring about good results. It also justifies the claim that people who live by noble principles are acting morally, even when some unforeseeable accident intervenes, and their action brings only bad results.

Kant had a deep reason (discussed in detail in the next chapter) for making the morality of an action depend on its maxim rather than its results: it is crucial that the morality of our actions depends entirely on what is within our control. We *can* control which maxims will govern our actions. We decide for ourselves what we intend to do and what reasons we endorse for doing it. Even in cases where my options are severely limited, as when a thug has a gun at my head, it is up to me to decide which choice to make.

By contrast, the results of our actions are often out of our hands. We can't always control them. And it is unfair to assign credit or blame for things we can't control. That is why we have an insanity defense. That is why we don't prosecute animals for the damage they sometimes cause. That is why we don't condemn infants for any harm they do.

So the morality of actions depends on their maxims. But how, precisely? Not every maxim is going to be a good one. We need a way to sort out the good maxims from the bad. That's where universalizability comes in.

How can we tell whether a maxim is universalizable? Here is a three-part test:

1. Formulate your maxim clearly—state what you intend to do, and why you intend to do it.
2. Imagine a world in which everyone supports and acts on your maxim.
3. Then ask: Can the goal of my action be achieved in such a world?

If the answer to this last question is *yes*, then the maxim is universalizable, and the action is morally acceptable. If the answer is *no*, then the maxim is not universalizable, and the action it calls for is immoral.

This should strike a familiar note. The test of a maxim's universalizability clearly echoes the rule consequentialist's test for optimific social rules (see the previous chapter) and the *what if everyone did that?* test discussed above. Indeed, Kant has us ask a version of that question in step 2 of this three-part test. But unlike these other tests, Kant doesn't ask about whether people would be much better off in the imagined world, or about whether disaster would strike there. Instead, he asks about whether we could achieve our goals in that world. But what is so important about that?

The importance, for Kant, is that this three-part test serves as the real way to determine whether we are being consistent and fair. If our maxim is universalizable, then we are pursuing actions for reasons that everyone could stand behind. We are not making exceptions of ourselves. Our goals are ones that everyone *could* support, even if, in the real world, some are dead set against them. We are asking whether our aims could be achieved if everyone shared them. If they can be, this shows that we are living by fair rules. Were we making an exception of ourselves, our maxims wouldn't be universalizable.

Consider the tax cheat again. The only reason he can get what he is aiming for (a lovely vacation) is because enough others are not adopting his maxim. The same goes for the careless driver who speeds down the emergency lane.

Kant sought to make this point with an example of his own. (I am embellishing a bit, but the essence of the example is Kant's.) Suppose that I am a compulsive gambler who is constantly in debt. One night I go to the tables to recoup my losses, only to dig myself further in the hole. The casino boss is having his men drop by tonight to collect. I can either pay them or have my kneecaps broken. I know which one I'd prefer.

The problem is, I don't have the money, the bank won't lend me any more, and I don't have anyone to turn to but you. Since you are aware of my reputation, I know that the only way to get the money is by lying to you. So I beg and plead and promise you, by all I hold dear, that I will repay you—even though I have no intention of doing so. I have just made what Kant calls a *lying promise*.

It seems clear that what I am about to do is immoral. And that is true even if, through a minor miracle, I then feel so much guilt that I repent of my ways, transform myself, and make the lie turn out for the best in the end. The morality of the action doesn't depend on its results, but on its maxim. And my maxim here is not universalizable. So my action is immoral, as Kant says, and as we believe.

Here's why. Suppose my maxim is: lie to a friend, in order to escape from being hurt. And suppose everyone acts on this maxim. They lie whenever they think that it is necessary to avoid some personal harm. In that situation, no one would trust the promises of others. And without that trust, people could not achieve the goals they are aiming for with their promises. In a world where no one believed the promises of others, I'd never be able to get money from you with my promise. And so the purpose of my promise would be defeated. And so my maxim is not universalizable. I am making an exception of myself, and am treating you unfairly. My action is therefore immoral.

11.3 Morality and Rationality

Kant claimed that when we act on a maxim that can't be universalized, we are contradicting ourselves. We are being inconsistent. We are assuming that it is acceptable to act in a certain way, even though our purposes could not be achieved if others acted in that very same way. When we make an exception of ourselves, we are acting as if we were more important than anyone else, and going on as if we were exempt from rules that others must obey. But we are not more important than others, and we are not exempt from these requirements.

It follows that when we behave immorally, we are reasoning badly. We are making mistaken assumptions—that we are more important than other people, that the rules applying to them do not apply to us. Those mistakes, and the inconsistent, contradictory reasoning behind them, show that *immoral conduct is irrational.*

That is a very striking claim, and one that most of us hope is true. We want to be able to convict rapists or terrorists of irrationality, of ignoring their strongest reasons. We want to be able to truthfully say that there were excellent reasons for them to do good and to avoid evil. Kant believed that we could do this.

But how could Kant be right? Consider the ruthless contract killer who knows precisely what he wants, knows exactly how to get it, and executes his plan without fail. Morality doesn't enter into his calculations. He knows that what he is doing is immoral, but that doesn't faze him. It seems that such a person is reasoning flawlessly. How can we defend the claim that he is irrational?

Let's call this the *Amoralist's Challenge.* The **amoralist** is someone who believes in right and wrong but doesn't care about morality at all. The amoralist has the same attitude to moral rules as I do to the rules of professional ice hockey—yes, they really exist, but they have absolutely no bearing on my life. Obedience to these rules is completely optional. If I am interested in playing the game, then I'll follow the rules. If not, then there is no reason to do so.

The Amoralist's Challenge supports this view in the following way:

1. People have a reason to do something only if doing it will get them what they care about.
2. Doing their moral duty sometimes fails to get people what they care about.
3. Therefore, people sometimes lack any reason to do their moral duty.

4. If people lack any reason to do their moral duty, then violating their moral duty can be perfectly rational.
5. Therefore, it can be perfectly rational for people to violate their moral duty.

The success of this argument would undermine the thought that morality, all by itself, supplies us with good reason to do as it says. It would also refute Kant's claim that immoral actions are always irrational.

Kant thought that you act irrationally when you act contrary to your strongest reasons. And he thought that when moral reasons apply to a given situation, they are always the strongest reasons. Moral reasons are more important than any other kind of consideration. If morality requires you to do something, then that is what you must do—even if you don't want to do it, even if you'll suffer for doing it, and even if the results of doing it cause only misery to others.

Kant admits that the ruthless contract killer, like so many other successful criminals, did, in a sense, reason perfectly well. He followed what Kant called **hypothetical imperatives**. Specifically, these imperatives (commands) are commands of reason. They command us to do whatever is needed in order to get what we care about. Hypothetical imperatives tell us how to achieve our goals. They require us, on pain of irrationality, to do certain things, but only because such actions will get us what we want.

For instance, if my goal is to lose twenty pounds (as it often is), then reason requires me to forgo that pint of luscious coffee ice cream. If I want to get that Wall Street job, then reason requires that I line up a good summer internship. Reason demands that I look both ways at a busy intersection if I want to remain alive. These rational commands apply to me because of what I care about. I am irrational if I disregard them or act in a way that violates them.

But what if I decide that I don't care about weight loss or the benefits that it can bring? What if I don't care about a Wall Street job? What if I want to die rather than live? In that case, I am no longer rationally required to pass on the ice cream, get the internship, or look both ways before crossing the street. These commands of reason are precarious. Their existence depends entirely on what I want. When my desires change, these rational requirements change or disappear.

Many people think that all rational requirements are like this—that they are all hypothetical imperatives. That's precisely what the first premise of the Amoralist's Challenge states: all of our reasons for action depend on what we care about.

Kant saw the implications of this argument very clearly, and knew that he had to challenge that first premise. In his jargon, what we need is to show how there can be such a thing as a **categorical imperative**. This is also a command of reason. But unlike hypothetical imperatives, categorical imperatives are rational requirements that do *not* depend on what we care about. They are requirements of reason that apply to everyone who possesses reason—in other words, everyone able to reflect on the wisdom of her actions, and able to use such reflections to guide her actions. Categorical imperatives command us to do things whether we want to or not, with the result that if we ignore or disobey them, we are acting contrary to reason (i.e., irrationally).

Kant thought that *all moral duties are categorical imperatives*. They apply to us just because we are rational beings. We must obey them even if we don't want to, and even if moral obedience gets us nothing that we care about.

One lesson Kant took from his thoughts about the golden rule is that the basic rules of morality do not depend on our desires. If they did, then moral rules would fail to apply to everyone, since our desires can differ from person to person. This would make morality too variable, and make it possible for people to escape from their moral duty just by changing what they want. Kant thought that he was defending common sense when he claimed that morality is, in this sense, universal—that everyone who can reason must obey its commands.

If moral duties really are categorical imperatives, then we act rationally when we act morally, and we act irrationally when we act immorally. Is that sort of view defensible? Can we really justify the claim that it is rational for everyone to act morally—even if we know that, for some people, moral conduct will only undermine their goals?

Kant thought he could do this. Consider his *Argument for the Irrationality of Immorality*:

1. If you are rational, then you are consistent.
2. If you are consistent, then you obey the principle of universalizability.
3. If you obey the principle of universalizability, then you act morally.
4. Therefore, if you are rational, then you act morally.
5. Therefore, if you act immorally, then you are irrational.

It does seem that rationality requires consistency, as the first premise asserts. And, as we have discussed, the principle of universalizability is a demand of consistency. So, while more could certainly be said about these first two premises, let us take them for granted here and focus on the third. This is the claim that obedience to the principle of universalizability guarantees that our conduct is moral.

Its location in this argument tells us that the principle of universalizability is a crucial element in Kant's reply to the Amoralist's Challenge. He needs to successfully defend the principle in order to secure the claim that rational people are moral people, and immoral people are irrational. Can he do it?

11.4 Assessing the Principle of Universalizability

Unfortunately, the principle of universalizability fails as a general test for the morality of our actions. Look at premise 3 of Kant's Argument for the Irrationality of Immorality. It says that a maxim's universalizability is a guarantee of an action's rightness. That is false. We can act on universalizable maxims and still do wrong.

The principle of universalizability seems to be a very attractive way of pointing out how unfairness and inconsistency lead to immorality. So, for instance, when a thief robs a bank in order to gain riches, Kant can show why the robbery is immoral. If everyone acted on the thief's maxim, there would be no money in the bank to steal, and the thief's goal could not be achieved. But what if the criminal had robbed the bank in order to cripple it and put it out of business? If everyone acted that way, then the thief's goal *could* be achieved. The principle of universalizability fails to condemn that robbery. And yet such an act is surely wrong.

Suppose that someone wants nothing more than to have a picture-perfect lawn. His basic maxim is to do whatever it takes to preserve the beauty of his grass. This would be strange, but that is no strike against his plans. The real thorn in this guy's side is the mail carrier, who always trots across the lovely yard on his way to delivering the mail. He has been warned, repeatedly, to use the sidewalk—but he never listens. So the homeowner decides to take matters into his own hands. The next time the mail carrier walks across the lawn, the homeowner pulls out a gun and kills him.

That's clearly the wrong thing to do. But this man's maxim is universalizable. It tells him to take whatever steps are necessary (including killing) in order to preserve the beauty of his lawn. What if everyone were to act upon this maxim? Could the homeowner's goal be met? Undoubtedly.

And so, if the principle of universalizability is true, this is no murder; it is justifiable killing. That has to cast serious doubt on the principle.

This unlikely example is just an instance of a general problem, one that we have seen before. Recall the case of the fanatic that came up when we were discussing the *what if everyone did that?* test. The goals of fanatics are ones that can often be met in a world in which everyone shares their aims. Fanatics (such as the lawn fanatic) need not make exceptions of themselves. The murderous aims of any number of groups could easily be achieved in a world in which everyone supported them. Thus fanatics can be consistent in the relevant sense: their guiding principles could be fulfilled if everyone else were to adopt them.

I think this shows that the principle of universalizability fails to give us an adequate test of fairness, for we can follow its advice while still singling out individuals or groups for discriminatory treatment. There can be consistent Nazis, after all. It doesn't follow that their policies are fair or morally acceptable.

11.5 Integrity

While utilitarians think of benevolence (the steady commitment to do good for others) as the central moral virtue, Kant touts integrity. Having integrity is living in harmony with the principles you believe in. It is the virtue of consistency. Integrity requires that you resist making an exception of yourself. It demands that you follow your principles even when doing so comes at a real cost. Kant is surely right that there is something admirable about integrity.

But integrity is not the only moral virtue, and it isn't even the most important one. The example of the fanatic shows this. We may be absolutely dedicated to our principles, but if those principles are deeply flawed, it would be better, morally speaking, for us to have less integrity. That's surely what we want of the Nazi commandant or the dedicated terrorist. It would be better were they less principled people. We want them to be more flexible, and more open to the possibility that their guiding ideals are mistaken. When Huck Finn beats himself up for continuing to hide Jim, the escaped slave who accompanies him down the Mississippi, we applaud Huck's lack of integrity. A Huck with greater integrity is also one who would betray Jim's location. We want Huck to be less than fully conscientious, since that will mean Jim's freedom.

Integrity is worthy of our admiration only when it is tied to morally legitimate principles. The problem, as we have seen, is that people of integrity may still be doing wrong. Refusing to make an exception of myself is no guarantee that my principles are morally acceptable. It's not that consistency is worthless. But it fails as a general test for the morality of the principles we live by.

11.6 Kant on Absolute Moral Duties

Kant thought that certain sorts of actions are never permitted. Lying is one of them. In a much-discussed case, that of the inquiring murderer, Kant has us imagine a man bent on killing. This man knocks at your door and asks if you know the location of his intended victim. You do. Should you reveal it? If you do, your information is almost certainly going to lead to murder.

Kant thought you had two decent choices. Ideally, you'd just say nothing. That wouldn't help the murderer, and it wouldn't involve lying. But what if you have to say something? In that case, you have to tell the truth—because you must never lie, under any circumstances.

I think that this is the wrong answer, and the interesting thing is that Kant's own theory does not require him to give it. Kant was so convinced that lying was wrong that he misapplied his own theory.

Kant never provided an argument for the claim that the moral rules prohibiting such things as lying and killing are **absolute** (i.e., never permissibly broken). The closest he came to supplying such an argument was in his belief that moral considerations are more important than anything else. In any conflict between moral duty and other demands—say, those of the law, self-interest, or tradition—morality wins.

Still, it doesn't follow that moral duties are absolute, for even if they always outweigh other kinds of considerations, moral duties might conflict *with other moral duties*. And if they do, they can't all be absolute. Some of them must give way to others.

And can't moral duties conflict with one another? It seems, for instance, that there is a duty to avoid hurting people's feelings, a duty not to start a panic, and a duty to protect innocent people from dangerous attackers. It also seems that fulfilling each of these duties will sometimes require us to lie, and that there is a moral duty not to do so. Perhaps none of these is really a moral duty. Or perhaps, implausibly, we'd never need to lie in order to respect these duties. But it's much more likely that these are real duties, and that they really can conflict with one another. And if that is so, then these duties cannot all be absolute.

This does not spell disaster for Kant. He does not need to defend the existence of absolute moral duties. His philosophy can, for instance, justify lying to the inquiring murderer. Kant's hatred of lying made him overlook a crucial element of his own view—namely, that the morality of action depends on one's maxim. He just assumed that anyone who lied would be operating with a maxim like this: *tell a lie so as to gain some benefit.* That maxim is not universalizable. In a world in which everyone did this, no one could trust the words of others, and people would be unable to obtain any of the goals they were trying to achieve through lying.

But Kant's maxim is not the only one you could have in such a situation. A maxim is a principle that you give yourself. No one forces it on you. When confronted with a potential killer, I might adopt this maxim: *say whatever I need to say in order to prevent the murder of an innocent person.* That maxim is universalizable. The goal I am aiming for—to save an innocent person's life—could be achieved if everyone acted this way.

For Kant, we can't determine whether an act is right or wrong until we know its maxim. And for any given action, there are countless maxims that might support it. After all, we make up our own maxims, and mine may be very different from yours. It follows that there is only one way for Kant to absolutely ban a type of action. And that is to be sure in advance that, of all the hundreds or thousands of maxims that might support an action, *none* of them is universalizable. It is hard to see how we could ever know that.

As a result, it is much harder than Kant thought to defend the existence of absolute moral duties. And in this particular case, that is all to the good, since it opens up the possibility that it is sometimes acceptable to lie—for instance, to the inquiring murderer. Of course, if Kant is right, then we would have to have a universalizable maxim that permits this. But nothing Kant ever said should make us think that this is impossible. Contrary to Kant's personal view, we don't have to regard all (or perhaps any) moral duties as absolute.

11.7 Discussion Questions

1. Explain the difference between the golden rule and the *what if everyone did that?* test. What problems arise for each? Do you think that they can be remedied?
2. What is a maxim, and what does it mean for a maxim to be *universalizable*? Why does the principle of universalizability fail to be a good test of the morality of our actions?

3. According to Kant, it is always irrational to act immorally. What reasons does he give for thinking this? Do you agree with him?
4. What is the difference between hypothetical and categorical imperatives? Why did Kant think that morality consists of categorical imperatives?
5. Why does the existence of fanatics pose a challenge to Kant's moral theory? How do you think that the Kantian should respond to this challenge?
6. Is integrity always a virtue? Why or why not?
7. Explain how one would show that a moral duty is absolute according to Kant's moral theory.

CHAPTER 12

.... ❧ ....

The Kantian Perspective
Autonomy, Free Will, and Respect

I s there anything wrong with slavery?

This probably sounds like an idiotic question. *Of course* slavery is wrong. So let me rephrase my question. Is there anything wrong, *in and of itself*, with enslaving other people?

In practice, slavery has always created much more harm than good. But what if that were not the case? What if the members of a slave society—slaves as well as masters—were, on the whole, wealthier, better educated, healthier, and more satisfied with their lives than most members of a free society? And what if the abolition of slavery was sure to undercut these greater benefits? In those circumstances, would slavery still be wrong?

This thought experiment was put to readers by an important twentieth-century moral philosopher, Richard Hare. In his article "What Is Wrong with Slavery,"[1] Hare defended the utilitarian view that denied that slavery is intrinsically wrong. Everything depends on the actual results of a slave system; in the imagined example, Hare had to admit that the slave society, since it created greater overall benefits, was the morally superior option. This despite the fact that Hare was once a slave himself. As a British soldier in World War II, he was captured by Japanese forces and interned in a camp that enslaved its inmates.

Hare emphasized that his views did not permit any slave system as actually practiced. He presented the story as a way to show that there is nothing wrong, in itself, with slavery. The utilitarian says that the morality

---

1. *Philosophy and Public Affairs* 8 (1979): 103–121.

of slavery, like that of any other practice, depends entirely on its results. In the picture Hare paints, slavery can be morally acceptable.

You might be outraged at such a view, convinced that slavery can never be morally right, because it grossly violates people's autonomy. Slavery allows people to be treated as mere things—as objects without any rights, of no intrinsic importance.

This is precisely the Kantian objection to slavery. Morality requires us always to treat human beings with the dignity they deserve. Slavery is inherently disrespectful. No one deserves such treatment. That is what explains why slavery is wrong.

Intuitively, this makes good sense. But it requires a bit of work to unpack it. We need to better understand why treating people as they deserve is so important, and what it means, specifically, to say that we deserve dignity and respect.

12.1 The Principle of Humanity

In the course of his work, Kant identified a number of different candidates for the role of ultimate moral principle. Although the principle of universalizability clearly emphasizes the moral importance of fairness, another of Kant's formulations directs our attention to the respect and dignity that serve as the basis of morality. This formulation is widely known as the **principle of humanity**:

> Always treat a human being (yourself included) as an end, and never as a mere means.

To understand this principle, we need to get clear about three things: humanity, ends, and means.

When Kant spoke of *humanity*, he wasn't thinking necessarily of *Homo sapiens*. Rather, he was referring to all rational and autonomous beings, no matter their species. Perhaps there are aliens, or some nonhuman animals, who are rational and autonomous. If so, then they count as human beings for purposes of Kant's principle.

Treating someone *as an end* is treating her with the respect she deserves. Treating someone *as a means* is dealing with her so that she helps you achieve one of your goals. This may be perfectly okay. I do this, for instance, when I hire a plumber to fix a broken water pipe in my kitchen. In an innocent sense, I am using him—he is needed to get me what I want (a functioning sink, in this case). Yet if I greet him at the door, give him any help he asks for, and then pay him as he leaves, I am also treating him with respect, and so, in Kantian terms, I am also treating him as an end.

But what if, while the plumber is checking the leak, I remove a wrench from his tool kit and whack him over the head with it? He's out cold—excellent. I then snugly fit his head into the space where the pipe has corroded, thus plugging the leak. While he's unconscious, I rush off to the hardware store and buy a cheap bit of PVC pipe. The plumber wakes up just as I am returning from the store. I scold him for falling asleep on the job and usher him out the door with a curt good riddance. Then I proceed to fix the leak myself, saving a hefty fee.

What has happened in this ridiculous scenario is that I've used the plumber literally as a thing, as if he were a piece of pipe. He might as well have been an inanimate object. I failed to treat him in a way that recognized any of his distinctively human features. That's why I have treated him as a *mere means*.

Although it often happens that people do treat one another both as an end and as a means, one can't treat people both as an end and as a *mere* means. Treating someone as an end implies a degree of respect that is absent when treating someone as a mere means.

Most of us think that there is something about humanity that lends us dignity and makes us worthy of respect. Most of us also think that human beings are worthy of greater respect than anything else in creation. Humans are more important than monkeys or sharks or daffodils or amoebas. Is this a defensible position, or is it just a self-interested prejudice?

Kant had an answer. He claimed that we are each rational and autonomous, and that these traits are what justify our special moral status. These two powers make us worthy of respect. Being rational, as we have seen, involves using our reason to tell us how to achieve our goals and to determine whether we can pursue them in a morally acceptable way. It takes a lot of brainpower to be able to formulate your goals, to imagine a world where everyone pursues them as you do, and then to ask about the consistency of your actions. Humans are the only beings on earth who can engage in such complex reasoning.

Being autonomous literally means being a self-legislator. Autonomous people are those who decide for themselves which principles are going to govern their life. Specifically, being autonomous is a matter of making free choices that determine how you behave. So long as your free choices are dictating your actions, you are autonomous. You are an autonomous person. You possess the ultimate responsibility for the choices you make, the goals you aim for, and the manner in which you pursue them. You are not a slave to your passions; you can resist temptation, check your animal urges, and decide for yourself whether to indulge them. You are not forced to act as you do, but are free to choose your own path.

Kant thought that our rationality and autonomy made each of us literally priceless. Despite the work of actuaries, and juries in wrongful death suits, you can't really put a dollar figure on a human life. The assumption that we are infinitely valuable explains the agony we feel at the death of a loved one. If we had to choose between the destruction of the most beautiful art object in the world and the killing of a human being, we should choose the former. No matter how valuable the object, the value of a human life exceeds it by an infinite amount.

12.2 The Importance of Rationality and Autonomy

Kant argues that rationality and autonomy support the dignity of each human being, and that everyone is owed a level of respect because of these traits. This makes excellent sense of a number of deeply held moral beliefs. Here are the most important of them.

1. It explains, in the first place, the immorality of a fanatic's actions. Such people don't regard human life as infinitely precious, but rather treat their despised opponents as mere obstacles to the achievement of their goals. The principle of humanity forbids such behavior, even when it is consistently undertaken, and thus allows us to address the most severe problem facing the principle of universalizability.

2. The importance of autonomy explains why slavery and rape are always immoral. Slavery treats the oppressed without regard for their own goals and hopes. Rape is treating another human being solely as a source of one's own gratification, as if the victim had no legitimate say in the matter. These are the most extreme examples of duress and coercion. They are immoral because of their complete denial of the victim's autonomy. As such, these crimes are perhaps the clearest cases of treating other people as mere means.

3. The principle of humanity easily explains our outrage at paternalism. To be paternalistic is to assume the rights and privileges of a parent—toward another adult. Paternalism has us limit the liberty of others, for their own good, against their will. It is treating autonomous individuals as children, as if we, and not they, were best suited to making the crucial decisions of their lives.

It is paternalistic, for instance, if a roommate sells your TV set because he is worried about your spending too much time watching *Seinfeld* reruns and too little time on your homework. Or imagine a classmate who thinks that your boyfriend is bad for you, and so writes him a nasty note and forges your signature, hoping that he'll break off your relationship. Anyone who has experienced paternalistic treatment knows how infuriating it can be. And the reason is simple: we are autonomous and rational, and the ability to create our own life plan entitles us to do so. We ought to be free to make a life for ourselves, even if we sometimes make a mess of things.

4. Our autonomy is what justifies the attitude of never abandoning hope in people. The chances that a very hard-hearted man will change his ways may be very small, but the probability never reduces to zero. No matter how badly he was raised, or how badly he has lived his life, he is still autonomous, and so can always choose to better himself. It is usually naïve to expect such a transformation. Changing your character and habits is hardly easy. But the possibility of redemption is always there, and that is only because we are free to set our own course in life.

5. Many people believe in universal human rights. These are moral rights that protect human beings from certain kinds of treatment and entitle each of us to a minimum of respect, just because we are human. Kant can explain why we have such rights. We have them because of our rationality and autonomy. These two traits are the basis for living a meaningful life. If you doubt this, just imagine a life without them. It is a life fit for an insect, or a plant. What endows our life with preciousness is our ability to reason and choose for ourselves how we are going to live it. Every person is rational and autonomous to some degree, and every person needs these powers protected in order to have the sorts of experiences, engage in the kinds of activities, and support the sorts of relationships that make life worth living. Human rights protect these powers at a very fundamental level.

6. Our autonomy is what explains our practices of holding one another accountable for our deeds and misdeeds. Because we are not robots, but rather free and rational human beings, we are morally responsible for our choices and actions. We are fit for praise and blame, and that is because our conduct is up to us. We don't blame sharks or falcons for killing their prey; neither do we condemn a wilted orchid or a nasty-smelling ginkgo tree. Plants and animals deserve neither moral credit nor blame, and this is because their lives are not autonomous ones.

7. Relatedly, most people believe that punishment, rather than conditioning, is the appropriate response to serious wrongdoers. When dogs "misbehave," we don't try to reason with them. We try to condition them to change their behavior through a set of rewards and punishments. They don't deserve to be punished when they break our rules, and that is because they lack the power to change their behavior by reasoning about it. By contrast, humans do sometimes deserve to be punished, precisely because they could have chosen to act well, but decided to act badly instead. People also deserve not to be manipulated into becoming obedient citizens. If we want criminals to behave differently, we must still respect their autonomy. The importance of autonomy explains why it is so objectionable to brainwash people, or to drug or torture them into doing what we want.

12.3 The Problem of Free Will

The seven features we've just reviewed reveal the deep importance we attach to autonomy. And as we've already seen, and will continue to note below, Kant's principle of humanity is intended to express this commitment to autonomy as the very heart of morality. But there is a worry, and I bet you've already thought of it: what if we aren't autonomous after all?

Recall that autonomy requires two things. First, it requires an ability to make free choices—philosophers call this **free will**. To have a will that is free is to be capable of making decisions that are genuinely your own, decisions that you author, ones that you originate and are responsible for. Second, autonomy requires that those free choices control your actions. You are autonomous just when your free will determines your behavior.

Given this analysis, it follows that there are two ways to fail to be autonomous. First, our choices may not govern our actions: there is some disconnect between what we decide to do and what we actually do. That's usually bad, and sometimes really terrible, but such cases are not the ones I'll focus on here. Instead, I'm concerned with the second way that our autonomy can be compromised. This occurs when our choices are themselves unfree. What if we don't have free will in the first place?

To get a sense of the concern, suppose that your choices actually do control your actions. But suppose that those choices are not free—you've been brainwashed, say, and are effectively programmed to choose as you do. This would be bad. Really bad. Now suppose that this isn't just a one-off episode in your life, but a fact about *all* of your choices. And all of mine. And all of everyone's. Suppose, in other words, that no one has free will. Because free will is a necessary condition of autonomy, it would follow that no one is autonomous. That would mean that Kant's ethical system would no longer have any relevance to our lives, since we would not be autonomous.

I do believe that I have free will. And so do you. We all do. When you reflect and ask whether, for instance, you could choose to stop reading this right now, the answer seems clear—of course you can. Whether you do so is *up to you*—it's your choice, not just in the sense that you are entitled to make that decision, but also in the sense, relevant here, that it's entirely within your control to choose to keep reading or to stop.

But our confidence in such freedom may be misplaced. The *Argument Against Free Will* explains why:

1. Either our choices are necessitated or they are not.
2. If they are necessitated, then we do not control them, and so we lack free will.
3. If they are not necessitated, then they are random, and so we lack free will.
4. Therefore, we lack free will.

Suppose our choices are necessitated. In other words, imagine that every choice we make is the only one we could have made in the circumstances. But how could that be? After all, don't you at this very moment have a choice about whether to put this book down or to continue reading? The choice is up to you. While we may not always be free to *act* in the ways we want—external obstacles may stand in our way—we are free to *choose* how we respond to the circumstances of our life.

But consider this: is anything influencing your choice? Of course. You choose to continue reading at least partly because you want to, because you believe you are able to, because you have no more appealing options, and because no one is forcing you to choose something else. *Given* all of these influences (and others, no doubt), it seems that you were bound to choose as you did.

True, it's not as if you are fated to keep reading *no matter what*. Rather, the idea is that you are destined to keep reading given your circumstances and your mindset (your beliefs, desires, aims, etc.).

But the causes of your choice (your beliefs, desires, etc.) are also caused. These further causes don't spring up from nothing. You chose to keep reading partly because you wanted to. And you wanted to keep reading because (perhaps) you have been assigned this chapter and want to do well in the course you are taking. But your desire to do well in the course also has an explanation. It was caused by other desires and beliefs of yours, which, in turn, were caused by other factors, and so on, and so on. Ultimately, our choices can be traced to causes over which we lack control—causes such as our genetic inheritance, our upbringing, and a variety of social influences. If we choose as we do because of factors that ultimately are out of our control, then our choices are ultimately out of our control. And so, if our choices are necessitated to be what they are, then we are not autonomous. That is what premise 2 says.

Now assume that our choices are *not* necessitated. Suppose that nothing determined that you would choose to continue reading, for instance. You just chose to do so. If that were the case, wouldn't that show that you chose freely?

No. If nothing causes us to choose as we do, then our choices seem completely random. Randomness undermines control, and hence undercuts free will.

Suppose I'm walking down the hall and see someone thrust out her arm and hit a bystander. Did she choose to hit him? Yes. Why? No reason. No cause. No explanation. It was just one of those things, completely out of the blue, unaccountable. But if that is really so—if nothing at all is causing her choice—then it seems that she isn't in command of her choices. They are something that happen to her, a passing fit of some sort, rather than something we can credit or blame her for. Her choices are out of her control. And that is what premise 3 says.

Thus, either way we go—whether our choices are necessitated or not—it seems that we lack autonomy. *If* that is so, then the Kantian basis of our dignity, and the source of our duty to respect others, is undermined.

Of course many philosophers (and almost all non-philosophers) think that something is wrong with this argument. Its logic is watertight, so if there is an error, it must be in one of the three premises. Premise 1 is pretty clearly true. So the problem, if there is one, must lie in premise 2 or 3. Philosophers who think that we really do have free will and autonomy have split on which premise to attack. Their work has been fruitful. (It has certainly multiplied—the issues of freedom and determinism nowadays form an entire subfield within philosophy.) So perhaps the pessimistic conclusion of this argument is false. But only a great deal more philosophy could show it so.

12.4   Four Problems with the Principle of Humanity

Despite its many attractions, the principle of humanity, with its emphasis on rationality and autonomy, is not trouble-free. In addition to the worry we've just discussed—that we may lack free will, and so not be autonomous after all—there are four especially serious concerns about the principle:

1. The notion of treating someone as an end is vague, and so the principle is difficult to apply.
2. The principle fails to give us good advice about how to determine what people deserve.
3. The principle assumes that the morality of our actions depends only on what we can autonomously control, but the existence of **moral luck** calls this into question.
4. The principle cannot explain why those who lack rationality and autonomy are deserving of respect.

Let's consider each of these problems in turn.

Vagueness

Unlike the three-step process used to apply the principle of universalizability, there is no straightforward test that tells us how to apply the principle of humanity. It tells us to treat humanity as an end—in other words, with the respect that people deserve. It's sometimes crystal clear whether the principle is being honored. No one doubts, for instance, that the principle is violated by treating a plumber as a piece of pipe or by shooting a trespasser for trampling the lawn. But the vagueness of the notion of treating someone as an end often makes it difficult to know whether our actions are morally acceptable. Do we respect celebrities by telling the truth about their private lives—even when this is damaging to their reputations? Is it disrespectful to enemy soldiers to set land mines at our borders? Are we failing to give due respect to famine victims if we spend money on a new computer rather than donating it to an aid agency?

We can't know the answer to these questions without a better understanding of what it is to treat someone as an end. Without a more precise test of when we are respecting others and treating them as they deserve (i.e., as their rationality and autonomy demand), the principle of humanity fails to give us the guidance that we expect from an ultimate moral principle.

Determining Just Deserts

The second concern is about whether it is always appropriate to give people what they deserve. Kant certainly thought so. Recall his thinking, from the last chapter, about the prime importance of doing justice. Doing justice involves giving people their just deserts—even if this is not going to benefit anyone.

Sometimes this seems clearly right. A murderer ought to be punished, even if a governor's pardon will make more people happier. An employee ought to get paid for her work, even if her employer could do more good by giving her salary to charity. But there are also problems, as we'll see.

Kant has a partial reply to the problem of vagueness, mentioned just above. He offers us a test for what *wrongdoers* deserve. That isn't the whole story, of course, since we also want to know how to apply the principle of humanity in cases where blame and punishment are not an issue. But even in contexts of condemnation, Kant's test—the famous **lex talionis**, or eye-for-an-eye principle—is fraught with difficulties. And so we are left with problems. In some cases, we don't know how to apply the principle of humanity, because it is unclear what treating a person as an end really amounts to. In other cases, it *is* clear—but also pretty clearly mistaken.

Lex talionis (the law of retaliation) tells us to treat criminals as they have treated their victims. Kant claimed that such punishment treats a criminal as an end, and thus with the respect he deserves, because it treats him as a rational and autonomous person. Punishment is justified, for Kant, only if criminals are autonomous, and so able to freely choose their maxims. Those who are insane, for instance, are not fit for punishment. Punishment also presupposes that criminals are rational, in the sense of trying to act on principles that they can consistently intend everyone else to act on. A criminal's rationality permits us to turn his principles back on him, and do to him what he did to his victim. That is just what lex talionis requires.

Punishment that is administered as lex advises can be deeply satisfying. It can get criminals to see things from their victims' perspective, and so open their eyes to the true nature of the damage they have done. Further, punishment in line with lex seems perfectly just, since the criminal can't rightly complain of being mistreated. As Kant says, we would laugh at a criminal who protested against a punishment that harmed him exactly as he harmed his victim. Lastly, in the difficult matter of determining how to punish criminals, lex often gives us concrete, practical advice. What to do with a murderer, for instance? Kant counsels us to avoid the "serpent-windings" of utilitarianism and banish all thoughts of whether the death penalty is going to reduce the murder rate. A murderer deserves to die—lex says so. Therefore, morality requires his execution.

These attractions account for lex's broad appeal. Despite the widespread enthusiasm, however, lex talionis is fatally flawed. Three reasons explain its failure.

First, lex cannot explain why criminals who intentionally hurt their victims should be punished more than those who accidentally cause the same harm. Lex tells us to set the punishment by reference to the suffering of the victim. But victims can suffer the same harm, whether the perpetrator has carefully planned to cause it or has caused it by accident. If I am recklessly practicing archery in my backyard and unintentionally skewer my neighbor, I deserve less punishment than a cold-blooded murderer. Or so we think. Lex does not allow for that, since the victims in both cases have suffered the same harm.

We could say that what criminals deserve is determined not only by the harm they have done, but also by how blameworthy they are in bringing it about. So a hired killer should be punished more than a reckless archer, because the murderer displays a kind of moral corruption that the archer lacks. This does give us the right answer—the callous killer *should* be punished more. But it comes at the cost of abandoning lex. That's because we are no longer required to treat the criminal as he treated his victim. If an assassin deserves to be executed, then those who kill, but are less guilty than an assassin, should receive a lighter sentence than death. That undermines the letter and spirit of lex talionis, since these less-guilty killers will not be harmed just as they have harmed their victims. And it also removes one of the great virtues of lex talionis—that of offering precise guidance on how much criminals should be punished.

Second, lex cannot tell us what many criminals deserve. This is most obvious in crimes that lack victims. Suppose an assassin attempts (but fails) to kill his victim, and the victim never discovers this. No harm, no foul? Suppose that someone leaves a bar well and truly drunk, and then manages to drive home without hurting anyone. Still, she deserves to be punished, but since there is no victim, lex offers no basis for punishment. Other crimes may have victims, and yet lex offers no advice about their punishment. What to do with a hijacker or a counterfeiter? A kidnapper? Someone who transports stolen mattresses across state lines? The idea of treating these people just as they've treated their victims makes little sense.

Third, the guidance that lex provides, when it does prescribe a punishment, is sometimes deeply immoral. It's a sad truth: any horror you can imagine people doing to one another has probably already been done. People have burned whole families as they slept in their homes, have severed their limbs, tossed acid in their faces, and thrown handcuffed victims out of airplanes and helicopters. Does morality really require that we do these things to the criminals who committed such deeds? We don't want official torturers and arsonists on the state payroll. Legal punishment is the state's business, and we insist that the state meet certain minimum moral standards. A state that rapes its rapists is failing, miserably.

These three problems show that lex cannot be the whole story about justice, because lex sometimes fails to give advice when it is needed, and sometimes gives bad advice. That means that when lex gets it right, it does so because its recommendations agree with those given by some more basic principle of justice. Homework: discover that basic principle.

In any event, most of us think that giving people the punishment they deserve sometimes has to take a backseat to other moral concerns. Our practice of allowing for parole, plea bargains, executive clemency, pardons, and suspended sentences attests to that. Each of these can be seen as an exercise in mercy—in treating people more kindly than they deserve. And mercy is a virtue. Kant's position requires that we never indulge in merciful treatment of criminals.

Suppose that maintaining a system of punishment required so much money that we had to drastically sacrifice funds for schooling, for health programs, and for national defense. In that case, perhaps we should punish criminals a bit less than they deserve, so as to save resources to meet these other social needs.

Suppose that punishing criminals as they deserve were to *increase* the crime rate rather than reduce it. Most would think this an excellent reason to lighten punishments.

Justice is very important. But these considerations should make us wonder whether Kant was right to think that justice must always be done, no matter its costs.

Moral Luck

Perhaps there is a flaw in the Argument Against Free Will that we considered earlier. I hope so. Let's indulge this hope for now and assume that we really do possess free will, and so *are* genuinely autonomous. Still, there are reasons to doubt that the morality of actions really depends on our autonomous choice.

Kant believes that we are rightly praised or blamed only for what we can control. That's why autonomy is so important. Autonomy *is* control—over our choices, and over our actions. Yet factors outside of our control apparently affect the morality of our conduct. If that is true, then autonomy may not play the central role in morality that Kant thinks it does.

The results of our actions are not fully within our control. And therefore they are morally irrelevant, from Kant's point of view. That is one of the main reasons that he so strongly opposes utilitarianism. And yet the results of our actions often *do* seem to make a moral difference.

I sometimes find myself effectively driving on autopilot. I've drifted over into the oncoming lane; I've failed to see a pedestrian at a crosswalk; I've missed a passing car in my side mirror. In each case it was pure luck that my inattention didn't cause a (possibly fatal) accident. Many people are not so lucky. When their negligence results in someone's death, they are blamed far more than I have ever been. Yet they may be no worse a driver (or a person) than I am.

This is an example of moral luck—a case in which the morality of an action or a decision depends on factors outside of our control. If Kant is right, moral luck cannot exist. And he may be right. But if he is, then we have to revise our moral views in each of these cases, and many others. A drag race down country lanes is fondly remembered—unless it leads to a paralyzing accident. The risky investment is harshly condemned if it forces bankruptcy, but celebrated if it establishes a family fortune. A revolutionary is a hero if his side wins, a despised traitor if it doesn't.

There is a tension at the heart of our moral thinking. We don't blame babies for any harm they cause. Adults who have been hypnotized or those who have been slipped an LSD tab are also immune from blame. Kant explained this perfectly: such people lack autonomy. They aren't in full control of their actions. But if Kant is right, and control is essential for moral responsibility, then we must abandon all of the moral judgments recorded in the previous paragraphs. It isn't an easy choice to make.

The Scope of the Moral Community

The final concern has to do with membership in the moral community. Kant's emphasis on rationality and autonomy forces us to draw the lines of this community very narrowly. We are in. Infants aren't. Those with severe mental illness or intellectual disability are out. So too are all nonhuman animals, and all plants and ecosystems. They all lack rationality and autonomy. By Kant's lights, they therefore have no intrinsic moral importance.

We owe them no moral concern, and so, it seems, we can treat them any way we want.

We can express this worry in the *Argument Against Animals*:

1. If the principle of humanity is true, then animals have no rights.
2. If animals have no rights, then it is morally acceptable to torture them.
3. Therefore, if the principle of humanity is true, then it is morally acceptable to torture animals.
4. It isn't.
5. Therefore, the principle of humanity is false.

Though this argument focuses on nonhuman animals, we could easily amend it to apply to infants, those with severe dementia, and so on. Kant's views exclude all of them from the moral community. But since Kant himself focused only on the case of animals, let's follow his lead. We can discuss the other cases as needed.

Kant thought that it is wrong to torture or otherwise mistreat animals. So he accepts the fourth premise of the argument. He also accepts its first premise. He thought that rights require autonomy, that animals lack it, and that they therefore lack rights. As he saw it, the second premise is the one that has to go.

Kant offered two arguments for rejecting the second premise. Both of them fail.

He first claimed that harming animals will harden our hearts, and so make it likely that we will mistreat our fellow human beings. Since that really would be immoral, we must not harm animals.

Kant's predictions about how we might be led to harm our fellow human beings are quite shaky. Most of us are easily able to make distinctions in our treatment of members of different groups. Abusive bosses usually treat their superiors with respect. Ruthless prison guards can be loving parents. Doctors who are condescending to their patients and nurses are often quite decent to their fellow doctors. So mistreating one group needn't lead to mistreating others.

Further, if Kant is right, we humans really do possess infinitely greater moral importance than animals. Anyone who takes that message to heart would resist harming his fellow humans—even if he felt comfortable hurting animals.

Kant faces a problem even if his predictions are right. For this argument is a classic instance of slippery slope reasoning, which depends for its plausibility on the truth of consequentialism.[2] Kant forbids us from mistreating animals just because doing so will have terrible results (it will lead to the mistreatment of humans). But as we have seen, Kant bases his theory on the view that results are irrelevant to the morality of actions. So this reply will not do.

He has a second. I own a desk. It obviously isn't rational or autonomous. And yet no matter how much someone wanted to take a hammer to it, it would be wrong to do so. Not because the vandal would be wronging the desk, but because he would be wronging *me*. The desk has no rights. But I do. And these must be honored. And so, even though my cat Oscar, for instance, has no rights, it would be immoral to hurt him, since in doing so, my rights (as his owner) would be violated.

There are two basic difficulties with this view. First, it offers no moral protections to wild animals. And second, domesticated animals will have no moral protection against their owners. If I decided to destroy my desk, just for the fun of it, I'd be doing nothing wrong. And since the Kantian view sees animals as morally on a par with my possessions, it can't explain why it would be wrong of me to destroy my animals simply because I wanted to.

That isn't the only bad news. Remember, this problem applies not only to animals but also to all human beings who lack rationality and autonomy. True, most of them (infants, the temporarily comatose, etc.) are loved by others. And so Kant might be able to claim that *our* rights (i.e., the rights of those who love such human beings) would be violated if anyone were to harm them. But what of the most piteous of humanity—the unloved, abandoned human beings who lack autonomy? Kant's theory gives them the same status as an unowned desk or animal. They are disposable and may be treated as we like. Kant thus excludes the most vulnerable among us from membership in the moral community.

12.5 The Good Will and Moral Worth

Kant's insistence on the importance of rationality and autonomy led him to a view of intrinsic value that is very different from that of consequentialists. The structure of consequentialist thought is simple. Identify what is worth pursuing for its own sake; your moral duty is to maximize this value. Kant rejected this picture in every way.

---

2. See the discussion "Slippery Slope Arguments" in chapter 9.

Kant rejected the idea that happiness (or well-being in any form) is the ultimate value. Happiness has *no* value, he said, if it comes as a result of wrongdoing. (The enjoyment that a sadistic criminal brings to his task does not add value to his crime, but only makes it worse.) And the same goes for other possible values. Wealth can be misused; so can power, and health, and understanding, and bravery. None of these is always valuable. There is only one thing that is valuable, no matter what—only one thing whose presence in any situation is bound to add value to it. That one thing is the **good will**.

The good will has two parts. It is the ability to reliably know what your duty is, and a steady commitment to doing your duty for its own sake. The good will works in a familiar way: we see what we are morally required to do, and we do it for that very reason. No calculations of costs and benefits, no worries about what impression we might be making, what enemies we might be gaining, what riches might be in store for us. Once we understand where our duty lies, we do it straightaway.

Kant had some very interesting ideas about how the good will worked. Two of these ideas are especially important. He thought, first, that acting from the good will is the only way that actions can be truly praiseworthy. (Kant referred to such actions as those that possessed **moral worth**.) He also thought that acting from such a motive is entirely an exercise of reason.

Consider the first point. Kant has us imagine two shopkeepers, each of whom does his duty by giving his customers the correct change. But the first does this only because he fears that if he were to cheat them, word would get out and he would lose business in the long run. He does his duty, but there is nothing morally worthy about his behavior.

The second store owner does the very same thing, but for completely different reasons. He treats his customers fairly because he thinks that cheating people is wrong, and he is committed to living up to the highest moral standards. This motivation earns the second shopkeeper the greatest praise. According to Kant, his actions and character display a worth that (like the value of humanity) is literally priceless. He is not for sale; he cannot be bought.

Kant's second point, about the importance of reason in motivating worthy conduct, is fairly complex. He thought that reason, operating alone and in the absence of any desires or emotions, could do double duty. It could reveal your moral duty, and it could motivate you to obey it.

To have a good will is, first of all, to know where your duty lies. According to Kant, reason alone can tell you this. We can know what is morally required of us without the help of our feelings and emotions. When we determine whether a maxim is universalizable or think about whether a proposed action will respect the humanity in others, we don't need to want or feel anything at all. We just need to carefully follow the three-step test for a maxim's universalizability, or to reflect on the importance of autonomy. We can reason our way to moral knowledge. Indeed, for Kant, neither our wants nor our emotions play any essential role in moral discovery. We must be able to determine what is right and wrong by rational thinking alone, without the aid of desires or feelings.

That's because Kant saw these as unreliable moral guides. Compassion can lead you to wrongly help an escaping criminal; the courage of a terrorist can make his actions worse; anger can cloud impartial judgment. Our emotions often lead us astray, says Kant. They need to be guided by sound principles before we can trust them. Without such guidance, we *might* end up doing our duty, but that would be just a matter of luck.[3]

Further, and importantly, Kant thought that moral wisdom should be available to everyone, regardless of their emotional makeup. All of us are rational. We each have the power to reason well, even if we often fail to use this power as we should. But our emotions are not always under our control, and they will differ from person to person. If a specific emotional makeup is needed to gain moral wisdom, then such wisdom might be out of reach for many of us. Kant thought that such a view is elitist and a denial of the fundamental equality of all human beings.

Knowing what you are required to do is one thing; actually doing it is another. Here Kant also downgraded desires and emotions in favor of reason. He denied the claim, made famous by David Hume, that our motivations always depend on our desires. Hume thought that beliefs alone

---

3. This thought is perfectly illustrated by a catty remark quoted in a biography of Napoleon's sister, Pauline. She was notoriously pampered and unfaithful, an irresponsible spendthrift with a full sense of entitlement. She was sometimes capable of bravery and generosity. But this was unpredictable, and for the most part she behaved very badly. Later in life, a former acquaintance gave the following account: "Although she was the most beautiful person one could imagine, she was also the most unreasonable. . . . [T]alking inconsequentially, laughing at nothing and at everything, she contradicted the most serious people and put out her tongue at her sister-in-law when Josephine wasn't looking. . . . *[S]he had no principles and was likely to do the right thing only by caprice*." (My italics.) As quoted in Flora Fraser, *Pauline Bonaparte: Venus of Empire* (New York: Alfred A. Knopf, 2009), p. 25.

could never move us, and that we must want something before we will ever act. By contrast, Kant thought that we could do things even if we didn't want to do them, and even if we didn't think they'd get us anything we wanted. When acting from the good will, we are acting solely from an understanding of what is morally required of us, not from any desire or emotion. If our action is to have moral worth, then this understanding, all by itself, must be enough to motivate us.

Anticipating Freud by a hundred years, Kant argued that our motivations are hardly transparent. In fact, we can never be sure that we have *ever* acted from a good will. Still, even if we can't be certain that our actions have ever earned moral worth, we *can* know what standard we should aim for.

Kant went so far as to write that dutiful actions motivated by emotions or desires lack any moral worth. Those whose generous nature causes them to lend a helping hand are to receive no credit. Aid workers motivated by compassion or sympathy are not to be praised for their good deeds. But those who overcome a complete lack of interest and nonetheless offer help, not because they want to but just because it is their duty to do so, will receive full moral credit.

There are two ways to interpret Kant's message here. The first says that the presence of emotions is enough to rob an action of moral worth. The second is more charitable. It says that actions done *solely* from desire or emotion cannot possess moral worth, but that some cases of mixed motives—cases in which the good will moves us to act, though helped along by an emotional push—can yet have moral worth. Kant scholars are still conflicted as to which interpretation best captures his intentions.

12.6 Conclusion

Kant's ethical views are rich and suggestive. They are extremely important in their own right, but it can also be quite helpful to contrast them with the consequentialist outlook that is so popular in political and economic circles these days. As we have seen, Kant's opposition to consequentialism was deep and thorough. These are the main points of disagreement:

1. Kant denied that benevolence is the central moral virtue, and thought instead that justice and integrity occupied that role.
2. Kant regarded many of the basic moral rules as absolute, and so insisted that it was never acceptable to break them—even if breaking them led to better results.

3. Kant denied that the morality of actions could depend on results or other factors outside of one's control, and claimed instead that they depend solely on what we can be held responsible for—our maxims and our free actions.

4. In a related point, Kant rejected the exclusive emphasis on the future and an action's results in determining what is right and wrong, and instead made past actions, and their just deserts, a central basis for moral evaluation.

5. According to utilitarians, all it takes to be a member of the moral community is a capacity to experience pleasure and pain; Kant thought instead that autonomy and rationality determined moral status.

6. Kant denied that happiness or well-being is always valuable in its own right, and instead believed that the good will—the steady commitment to do one's duty for its own sake—is the only thing that is valuable in all situations.

Many of the shortcomings of consequentialism are nicely handled by the Kantian theory. But consequentialists are pleased to return the favor: the Kantian theory isn't without its own problems, and many of those are neatly addressed by consequentialism. Let's now have a look at another important contender, the social contract theory, whose defenders hope to secure many of the benefits of these two ethical outlooks, while escaping the problems that confront them.

12.7   Discussion Questions

1. What is the relationship between Kant's principle of universalizability and the principle of humanity? Do the two ever give conflicting advice? If so, which do you think is a better guide to our moral obligations?

2. According to Kant, what is the source of human rights? What does his account imply about the rights of animals and disabled humans? Do you find his views on this subject plausible?

3. What does Kant mean by "the good will"? How is it possible for someone to do the right thing, but still lack a good will? Do you agree that actions are praiseworthy only if they are performed from the good will?

4. Kant endorsed the principle of lex talionis, which states that that we should treat criminals as they treated their victims. What do you think is the strongest objection to such a view? Can this objection be overcome?

5. Analyze this argument. If there is such a thing as moral luck, then we can be responsible for things that we cannot control. But we cannot be responsible for such things. So there is no moral luck.

6. What is autonomy? Do you think people have it? Why or why not?

7. If rationality and autonomy explain why we are as important as we are, how (if at all) can we explain the moral importance of infants and non-human animals?

12.8 Cases for Critical Reflection

Plagiarism

Consider the following thought experiment. Edward is a college student taking his first philosophy course, and the semester is soon coming to an end. Edward realizes that after weeks of slacking off, and hitting the bar most nights, he is in danger of failing the class. Further, his final essay on Immanuel Kant's moral theory is due in just a few days. Edward hasn't bothered to do the reading assignment, which looks like it will be difficult to understand. He asks his friend Debra if he can read her essay to help him understand the theory, and she happily agrees. Debra is an excellent student, and Edward has no doubt that her essay will receive a passing grade. Edward considers submitting Debra's essay instead of writing his own. Since Debra is taking the class with a different professor, Edward feels reasonably confident he would not get caught.

Questions

1. According to the golden rule, would it be wrong for Edward to submit Debra's essay as his own? Why or why not?

2. According to Kant's principle of humanity, would it be wrong for Edward plagiarize Debra's essay? Why or why not?

3. According to Kant's principle of universalizability, would it be wrong for Edward to plagiarize Debra's essay? Why or why not?

4. Suppose that Edward asked Debra for permission to plagiarize her essay, and Debra said she didn't mind. Would that change your answers to any of the previous questions?

Puffery

In the advertising business, there is a line drawn between stretching the truth and outright deception. It is against federal law in the United States for an advertisement to mislead consumers or make false statements about a product.[1] However, there is no law against "puffery," which means that marketers can exaggerate about a product as long as no reasonable person would take it literally. For example, advertisements for Axe Body Spray frequently suggest that any man wearing the body spray will become miraculously bombarded by beautiful women.[2] Even though Axe Body Spray has no such miraculous magnetizing effect, these advertisements are not considered misleading, since no one would take the suggestion literally. It's just a bit of puffery.

Some believe that the use of puffery in advertising wrongfully manipulates consumers. Imagine a motorcycle advertisement that appeals to a consumer's sense of adventure, displaying a motorcyclist driving through various exotic locations. The purchase of the motorcycle is certainly no guarantee of adventure, and most consumers wouldn't interpret the advertisement as providing such a guarantee. However, suppose someone watching the advertisement now finds herself interested, imagining the grand adventures she may take one day, even though she didn't previously desire a new motorcycle.

Questions

1. Do advertisements manipulate consumers? Can our autonomy be undermined by an exaggerated advertisement?
2. According to Kant's principle of universalizability, is there anything morally wrong with using puffery in advertising? Why or why not?
3. According to Kant's principle of humanity, is there anything morally wrong with using puffery in advertising? Why or why not?

Hooking Up

In a 2015 article in *Vanity Fair*, Nancy Jo Sales warned of a "dating apocalypse" among young people, brought on by hook-up culture and the dating app Tinder. The dating app shows users pictures of other nearby users, with the choice of swiping right for *yes* and left for *no*. Users who are matched can begin chatting with each other. Some Tinder users are looking for love. Others prefer to skip the traditional dating rituals and are instead looking for a casual hook up.

---

1. https://www.ftc.gov/news-events/media-resources/truth-advertising.
2. https://www.theloop.ca/the-surprising-and-arguably-bizarre-evolution-of-axe-body-spray-ads/.

One Tinder user, a marketing executive in New York, said, "Sex has become so easy. I can go on my phone right now and no doubt I can find someone I can have sex with this evening, probably before midnight." Several women interviewed by Sales complained of hook-up dating culture: "New York guys, they're not really looking for girlfriends. They're just looking for hit-it-and-quit-it on Tinder." Another woman said, "They start out with 'Send me nudes.' Or they say something like 'I'm looking for something quick within the next 10 or 20 minutes—are you available?' . . . It's straight efficiency." Sales warns that committed relationships are perhaps becoming rare, asking, "Can men and women ever find true intimacy in a world where communication is mediated by screens; or trust, when they know their partner has an array of other, easily accessible options?"[1]

Questions

1. Do you think there is anything morally dubious about hook-up culture? Why or why not?
2. According to the golden rule, is there anything morally wrong with casual sex? Why or why not?
3. According to Kant's principle of universalizability, is there anything morally wrong with casual sex? Why or why not?
4. Do casual hook ups involve treating someone as an object or as a mere means? According to Kant's principle of humanity, is there anything wrong with casual sex? Why or why not?

---

1. https://www.vanityfair.com/culture/2015/08/tinder-hook-up-culture-end-of-dating.

CHAPTER 13

.... ❧ ....

The Social Contract Tradition
The Theory and Its Attractions

13.1 The Lure of Proceduralism

One of the hardest and deepest problems for ethical inquiry is this: how to begin?

Should we assume, from the outset, that any plausible ethical theory will forbid slavery and torture, and require compassion and kindness? If so, then we can use these assumptions as a litmus test. Any theory that contradicts these assumptions would be rejected. For instance, if enslaving someone were ever in your self-interest, then ethical egoism would require you to perform such actions. It would therefore flunk our test. That would be enough to show that ethical egoism is false.

A question naturally arises: can we justify our basic assumptions and defend the practice of rejecting any moral theory that doesn't agree with them? If a theory contradicts our basic assumptions about right and wrong, why does that undermine the theory, rather than our assumptions? Aren't we just begging the question against the ethical egoist, for instance, by assuming that self-interest could never justify slavery or torture?

Defenders of this approach claim that there is no other alternative. We have to start moral thinking from somewhere—why not with those basic assumptions that almost everyone accepts, those that help support most of our other ethical claims? We can't prove that these assumptions are true. But that doesn't make them illegitimate.

Why not? Because the fundamental starting points in *every* area of thinking are beyond proof. It turns out, for instance, that the basic assumption behind all scientific inquiry—that there is a physical world outside of our own mind—cannot be proven. All the evidence we might collect in order to prove it already assumes that such a world exists. Yet that doesn't render every scientific claim implausible or unjustified.

Many philosophers remain dissatisfied with this approach. They believe that we can justify our basic moral views, rather than simply take them for granted. We can do that by coming up with a *procedure* that will tell us the steps for distinguishing right from wrong. The correct moral views are those that emerge from the correct procedure. I call this sort of approach **proceduralism**.

Proceduralism tells us that we should not begin moral inquiry by assuming, say, that slavery is wrong or that generosity is right. Make no moral assumptions at this stage. Instead, follow the correct procedure, and then see what the outcome is. Provided you've been careful, you'll land on the right answer to your moral question.

The golden rule is an instance of proceduralism. So is rule consequentialism. So is Kant's principle of universalizability. Each of these views tells us to follow certain steps in order to discover what is right and wrong. One of the main attractions of these views is that they do not take it for granted that slavery, for instance, is immoral; rather, they promise to *explain and justify* why slavery is immoral. They do this by showing, respectively, that (1) we wouldn't like it if we were enslaved, (2) no optimific social rule would permit slavery, or (3) no universalizable maxim would allow slavery.

If you have been reading these chapters in order, you know that there are significant problems with each of these proceduralist views. But that doesn't knock proceduralism out of contention, since there are many other proceduralist theories. Perhaps the most important of these is the **social contract theory**, nowadays known as **contractarianism**: the view that morality is based on a social contract.

13.2 The Background of the Social Contract Theory

Contractarianism originated as a political theory, and only later developed into a theory of morality. It tells us that laws are just if, and only if, they reflect the terms of a social contract that free, equal, and rational people would accept as the basis of a cooperative life together. Its view of morality stems directly from that political ideal: *actions are morally right just because they are permitted by rules that free, equal, and rational people would agree to live by, on the condition that others obey these rules as well.*

The theory's political origins can be traced back to the ancient Greeks. Early in the *Republic*, Plato's brothers tell Socrates that they find the social contract view both appealing and troubling. They challenge Socrates to tell them what is wrong with it. His answer takes up almost the whole of the book, a testament to the power of contractarianism.

Here is the story that Socrates heard. We are all by nature largely, or entirely, self-interested. What we want is power over others, physical security, plenty of money, and sensual pleasure. Our deepest goal is to lord it over everyone else. Who among us wouldn't want the power of the president or the wealth of Bill Gates—or, ideally, both?

This points to an obvious problem. Everyone wants to be at the top of the heap, and only a few can make it there. Further, no one wants to be a patsy, the person who gets stepped on as others climb the ladder of success. We each want to be number one. But we know that the chances of making it are slim, and we want to avoid being trampled as others claw their way to the top. So what do we do?

If we are rational, we will each agree to curb our self-interest and cooperate with one another. We'll do this *conditionally*—that is, on the condition that others do so as well. A complete free-for-all is going to make everyone miserable. If we all stop trying to get the better of each other, and instead agree to seek a little less for ourselves, then we'll all be better off.

That is what reason and morality require of us, according to the social contract theory. Starting with the assumptions that we each are largely motivated by self-interest, and that it is rational to be that way, contractarianism tells us that we each do best for ourselves by agreeing to limit the direct pursuit of self-interest and accept a bargain that gets us a pretty decent life. That everyone gets such a life means that we give up the chance of an absolutely fabulous life. But we also protect ourselves from a really terrible one, a life in which we are in the thick of a cutthroat competition, vulnerable to the attacks of everyone around us. That is a deal worth making. Here's why.

13.3 The Prisoner's Dilemma

Consider life's basic scenario. There is intense competition for scarce resources. We each want as much of those resources as we can get. Being rational, we each try to get as much as we can, knowing that more for us means less for someone else. Things are going to get very bad, very quickly.

This is what happened to the thousands of fishermen who sought ever larger catches, resulting in the emptying of the Chesapeake Bay—for centuries one of the world's greatest fisheries. This is what happened when baseball players, Tour de France cyclists, and Olympic weight lifters began to take increasingly dangerous anabolic steroids, in a bid to gain a competitive edge and lucrative championships. This is what happens when a politician starts a smear campaign and his opponent feels the need to ramp up the abuse in order to stand a fighting chance in the race. This is what always happens in turf battles over the spoils of an illegal drug trade.

These cases all share the same essential features. In each, there is mounting competition over a scarce resource, and many are trying their best to increase their share of it. That seems to be rational, and yet, if everyone stopped being so selfish, each person would be better off. There would still be fish in the Chesapeake, sustaining the communities surrounding it. Athletes would be safer, even if the world records in their fields were a bit less spectacular.

These sorts of situations, in which everyone would be better off by scaling back their pursuit of self-interest, are known as **prisoner's dilemmas**. The name comes from a scenario, introduced by economists, in which two thieves (call them Al and Bob) are caught and sent to separate detention cells. Being rational, Al and Bob previously made a deal with each other: if they get caught, they'll each keep silent, to thwart the police and protect themselves. Now that they have been captured, the police tell each one the same thing: "If you keep your promise to your partner by keeping quiet, and he rats you out, then he's off the hook, and you're looking at a six-year sentence. If *you* break your word and snitch on him, while he remains silent, you're home free, while he spends the next six years in jail. If you both keep quiet, you'll each get two years. But if you both confess, you'll each get four."

The following diagram will help you keep track of the options. Each number represents years in jail. The first number in each pair is Al's prison sentence; the second is Bob's.

		Bob	
		Remains Silent (Cooperation)	Confesses (Betrayal)
Al	Remains Silent (Cooperation)	2, 2	6, 0
	Confesses (Betrayal)	0, 6	4, 4

Suppose that both criminals know about the various outcomes, and that both have only one concern at this point: to minimize their jail time. If they are both rational, what are they going to do?

You might think that it's impossible to know the answer, since you don't know enough about Al or Bob, their bond with each other, their trustworthiness, and so on, to make an informed guess. But really, there is no doubt that each is going to confess. They are going to break their promise to each other, landing themselves a four-year sentence apiece. That's a far cry from getting off scot-free, and double the two years they'd get if they each kept quiet.

The important point is that remaining silent is the cooperative strategy. Silence here means keeping one's word, honoring the terms of the deal. Confession is a betrayal, breaking one's promise, abandoning a partner.

Al and Bob are going to betray each other. That's certain. They'll do this because they know the odds, because they are self-interested, and because they are rational.

Why will they confess? Because *no matter what his accomplice does, each criminal will be better off by confessing.*

Consider Al's choices. Suppose that:

Bob remains silent. Then if Al confesses, Al is home free. If Al keeps his mouth shut, Al gets two years. So if Bob remains silent, Al should confess. That will minimize his jail time. That is what he most wants. So, if Al is rational, he will confess.

Now suppose that:

Bob confesses. Then if Al confesses, Al gets four years in jail. Silence gets him six. So if Bob confesses, Al should confess, too.

Thus, either way, Al does best for himself by spilling the beans and breaking his promise to Bob. And of course Bob is reasoning in the same way. So they are both going to confess and end up with four years in jail.

The prisoner's dilemma isn't just some interesting thought experiment. It's real life. There are countless cases in which the rational pursuit of self-interest will lead people to refuse to cooperate with one another, even though this leaves everyone much worse off.

The Chesapeake fishermen were in a prisoner's dilemma with one another. So are world-class athletes, once they discover that some of their competitors are taking performance-enhancing drugs. So are gang members who are gunning for their competition. A cooperative strategy would have saved them their livelihoods or their lives.

13.4 Cooperation and the State of Nature

So why don't competitors cooperate? The answer is simple: because it is so risky. The criminals in the prisoner's dilemma could cooperate. But that would mean taking a chance at a six-year sentence and betting everything on your partner's good faith. Unilaterally keeping silent, reducing your catch, refusing the use of steroids, forsaking violence—these are strategies for suckers. Those who adopt them may be virtuous, but they are the ones who will be left behind, rotting in jail, economically struggling, off the Olympic podium, or the victim of an enemy's gunshot. If enough people are willing to do what it takes to ensure that they get ahead, then you've either got to join in the competition or be the sacrificial lamb.

Englishman Thomas Hobbes (1588–1679), the founder of modern contractarianism, was especially concerned with one sort of prisoner's dilemma. He invited the readers of his magnum opus, *Leviathan*, to imagine a situation in which there was no government, no central authority, no group with the exclusive power to enforce its will on others. He called this situation the **state of nature**. And he thought it was the worst place you could ever be.

In his words, the state of nature is a "war of all against all, in which the life of man is solitary, poor, nasty, brutish and short." People ruthlessly compete with one another for whatever goods are available. Cooperation is a sham, and trust is nonexistent. Hobbes himself lived through a state of nature—the English Civil War—and thus had firsthand knowledge of its miseries. If you've ever read *The Lord of the Flies*, you have an idea of what Hobbes is talking about. As I write this, I can turn on my television and see pictures of states of nature from around the world—in parts of Syria, Iraq, and Sudan. The scenes are terrible.

The Hobbesian state of nature is a prisoner's dilemma. By seeking to maximize self-interest, everyone is going to be worse off. In such dire circumstances, everyone is competing to gain as much as he can, at the expense of others. With so much at stake, an all-out competition is bound to be very bad for almost everyone. No one is so smart or strong or well connected as to be free from danger.

There is an escape from the state of nature, and the exit strategy is the same for all prisoner's dilemmas. We need two things: beneficial rules that require cooperation and punish betrayal, and an enforcer who ensures that these rules are obeyed.

The rules are the terms of the social contract. They require us to give up the freedom to attack and to kill others, to cheat them and lie to them, to beat and threaten them and take from them whatever we can. In exchange for giving up these freedoms (and others), we gain the many advantages of cooperation. It is rational to give up some of your freedom, provided that you stand a good chance of getting something even better in return. The peace and stability of a well-ordered society is worth it. That is the promise of the social contract.

But you need more than good rules of cooperation to escape from a prisoner's dilemma. You also need a way to make sure the rules are kept.

The state of nature comes to an end when people agree with one another to give up their unlimited freedoms and to cooperate on terms that are beneficial to all. The problem with agreements, though, is that they can be broken. And without a strong incentive to keep their promises, people in prisoner's dilemmas are going to break them. Just think of Al and Bob in our original example.

What's needed is a powerful person (or group) whose threats give everyone excellent reason to keep their word. The central power doesn't have to be a government—it could be a mob boss, who threatens Al and Bob with death if they were to break their silence. It could be the International Olympic Committee, with the power to suspend or disqualify athletes who test positive for illegal substances. But in the most general case, in which we are faced with anarchy and are trying to escape from utter lawlessness, what we need is a government to enforce basic rules of cooperation. Without a central government, the situation will spiral downhill into a battleground of competing factions and individuals, warlords and gang bosses, each vying for as much power and wealth as possible. A war of all against all won't be far behind.

13.5 The Advantages of Contractarianism

Contractarianism has many advantages. Here are some of the most important ones.

Morality Is Essentially a Social Phenomenon

For anyone all alone on a desert island or on a remote mountain retreat, there is no possibility of moral or immoral action. That is because moral rules are nothing other than special rules of cooperation, and when it comes to cooperation, it takes at least two to tango.

The contractarian emphasis on the social nature of morality implies that there are no self-regarding moral duties (duties that apply only to oneself).

True, we can fail ourselves in a number of ways. We can become strung-out addicts and ruin our potential. We can make poor financial decisions that leave us bankrupt. We can make an awful career choice and spend our days in drudgery. In all of these cases we are highly imprudent. But when such actions have no bearing on others (they often do, of course), then contractarians will deny that there is anything immoral about them.

Contractarianism Explains and Justifies the Content of the Basic Moral Rules

On the contractarian account, the moral rules are ones that are meant to govern social cooperation. When trying to figure out which standards are genuinely moral ones, contractarians ask us to imagine a group of free, equal, and rational people who are seeking terms of cooperation that each could reasonably accept. The rules they select to govern their lives together are the moral rules. These will closely match the central moral rules we have long taken for granted.

John Rawls (1921–2002), the most famous twentieth-century social contract theorist, had a specific test for determining the rules that the ideal social contractors would support. In his *Theory of Justice* (1971), by most accounts the most important work of political philosophy written in the last century, Rawls has us envision contractors behind a **veil of ignorance**. This is an imaginary device that erases all knowledge of your distinctive traits. Those behind the veil know that they have certain basic human needs and wants, but they know nothing of their religious identity, their ethnicity, their social or economic status, their sex, or their moral character. The idea is to put everyone on an equal footing, so that the choices they make are completely fair.

When placed behind a veil of ignorance, or in some other condition of equality and freedom, what social rules will rational people select? These will almost certainly include prohibitions of killing, rape, battery, theft, and fraud, and rules that require keeping one's word, returning what one owes, and being respectful of others. Contractarianism thus easily accounts for why the central moral rules are what they are—rational, self-interested people, free of coercion, would agree to obey them, so long as others are willing to obey them, too.

The rules of cooperation must be designed to benefit everyone, not just a few. Otherwise, only a few would rationally endorse them, while the rest would rationally ignore them. This allows the contractarian to explain why slavery and racial and sexual discrimination are so deeply immoral. Biased policies undermine the primary point of morality—to create fair terms of cooperation that could earn the backing of everyone. Even if oppressed people identify with the interests of their oppressors, and staunchly defend the system of discrimination, that does not make it right. The correct moral rules are those that free people would endorse for their *mutual* benefit—not for the benefit of one group over another.

Contractarianism Offers a Method for Justifying Every Moral Rule

Contractarianism is a prime example of proceduralism. Contractarians have a method for determining the morality of any given action. They invite us to think about whether free, equal, and rational people would agree to live by rules that allow the action in question. Contractarians do not assume that the standard moral evils are bad; rather, they can defend their verdicts by showing that rational contractors, getting together to select mutually beneficial rules of cooperation, would forbid such behavior.

Thus, we are never at the point where we have to say to people, "Don't you *just see* that _____ (fill in the blank) is wrong?" Contractarians never have to make this move, which is excellent, since it can't possibly convince someone who doesn't already agree with you. Rather, contractarians offer a method for justifying every single moral rule. Of course disagreements will arise when we apply this method. There is plenty of room for argument about what free, equal, and rational people would accept. Still, if contractarianism is correct, then we will always have something to say when it comes to justifying even the most fundamental moral claims.

Contractarianism Explains the Objectivity of Morality

Contractarianism offers an attractive picture of the status of morality. Moral rules, on this view, are objective. Anyone can be mistaken about what morality requires. Personal opinion isn't the final authority in ethics. Neither is the law or conventional wisdom—whole societies can be mistaken about what is right and wrong, because they may be mistaken about the principles that free, equal, and rational people would accept as the basis for governing their life together.

Thus contractarians have an answer to a familiar challenge: if morality isn't a human creation, where did it come from? If contractarianism is correct, morality does not come from God. Nor does it come from human opinion. Rather, morality is the set of rules that would be agreed to by people who are very like us, only more rational and free, and who are selecting terms of cooperation that will benefit each and every one of them.

Thus contractarians don't have to picture moral rules as eternally true. And they can deny that moral rules are just like the rules of logic or of natural science—other areas where we acknowledge the existence of objective truths. The moral rules are the outcomes of rational choice, tailored to the specifics of human nature and the typical situations that humans find themselves in. This removes the mystery of objective morality. Even if God doesn't exist, there can still be objective values, so long as there are mutually beneficial rules that people would agree to if they were positioned as equals, fully rational and free.

Contractarianism Explains Why It Is Sometimes Acceptable to Break the Moral Rules

Moral rules are designed for cooperative living. But when cooperation collapses, the entire point of morality disappears. When things become so bad that the state of nature approaches, or has been reached, then the ordinary moral rules lose their force.

One way to put this idea is to say that every moral rule has a built-in escape clause: do not kill, cheat, intimidate, and so on, *so long as others are obeying this rule as well.* When those around you are saying one thing and doing another, and cannot be counted on to limit the pursuit of their self-interest, then you are freed of your ordinary moral obligations to them.

The basis of morality is cooperation. And that requires trust. When that trust is gone, you are effectively in a state of nature. The moral rules don't apply there, because the basic requirement of moral life—that each person be willing to cooperate on fair terms that benefit everyone—is not met.

This explains why you aren't bound to keep promises made at gunpoint, or to be the only taxpayer in a land of tax cheats. It explains why you don't have to wait patiently in line when many others are cutting in, or to obey a curfew or a handgun law if everyone else is violating it. When you can't rely on others, there is no point in making the sacrifices that cooperative living requires. There is no moral duty to play the sucker.

13.6 More Advantages: Morality and the Law

Contractarianism Justifies a Basic Moral Duty to Obey the Law

The social contract theory also has plausible things to say about why we are sometimes morally allowed to break the law. Before explaining this, though, consider why such cases are the exceptions, why we are usually, on contractarian grounds, morally required to *obey* the law.

The law enables us to escape from the state of nature, and so to gain all of the good things that come from a stable, peaceful society. And the benefits are real. We can securely purchase items online, safely walk the streets, trust the mail service, and rely on legal contracts that we've entered, only because most people involved in these activities honor the rules that benefit everyone.

You have a role to play here. Your obedience to the law helps to support the institutions that make so many benefits possible. Those who break the law are undermining these highly beneficial institutions. They are also taking unfair advantage of the sacrifices made by their fellow citizens. That is immoral. Therefore, we all have a basic moral duty to obey the law.

The Contractarian Justification of Legal Punishment

Those who break the law are rightly punished. And the social contract theory has a natural explanation of this. Its account nicely blends some of the most attractive aspects of consequentialism and Kantianism, while solving a couple of hard problems in the philosophy of law along the way.

If punishment fails to deter crime, then the state cannot effectively serve its enforcer role, and so its ultimate justification is undercut. To achieve its aim of keeping the peace, the state's threats for lawbreaking have to be credible. To be credible, they must usually be carried out. And so, when people break the law, they need to be punished. That is the only way we can avoid falling into a state of nature.

Social contract theorists can also offer a Kantian rationale for legal punishment. When laws are good, they set out terms of fair play. When criminals break these rules, they take unfair advantage of their fellow citizens. They get all of the benefits of membership without shouldering the burdens that make the benefits possible. We right such wrongs by removing the criminal's ill-gotten gains. Punishment can do that. It can restore a level playing field. It can eliminate a criminal's unjust enrichment. It corrects the balance of benefits and burdens in society, and thereby sends a message that everyone is equal before the law.

Criminals have acted as if they could simply take what they wanted, without making the needed sacrifices that the rest of us have made. In doing so, criminals have placed themselves outside the protection of the law. They cannot complain if they are punished as a result.

Contractarianism Justifies the State's Role in Criminal Law

The contractarian justification of punishment neatly answers two related questions that have long perplexed philosophers: (1) why should the state, as opposed to private citizens, be the one who brings criminal charges and administers punishments? and (2) why should we have a criminal law in the first place? Why not just have the civil law (torts, contracts, etc.), and allow those who have been wronged to bring lawsuits against those who have harmed them?

The social contract theory has answers. The state's ultimate purpose is to aid our escape from the state of nature. This gives it special authority to determine who is posing a threat to social stability. The actions that are most dangerous to society—treason, assassination, hijacking, attacking government agencies—are prohibited by the criminal law. That makes perfect sense, given the different purposes of the criminal and civil law. The function of the civil law is to repair personal harms and wrongs; the function of the criminal law is to preserve the state, and all of the advantages it provides. That is why a state representative (say, a district attorney or federal prosecutor), rather than a private citizen, initiates criminal proceedings. And that is why criminal punishment is a state affair, rather than a private matter to be settled between citizens.

Contractarianism and Civil Disobedience

Contractarianism has attractive things to say about why we have a duty to obey the law, and why criminals are rightly punished for violating just laws. But what if the laws are unjust, and fail to set out fair terms of cooperation? What if the ideal social code and a society's actual laws are miles apart? In that case, the social contract theorist can explain why *breaking* the law (under certain circumstances) can be morally acceptable.

Laws are morally justified when they mirror the rules that free and equal people would accept. And so, when laws themselves are grossly unfair, or when fair laws are applied in a discriminatory way, the primary point of having a society under law is undermined. Those who always get the short end of the stick are being asked to sacrifice themselves for the sake of others. That isn't right, and the social contract theory explains why. The point of morality is to guarantee mutual benefit from fair terms of cooperation. Discriminatory policies and practices only frustrate this goal.

Governments must earn the allegiance of their citizens. They do this by making their citizens much better off than they would be in a state of nature. That is why it is rational for people to agree to be governed. But when whole classes of people are enslaved or discriminated against, then the government has lost its moral authority over them. And that seriously weakens the moral duty to obey the government's laws.

Indeed, this means that it is sometimes appropriate to disobey the laws. The precise conditions are very difficult to state. But certain cases seem clear. Think, for instance, of the protests that Gandhi initiated against British colonial rule, those of Chinese democrats at Tiananmen Square, or those led by Martin Luther King, Jr., against segregationist laws in the American South. These cases of civil disobedience each involved illegal activities. But the laws being challenged were deeply immoral. And the illegal actions were morally powerful precisely because (1) the protestors took the law into their own hands only as a last resort, after all feasible negotiations had failed; (2) they acted openly, not secretly, and were willing to pay the price by going to jail and suffering the beatings of police; (3) they acted nonviolently, often in the face of physical violence; and (4) they were clearly motivated not by the promise of personal gain, but rather by the hope of furthering the cause of justice. In just about every respect, these classic cases of civil disobedience are morally very different from the work of ordinary criminals.

In acting as they did, the nonviolent protesters were showing a respect for the rule of law. This sounds paradoxical, but their message was clear. They tried to change the law because it was deeply unfair. They didn't want to replace it with anarchy, but rather with a system of real legal justice. They recognized the great value of a society under law—under just law. When there is no choice but to remain oppressed, resort to violence, or opt for peaceful and open resistance to injustice, the social contract theory favors the latter course. Isn't that the most admirable choice?

13.7 Discussion Questions

1. What is proceduralism, and how does it differ from other approaches to ethics? Why is contractarianism a form of proceduralism?
2. What makes a situation a "prisoner's dilemma"? What is the rational thing to do in a prisoner's dilemma situation?
3. What is the state of nature, and why does Hobbes think that such a condition would be so bad? How does Hobbes think that people would be able to emerge from the state of nature?

4. How do contractarians justify moral rules against such things as slavery and torture? Do you find their justifications of such rules to be compelling?

5. Explain how a contractarian defends the objectivity of ethics. Do you find this defense plausible?

6. Do you find the contractarian justification of punishment attractive? Can you think of cases in which a contractarian would endorse punishment that turns out to be immoral? Can you think of cases in which certain behavior merits punishment, but contractarianism would fail to justify it?

7. Do we have a duty to obey the law? If so, is this duty absolute, or can there be exceptions? How would a contractarian explain the existence of a duty to obey the law?

CHAPTER 14

············ ❧ ············

The Social Contract Tradition

Problems and Prospects

14.1 Why Be Moral?

Most moral theories have tried to show how, on their terms, it is rational to be moral, and irrational to be immoral. Social contract theorists are no exception.

The classic statement of this contractarian aim is given in Hobbes's *Leviathan*. Hobbes discusses the views of the calculating amoralist, whom he terms the Fool. The Fool admits that breaking his promises is unjust, but he doesn't care about whether his actions are just or not. He cares only about his own self-interest. When keeping his promises will do him good, he'll keep his promises. When it won't, he won't. He reasons that he'll sometimes do best for himself by being unjust. When that is so, it is rational to act immorally.

Hobbes faces the challenge directly. He agrees with the Fool's basic assumption: that self-interest is the fundamental reason for acting. On this line of thinking, you are rational to the extent that you increase your chances of becoming better off. Thus Hobbes has to show that acting morally is always likely to promote self-interest. That's not so easy.

The specific case Hobbes considers is one in which the Fool has made a deal with someone else, and the other person has already done what he's promised to do. Should the Fool keep his side of the bargain anyway?

Many will say no. Their advice is simple: take the money and run. That's certainly immoral. But people might get away with their immorality. It has happened many times. In such cases, people get what they want without having to give up anything in return. It's a black eye for justice. But it seems the height of rationality.

Hobbes disagrees. He allows that people sometimes get away with injustice. But that doesn't make it rational to act unjustly. Unjust acts are rational only if they increase the *likelihood* of personal gain. And Hobbes says that they never do. Though people can sometimes get away with injustice, the chances of doing so are never good. So injustice is never rational.

One way to defend Hobbes's conclusion is to raise the possibility of divine wrath. If you are immoral, then God is going to punish you, and no matter the worldly riches you're after, they simply aren't worth that misery. But Hobbes tosses this aside—the Fool he is considering is the same Fool who has said in his heart that there is no God. So the threat of divine punishment isn't going to work.

We can make the challenge hardest for Hobbes by considering a classic puzzle of rationality: the **free-rider problem**. This occurs when lots of folks are cooperating in a way that brings some common good. So long as enough people are chipping in, this benefit can be enjoyed by all—even those who refuse to help out. These are the free riders. They are getting a free ride by exploiting the efforts of others, without making any sacrifices themselves. This refusal to contribute to the support of the common good seems highly unfair. But it also seems highly rational.

Let's make this more concrete. Consider some shared public goods: keeping a park clean; maintaining a high level of decency in society; having democratic elections; eliminating a dreadful disease; having a secure national defense; having government agencies ensure the safety of our food, medicines, and highways. These are genuine goods, and yet they can be achieved only if most people in a society are contributing to them. Such contributions involve sacrifice, sometimes small (making time to vote, not tossing a wrapper to the ground), and sometimes potentially large (serving in the military, paying your tax bill).

In many of these cases, the contribution that any single individual makes is negligible. Democracy isn't going to crumble if I decide not to vote. The park won't be totally spoiled if I drop my gum wrapper on the grass. The government agencies will continue to do their work with or without my tax payment. Since that's so, I might reason as follows: the particular resource doesn't depend on my contribution; it will still be there whether I contribute or not. So why make the sacrifice? I can gain the benefit of free elections or a secure national defense without taking the time to vote or serve in the military. I am not doing my fair share to support the common good. But I *am* getting something for nothing. How could that be irrational?

Of course, if you already care about not exploiting your fellow citizens, then it will be rational for you to make the needed sacrifices to help support these common goods. You won't see voting, getting immunized, or paying taxes as a nasty burden, but rather as your contribution to causes that you wholeheartedly support. But suppose you don't feel this way, or you do, but are starting to wonder whether you are being a dupe. Hobbes doesn't assume that we are generous and public-minded. He is trying to show the person who is entirely self-interested why it would be a good bet, even for him, to do his fair share. Can he do it?

There are two things we might say on Hobbes's behalf. First, we might argue, as he himself did, that the risks of doing wrong always outweigh its potential benefits. But this is simply mistaken. There are cases in which the chances of being found out are low, or the punishments are pretty mild and the benefits of injustice are really substantial. Since rationality, for Hobbes, is all about how much gain you can *reasonably expect* from an action, injustice can sometimes be highly rational.

What Hobbes could say is that it is never rational to behave unjustly *in a well-ordered society*. For him, such a society is one that offers reliable threats against breaking mutually beneficial rules. It won't be rational to cheat on your taxes, for instance, if the penalties for doing so are very severe and you are sure to get caught.[1]

However, in our imperfect world, where enforcement isn't foolproof, where punishments are sometimes pretty light, it can indeed be rational to take a chance at injustice. So long as we understand rationality as Hobbes does—as maximizing the chances of doing well for yourself—then he cannot show that injustice is always irrational.

But Hobbes might be able to show something nearly as comforting. Compare two claims:

1. No matter who you are, or what circumstances you find yourself in, it is always rational to act justly.
2. It is always rational to be a just person—the sort of person who values fairness, approves of just policies, tries to live an upright life, and becomes upset when learning of injustice.

---

1. It is interesting that on Hobbes's line of thinking, many criminal organizations will count as well-ordered societies. Think, for instance, of how badly police informants fare in the Mafia society or drug culture depicted in *The Sopranos* or *The Wire*. Going over to the feds or the cops is almost always a very bad bet, and that's because the punishments for doing so are as bad as they can be, and pretty reliably enforced.

Hobbes cannot defend claim 1. But he might be able to defend claim 2. And if he can, then he may also be able to show the following:

3. *For just people*, it is always rational to act justly.

And that would be a lot, even if it is a bit disappointing in leaving us without a surefire reply to the vicious person bent on doing evil.

Here is the best shot for Hobbes at defending claim 2. In the long run, just people are more likely to do better for themselves than unjust people. The upright person sleeps well at night. She has true friends. She has people she can share her delights with, be consoled by, confide her hopes and fears to. She isn't always looking over her shoulder, wondering whether an enemy is after her. She can review her life with satisfaction, knowing that she has earned the trust of others. The life of virtue has a lot going for it.

Compare such a life with that of an immoral criminal, one who is always worrying whether a vengeful victim or a turncoat conspirator is hard on his heels. It is a life of great insecurity. Those always on the lookout for the main chance, for the opportunity to cheat someone or exploit the system, are playing a losing game. They might win a few hands along the way, but there's not much in it as a long-term strategy. It isn't rational to be the cheating type.

If this is right, then it is rational to be a virtuous person. And that is what claim 2 says. Further, if it is rational to be such a person, it is rational to try to stay that way. The best strategy for maintaining your good character is to keep on doing good things. For once we begin to give in to temptation, immorality can slowly chip away at virtue. It can be very hard to put on the brakes and prevent a slide into real corruption. Thus, for good people, it is rational to continue to act justly and to resist the call to stray from the path of virtue. That is precisely what claim 3 says.

That is the best case to be made for claims 2 and 3. And yet it also fails—or, rather, it isn't a complete success. It may be rational to be a moral person in societies that are well ordered, stable, and largely just. But when corruption is rampant and the powerful can get away with most things, then virtue can be a recipe for disaster.

Take the case of Marlene Garcia-Esperat. She was a journalist investigating corruption in the Philippine Department of Agriculture. The corruption went deep, and it reached very high levels. In order to protect themselves, officials in the department ordered her death. In 2005, a man knocked at her door, wished her good morning, and then killed her in front of her children.

Between 1986 and 2019, more than 100 Philippine journalists were murdered, either in retaliation for their coverage or to prevent them from breaking the news of illegal activities among the wealthy elite. Garcia-Esperat's case was unusual in only one way—it was the first in twenty years in which the murderers were brought to trial.

These sorts of tactics aren't confined to the Philippines, of course. According to the Committee to Protect Journalists, more than 1,366 journalists were murdered around the world between 1992 and 2019.[2] Reporters and editors—and whistle-blowers, peace activists, and others intent on exposing immorality—often end up paying the ultimate price for their bravery.

Hobbes takes a hard-eyed view of human nature, and denies that virtue is its own reward. If he is right about that, then it pays to be good only when that promises a longer life, a more secure existence, or a better chance at getting what you want. It sometimes will. But not always. When it doesn't, Hobbesian rationality requires that you make injustice your master.

14.2 The Role of Consent

Most of us believe that we have a moral duty to honor our commitments. And a contract is a commitment—it is a promise given in exchange for some expected benefit. A social contract differs from other contracts only in the extent of the duties it imposes and the benefits it creates. Since we are morally required to keep our promises, we have a duty to honor the terms of the social contract.

But have we actually promised to live up to any social contract? The Pilgrims did, when they paused before the shores of Massachusetts and together signed the Mayflower Compact in 1620. In ancient Athens, free men were brought to the public forum and directly asked to promise obedience to their city—or leave, without penalty. Naturalized citizens in the United States have long been required to pledge allegiance to the nation's laws. But relatively few adults nowadays have done any such thing. It seems, therefore, that we are not really parties to any such contract, and so are not bound to obey its terms.

---

2. See https://cpj.org/data/killed/?status=Killed&motiveConfirmed%5B%5D=Confirmed&type%5B%5D=Journalist&start_year=1992&end_year=2019&group_by=year.

Some philosophers have tried to finesse this point by arguing that we actually *have* agreed to obey the law. True, most of us haven't signed any contract or stated out loud that we are prepared to follow the law. Instead, we have offered our **tacit consent**, which is expressed through silence and a lack of opposition to the government. Tacit consent is a possibility: when I ask my class whether it is okay to move on to a new topic, and no one replies, I reasonably take it that everyone agrees to proceed. Likewise, we might signal our consent to the government's laws by staying put, by not calling for its overthrow, by continuing to reap the benefits of civilized society.

But this is problematic. Some people loudly call for revolution; they are not tacitly consenting to obey the law. Others might be unable to voice their opposition freely, for fear of what the authorities will do. The fact that they remain where they are is no sign of their consent. It's simply evidence of a very practical decision. In many such cases, individual protest is unlikely to lead to better times, and is very likely to lead to imprisonment, torture, or an early death. How many political prisoners have learned this lesson the hard way? How many others have been deterred by their example?

Thus it seems that many people have neither explicitly nor tacitly consented to the rules that govern their society. The reasoning here is summarized by the *Consent Argument*:

1. We have a duty to obey the law only if we have consented to do so.
2. Many have not given their consent to obey the law.
3. Therefore, many people do not have a duty to obey the law.

I have just given some reason to think that the second premise is true. Still, the argument works only if the first premise is also true. Its supporters claim that governments can be terribly abusive, and so their power can be justified only if it respects the will of its citizens. And that requires that citizens consent to being governed. An essential part of government is its power to force its people to do what it says. But as a general matter, it is wrong to coerce people without their consent. Why should it be any different when the threat is coming from the government rather than a private citizen?

That is the strongest case for premise 1. Here is the strongest case against it.

Suppose you hate your country and reject its basic laws. You remain only because your government refuses to allow you to leave or because other, better countries won't let you in. You really, truly do not consent to your government's authority. Does that mean that you have no duty to obey its rules? That you are morally free to break laws against theft and slander and battery and murder, just because you renounce your membership in the social contract? That is the implication of premise 1. It is very hard to accept.

It is even harder to accept when we turn our focus away from questions of obedience to the law and ask, instead, about basic moral duties. It is *very* implausible to suppose that we are morally required to do only what we agree to do. We have a moral obligation to help the needy, even if we can't be bothered to think of their plight. Abusive bosses are morally required to be decent to their workers, even if the bosses deny this and have made no promise to do so.

Contractarianism would be in deep trouble if it claimed that our moral duties applied only to those who agreed to accept them. *But it makes no such claim.* The social contract that fixes our basic moral duties is not one that any of us has *actually* consented to; rather, it is one that we each *would* agree to were we all free and rational and seeking terms of mutually beneficial cooperation. So the fact that we have never signed a social contract or verbally announced our allegiance to one does not undermine the contractarian project.

Contractarianism does not require you to do whatever the existing laws and social customs tell you to do. Those standards are partly a product of ignorance, past deception and fraud, and imperfect political compromise. We are morally required to live up to the standards that free, rational people would accept as the terms of their cooperative living. It's safe to say that no existing set of laws perfectly lines up with those terms.

Thus contractarianism isn't a simple recipe to do whatever your society says. Rather, it provides a way to evaluate society's actual rules, by seeing how close (or how far) they are to the ideal social code that would be adopted if we were freer, more equal, and more rational than we are. If contractarianism is correct, this ideal social code is the moral law.

14.3 Disagreement among the Contractors

If the social contract theory is correct, then the moral rules are those that free, equal, and rational people would agree to live by. But what happens if such people disagree with one another? For instance, what if these idealized contractors can't reach a deal about the conditions under which a nation should go to war, or about the kind of aid we owe to the very poor? What happens then?

Rawls solved this problem by making every contractor a clone of every other. Behind the veil of ignorance, all of your distinguishing features go away. No one is any different from anyone else. And so there is no reason to expect any disagreement.

But Hobbes and other contractarians won't stand for this. They can't see why I should follow the rules of someone who is so completely unlike me—a person who is not only absolutely rational but also stripped of all knowledge of his social status, his friendships and family situation, his desires, interests, and hopes. Hobbes and his followers insist that the moral rules are those that we, *situated as we are*, would rationally agree to, provided of course that others would agree to live by them as well.

It's not easy to know how to solve this disagreement between contractarians. On the one hand, Rawls's view is likely to be fairer, since any information that could prejudice our choices is kept from us as we select rules to live by. But Hobbes also has a point, in that we want to make it rational, if we can, for everyone to live by the moral rules. Why should I live according to the rules set by some person who isn't at all like the real me? That's a pretty good question.

I'm sure that you've already figured out that I am not able to answer every good ethical question. This is another one I am going to leave for your consideration. Instead, let's return to our original problem: what should we say when the people choosing the social rules disagree with one another?

Perhaps Rawls is right, and there won't be any disagreement. But what if he's wrong? If contractors disagree, then the actions or policies they disagree about are morally neutral. They are neither required nor forbidden. That's because the moral rules are ones that *all* contractors would agree to. If there are some matters that they can't agree on, then these are not covered by the moral rules.

This could be pretty bad. Or it might be just fine. It all depends on where the disagreement arises (if it ever does). If there are only small pockets of disagreement, regarding relatively trivial matters, then this is hardly a problem. But what if contractors can't agree about war policy, about whether executions are just, about how to treat the poorest among us? Then this is really serious, since we do think that morality must weigh in on these issues.

So, how much disagreement will there be? There is no easy way to know. We can provide answers only after we know how to describe the contractors and their position of choice. Will they be clones of one another, situated behind the veil of ignorance? Or will they be aware of their different personalities and life situations? Will they be more or less equally situated, or are some going to have a lot more leverage than others? When we say that they are rational, do we have Kant's conception in mind? Or Hobbes's, according to which rationality amounts to reliably serving your self-interest? Or some other conception?

Answers to these questions will make a big difference in deciding on the specific moral rules that a social contract theory favors. These answers will also determine the amount of agreement we can expect from the contractors. There is no shortcut to discovering these answers. To get them, contractarians must defend their own specific version of the theory against competing versions. That is a major undertaking. Until it is done, we cannot know just what the moral rules are, or how much contractual disagreement to expect.

14.4 The Scope of the Moral Community

> The true measure of a man is how he treats someone who can do him absolutely no good.
>
> —*Samuel Johnson*

Who has rights? Who deserves our respect? Utilitarians have their answer: anyone (or any animal) who can suffer harm. Kantians have their answer: anyone who is rational and autonomous. And contractarians have theirs: anyone whose interests are protected by the rules that contractors will agree upon.

When coming together to negotiate rules to live by, who will the contractors decide to protect? Different social contract theorists give different answers. The key to understanding them, however, lies in the idea that the contractors are, above all, *rational and self-interested*. It's easy to see why they should be rational. But why assume that they are self-interested?

There is a two-part answer. First, the preliminary part: being self-interested is not the same thing as being selfish. Being self-interested is having a strong concern for how well you are faring in life. Being selfish is placing far too much importance on your own well-being and far too little on that of others. We don't have to assume that contractors are selfish. But they definitely do care about how well off they will be under the agreed-on rules of cooperation.

Okay, fair enough. But the real question is whether we should think of the contractors as also being generous, benevolent, and self-sacrificing.

And the answer that contractarians give is *no*. Why is that? Well, by assigning such virtues to the contractors, social contract theorists could be accused of stacking the deck in favor of moral principles that we already agree on. The attractions of proceduralism would be lost, since we would be starting our moral inquiry by making substantive assumptions about what is right and wrong. (Namely, that it is right to be generous, benevolent, and self-sacrificing, and wrong to be the opposite.) And we would also be making it much more difficult to show people why it is rational for them to obey the moral rules, since some of us are not that virtuous. Some people would take a look at the rules that a bunch of awfully nice, sweet people agreed to, and roll their eyes in disgust. There's no way that they are going to live by *those* rules.

The assumption, then, is that everyone is to some degree self-interested, and that it is rational to be that way.

Now back to our original question. If you are choosing from a position of equality, are free and highly rational, with a healthy dose of self-interest, who will you assign rights to? The answer is: other people like you. Contractors—those free, equal, and rational people engaged in the project of negotiating rules to live by—are the ones who will receive special treatment.

Contractors have a few defining features. First, they are both potential threats and potential benefactors. They can return our good deeds, but can also dish out some nasty treatment in response to being harmed. Second, they are, fundamentally, our equals. They have roughly the same powers as we do, including powers to help us and to hurt us. And third, *we must be unable to gain anything from them without their consent.* In other words, we must enter agreements with them in order to obtain benefits from them, and protection against them.

At first blush, it seems strange that membership in the moral community should be limited to contractors. But it makes good sense, once we recall the Hobbesian view of rationality. According to Hobbes, *sacrifice requires compensation.* When we escape from the state of nature, for instance, we give up a great many freedoms. But it is worth it, because of the promise of a better life, the sort that comes from being able to trust and rely on others.

Now here is the crucial question: if we can get what we really want, without having to sacrifice anything, then why should we make the sacrifice? If Hobbes is right, there is no answer to this question. There is no reason to make such a sacrifice.

We can get what we want from trees, from animals, from the very weak, without having to give up anything in return. And so we have no reason to treat such beings with respect. They don't meet the conditions of being a contractor. We *could* decide to be nice to them—we could choose, for instance, to let a chicken live, rather than kill it and eat it, or let a lab rat go free, rather than submit it to painful experiments. But that is charity. It isn't duty. We have no duties to such vulnerable beings, because our duties are limited to contractors—those we have reason to respect, because they can harm us if we don't and can benefit us if we do. We can't just take what we want from contractors. We need to give up something in exchange for their beneficial cooperation.

In short, you get moral status, have rights, and are owed respect just in case your cooperation is needed in order for others to benefit. You have to be a member of the social contract in order to have genuine moral importance. Plants aren't members, since we can use them as we like, without giving them anything in return. Ditto for animals, and the very weak among us. That is why membership in the moral community is limited to contractors. They are the only ones with whom it is rational to enter a social contract. For all other beings, we'd be giving something up (freedom to exploit them), without gaining anything in return. According to Hobbes, that is irrational.

Thus contractarianism offers no secure protection for the truly vulnerable. We could, if we like, ensure their protection, but reason does not require us to do so, since we can get what we want from them without having to sacrifice anything in return. We are to them as a much more powerful and indestructible alien race would be to us. Such creatures, if they felt like it, might be nice to us. But since there is nothing in it for them to treat us this way, neither reason nor morality requires that they offer us their respect. They'd be perfectly within their rights to snack on us day and night.

This is because morality, on the social contract view, comes from rules of beneficial cooperation that rational parties would agree to. Rational, all-powerful aliens wouldn't agree to limit their liberty in exchange for anything we might do for them, since we can't hurt them, and they can get whatever they want from us without giving anything up on their end.

If the social contract theory is correct, then animals, ecosystems, infants, and the severely mentally disabled are in the same position as we readers are in the fictional example I've just presented. It's very bad news for humanity if such a race ever pays the earth a visit. In the meantime, it's very bad news indeed for all the vulnerable among us.

14.5 Conclusion

Contractarianism starts with a very promising idea: morality is essentially a social matter, made up of the rules that we would accept if we were free, equal, and fully rational. The heart of the theory is an ideal social code that serves as the true standard for what is right and wrong.

This theory has a lot going for it, as we've seen. It offers us a procedure for evaluating moral claims, and so offers the promise of being able to justify even our most basic moral views. It has an interesting explanation of the objectivity of morality. It can explain why we are often bound to obey the law, and why we may sometimes break it. It has an appealing account of why we should punish criminals. It can explain why it is usually (though not always) rational to behave morally.

That's a very impressive list. Like all other popular moral theories, however, it is not perfect. There are those who are disappointed with the theory because it leaves open the possibility that immoral actions are rational. Whether this is a serious problem, however, is still up in the air, since it is very hard to know whether it is always rational to do your duty. Still, as we have just seen, the theory does have at least one truly worrying aspect. It denies that the neediest are members of our moral community, and so opens the way to their exploitation.

I want to remind you that every moral theory we consider in this book is still a work in progress. Very smart philosophers continue to develop these theories, building on their strengths and trying to shore up their weaknesses. It's no different here, when it comes to assessing the social contract theory. I haven't offered the last word on its success. I've offered only the beginnings of the full picture. Those who find its vision of morality elegant and compelling are invited to think more about how it might be supported, while fans of its competitors must do the same for their favored theory.

Let's now have a look at more of the competition.

14.6 Discussion Questions

1. Is it immoral to be a free rider? Is it irrational? Does the existence of free riders raise a serious problem for contractarianism? Why or why not?
2. How does Hobbes defend the claim that it is never rational to behave unjustly? Do you find his arguments convincing?

3. Some people might object that they never explicitly signed anything like a "social contract," and therefore cannot be bound by it. How might contractarians respond to such an objection?
4. Suppose that the existing laws of a society require something that you regard as unjust. Does the social contract theory automatically support the morality of the existing law? Why or why not?
5. Would a group of free, equal, and rational people necessarily all agree on a set of rules to live by? If not, is this a problem for contractarianism?
6. Do animals have rights? Do weak and vulnerable human beings? If so, can contractarianism account for this?

14.7 Cases for Critical Reflection

Doping

For many years, Lance Armstrong was considered to be one of the greatest cyclists to have ever lived. Between 1999 and 2005, he won seven titles in the Tour de France cycling competition. Years later, Armstrong was stripped of these titles when evidence showed that he had been doping, which is the practice of taking drugs in order to enhance athletic performance.

Doping in sport is widely considered to be wrong, because it undermines the fairness of the game. Sports federations often test athletes to detect illegal doping, though some athletes manage to evade detection. In some sports, doping is so common that athletes feel a strong pressure take drugs in order to maintain a competitive advantage. Meanwhile, the technology used to detect doping continues to improve. For example, in 2005, a laboratory test of Armstrong's urine found traces of erythropoietin, a banned substance. However, the urine sample had been taken years earlier and frozen in 1999, and at that time there was no reliable test to detect erythropoietin. Athletes who decide to dope will continuously seek out new drugs that are increasingly difficult to detect in laboratory tests.[1]

Questions

1. Do athletes face a prisoner's dilemma with respect to doping? Why or why not?
2. According to contractarianism, is doping in sport morally wrong? Why or why not?
3. Do you believe doping in sport is morally wrong? Why or why not?

---

1. https://www.wired.com/2012/10/lance-armstrong-and-the-prisoners-dilemma-of-doping-in-professional-sports/.

Climate Change

Climate change is currently an important global issue. Since the nineteenth century, the average temperature of the earth's climate has been rising, and the consensus among climate scientists is that this increase is driven by greenhouse gases that humans have put into the atmosphere. If nothing is done to stop the changing climate, the world will face risks of deadly heat waves, droughts, flooding, and extinction. Glaciers and ice sheets will melt, leading to the rise of global sea levels. The outcome for humanity could be catastrophic.[1]

Since climate change is a global phenomenon, there is very little that a single person or even a single nation could do to stop it. Cutting emissions isn't easy, and it is costly to find alternatives. The world gets much of its energy from fossil fuels, including oil, gas, and coal. Industries such as agriculture and manufacturing would need to change radically to reduce the impact of their emissions. Many countries have pledged to reduce their share of greenhouse gas emissions, but these pledges fall short of what is needed to bring climate change to a halt.

The problem of climate change has been compared to the prisoner's dilemma. Casper Hare, a philosophy professor at the Massachusetts Institute of Technology, teaches a course on the ethics of climate change. On whether climate change poses a prisoner's dilemma, Hare says:

With climate change, it may be that some of us are individually better off, short term, driving SUVs, but if we all emit carbon like crazy, we're all worse off than if none of us do so. Eventually, we might arrive at a point where everybody sees its in their best interest to cooperate and reduce emissions.[2]

Questions

1. Do we face a prisoner's dilemma with respect to global climate change? Why or why not?
2. Do you believe that individuals are morally obligated to reduce their share of greenhouse gas emissions? Why or why not?
3. What sort of principle regarding our obligations to reduce our share of greenhouse gases, if any, would the contractors agree to from behind the veil of ignorance? Why?
4. According to contractarianism, are we morally obligated to reduce our share of greenhouse gas emissions? Why or why not?

---

1. https://climate.nasa.gov/evidence/.
2. http://news.mit.edu/2018/philosophy-class-moral-calculus-climate-change-0605.

World Hunger

Global wealth and income are distributed unequally, and large numbers of people are at risk of starvation due to lack of food, shelter, and water. People who suffer from undernourishment live shorter lives, and meanwhile, they do not get the caloric energy necessary to lead a normal, healthy, and happy life. The groups who are disproportionately at risk of hunger include the rural poor, the urban poor, children in poor families, the elderly, women, and displaced people fleeing war and national disasters.[1] In 2018, half the country of Yemen was on the brink of famine, and nearly half a million Yemeni children were chronically malnourished.[2] Meanwhile, many well-off individuals across the world eat a diet of excess. Many governments and individuals provide charitable aid to world's poor, but so far, these efforts are not enough to end global poverty and hunger.

Questions

1. According to contractarianism, are we obligated to give aid to the poor in our own community? What about the world's poor?
2. Do we face a prisoner's dilemma with respect to providing charitable aid to individuals suffering from lack of food? Why or why not?
3. What sort of principle regarding charitable aid to foreign nations would the contractors agree to from behind the veil of ignorance? Why?

---

1. http://www.fao.org/FOCUS/E/WFDay/WFGra-e.htm.
2. https://www.cnn.com/2018/11/09/middleeast/yemens-plight-lister-analysis-intl/index.html.

CHAPTER 15

Moral Absolutism

Moral absolutism is the view that there are absolute moral rules. An absolute moral rule is one that you are *never* permitted to break. No exceptions. No matter the circumstances, no matter the outcome, an absolute rule, by definition, must always be obeyed. If you violate an absolute rule, you have automatically acted immorally. Some moral rules are clearly *not* absolute. Among many examples: those that forbid us from hitting others, or require us to tell the truth or honor our elders. If hitting someone is the only way to thwart a violent attacker, it's okay to do so. It is alright to lie to the inquiring murderer.[1] Morality doesn't require us to honor racist elders who fought to oppress their victims. Though these moral rules are permissibly broken on occasion, such examples pose no threat to moral absolutism. This view does not say that every moral rule is absolute—only that some of them are. Popular examples include rules that prohibit deliberately killing an innocent person, raping someone, or torturing a captive. Are such rules really absolute? Let's work toward an answer by focusing on a test case.

15.1 Is Torture Always Immoral?

You might reasonably think that if there are any absolute moral rules, then a ban on torture would be among them. Let's consider a real example to help sort things out.

---

1. See chapter 11, "Kant on Absolute Moral Duties."

On the evening of March 1, 2003, CIA officers deployed just outside of the Pakistani capital of Islamabad received a text message: "I am with K.S.M." The initials were those of Khalid Sheikh Mohammed, mastermind of the September 11 attacks on the World Trade Center. After waiting a few hours, so as not to compromise the identity of their informant, CIA officers stormed the house and apprehended Sheikh Mohammed. He was soon flown to Afghanistan and then to Poland, where he was detained in a "black site" facility—a detention center that did not officially exist and that was run without legal oversight.

Over the next two weeks, Sheikh Mohammed was sometimes prevented from sleeping for extended periods, was slapped, was subjected to frigid temperatures, and was "waterboarded" more than 100 times. Waterboarding is especially terrifying. It involves strapping a prisoner to a board and repeatedly pouring water over his mouth and nose to simulate the experience of drowning. As water fills his lungs, the prisoner almost immediately suffers a gag reflex and is overwhelmed by a feeling that he is about to die.

Waterboarding rarely results in death. It is always extremely painful, and it does sometimes kill, though it more frequently results in other sorts of harm (lasting psychological damage, lung or brain damage, and sometimes broken bones caused by struggling against the physical restraints).

In Sheikh Mohammed's case, the purpose of such treatment was clear—to extract useful information that would lead to the capture of other terrorists and the prevention of their murderous plans. Despite serious reservations by a number of CIA and FBI personnel, the most senior U.S. officials regarded such treatment as morally acceptable. Their argument was straightforward: though waterboarding isn't exactly a noble undertaking, it is the lesser of two evils. If faced with a choice between torturing a terrorist in order to save the lives of hundreds of innocent people and refraining from such torture at the risk of those many lives, it is clear which option is best.

Administration officials repeatedly denied that waterboarding is a form of torture. They appeared to embrace the absolutist idea that torture is always immoral. But is it? Despite widespread support for this view, it might not stand up to scrutiny. Perhaps we should accept that waterboarding is torture, but insist, forthrightly, that torture is sometimes morally acceptable—especially when many innocent lives are at stake. When vividly imagining bouts of torture, it can be hard to resist the thought that such actions are never morally acceptable. And yet, as we shall see, it can be very difficult to justify this view.

15.2 Preventing Catastrophes

Those who condemn all torture must be prepared to answer the perennial challenge of the ticking bomb terrorist, the one who knows the location of a bomb powerful enough to kill thousands of innocent people. Suppose that we were able to capture such a terrorist and that he refused to reveal the bomb's location. Wouldn't it be acceptable to torture him in order to gain knowledge of its whereabouts?

We should consider this challenge in its best light, so suppose that any torture we inflict will not be lethal and must first be authorized by at least two independent government officials. Further, it will be administered only after the prisoner has been given a chance to cooperate, and if he does, no torture will occur. Suppose all of these conditions have been met, but the prisoner refuses to cooperate. We then begin to torture him by means of an extremely painful technique that will cause no lasting physical damage— perhaps a series of sanitized needles inserted very deeply under the prisoner's fingernails. Given the stakes, isn't this sort of action justified?[2]

Those who say *yes* would do so for an obvious reason: torture in such a case might prevent a catastrophe. And morality should surely allow us to prevent catastrophes. The critic of absolutism relies on this thought in offering the *Argument from Disaster Prevention*:

1. If there are any absolute moral rules, then we are *never* permitted to break them.
2. Every moral rule may be permissibly broken, since doing so may be necessary to prevent a catastrophe.
3. Therefore, there are no absolute moral rules.

This is a powerful argument. Its first premise is certainly true, since absolute moral rules are, by definition, those that we are never allowed to break. And the second premise is quite plausible. After all, what could possibly be so important about obedience to a moral rule that would allow us to sacrifice thousands of innocent people for its sake? That is a very hard question to answer. If there is no satisfactory reply, then the second premise is true. Since this is a logically valid argument, the truth of both premises would entail the truth of the conclusion, and with it, the downfall of moral absolutism.

---

2. Harvard law professor Alan Dershowitz has offered a controversial defense of torture under these conditions. See *Why Terrorism Works: Understanding the Threat, Responding to the Challenge* (New Haven, Conn.: Yale University Press, 2003), ch. 4.

Notice that this argument makes no specific mention of torture. It is designed to be a perfectly general criticism of all absolute moral rules. But you might be suspicious. Perhaps torture isn't a good example. Maybe it's okay to torture people, in very unusual cases. But that doesn't settle the matter of absolutism's merits, since there might be better candidates for absolute rules. Could it ever be right, for instance, to rape someone? Or to deliberately kill an innocent person against his wishes?

Critics of absolutism will say that, yes, such actions may indeed be morally right, though these critics will also admit that any such cases would be extremely rare. For instance, if someone credibly threatens to detonate a nuclear bomb in a densely populated city, and agrees to defuse it only if we authorize the killing of an innocent person, then perhaps, morally speaking, we must agree to his terms. We should never celebrate having to torture, rape, or kill. But if doing such actions will prevent a horrible catastrophe, then critics of absolutism insist that we may be permitted, and perhaps even required, to do such things.

15.3 The Doctrine of Double Effect

Suppose that you are an emergency room physician and are faced with six patients who have just been rushed to your hospital. They were all at a dinner party and made the mistake of eating some innocent-looking mushrooms that turned out to be poisonous. Each of the patients is dying. After quickly running some tests, you discover that saving one of the patients requires giving him all of the available antidote. You also discover that you can save the other five patients by giving them each a fifth of the serum. Whom should you save?

Assuming that each of these six patients is a good person, with otherwise decent life prospects, it seems clear that you should save the five. It's not that the very needy patient deserves to die; rather, it is better that only one dies, rather than five.

We reach similar verdicts in other cases. Imagine that a runaway trolley is headed for five innocent people and that you can pull a lever that switches the trolley to a side track, where (you guessed it) one unfortunate person is trapped. Shouldn't you pull that lever?

Suppose that an important military operation can be conducted risking only one soldier's life, rather than five. If the one soldier is just as likely to complete the task, it seems clear that the right thing to do is to spare the five and send him out alone.

Reasoning in these cases, as in so many others, seems to push us directly to consequentialism. The mandate here (and in the Argument from Disaster Prevention) seems clear: minimize harm.

Yet we would also minimize harm if we were secretly to abduct a small number of healthy people, anesthetize them, and cut them up to distribute their vital organs to those who would otherwise die from organ failure. We could minimize misery by "culling" the population of those whose lives are wretchedly unhappy, with little prospect of improvement—even if they didn't want to die. We could dramatically reduce terrorism if we adopted a policy of reliably executing a terrorist's child or spouse in response. But these ways of minimizing harm are deeply offensive.

Consequentialist reasoning, so powerful in the Argument from Disaster Prevention and in the three initial cases we've considered here, seems to have led us astray. But if it is so plausible in the earlier cases, perhaps we should overcome our queasiness when it comes to the examples in the previous paragraph.

Absolutists reject that thought. Indeed, many people are tempted by absolutism precisely because they see it as the only way to resist consequentialism. But to make good on this hope, absolutists need to show how they can make sense of these various cases, without relying on hidden consequentialist assumptions. The absolutist must be able to distinguish the antidote, trolley, and military stories, on the one hand, from the murderous cases just described.

Absolutists have often relied on the **Doctrine of Double Effect (DDE)** to do this. The doctrine refers to two relevant effects that actions can have: those that we intend to bring about, and those that we foresee but do not aim for. This principle says the following:

> Provided that your goal is worthwhile, you are sometimes permitted to act in ways that foreseeably cause certain types of harm, though you must never intend to cause such harms.

The DDE does not say that it is always wrong to intentionally harm others. It allows, for instance, that harmful punishment is sometimes acceptable. The DDE simply tells us that *some* harms may never be aimed for, even though such harms may be permitted as side effects of one's actions (i.e., as "collateral damage"). Which harms are these? The ones prohibited by absolute moral rules.

The doctrine of double effect, if true, would have two very important implications: (1) it would provide a reply to the Argument from

Disaster Prevention, and (2) it would refute utilitarianism and all forms of **act consequentialism**.

A Reply to the Argument from Disaster Prevention

The Argument from Disaster Prevention advises us to impose certain terrible harms in order to prevent even more of them from occurring. Those who endorse this argument would have us set out to kill innocent people, for instance, if doing so would lessen the overall number of innocent deaths.

Against this, the DDE requires that we not aim at certain harms, even if that is the only way to prevent disaster. After all, the absolutist insists that certain acts must never be done, *whatever the consequences*. The DDE denies that the ends always justify the means. Certain goals are *never* to be pursued, even if pursuing them will help us minimize harm.

How the DDE Threatens Act Consequentialism

If the DDE is correct, then even if two actions predictably have the same bad results, one of these actions might be right and the other wrong. And that is something that utilitarians and other act consequentialists cannot allow. They determine the morality of an action based solely on its results. Any two acts with identical results must be morally equivalent.

By contrast, the DDE determines the morality of an action based partly on what is going on in the mind of the person performing it. If the DDE is correct, then some intentional harms may be immoral, even though causing the same harms while aiming at other goals may be permitted.

The DDE can be used by absolutists in the following way. Suppose, as many absolutists claim, that it is always wrong to deliberately kill an innocent person. Then it is always immoral to intend to kill a healthy patient to save others, to seek to eliminate the deeply miserable among us, and to aim to kill an innocent child to stave off terrorism. Since each of these actions involves the intention to kill innocent people, it is automatically wrong.

But by sending a soldier on a dangerous reconnaissance mission, knowing that he is likely not to return, we are aiming at some morally acceptable military goal rather than the soldier's death. In providing the antidote to five patients, we know that the neediest patient will die, but we would be delighted if he survived; we don't intend to kill him. In shifting the trolley to a side track, we are trying to save five lives, even though we foresee that one person will die as a result. These examples all involve morally acceptable actions; even though we foresee, in each case, that someone will probably die, we are aiming to do good, and do not intend to cause harm.

The DDE thus allows us to morally distinguish cases that yield identical results (in these cases, five lives saved, one lost). It does so by showing that we can respect an absolute ban on intentionally killing innocents. In drawing moral distinctions among cases with the same consequences, it directly challenges all forms of act consequentialism.

Distinguishing Intention from Foresight

So the DDE does a lot of good work for the absolutist. But there is a difficulty with the DDE, and it must be solved before absolutists can rely on it with confidence. The difficulty is that *we lack a clear basis for distinguishing between intention and foresight*. Without clarity on this point, the DDE will either fail to provide guidance about the morality of actions or will give us results that seem deeply mistaken.

Consider this challenge: Those who secretly abduct and carve up innocent people to distribute their organs could say that they intend only to save many innocent lives. They would be delighted if their innocent victims were (miraculously) to remain alive after the operation. Therefore, they *don't* intend to kill their victims. They merely foresee their death. Thus the DDE does not condemn their actions.

It is hard to imagine someone saying this with a straight face. But explaining precisely what is wrong with such a claim is not easy. It requires us to sharply define intention. Further, this definition must clearly distinguish intention from foresight, and also help us to see why intending harm is so much worse than foreseeing it. Can this be done? Have a look at these attempts:

(A) You intend to do X = You want X to occur as a result of your action.

But the surgeon carving up the kidnapped victims may not want them to die. He may want only to save the lives of the many patients who need these organs. So according to (A), the surgeon does not intend to kill the abducted patients. But he surely does, and that makes (A) implausible.

(B) You intend to do X = X is part of your plan of action.

Consider another variant on the trolley case. Here, the runaway trolley is heading toward five people, but there is no spur. The only way to stop the train is by pushing a huge bystander onto the tracks at the last minute. His bulk will stop the train—though he will surely die as a result. Here again, we save five at the cost of one. But this leaves an awfully bad taste in the mouth.

Yet if I were to push this guy, I could deny that his death was part of my plan. My plan was limited, let's say, to pushing this man and to stopping the train. I'd be pleased if the man were to escape with only bruises. According to (B), I didn't intend to kill the man. But I did. So (B) is problematic.

> (C) You intend to do X = You would regret it if X didn't occur as a result of your action.

Consider the last trolley case again. It seems clear that I intentionally killed the man I pushed to the tracks. But I would *not* regret it if he survived. Therefore, by (C), I did not intend his death. Again, something has gone wrong.

> (D) You intend to do X = X results from your actions in a nonaccidental way.

The problem here is that all merely foreseen results will now become results that we intend to produce. When the ER doctor gives the serum to her five patients, the sixth patient will die. The doctor knows this. And it isn't an accident. Therefore, by this definition, the doctor intends that the remaining patient die. But that, too, seems mistaken.

> (E) You intend to do X = You must cause X if you are to achieve your goals.

In the second trolley case, it is false that the huge bystander's death must occur if I am to achieve my goals. All that *must* occur is that he stop the train with his body. And so, with (E), I do not intend his death. And so the DDE does not condemn my action. But my action is surely condemnable.

These aren't the only possibilities for defining what it is to intend to do something, but it's been a very difficult task for absolutists to provide a definition of intention that manages to track the moral distinctions that we feel so confident about. So if you are a fan of the DDE, here is your task: clarify the distinction between intended and merely foreseen results, and do so in a way that shows why some intentional harms, just by virtue of being intended, are morally worse than harms that are foreseen—indeed, so bad that they may never be intentionally inflicted. Perhaps it can be done. But it won't be easy.

15.4 Moral Conflict and Contradiction

For those who find moral absolutism attractive, an invitation: put together your preferred list of absolute moral rules. Once you've completed the task, consider this question: what happens if these rules ever conflict with one another? If each of them is absolute, then moral conflict leads to contradiction. That is a deal-killer for a moral theory.

Consider a very simple case. Suppose that the correct list of absolute moral rules includes these two: keep your promises, and don't deliberately harm innocent people. The point I'm about to make doesn't depend on these rules actually being absolute—in fact, I think that neither of them is. But just imagine, for a moment, that they are. Now suppose that someone has done you a great kindness. As a gesture of thanks, you promise to help him whenever he needs it. He smiles, and then asks you to make good on your word by breaking into his rival's home and beating him senseless. The rival, let's suppose, is an innocent. He's done nothing to deserve such a beating.

In this case, you are morally required to keep your promise. But in doing that, you'd also be acting immorally, since you would be violating the rule against harming innocents. If you instead avoid hurting the innocent rival, you will be doing what is required of you. But this would also be forbidden, since it would involve breaking your promise. Either way you go, your action is both morally required and forbidden. That is a contradiction.

It's a simple case, as I've said. But it is meant to illustrate a crucial worry for theories that endorse absolute moral rules. When such rules conflict, the theory yields contradictory advice. And that will sink the view, since contradictions are fatal flaws for any theory. The *Argument from Contradiction* summarizes this challenge:

1. If there is more than one absolute moral rule, then those rules are bound to conflict at some point.
2. If absolute rules ever conflict, then this generates contradiction.
3. If a theory generates contradiction, then it is false.
4. Therefore, any theory that endorses the existence of more than one absolute moral rule is false.

Premises 2 and 3 are true. They won't attract any challenges from philosophers. The real debate focuses on premise 1. If you believe that there is more than one absolute moral rule, then you have to show that the rules will never, ever conflict.

There is a way to do this. We will have to assume that absolute moral rules have a certain limitation: they forbid us from acting in specific ways, but they never require us to act in any way at all. We may never do certain things—rape, torture, and terrorize, for instance. These rules, and others, can be honored entirely through *inaction*. So long as all absolute rules can be obeyed by doing nothing, then absolute rules will never conflict.

This means that most of the familiar moral rules cannot be absolute, since they require us to act in certain ways—perform easy rescues, prevent disaster, protect our children from harm, keep our promises. If moral rules require us to do things, rather than merely refrain from action, then they might require us to do incompatible things. That is the kind of conflict that leads to contradiction. If, instead, all absolute moral rules can be satisfied merely by sitting on our hands and doing nothing, then contradiction can be avoided.

15.5 Is Moral Absolutism Irrational?

Many people think that intentionally killing innocent people is never morally acceptable. What could explain this? Presumably, the incredibly important value of innocent human life. But if this is of paramount importance, then why shouldn't we kill an innocent person if we could save more innocent lives by doing so?

Optimists will say that such a thing could never happen. But it could.

In 1961, a man approached the chief rabbi of Warsaw, Shimon Efrati, and asked a question that had been troubling him for many years. This man was among a group of Jews who had hidden in a ghetto bunker during World War II, trying to avoid the Nazi patrols intent on killing them. There was a crying baby in the hideout. Someone pressed a pillow over the baby's face, in order to prevent it from making any more noise and revealing the group's location. The baby suffocated and died; their hiding place remained a secret.

You might think that there was no need to kill the baby. There must have been some way to avoid killing it while keeping the group's location a secret and saving everyone. But a terrible aspect of this story gives us reason to doubt such optimism.

The case brought to Rabbi Efrati was basically identical to a situation faced by the rabbi's own brother in 1943. He and his fellow refugees squeezed themselves into a small bunker in order to escape from the Nazi killing squads. One of the refugees was the mother of an infant whose cries threatened to reveal their hiding place. Members of the group tried all they could to quiet the baby, to no avail. One of them wanted to smother the baby, but the rabbi's brother intervened and prevented it. As a result, the baby's cries led soldiers directly to the hideout. Rabbi Efrati's brother, along with nineteen others, were rounded up and summarily executed.

Cases like these can make it seem irrational to defend an absolute ban on killing the innocent, since we can sometimes *better* protect innocent human life by violating this ban. That appears to show that the ban should not be absolute. The charge can be put in the form of an *Argument from Irrationality*:

1. If perfect obedience to a rule can frustrate the underlying purpose of the rule, then the rule is irrational.
2. Perfect obedience to any absolute moral rule can sometimes frustrate its underlying purpose.
3. Therefore, absolute moral rules are irrational.

This may look a bit like the Argument from Disaster Prevention, but there is an important difference. The charge here isn't that following absolute rules may produce a catastrophe. Rather, the complaint is that there is something fundamentally *inconsistent* about the absolutist position.

It is tempting to defend absolute rules by claiming that they protect all-important values, such as the value of innocent life. But if these values can be better served by violating those rules, then the rules *should* be broken. And that means that they aren't really absolute, after all.

Absolutists have replied to this challenge by rejecting the argument's second premise. To see how they do this, consider again an absolute ban on killing innocents. It's natural to think that the point of such a rule is to protect innocent life. But absolutists *deny* this. If our goal is to minimize the loss of innocent human life, then we *should* sometimes deliberately kill an innocent person, since that will best achieve our goal. But certain absolutists think that we should never, ever kill another innocent human being—even if doing so will thereby spare many more innocent people from being killed.

If the point of a ban on killing innocents is not to save innocent life, then what is it? The answer is simplicity itself. The point of such a ban is to forbid you from killing innocent people. The only way to honor that demand is by not killing innocents. Of course, it may be (as it was in the case of Rabbi Efrati's brother) that by obeying this requirement, you thereby open the door to a situation in which many more innocent people are killed. But the absolute requirement is not that you prevent the killing of innocents. It is that you kill none of them yourself.

In other words, the fundamental rationale for absolute moral rules is to forbid people from acting in certain ways, rather than to minimize the violation of these rules.

How can such a view be defended? The easy way is closed to us. The easy way tells us that innocent life is of the greatest importance, and so must be protected via an absolute rule. As we have seen, that way won't work, because this value can sometimes be better served by *violating* the rule against killing. That's what happens when we must kill one innocent person in order to save many others.

What we need instead is a defense of this key idea:

> We are always forbidden to act in certain ways, though we are not always required to prevent such acts from occurring.

Absolutists have found a way to defend this key claim. It is called the **Doctrine of Doing and Allowing (DDA)**.

15.6 The Doctrine of Doing and Allowing

At the finale of *Batman Begins*, Christopher Nolan's first movie about the comic book hero, Batman and his arch nemesis Ra's al Ghul are having their climactic battle aboard an elevated train. The train is about to plunge hundreds of feet to its destruction. Batman has finally pinned his enemy and could deal the killing blow. But he doesn't. Instead, the last words that Ra's al Ghul ever hears are these: "I'm not going to kill you. But I don't have to save you."

Batman's words reveal a commitment to a view that absolutists have long relied on. This is the Doctrine of Doing and Allowing (DDA):

> It is always morally worse to do harm than to allow that same harm to occur.

It is worse, for instance, to kill than to allow victims to be killed; worse to be a terrorist oneself than to allow others to perpetrate terrorism.

If it is always worse to do bad things than to allow them to occur, then we have a defense of the idea that absolute moral requirements apply only to what we do, and not to what we allow or fail to prevent. If the Doctrine of Doing and Allowing is true, we may be absolutely forbidden from killing, torturing, or raping, even though we are not absolutely required to prevent such behavior.

The DDA can therefore explain why there is something especially problematic about doing evil yourself. It can support the idea that you must keep your hands clean, even if doing so lets others cause even greater harm. The DDA directly supports the key claim that ended the previous section and is therefore essential to a defense of absolutism.

The Doctrine of Doing and Allowing thus allows us to deal with an especially tricky kind of moral dilemma—cases in which you are faced with a choice of doing something truly awful, or refusing to do so, knowing that your refusal will allow a less scrupulous person to take your place and do far greater harm.

Consider the case of certain Nazi military officers who came to view their cause as deeply unjust. They had much to fear, for if their views became known, they would be shot. If they resigned or sought to run away and were captured, they would also be shot. Apart from such fears, however, another consideration kept some of them from leaving their posts.

These officers often correctly thought that if they didn't follow orders, then some true believer, with no doubts about the Nazi program, would replace them. And that would be even more disastrous.

By remaining in their positions, these officers were aiding an evil cause. But they held the view, shared by many in situations like theirs, that the best way to lessen the harms of a morally bankrupt institution was to work from within. The problem, of course, is that one must often do evil to remain an insider. Immoral groups usually test the loyalty of their members, and this requires them to do all sorts of terrible things. Those who end up following orders often justify their cooperation with evil by arguing that any alternative would bring about even greater harm. And they may well be right.

Together with moral absolutism, the DDA forbids certain actions, without requiring that you prevent others from doing them. On the safe assumption that Nazi atrocities were evil, the DDA would forbid German officers from committing them. It would require those officers to step down from their posts, even though, in doing so, they were signing their own death warrant, and effectively allowing others to do even greater damage.

We are sometimes forced to choose between doing actions that will stain our lives forever, and refusing to do so, knowing that our refusal will create an opportunity for other people to do their worst. In such cases, the DDA requires that we abstain from evil, even if this means that more people get hurt or that our own life is thereby placed at greater risk. For those who favor the DDA, some things are more important than minimizing harm to others, or even remaining alive. Preserving our moral integrity is one of them.

But is the DDA true? It may be. Here are two cases that reveal its attractions.

> **Case 1:** I am morally allowed to eat at a decent restaurant, spending $30 on the dinner—even though, with that money, I could have prevented the death of three starving Somali children by sending a check to UNICEF. Most of us think it acceptable to spend the money on

dinner, thereby allowing those children to die. Yet it would definitely be wrong to kill them directly.

Case 2: I am a soldier on the battlefield and see a fellow infantryman shot at my side. I can't tell whether his wound is fatal. He is groaning and asking for help. It would definitely be wrong to shoot that soldier. It would not be wrong to let him die, if I had to ignore his pleas in order to obey a command to retreat from the battlefield.

We are forbidden from doing something in both of these cases, though permitted to allow it to happen. The Doctrine of Doing and Allowing perfectly explains why this is so.

But some have had their worries about the DDA. Consider these two cases:

Case 3: I am a nurse charged with giving a bedridden patient a life-saving pill every four hours. I am an evil nurse, however, and when the appointed time comes, I stand by, pill in hand, and do nothing, thereby allowing the patient to die. Suppose instead that I obtain a poison pill and give him that, rather than his real medication. He dies as a result. If the DDA is true, then giving the poison pill is morally worse than deliberately withholding the medicine. Is it?

Case 4: I am a switchman who notices a runaway trolley speeding down the tracks, headed for one innocent person trapped in a narrow pass. I pull a lever and switch the tracks so that the trolley heads off on a spur. I do this because five people are on that spur and I want to kill as many people as I can. They all die. Now suppose, instead, that the runaway trolley is headed for the five rather than the one, and I just stand there, gleefully passing up an easy chance to switch the trolley to the track with only one person on it. The DDA says that my action is morally worse than my omission, that pulling a lever is morally worse than not pulling it—even though both cases result in the same number of deaths, and in both I have the same motive, intentions, and knowledge of the likely outcomes.

These are all very schematic, underdescribed cases. Some of them are quite outrageous. But there is a point to relying on examples like these. We can appreciate it by thinking about the nature of scientific experiments. The ones that are well designed often place two groups in identical circumstances, and change just a single variable, to test for its importance. For instance, we offer a control group a placebo, and then test a new drug by seeing how members of a comparison group fare when taking it. This allows us to isolate the drug's powers (or lack of powers).

The tests we conduct in ethics are thought experiments. We think of different situations that are identical in all respects but one, and then ask whether that difference makes any *moral* difference. That is what is going on in the cases just described. Each case presents two scenarios that are perfectly similar in every way but one. In the first scenario, the person *does* something very harmful, but in the second, the person *allows* that same harm to occur. Keeping everything else the same enables us to filter out any distracting, irrelevant details that could skew our responses to these cases. We can then determine whether the difference between doing and allowing, in and of itself, is morally relevant.

The problem for the DDA is that it sometimes seems, as it might in cases 3 and 4 (and other easily constructed examples), that the mere difference between doing and allowing has no moral importance at all. That is a serious challenge to the DDA. But of course your views on these cases may differ from mine, and you might feel strongly that doing the harm is, in each case, worse than failing to prevent it.

Even if that is so, however, there is another potential problem for the DDA: the distinction between doing and allowing is actually very hard to draw. Consider the classic case of "pulling the plug" on a patient whose life is being maintained by a ventilator. It seems that this is a matter of doing something—removing a tube or flipping a machine's switch. The doctor or nurse is not just standing there, stock still. But many have argued that removing such life support is merely letting nature take its course—in other words, not doing anything at all, but rather allowing some ongoing chain of events to continue on its way.

Before we can apply the DDA, we need to have a plausible way to distinguish doings from allowings. I don't know how to do this in a general way. But there are many easy cases, ones in which an action counts very clearly as doing something, or an inaction counts as obviously allowing something to occur. Perhaps this is enough to give absolutists hope that we can someday formulate a criterion that will enable us to distinguish doings from allowings once and for all.

The point of investigating the merits of the DDA is to examine whether the absolutist position can be defended against the charge of irrationality. Absolutists can defend against this objection if they can show why we must never commit certain harms, even if doing so would reduce the number of those harms. The DDA is meant to provide this piece of the puzzle. It tells us that doing harm is morally worse than allowing that same harm to occur. Whether the DDA is plausible will depend, in the end, on whether absolutists can supply a test for distinguishing between doing and allowing, and whether the DDA is immune to counterexamples of the sort that cases 3 and 4 seek to provide.

15.7 Conclusion

When I reflect on my own moral views, I find it hard to resist the thought that certain kinds of actions just should never be done. At the top of my list is murderous terrorism—deliberately trying to kill civilians, with the aim of inspiring fear and thereby furthering some political goal. When I vividly consider such behavior, I can't help but feel deeply repelled and outraged. I'm inclined to think that terrorism is always immoral.

But I know enough about myself to recognize my fallibility. My sense of outrage is not a surefire test of morality. Perhaps terrorism, in rare cases, is morally acceptable. Ditto for other familiar cases of repugnant behavior—rape, for instance, or torture. Whether such practices are always wrong depends on whether absolutists can adequately defend against the Argument from Disaster Prevention, the Argument from Contradiction, and the Argument from Irrationality.

The worry about contradiction is the most serious, for any theory that generates contradictions is certainly false. So absolutists must show that their favored moral rules will never conflict. The only way to ensure this is to restrict the sort of things that are absolutely forbidden. There are two ways to do this.

First, we might be absolutely forbidden to *intend* certain harms. And, second, we might be absolutely forbidden to *do* certain harmful things. But why is it so important to refrain from intentional harms, or from doing harm—especially if what we intend or do, though harmful, will reduce the overall amount of harm in question? The DDE and the DDA are designed to provide an answer. The fate of absolutism hangs on whether these doctrines can be successfully defended.

15.8 Discussion Questions

1. Do you think it would be morally permissible to kill an innocent person to save a thousand innocent people? Defend your answer.
2. What is the doctrine of double effect, and how does it threaten consequentialism? Do you find the doctrine to be plausible? Why or why not?

3. Can you think of a general way to distinguish between what we intend and what we merely foresee, such that the harms we intend are morally worse than those we foresee?

4. If an absolute rule against deliberately killing innocent people is not justified by the need to protect innocent life, then what does justify such a rule (if anything)?

5. Why might the view that there are multiple absolute moral rules generate a contradiction? How can moral absolutists defend their theory against this possibility?

6. Is doing harm always worse than allowing harm? Is it always possible to draw a line between the two?

15.9 Cases for Critical Reflection

The Trolley Problem

Thought experiments are imagined cases that students of ethics use to aid in their reasoning about moral theories and principles. Recall our previous discussion of the trolley problem. Imagine that the driver of a trolley has passed out at the wheel, and his trolley is hurtling out of control down the track. Straight ahead are five people who cannot escape from the track. If the trolley reaches them, they will surely be killed. Fortunately, you are standing next to a lever, which you can pull in order to send the trolley down a side track. However, you realize that a single person is tied to the side track. Pulling the lever will save the five people on the main track but will result in the death of the person on the side track. Time is running out. You ask yourself: "Should I pull the lever?"

The trolley problem has been criticized by some for being too silly and unrealistic to help us understand real-world moral problems.[1] However, the thought experiment has received renewed attention due to developments in self-driving vehicle technology.[2] There are parallels between the dilemma posed by the trolley problem and real-life situations that self-driving cars could pose. For example, a driverless car may need to decide what to do if faced with a choice between colliding with another vehicle

---

1. https://www.theatlantic.com/health/archive/2014/07/what-if-one-of-the-most-popular-experiments-in-psychology-is-worthless/374931/.

2. https://www.wired.com/story/self-driving-cars-will-kill-people-who-decides-who-dies/.

or swerving into a crowd of people. Engineers may need to decide how to program self-driving cars to behave in these life-and-death situations.

Questions

1. What is your intuitive response to the trolley problem? Should you pull the lever? Why or why not?
2. How should engineers program self-driving cars to behave in scenarios like the trolley problem?
3. Recall the variant of the trolley problem in which you are standing on a footbridge looking down as the trolley hurtles toward the five people tied to the track. An extremely large man is standing next to you on the bridge. If you push him off the bridge, his large body will stop the trolley. That man will be killed, but the five people tied to the track will be saved. What is the morally right thing to do in this case, and why? If it's wrong to push the large man, is it also wrong to pull the lever?
4. What does the Doctrine of Double Effect counsel you to do in the original trolley problem, and the variant described in question 3? Does the Doctrine of Doing and Allowing give the same or different advice? Support your answer.

The Emergency Room

Imagine that you are a doctor in a hospital, and you have in your possession five doses of a scarce drug. Six patients arrive to the emergency room in critical condition, and each of them could be cured by the scarce drug. Untreated, each of the patients will die. Five of the patients are in a condition such that a single dose of the scarce drug would cure them. The sixth patient presents a special case and would require all five doses in order to be cured. You must decide who will receive the life-saving scarce drug.

Now consider this: you're a surgeon working in the hospital emergency room, with five patients in desperate need of organ transplants. Each of the five patients has a rare blood type, and between them they need a heart, two kidneys, a liver, and lungs. A new patient arrives at the emergency room. He is in excellent health and happens to have the same rare blood type as the five patients in need of organs. While you're alone with the new patient, you realize that you could harvest his organs in order to save the others. If you're especially careful, no one will ever discover the crime.

Questions

1. Who do you think should be given the scarce drug, and why?
2. Would it be wrong to harvest the organs of one patient in order to save five others? Why or why not?
3. What advice does the Doctrine of Double Effect and the Doctrine of Doing and Allowing offer for these scenarios?
4. Are there morally relevant differences between the two emergency room cases? If so, what are they, and can either the Doctrine of Double Effect or the Doctrine of Doing and Allowing account for any such differences?

············ ❧ ············

CHAPTER 16

Prima Facie Duties and Ethical Particularism

16.1 Two Assumptions

All of the moral theories we've canvassed share two key assumptions. The first is that there is just a single moral rule that is **fundamental**. A fundamental moral rule is moral bedrock: it does not derive its truth from any other moral rule, though it can explain why other moral rules are correct. The second assumption is that any fundamental moral rule is absolute (never permissibly broken).

We can easily see how these key assumptions underlie the moral theories we've surveyed. A sampling: for divine command theorists, there is one rule that is both fundamental and absolute—do whatever God commands. All other moral rules are derived from this one, which may never be broken. For ethical egoists, the fundamental, absolute rule requires that you promote your self-interest. All other moral guidelines are grounded in this rule, which is always in force and admits of no exceptions. For utilitarians, the rule demanding that we maximize happiness plays this special role. It serves as the basis for all other moral principles, and is never permissibly broken. If you ask utilitarians to explain why the principle of utility is true, they will deny that any other moral rule can do so. Moral questioning, like all other lines of investigation, must stop somewhere. Fundamental moral rules mark that stopping point.

The views we discuss in this chapter reject both of the key assumptions stated above. The first of these views says that there are *several* fundamental moral rules, and *none* of them is absolute. That's a pretty radical take on morality. The second is even more so. It not only denies that there are any absolute moral rules, but goes further in claiming that there are no fundamental moral rules at all. If either of these views is correct, then moral philosophers have for centuries been engaged in a wild goose chase; their search for a single moral rule, one that can unify the moral order by being both fundamental and absolute, has been bound to fail.

16.2 Ross's Ethic of Prima Facie Duties

With the publication of his book *The Right and the Good* in 1930, Oxford professor W. D. Ross (1877–1971) introduced a genuinely new moral theory that rejected the traditional view that morality was structured around a single fundamental, absolute rule. Instead, he argued for a more complex picture of morality that posits at least seven fundamental moral rules, none of which is absolute. He coined a special term for these rules, calling each of them a **prima facie duty**. We will stick with that label in what follows.

A prima facie duty is an excellent, non-absolute, permanent reason to do (or refrain from) something—to keep one's word, be grateful for kindnesses, avoid hurting others, and so on. As Ross saw it, each prima facie duty is of fundamental importance. None of these duties can be derived from one another, or from any more basic principle. Crucially, each prima facie duty may sometimes be overridden by other such duties. Though there is always good reason, say, to keep a promise or prevent harm to others, morality sometimes requires that we break a promise or do harm. Likewise for each of the other prima facie duties.

Ross was convinced that absolutism in all of its forms is implausible. Those theories that endorse more than one absolute moral rule are bound to yield contradiction. Those that endorse only a single absolute rule are too narrow, and fail to see that there are a number of independently important moral considerations. For instance, while Ross accepted the utilitarian emphasis on doing good and preventing harm to others, he also agreed with Kant that justice was morally important in its own right.

Ross identified seven prima facie duties, each of which is meant to be a fundamental moral rule:

1. *Fidelity*: keeping our promises, being faithful to our word.
2. *Reparations*: repairing harm that we have done.
3. *Gratitude*: appropriately acknowledging benefits that others have given us.

4. *Justice*: ensuring that virtue is rewarded and vice punished.

5. *Beneficence*: enhancing the intelligence, virtue, or pleasure of others.

6. *Self-improvement*: making oneself more intelligent or virtuous.

7. *Non-maleficence*: preventing harm to others.

Ross did not claim that this list was complete. He allowed that there might be other prima facie duties. But each of these seven duties, he thought, definitely did belong on the list.

The term *prima facie duty* can be misleading. That's because these things are not really duties, but rather permanent moral reasons that partly determine whether an action truly is, in the end, morally required. To say, for instance, that there is a prima facie duty of beneficence is to say the following:

1. There is *always* a strong reason to benefit others.
2. This reason may sometimes be outweighed by competing reasons.
3. If this reason is the only moral reason that applies in a given situation, then benefiting others becomes our all-things-considered duty—in other words, what we are really, finally morally required to do in that situation.

Focus for a moment on the first item. It provides us with a way to test Ross's specific roster of prima facie duties. Suppose that there are situations in which there is *no reason at all* to benefit others. If that were so, there would be no prima facie duty of beneficence.

I will let you do the testing yourself, because I am most interested in the general theory of prima facie duties, rather than in any specific version of it. Even if Ross's group of seven rules includes too much, or too little, this would not undermine the ethic of prima facie duties. What it would show (and this would certainly be important) is that Ross's own list was off base. But even if it were, a better list might make the cut.

So let's instead consider the big picture, and reveal the attractions, and difficulties, of the general model of morality that Ross advanced. First, as usual, the attractions.

16.3 The Advantages of Ross's View

There Are Many Fundamental Moral Considerations

The greatest attraction of the ethic of prima facie duties is its ability to accommodate our sense that there is, indeed, more than just a single fundamental moral consideration. To Ross, and to most of the rest of us, it does seem that the very fact of our having promised to do something generates *some* reason to follow through, even if keeping our promise fails to bring happiness, reward virtue, prevent misery, or do anything else. That we have given our word is reason enough to do what we have promised.

But no one believes that promising is the only thing like this. There does seem to be something immoral, for instance, when someone repays a kindness with ingratitude—even if, in unusual circumstances, being ungrateful is the right way to go.

Whether or not you agree with the whole of Ross's list, you may well sign on to the idea that fidelity and gratitude, at the very least, each possess moral importance in their own right. If you do, that is enough to force a shift away from the idea that there is only one fundamental moral rule. And once moved in that direction, we should be open to the possibility that there are still other fundamental sources of moral duty—perhaps as many as seven of them, as Ross affirmed.

We Are Sometimes Permitted to Break the Moral Rules

Ross's position also easily explains the widespread belief that the moral rules may sometimes acceptably be broken. There is always something to be said in favor of keeping a promise—but I should break my promise to meet a student for coffee if my daughter has a medical emergency and needs to be taken to the hospital. We all accept that there are circumstances in which it is morally acceptable to break a promise, allow harm to others, pass up a chance at self-improvement, and so on. Ross's theory straightforwardly explains this.

Moral Conflict

The ethic of prima facie duties also appears to make good sense of our experience of moral conflict. Duties conflict when they can't all be fulfilled. On absolutist views, such conflict yields contradiction. But Ross's theory easily avoids this.

Consider the case of a poor single mother whose child is too sick to go to school. The mother has a duty to report to work. By taking the job, she has promised to reliably show up as scheduled. But suppose that she has just moved to town, has no friends or family there, and isn't allowed to bring her child to work. She also has a duty to care for her child, especially if no one else is available to do so. What should she do?

The Rossian can say of such a case that there is a conflict of prima facie duties. There is a strong case for showing up to work. There is a strong reason to care for one's child. Sometimes we can't do both. But no contradiction occurs, because we can distinguish between a standing reason (a prima facie duty) to do something and an all-things-considered, final duty to do it. When these final duties conflict—when we say, *in the end*, that you are fully required to show up at work and are also fully required to care for your child—then there is contradiction. Ross's view avoids this problem entirely.

I'm not intent on defending a specific verdict in this example. If Ross is correct, the key thing is that context will determine just how important a prima facie duty is. The consideration at the heart of such a duty (promise keeping, preventing harm, righting one's wrongs, etc.) is always morally *important*. But it is not always morally *decisive*. That is precisely what distinguishes a prima facie duty from an absolute one.

Moral Regret

Another way in which Ross's theory nicely handles moral conflict is in its view of moral regret. When moral claims conflict and we can't honor them all, we think that it is right to feel regret at having to give up something important. Regret is evidence that something of value has been sacrificed. When prima facie duties conflict and one takes priority over the other, the lesser duty doesn't just disappear. It still has some weight, even though in the circumstances it is not as morally powerful as the conflicting duty. Regret is our way of acknowledging this forsaken duty, our way of recognizing that something of value was lost in the conflict.

Indeed, this provides us with a reasonable test for knowing what our prima facie duties are. The test is simple: there is a prima facie duty to act in a certain way only if it would always be appropriate to regret our failure to act that way. If there were nothing valuable about gratitude, for instance, then missing a chance to express it would not be a cause for regret. But it is. And that shows that there is *something* important about gratitude, even if it isn't *all-important*. That's just what Ross believed.

Addressing the Anti-absolutist Arguments

Ross's view also provides a direct reply to all three of the anti-absolutist arguments in the previous chapter. The Argument from Contradiction is easily handled, as we've seen. For Ross, conflict among moral rules does not entail contradiction, since the moral rules that he favors are not absolute.

Ross's view can also make quick work of the Argument from Disaster Prevention. This argument claims that any moral rule may permissibly be broken if that is what it takes to prevent a catastrophe; as a result, no moral rules are absolute. Ross agrees with this. None of his moral rules is absolute. When the stakes are high enough, each of them may acceptably be sacrificed.

The Argument from Irrationality charges that absolutism is inconsistent, since the values at the heart of its rules can sometimes be better served by violating those rules. Ross can agree with this criticism as well. If we must break a promise in order to ensure that many more are kept, Ross can allow that this promise ought to be broken. The charge of irrationality stems from the absolutist claim that certain rules must be obeyed no matter the consequences. Ross rejects this absolutist claim.

But Ross also denies the push to consequentialism that lies at the heart of the last two arguments. Both of them try to show that the morality of our actions always depends on their results. Think of those two arguments like this: if obeying a rule leads to a catastrophic outcome, or results in greater violations of that rule, then that rule cannot be absolute. These are consequentialist reasons for rejecting absolutism.

Ross believed, of course, that the moral rules are not absolute. But he did not get there by assuming, with consequentialists, that our moral duty is always to maximize good results. Though he agreed with utilitarians that results are morally important, he denied that they are all-important. Doing justice, for instance, or improving oneself, is sometimes more important than doing what is optimific.

Indeed, to make his case against consequentialism, Ross had us imagine a situation in which we are faced with a choice. We can benefit person A or B. We can benefit person A by fulfilling our promise to him. Or we can benefit person B just slightly more, though we have made no promise to him. If we benefit B, we break a promise to A. Further, B has no expectation that we will benefit him. Ross thought it obvious that we ought to keep our promise to A, even though we would do more good by benefiting B.

This thought experiment convinced Ross of two things. First, there is a prima facie duty of **fidelity**. There is always something morally important about keeping our word. And second, consequentialism is mistaken, since the case just described includes an option (benefiting B) that produces the most good, but is morally wrong nonetheless. So, while Ross agrees with the conclusion of the anti-absolutist arguments, he denies that we should be led to consequentialism as a result.

16.4 A Problem for Ross's View

In Ross's view, preventing harm (i.e., fulfilling the prima facie duty of **non-maleficence**) is always morally important. Sometimes it is the most important thing you can do. But not always. Seeing that the guilty get their just deserts is also, and always, very important. If Kant is right, it always takes priority over preventing harm. If utilitarians are right, it never takes priority. If Ross is right, it sometimes does, and sometimes doesn't.

This leads us naturally to what may be the hardest problem for Ross's view. Ross denies that there are any absolute moral rules. So each moral rule may sometimes be broken. *But when?*

The easiest way to answer that question would be to create a permanent ranking of the prima facie rules, by placing them in order from least to most morally important. Whenever a lower ranked rule conflicts with a higher ranked one, the higher rule wins out and determines our moral duty.

Ross rejects this strategy. He thinks that there is no fixed ranking of the various prima facie rules, no permanent ordering in terms of importance. And he is not alone in this. Though a ranking system is possible in principle, in practice no one has ever made it work. Sometimes it is morally more important to be grateful than to prevent harm. But not always. Sometimes it is more important to be honest with people than to spare them the hurt feelings that honesty may cause. And sometimes not. You get the picture.

The problem is that if we can't provide a fixed ranking of moral principles, then it isn't clear how we are to decide what to do when they conflict. That is because none of the prima facie duties has any kind of built-in moral weight. They are always important. But just how important? That depends on the specifics of the situation. Yet there are no guidelines that we can use from case to case to help us to know when a prima facie duty takes precedence over a competing duty. If a duty is sometimes, but not always, more important than another, then how do we know which one to obey when we cannot obey them both?

This is an extremely hard question. But before we can answer it, it seems we must answer an even harder one: How can we know which prima facie duties are real and which are mere pretenders? For instance, is there really a prima facie moral duty of self-improvement? Ross thought so, but many people think that letting oneself go isn't a moral failing at all. How do we settle the matter? It seems we must first know the true list of prima facie duties, before we can get to the more specific question of how to strike an appropriate balance when prima facie duties conflict.

16.5 The Appeal to Self-Evidence

How can we know what the fundamental moral rules are? The standard way of justifying a rule is not open to us here. We cannot cite a more general rule to back up the one in question. If the rule is really fundamental, then there are no deeper rules to derive it from. When we call such a rule into question, how can its correctness be defended?

Ross had an answer. He claimed that his prima facie duties were **self-evident**. A claim is self-evident just in case it is true, and adequately understanding it is enough to make you justified in believing it. Self-evident truths are those that you are justified in believing on the basis of careful reflection alone. If you think hard about such claims, and come to believe them as a result, then you will have knowledge.

I think that there are some self-evident claims. Here are a few:

- All bachelors are unmarried.
- If Alice is taller than Bob, and Bob is taller than Charlie, and Charlie is taller than Denise, then Bob is taller than Denise and Charlie is shorter than Alice.
- Anything that happened a decade ago occurred prior to today's events.

Some of these claims are just obvious; others may take a bit of time to sort out. Self-evident claims need not be obvious. What is crucial is that careful reflection is all it takes to know them.

Suppose that some moral rules are self-evident. Then we have a way of calling a halt to an otherwise infinite chain of moral questioning. Our stopping points will be self-evident claims that require no further justification.

If Ross is right, then all seven of his principles are self-evident. We can know them just by thinking about what they really stand for. If we can rid ourselves of distorting influences—such things as bias, hasty judgments, and excessive emotional involvement—we will be convinced that there is always something right about keeping promises, preventing harm, doing justice, showing gratitude, and so on.

Critics of self-evidence often level the charge that one generation's self-evident truths are the next generation's outdated pieties. According to such critics, there are no self-evident moral truths at all—these are simply moral views that cannot be defended, and their ardent supporters, finding themselves unable to argue on behalf of their favorite moral claims, are forced to fall back on insisting that they are self-evident. This has definitely happened, and not in a good way. People have declared it self-evident that women are unfit for political office, that the "White" race is superior to all others, that all Jews are morally corrupt. These claims are false. Therefore they can't be self-evident, despite the fact that countless people have believed them to be.

But it would be too hasty to dismiss the possibility of self-evident moral truths just because appeals to them can be abused. For Ross, there is no precise test for sorting the genuine self-evident moral claims from mere pretenders. Only careful, mature reflection is able to reveal whether a given moral claim is true, and there is no algorithm for undertaking such reflection. Ross realized that his view offered little comfort to those who did not agree with his seven principles. But he was unapologetic. To someone who thought about justice, for instance, and failed to see its moral importance, Ross could do only one thing. He would invite that person to think more carefully about what justice really is. This can be done in many ways. We can offer the person examples to consider; draw analogies to cases that reveal the importance of justice; distinguish justice from other, possibly related, notions; ensure that particular beliefs opposing the importance of justice are not based on error. But suppose that the person remains unconvinced even after all of this further reflection. According to Ross, moral discussion now comes to an end, and the only verdict to render is that this person is mistaken. Nothing you can say will show him that he is wrong.

That may strike you as closed-minded. But two things can be said in Ross's defense. First, what are the alternatives? Why must it always be possible to offer something more in support of one's beliefs? If the process of offering justification for one's beliefs (whether ethical or non-ethical) ever does stop somewhere, then once we have reached that stopping point, all that could possibly be done is to invite the doubters to reconsider.

Second, we should consider the possibility, in *nonmoral* contexts, of finding ourselves without any support for a claim that we rightly continue to believe. For instance, there may be nothing you can say that will convince a member of the Flat Earth Society of his mistake; no way to convince someone who believes in vampires that he is wrong; no clear path to showing a stubborn person that creating a square circle is impossible.

You may be justified in your beliefs even if you can't always convince those who disagree with you. That holds for moral as well as for nonmoral beliefs.

16.6 Self-Evidence and the Testing of Moral Theories

Ross thinks that his theory of prima facie duties, and his confidence in their self-evidence, are in deep harmony with common sense. And as he sees it, this is a great benefit of his theory. We should not overturn the biddings of common sense just because it conflicts with a pet theory.

Ross used the example of beauty to establish this point. Many of us feel sure that the *Mona Lisa* is a beautiful work. We should not abandon our belief in its beauty just because some theory of art declares that only Impressionist paintings or medieval altarpieces are really beautiful. We should give up the theory before tossing aside our deepest, most secure beliefs about art.

What is true of our artistic judgments is also true of our moral ones. We can see how this plays out by considering Ross's rejection of consequentialism. Ross was quite clear-eyed about how tempting consequentialism can be. But he insisted that it was fatally flawed because it failed to appreciate the variety of fundamental moral concerns. Consequentialism imposes order, system, and a unifying principle onto our moral thinking. But he argued that we must resist such charms, because they conflict with our deepest beliefs about what is truly morally important. Our confidence in the independent value of promise keeping—or justice, or repairing our wrongs—should not be held hostage to a theory's demands.

If Ross is right, we use our deepest commonsense beliefs, some of which will be self-evident, as the way to test moral theories. Our self-evident beliefs have a kind of priority in moral thinking. It isn't as if each moral belief we have is beyond scrutiny. Far from it. Some of our moral views, perhaps even our most cherished ones, may have to go, once we see that they conflict with beliefs that are even better justified. Still, the data of ethical thought, as Ross puts it, are those moral beliefs that have survived very careful reflection. Self-evident principles are where our moral thinking must begin. They are what moral theories must account for. These basic beliefs are to be given up only if we can show that they can't all be true.

To the extent that a moral theory cannot make room for such beliefs, it is the theory that must go. This was Ross's diagnosis of both consequentialism and Kantianism, for instance. They both understood morality too narrowly, as limited to a single fundamental moral rule. He thought that careful reflection would show us that there are at least seven such rules—none of them absolute.

It might be helpful to contrast this reliance on self-evidence with the proceduralist's insistence that justified moral beliefs emerge from a certified procedure. According to proceduralism,[1] the place to start in our ethical reflections is with a procedure whose outputs are the moral views we can trust. Examples of proceduralism include the golden rule, Kant's principle of universalizability, and the contractarian view that focuses on the outputs of a process of reflection by free, equal, and rational people. According to proceduralism, we cannot know what is right or wrong until we have applied the correct moral procedure and discovered its results.

Ross will have none of that. The golden rule, for instance, allows me to break my promises, so long as I'm okay with others breaking their promises to me. For a Rossian, that's enough to show that the golden rule is false. We can appreciate the importance of fidelity (keeping our word) by reflection alone—if a theory, such as the golden rule, gives fidelity only trifling importance, so much the worse for the theory. The principle of universalizability licenses the Nazi's behavior, so long as he can achieve his goals in a world of like-minded fanatics. He can. But that doesn't make Nazi behavior morally ok; rather, it shows that the principle of universalizability is false, since it clashes with self-evident principles that affirm the value of justice and non-maleficence.

It's important to note that the Rossian need not be opposed to all procedures for assessing the merits of a moral view. It's just that any legitimate procedure must itself be ratified by the fact that its outputs are consistent with the self-evident moral truths that emerge from careful reflection. These represent the proper starting points for our investigations in moral theory. (Compare the list of ethical starting points in the Introduction.) Procedures might be helpful in shaping our beliefs in difficult cases where there are no self-evident truths awaiting our discovery. But any such procedure needs to be in good standing, and for Ross, the only way to earn that status is to show that it aligns with self-evident moral truths.

---

1. See chapter 13, "The Lure of Proceduralism."

16.7 Knowing the Right Thing to Do

Even if our prima facie duties are self-evident, we are still faced with the problem of knowing what to do when they conflict. And Ross has very little to say here, except that we can never be certain that the balance we strike is the correct one. Ross acknowledged that our actual, all-things-considered moral duty on any given occasion is *not* something that is self-evident. That doesn't mean that correct moral verdicts are out of reach. Indeed, there are many easy cases in morality, ones where the right (or wrong) thing to do is plain to see. It's clearly wrong to kill or humiliate people just for fun, to slander them to advance your career, to create Ponzi schemes for personal enrichment. The list is easily expanded. Still, despite the ease with which we come to a moral verdict in such cases (and the difficulty that confronts us in others), Ross believes there is no surefire method for guiding us from an understanding of the prima facie duties to a correct moral verdict.

We must start our moral thinking about specific situations by understanding the kinds of things that can be morally important. This is a matter of clearly grasping the prima facie duties. These tell us what to look out for. Has a promise been made? A wrong been done? Is there an opportunity for self-improvement here? And so on. But once you answer such questions, you're on your own. You must bring your experience and insight to bear on the details of a given case. The bad news is that there is no mechanical procedure that tells us how to do this.

This can be very dissatisfying. There are several aims of moral theory, and one of them, surely, is to offer advice on deciding how to live. Ross denies that there is any general rule to follow in order to provide answers here. What a letdown.

But again, there are a few things we might say in order to make this a bit easier to swallow. First, the idea of a comprehensive moral decision procedure, one that can be consulted to provide definite answers to all moral questions, may not be so plausible. When faced with puzzling ethical questions, we may *want* a concrete set of guidelines to help us along. But do we really believe that there is such a thing? Each of the familiar options (e.g., the principle of utility, the golden rule, the *what if everyone did that?* test) has its problems. Perhaps the best explanation of this is that we are looking for something that does not exist.

Second, Ross's theory is not the only ethical view that abandons the idea of a moral decision procedure. The theories that we next consider—both virtue ethics and feminist ethics—also deny that there is any method guaranteed to lead us to the moral truth. And as we've seen, even consequentialism can fail to supply a procedure for determining our moral duty.[2] If more than one thing is intrinsically valuable, then it will be unclear what to do when we can maximize one value without maximizing the other.

Finally, the absence of a decision procedure for arriving at conclusions is actually the *default* situation across all areas of thinking (except mathematics and its associated disciplines). For instance, scientists faced with a conflict between their data and some favored theory have no uniform method for determining whether to modify the theory or rethink their data. Further, even when the data are uncontroversial, selecting the best theory to account for it is anything but a rote, mechanical undertaking. Scientists must rely on good sense, too, since choosing which theory to believe is a matter of balancing the virtues of the competing theories. There is no precise rule to tell a scientist how to do this.

There are many theoretical virtues: parsimony (employing fewer assumptions than competing theories); conservatism (preserving as much as possible of what we already believe); generality (explaining the broadest range of things); testability (being open to experimental challenge and confirmation); and others. Suppose that one theory is more parsimonious and also more conservative, but another theory is more general and more testable. Or suppose that one theory is far more conservative than any competitor, but is also somewhat less general, and a fair bit less parsimonious. Science does not offer us a definite procedure for identifying the better theory. Sometimes it is just obvious that one theory is better or worse than another. But in close cases, scientists have no alternative but to use their judgment.

And that is precisely our situation when it comes to morality. There are many easy cases where the moral verdict is just obvious. These rarely get our attention, since they don't call for any hard thinking. It's the difficult cases—where different options each respect some prima facie duties

---

2. See "Measuring Well-Being" and "The Problem of Injustice" in chapter 10.

but violate others—that require judgment. We can never be sure that we've exercised good judgment. We may be unable to convince ourselves, much less our opponents, that we have landed on the right answer to a hard ethical question. The lack of guidance we get from Ross's view of ethics can leave us feeling insecure and unsettled. That is regrettable. But it may also be inescapable.

16.8 Ethical Particularism

The ethic of prima facie duties offers a serious challenge to the idea that there is just a single moral rule that is both fundamental and absolute. Yet there is a view, known as **ethical particularism**, that is an even more extreme challenge. Like Rossians, particularists reject moral absolutism. But unlike Rossians, particularists also deny the existence of any prima facie duties.

Recall that a central feature of such duties is that they represent moral reasons that are always important. Every time you do wrong, for instance, there is excellent reason to repair the damage. There is, without exception, something to be said for keeping the promises you've made. True prima facie duties point to features that are always morally important.

Particularists deny that anything meets this description. As they see it, something's moral importance depends entirely on context. If they are right, then sometimes there is nothing good *at all* about righting a wrong, or benefiting someone else, or preventing harm to others. The moral value of such things depends entirely on the details of the case.

Prima facie moral rules claim that certain features (e.g., promise keeping, self-improvement, preventing harm) are always morally important. Absolute moral rules state that certain features are not only always morally important, but also morally decisive—these features settle the matter of our moral duty once and for all. Particularism, then, is the view that *there are no prima facie or absolute moral rules*. If particularists are right, then morality is entirely particular to specific situations; there are no moral rules at all to help us navigate our way in the world.

Consider an example of particularist thinking: it is often important to keep our promises, but not always, and so Ross was mistaken to think that promise keeping is a prima facie duty. A promise made by a hostage to her kidnapper carries no weight. Nor is there anything good about returning a promised weapon to its now obviously homicidal owner. If particularists are right, there is sometimes no reason at all to keep a promise.

Particularists think that every prima facie rule is subject to this sort of criticism. For each of Ross's prima facie duties, and for any other candidates, particularists will try to offer counterexamples to the rule. A prima facie rule says that X (self-improvement, doing justice, etc.) is always morally important; particularists will try to come up with cases in which X has no moral value at all. If they are right, nothing possesses any fixed moral importance. Whether something has moral value always depends on the other features in a situation.

Particularists often use nonmoral examples to soften us up to their core idea. The intense coloring of a Turner painting is an essential part of what makes it so beautiful. But such colors would ruin a piece by Whistler. The paint drips that make Jackson Pollock's work so interesting would completely spoil a Velasquez. The lesson here is that whether something makes a difference to the beauty of an object depends entirely on context. There are no rules of beauty, because there are no features that always enhance (or spoil) the beauty of an object.

That a person told me something is sometimes a reason to believe it. And sometimes not (if we are playing a bluffing game, for instance). That an act is against the law is usually a reason not to do it. But not always (think of cases of justified civil disobedience). That I want something is often a reason for me to do it. And sometimes it isn't (consider an addict's desires). Here we have cases in which things sometimes but not always count as a reason. When this is so, the features in question have no place in either a prima facie or an absolute rule.

Particularists rely on such examples to show us that theirs is the ordinary view when it comes to nonmoral matters. And yet when applied to morality, it has met with great resistance. There are three primary sources of opposition.

16.9 Three Problems for Ethical Particularism

Its Lack of Unity

This criticism, and the next, should be familiar from our discussion of prima facie duties. Defenders of standard moral theories attacked Ross's view because, in the words of one critic, it offered us nothing more than "an unconnected heap of duties." Such critics felt uncomfortable with the idea of several fundamental moral rules, rather than just one. Indeed, as we have seen, philosophers are strongly tempted to look for a certain sort of moral theory—a body of unified, systematically interconnected claims that stem from a single fundamental truth. Ross's theory was a disappointment in this respect; particularism completely dashes such hopes. On the particularist picture, the moral realm is hugely complex, and there are no moral rules at all to help guide us on our way.

But this cannot be a decisive criticism of particularism. We might hope for simplicity and elegance, but the moral realm may be much messier than we had thought. We can't assume from the outset that moral reality is structured around a single fundamental rule, and then criticize particularism for flouting that picture. Whether the moral realm is neatly ordered, as standard theories would have it; whether it is somewhat structured, as Ross argued; or whether it is highly disordered, as particularists insist, is a matter that can be settled only after a great deal of further moral debate.

Accounting for Moral Knowledge

The second criticism leveled against particularism is that it provides us with no guidance for gaining moral knowledge. Ross's theory, as we know, came in for criticism on this front, since he failed to offer general advice about how to balance prima facie duties when they conflict. But particularism takes this worry to a new level, since Ross, at least, was able to instruct us on what to look out for in all of the cases we might face. The prima facie rules serve as useful signposts to indicate the features that are relevant in discovering our moral duty.

By contrast, particularists tell us that anything that has once been a force for good may, at other times, be either morally neutral or positively bad. There is no way to know in advance how things are going to play out. Nor is there any method guaranteed to reveal the correct moral verdict in a given situation. We don't have any rules to tell us what is morally important. And we lack rules to tell us how to figure out our moral duty in specific cases.

If the moral importance of everything depends on context, then there is no general roadmap to follow for those who want to know their moral duty. Indeed, particularists can offer almost no such advice at all, other than some very broad tips (take careful note of details, don't confuse self-interest with morality, get the facts straight, etc.). Basically, they must insist that our moral knowledge comes only through a comprehensive appreciation of all of the relevant features of a situation. Just as we can take in the beauty of a canvas only by noticing how each distinct feature plays off the others, so too can we detect the morality of an action only by taking careful note of all of its important features and their interplay with one another. The features that are relevant in any given situation cannot be known in advance, since no features possess permanent moral importance.

So particularism fails to supply a general blueprint for gaining moral wisdom. Yet this is a serious failing only if there *is* such a blueprint. There may be. But that remains to be seen.

Some Things Possess Permanent Moral Importance

We can best appreciate the deepest criticism of particularism by considering the central argument in its favor. Call this the *Particularist Argument*:

1. If nothing possesses permanent moral importance, then there are no prima facie or absolute moral rules.
2. Nothing possesses permanent moral importance.
3. Therefore, there are no prima facie or absolute moral rules.
4. If there are no prima facie or absolute moral rules, then particularism is true.
5. Therefore, particularism is true.

This argument has only three premises. Premise 1 is completely uncontroversial. Premise 4 is also secure—so long as there are any moral truths at all. (We'll consider the possibility that there aren't any, and that morality is all make-believe, in chapter 20.) So if you have doubts about particularism, then you need to focus on that second premise.

And that is just what critics will do. They will insist that the central claim of particularism, stated in premise 2—that there are no features that are always morally important—is mistaken. If that premise is false, then there are at least some prima facie moral rules. Whether there are any absolute rules depends, of course, on whether there are any features (e.g., maximizing happiness, being commanded by God) that are morally decisive in every possible context.

To undermine particularism, we would have to provide examples of features that are always morally important. Perhaps Ross managed to do this. Consider doing justice, for example. Relying on the "regret test" mentioned earlier (see "Moral Regret"), it seems that there is always some reason for regret when we commit injustice, even if injustice really is the way to go in a given case. But I don't want to rest anything on my view of this matter. That's because we can leave justice aside and still show that particularism is in trouble. There seem to be a number of prima facie duties, even if they are not the ones that Ross himself favored.

For instance, I think that there is always an excellent reason against humiliating people, hurting others strictly for the pleasure it gives you, intentionally killing an innocent person who wants to live, betraying a friend's trust, knowingly violating an oath because of greed, and committing rape. Maybe none of these represents an absolute rule; perhaps, in very unusual circumstances, it can be morally acceptable to commit each of these acts. But there would always be something to regret in doing so, and that is good evidence that there is a prima facie duty not to do such things.

This list is certainly not complete. But if my list (or a better one that you can construct) is plausible, then particularism is mistaken. Morality would have more order and structure than particularists allow. They claim that we can never know in advance, independently of context, whether something is morally important. If there are any prima facie moral rules, that claim is false.

16.10 Conclusion

The ethic of prima facie duties has a lot of things going for it. It affirms the independent moral importance of several distinct considerations. It rejects absolutism, and so explains why it is sometimes permissible to break legitimate moral rules. It easily handles moral conflict without falling into contradictions. It offers an interesting role for regret in thinking about what is morally important. And it nicely handles some of the most difficult arguments designed to undermine moral absolutism.

Yet like all of the moral theories we have discussed, Ross's view is not without its problems. Perhaps the hardest of these concerns the question of how we can know what to do in particular situations. Since there is no permanent ranking of the prima facie rules, and no precise method for knowing how to strike a balance when the prima facie rules conflict, this leaves us with very little guidance for discovering what morality actually requires of us.

Ross also has the worry of explaining how we might gain knowledge of his prima facie rules. I think that the question of how we can know the fundamental rules of morality is very, very hard. And Rossians can take some comfort in the knowledge that *every* moral thinker shares this problem.

I sketched Ross's preferred solution, one that invokes self-evident truths, but this of course offers only the very beginning of the needed discussion.

As we have seen, those who resist the idea that there is just a single moral rule that is fundamental and absolute need not go in for prima facie duties. They may embrace ethical particularism, which denies that there are any absolute or even prima facie moral rules. On this view, nothing is always morally important, much less always morally decisive. Particularism is a bold thesis. But despite its boldness, it does seem that there are some things that are permanently morally important. And if that is so, then there are some prima facie rules after all.

The particularist can still level a challenge to those who think that morality is rule-based. Imagine that after a great deal of thought, we were able to identify a dozen prima facie duties. It might still be the case that *most* of the morally important features we encounter in our lives were not mentioned in any of those rules, because these features are only sometimes, and not always, morally important.

For instance, suppose that my earlier remarks about promise keeping were on target, and that there really are cases in which nothing at all favors our keeping a promise. Still, the fact that we promised to do something usually *is* morally important, even though (on the present assumption) there is no absolute or prima facie moral rule that tells us so. Likewise for telling the truth—there is ordinarily a strong reason to be truthful, even if there are some cases where there is no moral value at all in telling the truth.

If morality is really like this, where many features that are morally important are not always so, then we have a kind of hybrid view, a mix of Ross's theory and particularism. Some types of action possess permanent moral importance, as Ross said. Others do not. If that were so, then we would be faced with a moral world that was *far* less simple and unified than the one presented by monists and absolutists. Is that our world? That is for you to decide.

16.11 Discussion Questions

1. What exactly is a prima facie duty? How does an ethic of prima facie duties differ from absolutist ethical theories?
2. Do you think that Ross's list of prima facie duties is accurate and complete? If not, either explain why some of those on the list do not qualify as prima facie duties or provide examples of other prima facie duties that should have been included in his list.

3. Does the phenomenon of regret lend any support to Ross's theory? Why or why not?

4. To what extent does Ross's theory provide us with a method for deciding what the right thing to do is in particular situations? Is this a strength or a weakness of the theory?

5. Do you think that there is a formula for determining in every case what our moral duty is? If so, what is it?

6. What is it for a belief to be self-evident? Do you think that there are any self-evident moral truths?

7. How does ethical particularism differ from Ross's ethic of prima facie duties? Can you think of any counterexamples to the particularist's central claim?

16.12 Cases for Critical Reflection

Should I Stay, or Should I Go?

In a 1946 essay, the French existentialist philosopher Jean-Paul Sartre described a dilemma faced by one of his students. The young man's oldest brother had been killed in the German offensive of 1940, and the young man felt compelled to avenge him. Meanwhile, he lived alone with his mother, who was frail and still deeply affected by the death of her oldest son. The young man was her only consolation. According to Sartre's retelling, he realized that his disappearance or death in war would plunge his mother into despair. The young man found himself torn between his personal devotion to his mother and the noble cause of fighting with the anti-Nazi resistance. Sartre suggested that the dilemma could not be answered by an ethical theory, writing, "Nothing remains but to trust our instincts."[1]

Questions

1. Which of W. D. Ross's seven prima facie duties is relevant to the young man's dilemma? Which of these duties do you think should be given the strongest weight, and why?

2. According to the ethic of prima facie duties, what should the young man do, and why?

---

1. Jean-Paul Sartre, "Existentialism Is a Humanism," in *Existentialism from Dostoyevsky to Sartre*, ed. Walter Kaufman (New York: Plume Publishing Company, 1975).

3. Do you think a standard ethical theory, such as act utilitarianism, can settle the young man's dilemma? Why or why not?
4. Sartre thought that the young man's dilemma couldn't be resolved by any ethical theory and that the young man would have to decide based on instinct. Are there some moral dilemmas without an answer? In such cases, should we simply trust our instincts?

One Tortured Child

In his 1880 book *The Brothers Karamazov*, Fyodor Dostoevsky described the following moral dilemma:

> Tell me yourself—I challenge you: let's assume that you were called upon to build the edifice of human destiny so that men would finally be happy and would find peace and tranquility. If you knew that, in order to attain this, you would have to torture just one single creature, let's say the little girl who beat her chest so desperately in the outhouse, and that on her unavenged tears you could build that edifice, would you agree to do it? Tell me and don't lie![1]

This thought experiment was developed further in Ursula K. Le Guin's 1973 short story "The Ones Who Walk Away from Omelas," which describes a utopian city called Omelas. Omelas is a paradise, but the prosperity of the city depends on the misery of a single child. The child is locked away in a dark basement closet, left alone to suffer from fear, malnutrition, and neglect. Meanwhile, the people in the city above live in peace and happiness.[2]

Questions

1. Dostoevsky's thought experiment and Le Guin's short story are, of course, works of fiction. However, suspend your disbelief and consider: Would it be wrong to allow for the suffering of a single child if it led to prosperity for all of humanity? Why or why not?
2. Consider your answer to question 1. Which of W. D. Ross's seven prima facie duties were relevant to your answer? Are there other relevant prima facie duties not included in Ross's list? Which of these duties do you give the strongest weight in this case, and why?

---

1. Fyodor Dostoyevsky, *The Brothers Karamazov*.
2. Ursula K. Le Guin, *The Ones Who Walk Away from Omelas* (Mankato, Minn.: Creative Education, 1993).

3. Do you think a standard ethical theory, such as act utilitarianism, can give a satisfactory answer to the dilemma? Why or why not?
4. Can the ethic of prima facie duties give us a satisfactory answer to the dilemma? Why or why not?

Robin Hood

Gilberto Baschiera has been called a modern-day Robin Hood. He worked as a bank manager in Forni di Sopra, a small town in northeast Italy, until it was discovered that he had stolen €1 million from the accounts of wealthy customers in order to distribute the money to the poor.

It began during the 2009 financial crisis. Baschiera was approached by a local man who sought a small loan yet didn't qualify. So Baschiera decided to transfer a small amount of money from a rich client to the man's account, which allowed him to qualify for the loan. Baschiera went on to do the same for other locals who struggled to access credit. He never took money for himself, and trusted that his customers would pay the money back. Some of them didn't.

Baschiera was eventually charged with embezzlement and fraud. In 2018, he was sentenced to two years in prison, but since it was his first offense, he didn't serve any time. Baschiera described his actions to a Milan newspaper:

> I just wanted to help people who couldn't access loans. . . . I would have returned all that money. I have always thought that in addition to protecting savers our task was to help those in need.[1]

Questions

1. Imagine that you are in Baschiera's shoes, considering whether or not to take money from the rich to help the poor. Which of W. D. Ross's seven prima facie duties seem relevant? Are there any other relevant prima facie duties not included in Ross's list? Which of the prima facie duties do you give the strongest weight in this case, and why?
2. According to the ethic of prima facie duties, were Baschiera's actions morally wrong? Were his actions morally good? Why or why not?
3. According to a standard ethical theory, such as act utilitarianism, did Baschiera do the right thing? Why or why not?

---

1. https://www.theguardian.com/world/2018/oct/04/robin-hood-of-the-alps-pays-for-costly-mistake-after-banking-on-trust.

CHAPTER 17

.... ❧ ....

Virtue Ethics

W hat sort of person should I be? An answer to that question provides some of the most vital information you can ever have. And yet none of the ethical theories we have examined thus far does much to address it. Each will say: You ought to be the sort of person who . . . maximizes happiness, or treats others with respect, or adheres to rules that free and equal people would endorse, or honors absolute rules. That's a pretty thin sort of answer.

To see what might be missing, consider what we might say of a police officer who obeys the law, but only reluctantly. He always does the minimum required of him. If he could get away with it, he would extort money from business owners on his beat, brutalize prisoners, and doctor evidence. He doesn't actually do any of these things. But that's only because he's afraid of what would happen if he were caught.

If we focus just on what the officer has or hasn't done, we will be missing a large part of the ethical picture. To fill things out, we must consider the kind of character he has. It's not a good one. We don't admire such a person; we don't want our children growing up like him. He is lazy, abusive, and untrustworthy, even if his conduct is satisfactory. If we think only about whether he has done his duty, there is nothing to criticize him for. But that just shows that we need to broaden our thinking. We should focus less on matters of moral duty, and concentrate much more on ideals of character. Following that advice leads us directly to a consideration of **virtue ethics**.

All of the moral theories we have reviewed thus far share a common assumption: that the moral philosopher's primary task is to define the nature of our moral duty. On this view, *What should I do?* is the crucial moral question. Once we have an answer to that, I can know what sort of person I should be—namely, the sort who will do my duty as reliably as possible.

But what if we approached ethics from a different starting point? What if we began by considering what makes for a desirable human life, examining the conditions and the character traits needed to flourish? Rather than begin with a theory of moral duty, we would start with a picture of the good life and the good person, and define our duty by reference to these ideals. That is precisely what virtue ethics recommends.[1]

Virtue ethics is not a single theory, but rather a family of theories that can trace its history (in the West) to the philosophy of the ancient Greeks. Aristotle's *Nicomachean Ethics*, written about 2,400 years ago, has had the greatest influence in this tradition and remains a primary inspiration for most who work in it. Aristotle's book develops most of the major themes that even today define the virtue ethical approach to the moral life. Let's consider some of the most important of these themes.

17.1 The Standard of Right Action

Many virtue ethicists have preferred not to talk about what is morally required or forbidden. They want to keep the focus on the nature of the good life and on the character traits needed to live such a life. Recently, however, many virtue ethicists have become more comfortable trying to identify a fundamental principle that spells out our moral duty. In doing so, they insist that we understand right action by reference to what a virtuous person would characteristically do. To put it a bit more formally,

> (VE) An act is morally right just because it is one that a virtuous person, acting in character, would do in that situation.

According to virtue ethicists, actions aren't right because of their results, or because they follow from some hard-and-fast rule. Rather, they are

---

1. There is a strand of virtue ethics that abandons talk of moral duties and moral requirements altogether, and instead suggests that we restrict our assessments to what is good and bad, virtuous and vicious. I invite you to reflect on whether it would be a gain or loss to give up on the concepts of moral duty and requirement, but for the remainder of the chapter, I will assume that virtue ethicists will allow a place for these notions.

right because they would be done by someone of true virtue. This person is a **moral exemplar**—someone who sets a fine example and serves as a role model for the rest of us. The ideal of the wholly virtuous person provides the goal that we ought to aim for, even if, in reality, each of us will fall short of it in one way or another.

Though virtue ethics affirms a single ultimate standard—do what the virtuous person would do—there are many cases where this advice is too general to be of use. At such times we need a set of more specific moral rules. Virtue ethics can provide these, too. For each virtue, there is a rule that tells us to act accordingly; for each vice, a rule that tells us to avoid it. So we will have a large set of moral rules—do what is honest; act loyally; display courage; deal justly with others; show wisdom; be temperate; avoid gluttony; refrain from infidelity; don't be timid, lazy, stingy, or careless; free yourself of prejudice; and so on.

When these rules conflict, how do we know what to do? We should follow the lead of the virtuous person. True, there will inevitably be disagreement about who counts as virtuous, and about the actions such a person would pursue. But this needn't cripple us. There is lots of room for critical discussion about who is virtuous and why. In the end, we may have to agree to disagree, since there may be no way to convince someone whose moral outlook is fundamentally opposed to our own. Those who have been raised to idolize Hitler or Stalin are going to have a skewed moral vision, and there may be no way to convince them of their error. Virtue ethicists deny that this undermines the existence of correct moral standards. It just shows that some people may always be blind to them.

17.2 Moral Complexity

Many moral philosophers have hoped to identify a simple rule, or a precise method, that could tell us exactly what our moral duty is in each situation.[2] What's more, this rule or method could be reliably used by anyone, so long as he or she is minimally intelligent. A classic example of this is the golden rule. Even a five-year-old can apply this test.

---

2. See the following discussions for more in-depth treatment of why people would have such hopes: on the structure of moral theories, Introduction, "Moral Philosophy and Moral Theories"; on proceduralism, chapter 13, "The Lure of Proceduralism"; and on knowing one's duty, chapter 16, "The Appeal to Self-Evidence."

Virtue ethicists reject the idea that there is any simple formula for determining how to act. At the beginning of the *Nicomachean Ethics*, Aristotle cautions that we must not expect the same degree of precision in all areas of study, and implies that morality lacks rules and methods of thinking that are as precise as those, say, in mathematics. When it comes to morality, we must be content with general principles that allow for exceptions.

Virtue ethicists have followed Aristotle in this thought. To them, ethics is a complex, messy area of decision making, one that requires emotional maturity and sound judgment. One of the *problems* of the golden rule, for instance, is that even a child can use it with authority. Aristotle thought it obvious that even the most perceptive children are far short of true moral wisdom.

Virtue ethicists sometimes invite us to appreciate the complexity of morality by having us imagine a moral rule book. The book would contain all the true rules of ethics and all of the precise methods for applying them. It would state when exceptions were called for and when they were forbidden. It could be applied in a mechanical way, without any need of judgment.

Is this a real possibility? Not likely, according to virtue ethicists. Morality is not like geometry or civil engineering. We have moral rules of thumb that can help us in most situations. But strict obedience to such rules is bound to lead us into error. And the rules, of course, will sometimes conflict. What we need in all cases is a kind of sensitivity. It is something very different from a rote application of preset rules.

This does not mean that everything is up for grabs in ethics. The precision of a discipline is one thing; whether its principles, methods, and results are merely a matter of opinion—each one as good as the rest—is quite another. Morality may be an imprecise discipline, but that does not mean that each person's moral views are as plausible as another's. Aristotle and most of his followers believe in objective standards of morality (those that are true independently of personal feelings or opinions). Whether they are right about this is something that we consider at great length in the final part of this book.

17.3 Moral Understanding

As virtue ethicists see things, moral understanding is not just a matter of knowing a bunch of moral facts. If it were, then a child prodigy might be one of the morally wisest among us. As we have seen, virtue ethicists deny this possibility. Imagine turning to such a child for advice about dealing with difficult coworkers, or helping a drug-addicted friend through recovery, or determining the best way to break off a relationship.

Moral understanding is a species of practical wisdom. Think of some familiar kinds of practical wisdom—knowing how to fix a car engine, how to skillfully play an instrument, or how to inspire teammates to come together behind an important project. Such knowledge does require an understanding of certain facts, but it is much more than that. We all know people with plenty of book smarts and very little in the way of good sense. Moral wisdom is a kind of know-how that requires a lot of training and experience. What it doesn't require is a superior IQ or a vast reading list.

We need experience, emotional maturity, and a great deal of reflection and training in order to acquire moral wisdom. We have to know how to read people, to be familiar with the sorts of troubles people can fall into, to understand the kinds of personality issues that can prevent us from flourishing, to have a keen ability to pick up on social cues. We can't learn such things only from books.

One way to reinforce this idea is to appreciate the crucial roles that emotions play in moral understanding. There are three that are especially important.

1. *Emotions can help us to see what is morally relevant, by tipping us off to what matters in a given situation.* Fear can signal danger; guilt can reveal our moral faults; compassion can tell us that someone needs our help. It's no use knowing that you ought to aid those in need if you always walk around with blinders on, never aware of the struggles or potential discomfort of others. The person with the virtues of compassion, sympathy, and kindness will see things that others miss. Our emotions, when they are well trained, reliably alert us to the morally important features of our lives.

2. *Emotions can also help to tell us what is right and wrong.* If we are virtuous, the anxiety we feel when considering certain actions is excellent evidence that these actions are immoral. We often feel that certain paths are simply off limits, or that other things definitely must be done, before we have a good intellectual account of why this is so. That a good man feels proud of his actions is reason to think that he has done well. His anger is a reliable indicator that someone has done wrong.

3. *Emotions also help to motivate us to do the right thing.* They support and reinforce our thoughts about what we ought to do. Knowing the right course of action is one thing; following through is another. The morally wise person will have an easier time of things here, because her emotions will be in harmony with her understanding of what morality calls for. Unlike a weak-willed person or someone who manages to control her inappropriate impulses, the morally wise person wholeheartedly does what is right. She is relatively free of inner conflict and takes pleasure in doing the right thing.

Moral wisdom is an extremely complicated kind of skill. It does require knowledge of the way the world works, but it demands more than that. We must have a great deal of emotional intelligence as well. The moral virtues, which all require moral wisdom, therefore also require a combination of intellectual and emotional maturity. A person with only a crude appreciation for life's complexities, or a blank emotional life, is bound to be morally blind. Virtue ethics perfectly explains why that is so.

17.4 Moral Education

Virtue ethicists, again following Aristotle, believe that moral understanding can be gained only through training, experience, and practice. True, some people are by nature kinder or more generous than others. Yet an impulse in these directions is not enough. Without wisdom, these traits will only occasionally lead to appropriate action. We shouldn't always give to others or tend to their needs. They may be engaged in evil projects. They may need tough love, rather than indulgence. The wise person will know when to give, and when to withhold.

So virtue is not inborn. It takes time to acquire. And it also takes the right sort of environment and teachers. Indeed, Aristotle thought that whether we are virtuous or not is partly a matter of moral luck.[3] Our upbringing plays a crucial role in whether we are able to become virtuous, and we obviously cannot control the environment we are raised in. If we are lucky, we will have wise and caring parents and teachers to guide us on the path of virtue. But many are not so fortunate. Those who grow up in a corrupt society with terrible role models may (through no fault of their own) lack the opportunity to develop virtues. The most important

---

3. For more on this topic, see chapter 12, "Moral Luck."

elements of moral education occur in our youth—so much so that Aristotle doubted that a person raised in vice could later change his character very significantly.

The point of giving children a moral education is straightforward—to help them acquire the virtues. The key to this is to develop their capacity for moral wisdom. The virtue ethicist invites us to think of children as apprentices being taught to gain a very complex skill, that of moral wisdom.

Think first about how apprentices in other areas are trained. An apprentice in a professional kitchen begins with a list of dos and don'ts, a set of hard-and-fast rules. Over time, she learns the limits of these rules, when to honor and when to break them. There is no master rule book that can give her this knowledge. She acquires it through trial and error, through the advice of experts, through a deeper understanding of cooking methods and of her ingredients. By the end of a successful education, she is something of an artist.

The same holds true of moral education. We begin as apprentices, following in an unquestioning way the rules handed down by our parents and teachers. In the early stages of their moral training, children learn simple rules, and are told to treat them as absolute: never, ever lie, steal, hit others, tattle, and so on. These rules are crude, but it's right to ask our children to obey them. We address our learners where they are.

As children mature, they will, through experience and guidance, come to appreciate when exceptions are called for. We gradually step back from the rules we learned on our mother's knee, and subject them to careful scrutiny. A successful education will produce an independent thinker, one who doesn't need the old, over-simple rules as a crutch to get through each new situation. We understand, for instance, that honesty is the best policy. But sometimes honesty would be so hurtful and gain so little that evasion is the right way to go. As a rule, friends deserve our loyalty. But that doesn't mean that we must cover up for them if they steal from their employer and ask us to lie about it.

This line of thought supports the virtue ethicist's rejection of a simple moral litmus test, a formula that could be used by anyone, no matter her degree of moral sophistication. Such a test not only overlooks the great complexity of morality, but also ignores the point that people possess moral wisdom in degrees. Advice that is suitable for a novice will be too crude for an expert, and vice versa.

17.5 The Nature of Virtue

The ultimate goal of a moral education is make ourselves better people. A better person is a more virtuous person—someone who is more courageous, just, temperate, and wise (among other things).

A virtue is an admirable character trait that enables its possessor to achieve what is good. It's not a mere habit, or a tendency to act in certain ways. Habits don't define a person; character traits do. Some people are habitually loyal or generous. Yet they may lack virtue, because they don't really understand why it is appropriate to act this way. Virtues require wisdom about what is important, and why. While habits are defined as certain patterns of behavior, virtues require much more. In addition to routinely acting well, the virtuous person also has a distinctive set of perceptions, thoughts, and motives.

Let's make this concrete. Consider first the virtue of generosity. A generous person will often have different *perceptions* from a stingy person. Generous people will see the homeless person on the street, will take note of the shy child in the classroom, will realize that an injured person is having trouble with the door. Stingy people tend to look the other way.

A generous person has different *thoughts* from those of an ungenerous person. A generous person will think about how to be helpful, will not think only of his own needs, will value being of service, and will believe in the goodness of caring for the less fortunate.

A generous person's *motives* will differ from those of a stingy person. Generous people are not begrudging of their time, they are moved by the distress of others, and they take pleasure in freely giving what they can to those in need.

We can offer similar accounts of all of the other virtues. Courage, for instance, requires that we correctly perceive various threats or dangers, control our fear in a reasonable way, be moved by a noble end, and act accordingly. Though Aristotle considered courage primarily in the context of the battlefield, this virtue, like all virtues, has its place in any number of more ordinary situations. The new kid in school displays courage when taking an unpopular stand among those whose approval and companionship he hopes for. Gandhi displayed courage in peacefully resisting the nightsticks and attack dogs of the British colonial police. A whistle-blower is courageous in revealing the corruption of her employers, knowing that she may be fired or sued for telling the truth.

Virtuous people are therefore defined not just by their deeds, but also by their inner life. They see, believe, and feel things differently from vicious people. They see what's important, know what is right and why it is right, and want to do things because they are right.

People are virtuous only when their understanding and their emotions are well integrated. A virtuous person who understands the right thing to do will also be strongly motivated to do it, without regret or reluctance, for all the right reasons. In Aristotle's view, and in the virtue ethical tradition, this is what distinguishes the truly virtuous from the merely **continent**— those who can keep it together, manage to do the right thing, but with little or no pleasure, and only by suppressing very strong contrary desires. As Aristotle insists, "Virtuous conduct gives pleasure to the lover of virtue."[4] This is one way to distinguish the truly virtuous from the merely continent.

17.6 Virtue and the Good Life

Aristotle thought it obvious that all of us seek **eudaimonia**, which translates as "happiness," or "flourishing." A life of eudaimonia is an excellent life for the person living it. The happiness Aristotle speaks of is not mere enjoyment. It isn't only a state of mind, but rather a combination of activity and pleasure. Aristotle thought that the good life is an active one filled with wise choices and worthy pursuits. No matter how much pleasure you get from sitting in front of the TV and watching *The Simpsons* (a lot, in my case), a life devoted to that fails to qualify as a good life. Aristotle was no hedonist.

Aristotle argued that virtue is an essential element in a good life. In this he agreed with his teacher, Plato. Unlike Plato, however, Aristotle did not think that we could be happy on the rack. Virtue does not guarantee a good life; it is necessary, but not sufficient, for our flourishing. Most contemporary virtue ethicists side with Aristotle on this one—enough misfortune can damage a life so greatly as to make it, on the whole, an unenviable one. If a virtuous person loses her beloved family to war or disease, or falls prey to nasty rumors, crushing debt, and crippling disability, then no matter how virtuous, she can fail to gain true happiness.

But is virtue really essential to a good life?[5] What about all of those criminals who get away with their crimes and enjoy a lavish retirement?

---

4. *Nicomachean Ethics* 1099a12.

5. For more on this topic, see "Why Be Moral?" in chapters 8 and 14, as well as the general discussion in part 1.

What of the powerful tyrant who dies at the end of a long reign, peacefully and in his sleep? Few would argue that such people are virtuous. Yet they seem to live very good lives.

Virtue ethicists argue that appearances here are deceiving. Such people may indeed be pleased with how things are going, and get a lot of enjoyment from their lives. (Then again, a closer look at the criminal's fear and insecurity, his emotional immaturity and the complications this brings, may make us think twice.) But virtue ethicists deny that pleasure is the be-all and end-all of a good life. Pleasure without virtue is not worth much. The most pleasant life may be a poor one indeed.

How can such a view be defended? Aristotle set up a three-part test to determine our ultimate good, in part to show that pleasure, wealth, power, and fame are *not* what life is all about.

First off, our ultimate good must not be something that is only instrumentally valuable. This explains why money and fame are ruled out, since these things have no worth of their own. They are merely a means to gaining other things of value.

Our ultimate good must also be *self-sufficient*. Possessing it is, all by itself, enough to make a life a worthy one. Political power fails this test. Having power over others is not what makes life valuable. Power is important, when it is, just because of what it enables a leader to do.

Finally, our ultimate good must involve something that is *distinctive* about us, something that is uniquely human. We need food to survive. But being nourished cannot be our final good, since we share this need with plants and animals. And since animals can experience pleasure, the point of our lives cannot be to gain pleasure, either.

What sets us apart from everything else in the world is our rationality. Our ultimate good, then, must take the form of exercising our rationality. But there is little good in reasoning poorly. Rather, our ultimate good consists in the excellent use of our reasoning powers. And that is precisely what the virtues involve.

How attractive is a life of virtue? Very. Just think of what we hope and try for when raising our children. We want them to be kind, fair, generous, appropriately self-confident, and wise. We hope that they develop courage, that they know how to be a good friend, that they can sensitively offer comfort to others in need. Each of these is a virtue; a person who manages to have them all is in most ways living an excellent life. True, if Aristotle is correct, having these traits will not guarantee a good life. The admirable nature of a virtuous person may, for instance, attract the envy and hatred of others, who will sometimes make a martyr of a noble soul. But this should not lead us to think that the virtues are unnecessary for a good life. Even if a life of virtue is not a guarantee that you will flourish, a life without virtue is a poor one.

The virtue ethicist thus has an answer to a skeptic who charges the good person with being a dupe, with sacrificing self-interest on the altar of virtue. Being virtuous will (barring disaster) make you better off. It will ensure that you aim at things worth trying for. Virtuous people ordinarily do very well for themselves, even if the vicious sometimes have more fun. That is because human well-being is *defined* in terms of the virtues. Virtues are those excellences of character that contribute to one's well-being. Without them, one is leading the life of an animal—or worse.

17.7 Objections

The virtue ethical approach to life has a number of attractive features. I've tried to sketch some of the more important of them here. But given its unorthodox approach to morality, it is hardly surprising that virtue ethics has come in for its share of criticisms. Here are some of the more significant ones.

Tragic Dilemmas

Consider two central claims of the virtue ethical approach to morality:

1. Actions that would be done by a virtuous agent, acting in character, are morally right.
2. Such actions, when motivated by virtue, deserve our praise.

If these views are problematic, then virtue ethics is in deep trouble. Tragic dilemmas highlight the difficulty here.

A tragic dilemma is a situation in which a good person's life will be ruined, no matter what she does. All of her options will lead to disaster. Virtuous people will usually be able to avoid these situations, since they typically arise as a result of some serious moral mistake. Think, for instance, of the premise of so many movies—simple-minded guy finds bundle of cash, stupidly walks away with it rather than reporting it, and eventually faces a host of deadly choices.

But it is possible to find yourself in a tragic dilemma through no fault of your own. Consider the title character in William Styron's *Sophie's Choice*, who is detained in a concentration camp and then given the terrible news: one of her two children will be sent to the gas chamber. She must choose which one. If she refuses, both children will be killed.

Sophie's life will be ruined no matter what she does. But she should not withdraw from the situation; she must make a choice. A virtuous person (acting in character) would do so, since that would mean saving one of her precious children. If virtue ethics is correct, then selecting one of her children to be murdered is morally right and morally praiseworthy. But that seems wrong.

Here is an *Argument from Tragic Dilemmas* designed to set out the worry:

1. If virtue ethics is the correct account of morality, then Sophie's selection of one of her children to be murdered is morally right and morally praiseworthy.
2. It is neither.
3. Therefore, virtue ethics is not the correct account of morality.

Premise 1 assumes that a virtuous person would do as Sophie did—namely, select one of her children to die. Further, it assumes that there is a right way and a wrong way to do this. A virtuous person will see the tragedy for what it is, will not leap at the chance to make the selection, will not express joy at what is about to happen. And that was Sophie's response. She was motivated as a virtuous person would be motivated—with a recognition of the terrible burden she faced, with love for her children, and with the greatest possible regret.

The only way to challenge premise 1 is to deny that a virtuous person in Sophie's shoes would select one of her children to be killed. That *might* be right—a virtuous person might refuse to make a deal with evil, and so try to keep her hands clean by not playing along with the sadistic choice offered to her. But recall that this means the death of both of her children, and it is hard to think that a virtuous person would prefer that to the death of one. I might be wrong about this. If so, then we have a way of rejecting the first premise.

That said, I think that the better option for the virtue ethicist is to criticize premise 2. *Under the circumstances*, a virtuous person *would* try to minimize the number of innocent deaths. And that means having to make a tragic choice, rather than refusing to do so. Choosing is indeed the right thing to do—even if it is absolutely heartbreaking.

It may also be praiseworthy. We might say of a person who refused to make this choice that, however understandable it may be, she was still being squeamish, and showed a lack of nerve. Having to make such a choice under these circumstances requires courage and fortitude, which is praiseworthy. Sometimes life presents us only with a choice among evils. Finding the inner strength to choose the lesser evil on that occasion need not be a moral failing, but may instead be something quite admirable. Our admiration should only increase when the choice involves an outcome that predictably destroys all of one's hopes for happiness.

If this analysis is correct, then virtue ethicists have an adequate reply to the Argument from Tragic Dilemmas. They can argue that certain choices in these situations are virtuous and that such choices are therefore right and admirable, even if, in more ordinary circumstances, any such choice would be purely evil.

Does Virtue Ethics Offer Adequate Moral Guidance?

Critics of virtue ethics often accuse it of failing to provide enough help in solving moral puzzles. When we are trying to figure out how to behave, we'd like to have something more than this advice: do what a virtuous person would do.

But virtue ethics *can* provide more advice. It will tell us to act according to a large number of moral rules, each based on doing what is virtuous or avoiding what is vicious: do what is temperate, loyal, modest, generous, compassionate, courageous, and so on. Avoid acting in a manner that is greedy, deceitful, malicious, unfair, short-tempered, and so on. The list of virtues and vices is a long one, and this may really be of some help in figuring out what to do.

Still, the virtue ethicist has to face the familiar problem of moral conflict. What happens when these virtue rules conflict with one another? Suppose, for instance, that you are on vacation and happen to see your best friend's husband intimately cozying up to another woman. Would a virtuous person reveal what she has seen? Well, there is a virtue of honesty, and that points to telling your friend. But being a busybody and rushing to judgment are vices; it's their marriage, not yours, and poking your nose into other people's business isn't a morally attractive thing to do.

That's all well and good. But you must do something. How to resolve this conflict (and countless others)? There *is* a right answer here, because there is something that a virtuous person would do. But virtue ethicists have offered very little instruction for deciding what that is. Once you appreciate which virtues and vices are involved in the situation, it is up to you to sort out how to balance them against one another.

This, of course, will be deeply unsatisfying to many people. They want their ethical theory to provide a clear rule that can tell them exactly what is required for each new situation. With expectations set this high, virtue ethics is bound to disappoint.

Unsurprisingly, however, virtue ethicists think that such expectations are implausible and far too demanding. They deny that ethics is meant to provide us with a precise rule or mechanical decision procedure that can crank out the right answer for each morally complex case. Recall the virtue ethicists' earlier criticisms of such an idea, and their claim that moral advice must be offered based on a person's level of wisdom and experience. There is no uniform moral guidebook, no formula or master rule that can tell us how to behave. We must figure it out for ourselves, through reflection, discussion, and experience.

Virtue ethicists can also argue that their theoretical competitors face similar problems. Most ethical theories incorporate a rule requiring promise keeping. But isn't it sometimes okay to break this rule? If so, is there any *other* rule that could tell us precisely when we may break our promises? Try it out. "You are allowed to break a promise if and only if _____." I don't know how to fill in that blank. That, of course, doesn't show that it can't be done. But anyone who can do it will also be able to know, in difficult situations, how to balance the virtue of fidelity against other considerations.

The bottom line is that almost every moral theory will require us to exercise good judgment in applying its rules. Virtue ethics requires more of us in this regard than some other theories, but that is a drawback only if morality can be made more precise than virtue ethicists believe. Whether that is so remains to be seen.

Is Virtue Ethics Too Demanding?

Virtue ethics tells us to do what a virtuous person would do in our situation. But what if a truly virtuous person sets a standard of excellence that is (almost) impossible to reach?

In 1933, Mohandas Gandhi went on a hunger strike that nearly killed him. Others have protested injustice by fasting unto death. Some of these protests were not based on personal grievances, but were expressions of outrage at social injustice. Assuming that some hunger strikers are virtuous people, acting in character, it appears that virtue ethics requires us to follow their lead.

Morality can sometimes require a great deal of us, but this may be going too far. One possibility, of course, is that it isn't. Perhaps we should be much readier than we are to give up our health or even our lives in political protest. Virtue ethicists could argue, as consequentialists have long done,[6] that morality really does demand much more of us than we think. They might say that the expectations we've been raised with are too lax. If we were raised in a way that repeatedly reminded us of the importance of noble sacrifice, then we would be much more inclined to follow such examples. Our reluctance to sacrifice ourselves is no strike against virtue ethics, but rather against our own self-indulgence and desire for comfort and security.

Virtue ethicists could take a less severe stance, however, and argue that such extreme measures are appropriate only in rather special circumstances. If Russ Shafer-Landau went on a hunger strike, few would pay any attention, and so my extended fast would likely do more harm than good. The test of right action is to ask how a virtuous person, *in my circumstances*, would act. Since my circumstances are quite different from those of a world-renowned political leader, it doesn't follow that a hunger strike is something I should try myself.

That doesn't quite let me off the hook. For a truly virtuous person might do much more for others, and far less for himself, than I typically do in my everyday existence. And were he in my shoes, this might *still* be the case. So virtue ethics may indeed demand quite a lot from us.

Who Are the Moral Role Models?

If virtue ethics is correct, then we can solve moral puzzles only by knowing how a virtuous person would act in our situation. Yet who are the moral exemplars? How do we decide who our role models should be, especially if different people endorse different candidates?

This is a very hard problem. After all, we pick our role models in large part by seeing how well they live up to our preexisting beliefs about what is right and wrong. Some people exalt suicide bombers as role models; others get sick just knowing that's so.

One solution to this problem is relativism—the idea that appropriate role models will differ from person to person, or culture to culture. This leads to the view that moral standards, too, will differ in this way. Since we spend a good deal of time on relativism in chapter 19, I suggest we move on and consider some alternative solutions here.

---

6. See chapter 10, "Utilitarianism Is Very Demanding," for more on this topic.

People can be truly virtuous even if we don't realize that they are. When we fail to choose the right role models, this is often explained by our own failure of virtue. Winston Churchill, for instance, though possessed of a great many virtues himself, was nevertheless so committed to maintaining British rule over India that he never saw past his racist attitudes toward Indians. Churchill once announced, "I hate Indians. They are a beastly people with a beastly religion." His racism prevented him from seeing Gandhi as a moral exemplar; indeed, Churchill was fully prepared to let Gandhi die in one of his hunger strikes. Churchill declared that Gandhi "ought to be lain bound hand and foot at the gates of Delhi and then trampled on by an enormous elephant with the new Viceroy [the British ruler of India] seated on its back."[7] Churchill's failure of virtue clouded his judgment so badly that he regarded Gandhi as deserving to die because of his threat to British imperial ambitions.

We become more insightful in selecting moral exemplars only by becoming morally wiser in general. And as we have seen, there is no fixed recipe for doing this. Moral education is a lifelong affair, and we are never fully wise. So we may indeed be off target in selecting our role models.

This isn't the whole story, of course. The whole story would involve a much more detailed account of how we gain moral knowledge, including knowledge of how to correctly identify our role models and how to resolve disputes about this matter. But in this respect, the virtue ethicist is in the same boat as everyone else. *Every* moral theorist has to answer hard problems about how to gain moral wisdom, and how to resolve disagreements about fundamental moral issues.

Conflict and Contradiction

We have seen in previous chapters how certain kinds of moral conflict can yield contradiction.[8] Contradictions are a fatal flaw in any theory. Virtue ethics may be saddled with contradictions, and if that is so, then it is sunk.

The problem is simple. If there are many virtuous people, then what happens if they disagree about what to do in a given situation? If, in my shoes, some good people would act one way, and others would behave

---

7. These quotes appear in Johann Hari, "The Two Churchills," *New York Times Book Review* (August 15, 2010), p. 11. Hari was reviewing Richard Toye's book *Churchill's Empire* (New York: Henry Holt, 2010).

8. See especially chapter 15, "Moral Conflict and Contradiction." This matter is also discussed at some length in chapter 19, "Ethical Subjectivism and the Problem of Contradiction."

differently, then it seems that the same action would be both right (because some role models would do it) and not right (because others would not do it). This is a contradiction.

The very wise people I have known do not all think alike. They don't see every case in the same light. They temper justice with mercy to varying degrees. They disagree about the role and form that discipline should take in good parenting. Some are more optimistic than others; some are more willing to demand more personal sacrifice than others. It thus seems possible that virtuous role models, acting in character, would do different things in the same situation. And that would yield contradiction.

There are a few ways out of this problem.[9] The first is to insist that there is really only a single truly virtuous person, and so the differences that cause the contradictions would disappear. The second is to insist that every virtuous person, acting in character, would do exactly the same thing in every situation. I don't find either of these replies very plausible, but perhaps there is more to be said for them than I am imagining.

The better option, I think, is to slightly modify the virtue ethical view of right action, given earlier in this chapter (in the section "The Standard of Right Action") by the thesis labeled (VE). Assuming that virtuous people, acting in character, will sometimes do different things in the same situation, we should say the following:

1. An act in a given situation is morally required just because *all* virtuous people, acting in character, would perform it.
2. An act in a given situation is morally permitted just because *some but not all* virtuous people, acting in character, would perform it.
3. An act in a given situation is morally forbidden just because *no* virtuous person would perform it.

This really will solve the contradiction problem. If different virtuous people would act differently in the same situation, then we are no longer forced to say that an act is both right and wrong. Rather, we say that it is simply permitted, neither required nor forbidden. If different virtuous people would act differently were they in our shoes, then we are permitted to act as any one of them does. In that case, the theory will not tell us which role model to follow—it will be, morally speaking, up to us.

---

9. A similar problem confronts the social contract theory; see chapter 14, "Disagreement among the Contractors."

The Priority Problem

How do we get a handle on the nature of virtue? Here is the standard way. We first get clear about our duty, and then define a virtue as a character trait that reliably moves us to do our duty for the right reasons. So, for instance, to understand the virtue of generosity, we first note that we are duty-bound to help the needy, and then define generosity as the character trait of giving to others in need, for the right reasons.

Virtue ethicists reject this strategy, because they deny that we can know our duty before knowing how virtuous people characteristically behave. For them, virtue has a kind of priority over duty—we must know what virtue is, and how the virtuous would behave, before knowing what we must do.

Virtue ethics is unique in this regard. All other moral theories think of duty as the primary moral concept. For them, we can understand virtue only after we have the concept of duty under our belt.

The issue is about which concept is morally fundamental—virtue, or right action. To help see the stakes here, consider this question: are people virtuous because they perform right actions, or are actions right because virtuous people perform them? Other moral theories go with the first option. Virtue ethics takes the second. And this raises a number of concerns.

Consider the evil of rape. The virtue ethicist explains its wrongness by claiming that virtuous people would never rape other people. But that seems backward. It is true, of course, that virtuous people are not rapists. But their rejection of rape is not what explains its wrongness. Rape is wrong because it expresses contempt for the victim, sends a false message of the rapist's superiority, violates the victim's rights, and imposes terrible harm without consent. We explain why virtuous people don't rape others by showing why rape is wrong. We don't explain why rape is wrong by showing that good people will not rape others.

The same goes for right actions. A bystander who sees a toddler about to walk into traffic should rush over to prevent the accident. Why? Not because a virtuous person would do such a thing (though of course she would). The real reason is to save a child's life, or at least to prevent her from being seriously injured. It's not that intervention is right because virtuous people would do it; rather, they would do it because it is right.

If this has a familiar ring to it, that's because the structure of this theory closely mirrors that of Euthyphro's preferred view, the divine command theory (discussed in chapter 5). That theory denied that we could understand our duty apart from the decisions made by God, because God's commands are what create our duty. Virtue ethics takes a similar approach to morality, though many of its versions, including Aristotle's, are secular.

Virtue ethics tells us that it is the actions of virtuous people, rather than God's commands, that determine what is right or wrong. According to virtue ethicists, people aren't virtuous because they do right; actions are right because they are done by the virtuous.

Virtue ethics and the divine command theory share a basic structure. And they share a basic weakness. We can see this by posing a familiar dilemma. Virtuous people either have, or don't have, good reasons for their actions. (1) If they lack good reasons, then their actions are arbitrary, and can't possibly serve as the standard of morality. (2) If they do have good reasons to support their actions, then these reasons, rather than the choices of good people, determine what is right and wrong.

The second option is the better one. We must suppose that virtuous people act on good reasons, or else they wouldn't really be virtuous. Consider again the immorality of rape, and the many reasons why it is wrong. A virtuous person is one who is aware of these reasons and takes them to heart. Rape is wrong not because good people oppose it. They oppose it because it is wrong.

This approach preserves the integrity, the wisdom, and the goodness of the virtuous person. But there is naturally a cost. And it is steep. The cost is that the virtue ethicist's account of right action is directly threatened. That account tells us that acts are morally right *just because* all virtuous people would perform them in the circumstances, and wrong just because such people would refrain. But as we have seen, the choices of virtuous people do not make actions right or wrong.

We can still look to virtuous role models for reliable guidance on how to act. But their choices do not turn otherwise neutral actions into ones that are right (or wrong). They are not so powerful as that. Virtuous people have keen insight into the reasons that make actions moral or immoral. They feel the compelling force of these reasons and act accordingly. That is what makes them virtuous.

If this line of criticism is on target, then we have an explanation of why so many moral theories give priority to duty over virtue. We need to explain virtue in terms of duty, because we would otherwise be left with a picture of virtuous people that makes their choices arbitrary. But if that is so, then virtue ethics is in trouble, since one of its fundamental points is that rightness is defined in terms of the choices of the virtuous.

17.8 Conclusion

Virtue ethics represents an exciting continuation of an ancient tradition. It has a variety of attractions, not least of which is its emphasis on the importance of moral character. It has interesting things to say about ethical complexity, moral education, the importance of moral wisdom, and the nature of the good life. Many of the criticisms that have been leveled at it can be met once we dig a bit deeper, or introduce small changes to the theory.

But no ethical theory, at least in its present state, is immune to all real difficulties, and virtue ethics, too, has its vulnerable points. The greatest of these takes aim at one of its central claims: that right action must be understood by reference to virtue, rather than the other way around. Perhaps virtue really does enjoy this sort of priority. But it will take a great deal of further work to show it so.

17.9 Discussion Questions

1. How might a person do the right thing but still fail to be morally admirable? How does virtue ethics account for this?
2. How do we come to know what the right thing to do is in a particular situation, according to virtue ethics? How does this account of moral knowledge differ from the accounts given by previously discussed theories? Which do you find more attractive?
3. Aristotle believed that being a virtuous person was essential to one's life going well. Do you agree? What reasons can be given in support of this position?
4. What are tragic dilemmas? How might they pose a problem for virtue ethics?
5. Does virtue ethics demand too much of us? Why or why not?
6. Virtuous people sometimes disagree with one another about which actions are right. Is this a problem for virtue ethics? Why or why not?
7. What is the priority problem for virtue ethics? Do you think the virtue ethicist has an adequate reply to this problem?

17.10 Cases for Critical Reflection

Whistle-Blowing

During the 1990s, Jeffrey Wigand made national headlines as a tobacco industry whistle-blower. He had worked as an executive at Brown

& Williamson, an American tobacco company. In 1989, Wigand was hired as the head of research and development at the company to help produce a safer cigarette. The project was dropped in March 1993, and Wigand was fired. Wigand signed a confidentiality agreement with the company.

In 1996, Wigand gave an interview on CBS's *60 Minutes* in order to alert the public that Brown & Williamson intentionally added harmful chemicals to cigarettes to increase the nicotine effects. Wigand also said that the company had been aware of addiction and health hazards associated with cigarettes, which they had been publicly denying. In doing so, Wigand broke his confidentiality agreement and risked a lawsuit.

The costs to Jeffrey Wigand were enormous. Anti-smoking advocates hailed Wigand as a hero for his act of whistle-blowing, but he was vilified by the tobacco industry. He lost a $300,000 salaried job at Brown & Williamson and severely hurt his chance at being hired elsewhere as a high-level researcher. In the aftermath, Wigand and his family received death threats, his marriage fell apart, and he became the subject of a surveillance and smear campaign.[1] Still, Wigand felt that he did the right thing: "I felt that I had the moral imperative that I had to do something with the knowledge I have. . . . I would most certainly do it again."[2]

Questions

1. Whistle-blowers such as Jeffrey Wigand often expose truths to the public at great cost to themselves and their families, and reasonable people may disagree about whether a particular situation calls for an act of whistle-blowing. When do you think a virtuous person would decide to become a whistle-blower? Why?
2. Do you think whistle-blowers such as Jeffrey Wigand are moral exemplars? Why or why not?
3. According to virtue ethics, did Jeffrey Wigand do the right thing? Why or why not?

Mother Teresa

Mother Teresa was an Albanian-Indian Catholic nun and missionary who has been hailed for her service to the world's poor. She devoted her life to working among the poorest people in the slums of Calcutta and

---

1. https://www.vanityfair.com/magazine/1996/05/wigand199605.

2. http://www.nbcnews.com/id/8077025/ns/msnbc-hardball_with_chris_matthews/t/inside-mind-whistle-blower/#.XA2YjnRKhPY.

founded the Missionaries of Charity, an organization "whose primary task was to love and care for those persons nobody was prepared to look after."[1] Mother Teresa and her associates built homes for orphans, shelters for people suffering from leprosy, and hospices for the terminally ill. In 1979, she was awarded a Nobel Peace Prize. After her death, she was declared a saint by Pope Francis.

Not everyone thought Mother Teresa was a saint. Her critics point out that she sometimes baptized terminally ill patients without their knowledge and that her hospices failed to meet contemporary medical standards.[2] Christopher Hitchens famously criticized Mother Teresa, calling her a fanatic and a fraud, and pointing out that her congregation received misappropriated money from the Duvalier family in Haiti. She was also criticized for utilizing contemporary medical technology to protect her own health, a luxury not afforded to the patients in her hospices.[3] Others have come to Mother Teresa's defense:

> Regarding the "poorest of the poor," those who today die neglected, there would seem to be two choices. First, to cluck one's tongue that such a group of people should even exist. Second, to act: to provide comfort and solace to these individuals as they face death. . . . Mother Teresa, for all of her faults, chooses the latter.[4]

Questions

1. Some regard Mother Teresa as a moral exemplar who helped the poorest of the poor and inspired others to do the same, while others have criticized her harshly for her various faults. What do you think it takes to be a moral exemplar? Does someone like Mother Teresa count? Should moral exemplars be morally perfect?

2. One criticism of Mother Teresa is that she received donations from the Duvalier family, who have been blamed for corruption and devastation in Haiti. What, if anything, does the company we keep say about our own character? Can a virtuous person have unvirtuous friends? Why or why not?

---

1. https://www.nobelprize.org/prizes/peace/1979/teresa/biographical/.
2. https://www.washingtonpost.com/news/worldviews/wp/2015/02/25/why-to-many-critics-mother-teresa-is-still-no-saint/?noredirect=on&utm_term=.b6b8005a5d53.
3. https://slate.com/news-and-politics/2003/10/the-fanatic-fraudulent-mother-teresa.html.
4. https://www.nybooks.com/articles/1996/09/19/in-defense-of-mother-teresa/.

3. Can we learn anything about virtue from the life of Mother Teresa?
4. According to virtue ethics, what is the correct response to poverty in the world?

Benjamin Franklin's Virtues

Benjamin Franklin was a diplomat, inventor, and scientist; he is best known for his role in drafting the Declaration of Independence and the Constitution of the United States. He is less well known for his method of self-improvement, which he came up with after critically reflecting on his habits. He realized that he ate and drank too much, talked about himself too much, spent more money than he wished to, and didn't always accomplish his goals. So he developed a list of thirteen virtues that he believed would counteract his behavioral vices. Franklin's list included temperance, silence, order, resolution, frugality, industry, sincerity, justice, moderation, cleanliness, tranquility, chastity, and humility. Rather than attempt to adopt all the virtues at once, Franklin would work on one virtue a week before moving on to the next, tracking his progress with a chart throughout the year. He called this process as "a bold and arduous project of arriving at moral perfection." Franklin never felt that he fully mastered the virtues, but did think he made progress over time:

> On the whole, tho' I never arrived at the Perfection I had been so ambitious of obtaining, but fell short of it. Yet as I was, by the Endeavor, a better and a happier Man than I otherwise should have been if I had not attempted it.[1]

Questions

1. Do you agree that each of the traits included on Benjamin Franklin's list is a virtue? Are some of the traits controversial? If so, which ones, and why?
2. How should we go about determining which traits are virtues or vices?
3. Is it a problem for virtue ethics if it isn't easy to decide whether a particular trait is a virtue? Why or why not?
4. How does one become a virtuous person? Does Benjamin Franklin's method seem like a good way to do it? Why or why not?

---

1. https://www.cnn.com/2018/03/01/health/13-virtues-wisdom-project/index.html.

CHAPTER 18

.... ❧ ....

Feminist Ethics

18.1 The Elements of Feminist Ethics

The most prominent authors and supporters of the ethical theories that we have considered so far have one thing in common. They are all men. Most of them lived in societies that systematically discriminated against women. Since even the most high-minded thinkers are bound to reflect some of the common assumptions of their times, it should come as no surprise that many important philosophers held views about women that nowadays make us cringe.

Aristotle said that "the male is by nature superior, and the female inferior; the one rules, and the other is ruled."[1] Aquinas claimed, "As regards her individual nature, each woman is defective and misbegotten."[2] Kant wrote that "laborious learning or painful pondering, even if a woman should greatly succeed in it, destroy the merits that are proper to her sex . . . [and] they will weaken the charms with which she exercises her great power over the other sex. . . . Her philosophy is not to reason, but to sense."[3] Rousseau said, "Women do wrong to complain of the inequality of man-made laws; this inequality is not of man's making, or at any rate it is not the result of mere prejudice, but of reason. . . . [Women] must be trained to bear the yoke from the first, so that they

---

1. Aristotle, *Politics* 1254 b13.
2. Thomas Aquinas, *Summa Theologica*, question 92, first article.
3. Immanuel Kant, *Observations on the Feeling of the Beautiful and the Sublime*, section 3.

may not feel it, to master their own caprices and to submit themselves to the will of others."[4]

We might be tempted to downplay these slights by claiming that they did not influence the main lines of argument of these thinkers. And there is a sense in which this is correct—almost none of the major male philosophers of past centuries wrote very much about women. But there is also a sense in which it is incorrect, for there are two ways in which philosophers have shortchanged the lives of women. The first is to make false and damaging claims about them. The second is to ignore female experiences and perspectives. Both have been the norm in ethical thinking for centuries. **Feminist ethics** seeks to remedy both of these flaws.

Feminist ethics is not a single theory, but rather a general approach to ethics that is defined by four central claims:

1. Women are the moral equals of men; views that justify the subordination of women or downplay their interests are thus mistaken on that account.

2. The experiences of women deserve our respect and are vital to a full and accurate understanding of morality. To the extent that philosophers ignore such experiences, their theories are bound to be incomplete, and likely to be biased and inaccurate.

3. Traits that have traditionally been associated with women—empathy, sympathy, caring, altruism, mercy, compassion—are at least as morally important as traditionally masculine traits, such as competitiveness, independence, demanding one's fair share, a readiness to resort to violence, and the insistence on personal honor.

4. Traditionally feminine ways of moral reasoning, ones that emphasize cooperation, flexibility, openness to competing ideas, and a connectedness to family and friends, are often superior to traditionally masculine ways of reasoning that emphasize impartiality, abstraction, and strict adherence to rules.

Two cautionary notes. First, no one believes that every woman is compassionate and caring, or that every man is aggressive and competitive. These are generalizations that hold only to some extent, and allow for many exceptions. Second, when I speak of *traditionally* masculine and feminine traits, I mean just that. These are features that our cultures have long

---

4. Jean-Jacques Rousseau, *Emile: On Education.*

associated with men and with women, respectively. But there is no claim that such traits are innate. Many characteristics we associate with certain groups are a by-product of social influences. Stereotypes often fail to have any basis in fact. But even when they do, these facts are often a result of difficult circumstances and limited opportunities, rather than the expression of some inborn character.

18.2 Moral Development

Feminist ethics really came into its own in the 1980s. Before that, scattered writings by feminist philosophers had been appearing for at least two centuries. But in 1982, Harvard psychologist Carol Gilligan published *In a Different Voice*.[5] It's fair to say that this book did more than any other to launch this new movement in philosophical thinking.

Gilligan argued that women think and experience the world differently from men. This was not news—psychologists had long agreed on this point. The difference, though, was that Gilligan rejected the mainstream views that saw women's thinking as inferior to men's.

One of the most influential models of moral thinking in the 1970s was put forth by Lawrence Kohlberg, a teacher and colleague of Gilligan's. Kohlberg defended the idea that there are six stages of moral development. At the earliest stage, as children, we see moral rules only as potential threats, and we behave well only out of fear of punishment. As we grow, we view morality (at Kohlberg's third stage) as depending on our social roles and on our relations. Moral demands come from these roles and relationships; the point of morality is to reinforce them. Ultimately, at the sixth and highest stage, we think of morality as requiring obedience to abstract rules of impartial justice. These rules require us to see our situation dispassionately. They assign everyone equal importance. These rules are universal, and do not depend on, or refer to, the particulars of our character or our situation.

Gilligan noted that many women fare poorly on Kohlberg's scale—they never advance beyond the third stage. She argued that women brought an attitude of care and sympathy to their decision making, an attention to the concrete particulars of the cases with which they were confronted. They rarely appealed to abstract moral principles. They did not regard justice as all-important. They were partial to certain people—family members,

---

5. Harvard University Press, 1982.

friends, lovers—rather than seeking to give everyone the same degree of concern. In deciding what to do, they sought compromise where possible, and did not regard the relevant moral rules as absolute. They tried to "split the difference" in cases of conflict, and showed greater respect for views that differed from their own. They were inclined to voice their views with hesitation and humility, rather than with great confidence and assurance.

Gilligan did not argue that *all* women thought in these ways. Nor did she claim that women, *by nature*, were attracted to these ways of thinking. Still, she claimed to have identified a very strong tendency among the women she studied to react to cases of moral conflict in the same way—a way very different from that of the men she interviewed. Gilligan argued that this was not evidence of the moral immaturity of these women. Rather, it indicated the failure of Kohlberg's six-stage model. As she saw it, it was only a prejudice—a very well-entrenched and long-standing one, to be sure—that elevated Kohlberg's emphasis on justice, impartiality, and rules over traditionally feminine ways of moral reasoning.

Gilligan is a psychologist, not a moral philosopher. She saw her work as describing the differences between male and female thinking, and did not focus on drawing out the ethical implications of her research. But philosophers soon took up this task, developing a new model of moral thinking that set out to challenge the prevailing ethical wisdom on a number of fronts. Let's turn our attention to some of the most important of these challenges.

18.3 Women's Experience

There is always a danger of oversimplifying things when discussing "the female perspective." There is no such thing, strictly speaking. Women's experiences, their outlooks on life and their responses to it, are extraordinarily diverse. On any issue of importance, there are women on opposite sides of the fence—just as there are men. Many men share the outlook that Gilligan associated with women, and many women share a more "masculine" approach to moral thinking.

And yet . . . even though there is no one thing that is "the female outlook," there are some distinctively female experiences (giving birth and mothering, most obviously), and many others that are widely shared by women, less so by men, and that have been largely neglected by philosophers. One of these is a vulnerability to rape. Another is the threat of domestic abuse. Yet another is the systematic disparity in pay for the same work. Another is women's total or near total exclusion from a variety of professions (president, airline pilot, welder, mason, firefighter, electrician, etc.). This list could be expanded, surely. And it could go on for pages if we broadened the scope of our investigation to consider the status of women in other countries that have done less to reduce overt sexual discrimination.

Women are not the only ones who have suffered these threats and limitations. Many men have been raped and beaten, have experienced discrimination of various forms. But the likelihood of such suffering is greatly increased if one is a woman. And yet prior to the early 1980s, philosophers had almost completely ignored these issues, devoting little if any thought to the ethical problems they raised. One goal of feminist philosophers is to put these issues on the map, and to get philosophers and policymakers to devote their time and attention to solving them.

There is another, related aspect of ordinary female experience that bears mentioning here: an increased dependence and diminished autonomy. Compared to men, women have almost always had far fewer choices open to them, and have enjoyed far less control over important aspects of their lives. In many countries, women still need the permission of either their husbands or a close male relative to travel outside of their region. Women have been, and in many places continue to be, unable to choose a spouse for themselves. Women are far likelier than men or boys to be sold into sexual slavery. Many kinds of jobs, all political offices, and a variety of social positions have been closed to women, just because they are women.

These are commonplace observations—no less true and no less worrisome for that. We can summarize them by noting that two central facts of most women's lives are their dependence and the frequent demands to place their own interests on the back burner. Married women have traditionally had very little choice about where to live, for instance—if their husband's job required a family move, then that was that. It is still the case that a mother is usually the one to sacrifice job prospects if a couple decides that one of them must stay home to care for their child. Historically, and still in most areas around the world, women are dependent on men for their economic survival. They are vulnerable to physical abuse by husbands or male relatives. They are legally at the mercy of judicial systems ruled by men.

Dependence on others often requires us to rethink our moral assumptions. Consider this popular one: we should stand up for our rights and defend our honor against attacks. But if a woman has little education and less job training, does she walk out on an abusive husband who is paying the bills? Does she confront him and go so far as to seek a divorce— knowing the terrible statistics of spousal murder, and not knowing where her next meal will come from?

The choices of most women (and most men, for that matter) reflect their role within a family—as a grown child of elderly parents, as a spouse of someone whose needs and wants will not always match your own, as a sibling whose brothers or sisters may sometimes require your immediate, significant assistance. We do not choose our parents or our siblings. Consent does not enter into it, and yet here we are, with duties to them whether we like it or not. What morality requires of us often depends on who we are related to. And this is usually something that we cannot control.

Vulnerability, not having control over important aspects of one's life, dependence, and connectedness to others are all features of the moral life highlighted by feminist ethics. What we ought to do with our lives, from the big picture to our everyday choices, is often a matter of having to recognize the importance of those we care about. The interests and desires of our partners or spouses must be taken into account. Those of us with children know how needy they can be—even the least needy among them. True friends are sometimes very demanding. Fulfilling our duties across this range of relationships often means setting aside our own interests, or seeing our interests as crucially dependent on the interests of those we care for.

It's not that women alone are deeply connected in this way. *Most* of us are enmeshed in a network of personal relationships, many not of our own choosing. Feminists argue that this should force us to rethink the ideal of a person as a free agent, isolated, and wholly independent. Once we really appreciate how connected we are to others, the moral philosophies that are based on ideals of self-interest or full autonomy may become less appealing.

A way of reinforcing this point comes from feminists who emphasize the importance of caring in establishing and sustaining our vital relationships. Women have usually been cast in the role of nurturer—the one who sensitively cares for others in need. Of course not all women are tender and nurturing. But it is important to understand how much of what goes on in society depends on domestic work being well done—children fed and well raised, house and household well maintained. Society is possible only if there are people devoted to caring for others. Without caretakers, children would die, the sick and the infirm would die, and many of the mentally disabled and mentally ill would die. Most of those whose work does not involve caring for others are able to keep their jobs only because there is someone back at home who is managing the household. That someone is usually a woman. Where it is not a wife or mother, it is a usually a domestic employee or servant—and this, too, is almost always a woman.

Where standard ethical theories see morality as primarily about the pursuit of self-interest (egoism), doing justice (Kantianism), seeking mutual benefit (contractarianism), or impartial benevolence (utilitarianism), many feminists point to care—especially a mother's care—as the model of moral relations and the basis of ethics. This maternal model has generated what feminist philosophers now call an *ethic of care*. Let's take a closer look at this new moral theory.

18.4 The Ethics of Care

The major moral theories we have discussed thus far are not designed with home and family life in mind. But since so many of our most important moments are spent with those we love, and since so many moral choices are made within the context of close relationships, why not imagine what an ethic would look like that took these as its starting points? In particular, some feminist ethicists have argued that we should think of a loving mother's care for her children as a model for all moral behavior.

We can better understand an ethics of care by first seeing what it is not. Unlike ethical egoism, care ethics does not insist that we always look out for number one. Mothers often rightly sacrifice their own interests in order to advance those of their children. Unlike Kantianism, an ethics of care does not place supreme importance on justice. Matters of justice are not entirely absent from parent-child relations, but they are certainly not the primary focus here. It is important that a parent not try to swindle her children, and that children show respect for their parents. But standing on one's rights, insisting on a fair share, and ensuring that the guilty are given their just deserts are not at the heart of loving relationships.

Contractarian theories see the authors of the moral law as indifferent to the needs of others, willing to make sacrifices for them only if there is a reasonable chance of being compensated in return. Good parents don't see things that way. A mother's care is not conditional on her child's obedience to a set of mutually beneficial rules. The rational pursuit of self-interest is not the ultimate goal; if the only way to help your child is to take a serious hit yourself, a good parent will often do just that.

And contrary to utilitarian demands for impartial benevolence, loving parents are much more concerned about their own children than about other people's kids. There is no thought of being impartial here; a good mother will be partial to her children, will give them more care and attention than she does anyone else's children. Love and care cannot be parceled out to everyone equally.

In addition to these specific differences, the ethics of care incorporates the following features. Most of these represent a point of departure from most traditional ethical theories, though as we'll see, there are some points of similarity between the ethics of care and both virtue ethics and Ross's ethic of prima facie duties.

The Importance of Emotions

Care is an emotion, or a network of reinforcing emotions that involve some combination of sympathy, empathy, sensitivity, and love. Like all emotions, care has elements that involve thinking and feeling. The relevant thoughts are focused on the wants and needs of the one being cared for. The feelings are positive, friendly, helpful, nurturing, and often loving. Care helps us know what others need—parents often understand what their own child needs much better than anyone else. And care helps to motivate us to tend to those needs, even when we are exhausted, grudging, or angry. How many mothers and fathers have roused themselves from a sound sleep to soothe their crying infant? Care helps ease those parents out from under the covers.

Utilitarians don't place much importance on the emotions in knowing what's right and wrong. Calculating amounts of happiness and misery isn't an emotional task. And we have seen how dismissive Kant was of the emotions, claiming that reason alone could both tell us where our duty lay and get us to do it.[6] Kant was surely right in thinking that our emotions cannot go unchecked—we need an ethic of care, and not just care itself. But care ethicists argue that care and its associated emotions are central to moral motivation and moral discovery, even if they are not the whole story.

Those who defend an ethics of care sometimes see themselves as working within a virtue ethics tradition. And this makes sense, given the emphasis not only on what we do, but on how we do it. The manner in which we do things is often as important as what we do.

---

6. See the discussion "The Importance of Rationality and Autonomy" in chapter 12.

Suppose, for instance, that my mother calls me up and asks that I spend the afternoon helping my aged father with some household chores. I do as she asks, but only grudgingly, and make it clear with my body language and my brusqueness that I resent being there. I've done the right thing, but in the wrong manner. I am not acting virtuously and am not displaying an appropriate level of care.

Against Unification

Most of the traditional ethical theories offer us one supreme moral rule that determines the morality of all actions. Care ethics rejects this picture. I can't offer a short formula to describe the its conditions of right action, because on this view there is no such formula. Ethics cannot be systematized. If care ethicists are correct, there is no ultimate rule that can explain or justify all of our moral duties.

This has a number of important implications.[7] One of these is that there is no surefire test for knowing what morality demands of us. Morality is complicated and messy. The drive to try to unify all of morality under a single supreme rule is an understandable one. Such a rule would lend clarity and structure to ethics. But care ethicists argue that this is a pipe dream.

We can see this as it plays out in the lives of many women (and men) faced with conflicting demands from children, work, spouses, and other sources. Suppose your parents call you up and proceed to criticize your boyfriend. He later asks you what you and your parents talked about. Do you tell him what they've said, knowing that he'll be hurt and that this is going to make a good relationship between him and your parents even harder to achieve? Or suppose your husband believes in disciplining children with a very firm hand. You disagree. He spanks his son—your son—after some minor misbehavior. Then he does it again. What do you do?

These aren't life-or-death cases. Rather, these are ordinary situations that arise in homes all the time. Care ethicists say of such examples that while there is often a right thing to do, we can't read off a recommendation from some simple rule. Rather, we have to appreciate the different sources of our moral duties. These stem primarily from relationships we have with

---

7. Most of these have been discussed in detail in chapter 16, the bulk of which is devoted to considering Ross's view that there are a number of different fundamental moral duties, rather than just one. Virtue ethics also endorses this idea; see chapter 17, "Moral Complexity," for more discussion.

other people. And they can conflict with one another. When they do, it can be very hard to know what to do. At such times, we may wish for some easy formula that could give us instant advice about how to behave. But if care ethicists are right, there is no such thing. Part of gaining moral maturity is recognizing this, facing life's difficult choices, and not pretending that overly simple answers will solve our problems.

Against Impartiality and Abstraction

There are many reasons why philosophers have been so attracted to the idea of a supreme moral rule. Here is one of them. The more general and abstract the rule, the less likely it is to include bias. A rule that applies only to certain people or to certain situations may reflect only a limited perspective. Philosophers have long sought an outlook that is free of prejudice and distortion, one that takes into account all people at all times.

But why is this so important? The traditional answer is that it gives us a way to ensure impartiality. We must think of everyone as moral equals, and that means giving each person equal weight when we determine what is right and wrong. But as we have seen, care ethicists reject the idea that we must proceed in this way. It is right that we give priority to those we care about. It is good to be partial to our loved ones.

Care ethicists resist the push to abstraction that we see so strongly in philosophy. Moral reasoning should not be centered on a single, very general rule, but rather should be guided by a more complicated understanding of the specifics of situations.

For instance, care ethicists reject Rawls's attempt to strip away all concrete, particular knowledge of who we are when determining the principles of justice (see chapter 13, "Contractarianism Explains and Justifies the Content of the Basic Moral Rules"). They reject the utilitarian emphasis on impartiality. They deny that any general rule, such as lex talionis (see chapter 12, "Determining Just Deserts"), can illuminate the nature of justice. We must instead substitute a sensitive appreciation of the details and complexities of a situation, and not try to solve moral problems by seeing how these features fall under some general moral rule. If an ethic of care is correct, there is no master rule that can successfully guide our moral decisions.

Against Competition

It shouldn't be surprising that the virtues of competition are so often touted by men. Competition governs the business world, the realm of politics, and the world of sports—for so long exclusively male domains, only recently opened to women. Moral theorists have sometimes borrowed this emphasis on the importance of competition. Ethical egoists require us to harm others if their interests compete with our own. Contractarians think of social interactions as a series of prisoner's dilemmas (see "The Prisoner's Dilemma" in chapter 13), in which each person's interests are pitted against those of others.

An ethic of care seeks to replace this picture with one that values cooperation over competition. A healthy mother-child relationship is not a competitive one. It does not set the interests of parents against their children. It is marked by kindness and a willingness to sacrifice for one another. Good parents will see their interests as very closely bound up with the interests of their children, rather than in competition with them.

Care ethicists argue that we should try to turn competitive situations into cooperative ones. Rather than highlight the areas in which our interests clash, we should try to seek reconciliation. We should turn demands into requests, try to understand where the other person is coming from, and be flexible in our dealings with others. We can't show the same degree of care toward others as we do toward our loved ones, but we can approximate this, and look to care as the basis of our relationships. Imagine how different the business, political, and social worlds would be if people were animated by care rather than by self-interest and competitiveness. It's a far cry from the world we live in—and a far better one, if care ethicists are right.

Downplaying Rights

Care ethicists often argue that moral theories have placed too much emphasis on justice. Demanding our rights, insisting that others honor our claims, and making sure we get what we are entitled to—these are ways of asserting our independence from one another, rather than our connectedness. Talk of rights can divide us more quickly. This is a common complaint about the abortion debates, for instance. Once we start speaking of the rights of a fetus and of a woman, the debate becomes bogged down, making it very difficult to find common ground with those on the other side of the fence.

Imagine that we instead emphasized our responsibilities to one another, based on the model of a caring parent toward her children. Society would be seen not as a venue for the pursuit of rational self-interest, but rather as a stage for cooperation where we took responsibility for one another, and especially for the most vulnerable among us. In the area of social policy, for instance, this would lead to placing much greater importance on education, on support for poor families, and on making sure that everyone has access to excellent medical care.

The emphasis on rights has often meant giving priority to our being free from coercion and unwanted interference. Rights protect autonomy and independence. And so we have rights, for instance, to say and to read what we want, or to do what we like within the privacy of our own homes.

But many (though not all) feminists have launched pointed criticisms of such priorities. They argue that rights tend to place us in opposition to others, creating a barrier beyond which no one may pass without permission. Individual rights often allow people to pursue their own paths at the expense of the community. Rights emphasize the ways in which we are separate from one another, rather than the ways in which we might be brought together.

After all, loving parents do not stand on their rights when their child needs them. They do not want to assert their independence from their child. Care ethicists argue that rather than finding ways to insulate ourselves from others, we should be looking to create more opportunities for people to help one another. We should emphasize our responsibilities to others, rather than our rights against them. To the extent that rights stand in the way of building community and forging close ties with others, care ethicists regard them with suspicion.

18.5 Challenges for Feminist Ethics

Feminist ethics is an approach to morality, rather than a single unified theory with specific claims that all feminists endorse. As a result, a presentation of this family of views must settle for highlighting general lines of thought, rather than particular arguments and views that all feminists will accept.

Feminist ethicists currently deal with several challenges. And this is unsurprising, given that extensive work in the area is only a few decades old. Here are some of the most important of these challenges.

1. *The feminist ethics of care threatens to restrict the scope of the moral community too greatly.* Indeed, early care ethicists argued that we have moral duties only to those we care about. This view is no longer

defended, as it leaves us without any moral duties to strangers or to those we thoroughly dislike. But if we are to model our moral behavior on the mother–child relation, then we need extensive advice about how this is supposed to work in the case of those we don't know or care about. After all, one way in which we seem to have made moral progress is by extending the scope of the moral community beyond those who are near and dear to us.

2. *The role of the emotions in helping us to know the right thing to do, and in moving us to do it, needs further exploration.* Moral clarity sometimes requires that we overcome our indifference and become more emotionally invested in an issue. But in other cases, emotions can cloud our judgment. We need a view of which emotions are appropriate, and when they are appropriate, since the very same emotion can sometimes be enlightening and at other times anything but. An emotion such as anger often blinds us to the truth and prevents us from doing right. And so it needs to be regulated. But anger can also correctly alert us to serious immorality and will sometimes move us to overcome our fear and do the right thing. We need a much fuller story about the role of the emotions in the moral life.

3. *Downgrading impartiality has its costs.* As we saw in an earlier chapter (9, "Impartiality"), there is a great deal to be said for the importance of impartiality. It is a definite virtue of judges and others who hold positions of civic responsibility. It is an important corrective for prejudice and bias. It is one of the best reasons for taking the interests of women as seriously as those of men. Impartiality may not always be the right way to go, but it is, at least sometimes and perhaps usually, the best perspective from which to make important moral decisions.

4. *Rejecting any supreme moral rule leaves it hard to know how to solve moral conflicts.* A virtue of the principle of universalizability, or the principle of utility, is that we have a definite standard to appeal to in trying to decide how to act in puzzling cases. Without such a standard, we may be left largely in the dark about what morality allows or requires of us.

5. While cooperation is often an excellent thing, we also need to have strategies for dealing with uncooperative people or governments. The world would be a much better place if we were all able to get along and put our differences behind us. But as we all know, good faith and flexibility are sometimes met with a sneer and an iron fist, and moral philosophy needs

to have something to say about such occasions. Caring for our enemies will sometimes mean that they kill us or those we are entrusted to protect. Further, competition is sometimes a good thing. It can enhance efficiency in business. It can make for inspiring athletic events. It can spur us to personal excellence. So we shouldn't give up on competition entirely. And that means developing a sophisticated view of when it is and isn't appropriate to prefer cooperation over competition.

6. *While justice and rights are not the whole of morality, they are nonetheless a very important part of it.* We can explain what is so immoral about the oppression of women by citing the rights that are violated by sexist actions and policies. Women have rights to be free of physical abuse; they have a moral right to be paid the same amount of money for doing the same work; it is a gross injustice to forcibly circumcise a teenage girl (or a grown woman, for that matter). Rights are a form of moral protection, and women are often the ones in need of the strongest protections. A plausible feminist ethic must therefore make room for the importance of moral rights and the demands of justice that they support.

18.6 Conclusion

Feminists have often been described as those who think that women ought to be treated exactly as men are treated. But this is a mistake. Feminists argue not for equal *treatment*—after all, many of the ways that men typically get treated are morally questionable. Rather, feminists argue for *equal consideration*. The interests of women are to be given the same importance as those of men. When setting social policies, when evaluating traditions, or when trying to settle conflicts between men and women, it is immoral to downgrade the interests of women just because they are women. Women are the moral equals of men. This simple idea, if taken seriously, would lead to radical change in most areas of the world.

Perhaps Carol Gilligan was right in arguing that women's moral thinking typically differs significantly from that of men. Many neurobiologists and cognitive scientists have since endorsed this basic idea. But even if Gilligan got it wrong (as some have argued—you didn't expect everyone to agree on such a matter, did you?), we can still learn a great deal about ethics by reimagining moral philosophy through the lens of traditionally feminine concerns.

Many of us are more vulnerable and dependent than traditional moral theory allows. In the real world, there are severe inequalities of wealth and power, and it pays to be sensitive to such things when deciding on our moral ideals. Making care the centerpiece of our moral life, and allowing emotions and our loving relations a larger role in moral thinking, can make a substantial difference in our ethical outlooks.

Feminist ethics is not just for women. Its recommendations are intended for all human beings. The importance of care, and emotions generally; the emphasis on cooperation; the attractions of flexibility and compromise; the need for more than justice—each of these is morally important for everyone, not just women.

Feminist ethics is best seen as a general approach to morality, rather than as a single, unitary moral theory that can at this point compete directly with the traditional moral theories. But this is not necessarily a weakness. Rather, it is evidence of the wide variety of views that can be developed by those who take the interests of women just as seriously as we have long taken those of men.

18.7 Discussion Questions

1. What distinctively "female" experiences do feminists claim are neglected by traditional ethical theories? Do you agree that moral philosophy should be more attentive to these experiences? If so, how should our ethical theories incorporate them?
2. Most ethical theories stress that impartiality is important to acting ethically. Why do care ethicists deny this? Do you think they are correct to do so?
3. Like Ross's ethic of prima facie duties, care ethics rejects the notion of a single supreme principle of morality. What are the advantages of this approach? What are the disadvantages?
4. How plausible do you think it is to model the moral relations between people on that of a caring mother to her child?
5. Compare and contrast the role that Kantian ethics, virtue ethics, and feminist ethics assign to the emotions.
6. Given that feminism is often associated with the idea of women's rights, it might seem strange that care ethics downplays the importance of rights. What are the reasons care ethicists give for doing so? Do you find this an attractive feature of this approach to ethics?

18.8   Cases for Critical Reflection

The Heinz Dilemma

Consider the following thought experiment from psychologist Lawrence Kohlberg:

> In Europe, a woman was near death from cancer. One drug might save her, a form of radium that a druggist in the same town had recently discovered. The druggist was charging $2,000, ten times what the drug cost him to make. The sick woman's husband, Heinz, went to everyone he knew to borrow the money, but he could get together only about half of what it cost. He told the druggist that his wife was dying and asked him to sell it cheaper or let him pay later. But the druggist refused. The husband got desperate and broke into the man's store to steal the drug for his wife. Should the husband have done that? Why?[1]

Questions

1. What is your intuitive response to the dilemma? Did Heinz do the right thing? Why or why not?
2. According to an ethics of care, what would be the best response to the dilemma? Why?
3. Do you think Heinz dilemma can be resolved by a supreme moral rule? If so, what is the rule?
4. What sort of approach to the dilemma would feminist ethics require? What are the advantages or disadvantages to this approach?

Women in Combat

Traditionally, military combat has been restricted to men, but in 2013, the Pentagon lifted its prohibition on women in combat in the U.S. military. This gave women expanded access to career opportunities in the military, which could be seen as a win for the feminist movement, which seeks equality for women. Feminists have long been concerned with providing women with access to the same opportunities as men. However,

---

1. Lawrence Kohlberg. *Essays on Moral Development, Vol. I: The Philosophy of Moral Development* (San Francisco, Calif.: Harper & Row, 1981).

historically, many feminists have also criticized war for exemplifying patriarchal ideals that glorify dominance. For example, Virginia Woolf wrote:

> Though many instincts are held more or less in common by both sexes, to fight has always been the man's habit, not the woman's. Law and practice have developed that difference, whether innate or accidental. Scarcely a human being in the course of history has fallen to a woman's rifle; the vast majority of birds and beasts have been killed by you, not by us.[1]

The history of war and combat is overwhelmingly male, but even before the combat prohibition was lifted, women were already fighting in war. Tens of thousands of women helped fight in Iraq and Afghanistan as medics, military police, and intelligence officers. While these women were technically banned from combat on the ground, they would often find themselves on the front lines.[2]

Questions

1. Fighting in combat is a traditionally masculine enterprise. What are some other traditionally masculine roles in which women's opportunities have been limited?
2. Are there any traditionally masculine activities or roles (such as engaging in combat) that should remain that way? If so, why? If not, why not?
3. Would an ethics of care endorse the military policy to allow women to fight in combat? Why or why not?

Favoring Friends

Consider the following thought experiment: Elizabeth is the hiring manager at a start-up technology company that is seeking a new software developer. Her good friend, Janice, just completed a degree in computer science and is seeking her first job out of college. When Janice's resume crosses Elizabeth's desk, she immediately adds Janice to the shortlist for the job. Elizabeth thinks to herself that it would be a very good thing to help Janice break into the industry, and she imagines it would be fun working with her good friend. However, when comparing Janice's resume to

---

1. https://www.theatlantic.com/sexes/archive/2013/01/the-feminist-objection-to-women-in-combat/272505/.
2. https://jezebel.com/5978607/women-have-been-in-combat-all-along.

the other shortlisted candidates, Elizabeth begins to realize that there are better candidates for the job. Janice is inexperienced and would require more training than the other potential hires. Still, Elizabeth feels that she has a special duty to help her friend.

Questions

1. What sort of approach to Elizabeth's decision would feminist ethics require? Are there advantages or disadvantages to this approach?
2. Would it be unfair for Elizabeth demonstrate partiality by hiring her friend? Why or why not?
3. Do we have special duties to our friends that we don't have to others? Why or why not?
4. According to the ethics of care, what should Elizabeth do? Why?

PART THREE

Metaethics:
The Status of Morality

CHAPTER 19

.... ❧ ....

Ethical Relativism

19.1 Doubts about Objective Morality

Each of us has our doubts about morality. Most of these reflect our occasional puzzlement about what's right and wrong—we aren't sure, for instance, whether it is ever okay to lie, or to break a deathbed promise.

But there is another kind of doubt, one that can undermine all of our confidence in morality. This sort of puzzlement is not about the content of morality—what it requires or allows—but about its status. The worry, specifically, is that there are no **objective moral standards**,[1] and that morality therefore lacks any real authority.

Objective moral standards are those that apply to everyone, even if people don't believe that they do, even if people are indifferent to them, and even if obeying them fails to satisfy anyone's desires. Moral claims are objectively true whenever they accurately tell us what these objective moral standards are or what they require of us.

There are millions of objective *non-moral* truths. Here are three, at random. The planet Jupiter has a greater mass than Mercury. Virginia Woolf wrote *Orlando*. Galileo is dead. It doesn't matter what you think of these claims, and it doesn't matter what I think of them. It doesn't matter whether I care about these claims, and it doesn't matter whether believing them satisfies any of our desires. Neither personal opinion nor

---

1. All terms and phrases that appear in **boldface** are defined in the glossary at the end of the book.

conventional wisdom makes these claims true. They are true and would remain true even if no one believed them.

But are there any objective *moral* truths? That's not so clear. There are plenty of reasons for doubt; the most popular and important of these will be the focus of chapter 21. If such doubts are correct, then **ethical objectivism** is false. Ethical objectivism is the view that some moral standards are objectively correct and that some moral claims are objectively true.

Before having a look at these criticisms of ethical objectivism, let us consider the alternatives. This requires just a little more jargon. (I'm sorry.) There are basically two families of views that reject ethical objectivism: **moral nihilism** and **ethical relativism**.

Moral nihilism is the view that there are no moral truths at all. Taking a close, hard-nosed look at what is real and what isn't, nihilists place morality squarely in the latter camp. The world contains no moral features. Don't be fooled by our common talk of genocide's immorality or a murderer's evil nature. That sort of talk is either just plain false, or a disguised way of venting our feelings (of hatred, disgust, etc.).

According to the moral nihilist, when we take a step back from the issues that engage our emotions, we can see that nothing is right and nothing wrong. The world will one day be fully described by science, and science has no need of moral categories. In the words of the brilliant Scottish philosopher David Hume (1711–1776), we *gild* and *stain* a value-free world with our feelings and desires. When we declare a murderer wicked or a relief worker good and kind, we are expressing our anger or our admiration. We are not stating a fact. We couldn't be, since there is no moral reality to describe. As a result, no moral claims are true.

By contrast, ethical relativists claim that some moral standards really are correct, and that these determine which moral claims are true and which false. Many are true. People sometimes get it right in ethics, and they do that when their beliefs agree with the correct moral standards.

But these standards are never objectively correct. Rather, these standards are correct only *relative to* each person or each society. A moral standard is correct just because a person, or a society, is deeply committed to it. That means that the standards that are appropriate for some people may not be appropriate for others. There are no objective, universal moral principles that form an eternal blueprint to guide us through life. Morality is a human construct—we make it up—and, like the law, or like standards of taste, there is no uniquely correct set of rules to follow.

Moral nihilism and ethical relativism, though joined in their opposition to ethical objectivity, are quite different from each other. It pays to treat them separately. We'll keep the focus on ethical relativism in this chapter, and turn to moral nihilism in the next.

19.2 Two Kinds of Ethical Relativism—and Their Attractions

As you may already have noticed, ethical relativism isn't just a single doctrine. It actually comes in two varieties: **cultural relativism** and **individual relativism** (usually referred to as **ethical subjectivism**, a name I'll use from now on). Cultural relativism claims that the correct moral standards are relative to cultures or societies; ethical subjectivism claims that the correct moral standards are those endorsed by each individual. The difference amounts to whether society, or each person, has the final say about what is right and wrong. This is undoubtedly an important difference, but as we'll see, both the advantages and the drawbacks of cultural relativism and ethical subjectivism are remarkably similar.

Consider subjectivism first. It says that *an act is morally acceptable if, only if, and because (a) I approve of it, or (b) my commitments allow it. An action is wrong if, only if, and because (a) I disapprove of it, or (b) my commitments forbid it.* My commitments are the principles I support, the values I stand for. On this line of thinking, personal conviction is the ultimate measure of morality.

Subjectivists think that there are right answers in ethics, but that these are always relative to each person's values. There is no superior moral code that can measure the accuracy of each person's moral outlook. If subjectivism is correct, each person's ultimate moral standards are equally plausible.

Cultural relativism instead locates the ultimate standard of morality within each culture's commitments. It says that *an act is morally acceptable if, only if, and because it is allowed by the guiding ideals of the society in which it is performed, and immoral if, only if, and because it is forbidden by those ideals.* The fundamental difference between these two views is whether each person, or each society, gets to have the final say in ethics.

People find subjectivism or relativism attractive or a variety of reasons. Many of these reasons are negative—they amount to criticisms of ethical objectivism, criticisms that we will take up in chapter 21. So let us focus now on their sources of positive support. One of these is that relativism easily explains the origins of morality. Morality originates with human beings and their attitudes—those of each individual, if subjectivism is true, or those of collectives, if cultural relativism is correct. Before humans entered the picture, there was no such thing as morality. And once our planet heats up to intolerable levels, or the big asteroid hits, our species will vanish, and morality will be extinguished along with us.

A second attraction of these views is that they can also easily account for why morality is restricted to human beings. Moral requirements don't apply to snakes or cockroaches or blue jays, and subjectivism and relativism can easily explain why—morality is a set of rules that humans invented for their own use; these animals lack the brainpower to create or obey such rules. On this view, morality is made by and for human beings.

This leads to a third attraction—subjectivism and relativism provide a scientifically respectable account of morality. There is nothing mysterious about its decrees—morality is a code that reflects personal or cultural taste, nothing more (or less). The origins of morality can be scientifically confirmed (morality arose when humans did), and the contents of morality are also scientifically verifiable. We can use the social sciences of psychology, sociology, and anthropology to figure out what human beings really favor; if either form of relativism is correct, these findings will, in turn, tell us what is really right or wrong.

And this in turn leads to a fourth source of appeal—the ease with which subjectivists and relativists can explain the possibility of moral knowledge. For subjectivists, you can know what you are morally required or forbidden from doing just by knowing what you are truly committed to. For relativists, moral knowledge comes from having your finger on the pulse of society. That is all that's needed to know right from wrong.

Finally, these theories are egalitarian in ways that many people find deeply attractive. According to subjectivism, almost everyone is an excellent judge of morality, since almost everyone is pretty knowledgeable about their own commitments. While there are various specialists in physics, engineering or math, subjectivists deny that there are any moral experts (or insist that we are all moral experts), since everyone is equally well placed to gain moral knowledge. And according to relativism, we are unable to judge one culture's moral code as morally superior (or inferior) to another's; this has seemed to many like a refreshing kind of equality in the moral sphere.

Despite their disagreement about whose views are morally authoritative, both ethical subjectivism and cultural relativism share a number of features that make it easy to evaluate them together. Let's have a look.

19.3 Some Implications of Ethical Subjectivism and Cultural Relativism

Moral Infallibility

Subjectivism and relativism occupy a middle ground between moral nihilism and ethical objectivism. There are legitimate moral standards (contrary to nihilism), but their legitimacy depends crucially on our support (contrary to objectivism).

Though united in their opposition to nihilism and ethical objectivism, subjectivists and relativists do not always see eye to eye. Subjectivists are suspicious of cultural relativism because of the subjectivist belief that societies can be deeply mistaken about what is right and wrong. If the core principles of a social code can contain some serious moral errors, then cultural relativism is in trouble, since it says that whatever society holds most dear is morally right.

Relativists admit that some social beliefs can be morally mistaken. These are the ones that clash with society's most cherished ideals. But if relativists are right, those ideals can never themselves be immoral, since they just are the ultimate moral standards for each society.

The subjectivists seem to have a valid criticism here. The basic ideals of some cultures do appear to be deeply mistaken. Consider the case of Nuran Halitogullari, a fourteen-year-old girl from Istanbul who was abducted on her way home from the supermarket. She was raped over the course of six days and then rescued by police. After being reunited with her family, her father decided that she had dishonored their family by having been raped. He then exercised what he regarded as his rightful authority. As he told a newspaper reporter, "I decided to kill her because our honor was dirtied. I didn't listen to her pleas; I wrapped the wire around her neck and pulled at it until she died."[2]

Such "honor killings" usually go unpunished. That's because the cultures in which they are committed often regard them as justified. In such cultures, a family's honor is often dependent on the "purity" of its women. And this purity is measured in how its women dress, in who they have relationships with, and in whether they have been victimized in various ways. Thousands of girls and women over the past two decades alone have been killed because they have worn "Western" clothes, have had premarital sex, have had a boyfriend of a different religion, or have been raped.

---

2. Suzan Fraser, "Turk Kills 14 Year Old Daughter," AP newswire (April 29, 2004).

Such killings are supported by deep cultural assumptions—(i) that men should have the power of life and death over women; (ii) that women ought to obey their husbands, fathers, and brothers unconditionally; (iii) that a man's feeling of shame is enough to justify killing a woman who has made him feel that way.

These assumptions are found at the heart of many cultures. If ethical relativism is correct, then men in those cultures may be morally required to kill their wives, daughters, or sisters for having shown their bare calves, having kissed the wrong person, or having been raped.

The extreme sexism at the heart of honor killings is but one of many examples that raise doubts about cultural relativism. After all, societies are sometimes based on principles of slavery, warlike aggression, religious bigotry, or ethnic oppression. Cultural relativism would turn these core ideals into ironclad moral duties, making cooperation with slavery, sexism, and racism the moral duty of all citizens of those societies. The **iconoclast**—the person deeply opposed to conventional wisdom—would, by definition, always be morally mistaken. This has struck many people as seriously implausible.

Subjectivism faces a similar problem. The cultural relativist makes societies morally infallible (incapable of error), at least with regard to their foundational principles. Yet subjectivists make *each person's* basic commitments morally infallible. True, subjectivism allows that people can make moral mistakes, but only if they fail to realize what follows from their own commitments. When it comes to the basic commitments themselves, subjectivism denies that these can ever be false or immoral.

The problem with such views is that the ultimate moral principles—whether fixed by each individual or by each society—can be based on prejudice, ignorance, superficial thinking, or brainwashing, *and still be correct*. According to both kinds of relativism, the origins of our basic moral beliefs are irrelevant. No matter how we came by them, the relativist claims that our fundamental moral beliefs cannot be mistaken.

If morality is in the eye of the beholder, then everyone is seeing things equally well. Millions of people have very sincerely endorsed programs of ethnic cleansing, male domination, and chattel slavery. Subjectivism turns these prejudices into moral truths.

Moral Equivalence

Subjectivists grant that your moral values, which very likely oppose the ones just mentioned, are also correct. The biased and the bigoted have no monopoly on the truth. Ethical subjectivism is a doctrine of moral equivalence; everyone's basic moral views are as plausible as everyone else's. This can sound liberating and tolerant, and can be put to good use in cutting arrogant people down to size. Such people usually claim to have found the Truth, and often think that they have a special license to force this Truth on others. If subjectivism is correct, the views of such zealots are no better than those of their intended victims.

But they are no worse, either. If ethical subjectivism is correct, then the moral outlooks of Hitler or Stalin are just as plausible as those of a Nobel Peace laureate. And, as we will see below (have a look at chapter 21, "Moral Objectivity Supports Intolerance"), if all moral views are on a par with one another, then this is a *threat* to tolerance, rather than support for it. That's because those with intolerant outlooks would have a moral view as good as that of their opponents.

Cultural relativism fares a bit better here. It denies that everyone's moral views are equally plausible. Some people are much wiser in moral matters than others, since some people are better attuned to what their society really stands for. But when it comes to evaluating the basic codes of each society, relativists must allow that every code is equally good. Since the ultimate moral standards are those endorsed by each society, none is better than any other. That may sound egalitarian and open-minded. But what it means in practice is that social codes that treat women or ethnic minorities as property are just as morally attractive as those that don't. That's not an easy thing to accept.

Questioning Our Own Commitments

If subjectivism is correct, then I know what is right so long as I know what I approve of. That's because my approvals (according to subjectivism) are the ultimate measure of morality. But what about the situations where I want to know whether my commitments are worthwhile? In these cases, I know what I like, but am still up in the air about its value.

This sort of puzzlement seems to make sense. I have been in such situations before, where I am unsure of whether I am right to like someone so much, or wrong to be so critical of some action. But if subjectivism is true, this *cannot* make sense, since my approvals and disapprovals are the ultimate test of right and wrong.

The same sort of problem faces cultural relativism. There is no room in this theory to second-guess the guiding ideals of one's own society, since (by definition) they are the correct moral standards of that society.

And yet it seems to make sense to ask whether the basic principles of your society are morally acceptable. If relativism is correct, however, such questioning shows that you don't really understand what morality is all about.

Moral Progress

It seems that both individuals and societies can make moral progress. We can do this when our actions become morally better than they used to be. But I am thinking here of progress in our moral beliefs. This occurs when more of them are true and, in particular, when our most fundamental beliefs change for the better.

The gradual reduction in racist and sexist attitudes in the United States seems to represent this sort of moral progress. The kind of repentant self-examination that German society undertook (and continues to undertake) after World War II also seems a clear improvement over Nazi ideology. When I examine my own life, I see several moral views that I held when I was younger that I now regard as seriously mistaken. Maybe you do, too.

The problem for relativism and subjectivism is that it can't make sense of the most basic kind of moral progress. If a person's or a society's deepest beliefs are true by definition, then they *cannot* change for the better. They can change, of course. But no such change would mark a moral improvement.

To measure moral progress, you need a standard. If subjectivism is correct, that standard is personal opinion. If relativism is correct, that standard is given by a society's basic ideals. These cannot be mistaken. If a society gradually eases out of its deeply sexist attitudes, for instance, that cannot be moral progress. That can only be a change to a different moral code. And if relativism is correct, different moral codes are not better or worse than one another. They are morally equivalent.

If subjectivism is correct, then inmates who experience a change of heart while in prison, who adopt new aims of charity and repentance, cannot be showing moral progress. If relativism is correct, then a society that rejects its earlier ideals of racial purity and genocide cannot be making moral progress. That is difficult to believe.

Ethical Subjectivism and the Problem of Contradiction

A final problem for both theories is one that you've probably already thought of. It is the problem of contradiction. A contradiction occurs when a statement is said to be both true and false at the same time. It's a contradiction, for instance, to both assert and deny that the Empire State Building is in New York. Theories that generate contradictions are incoherent. They can't be true; they are muddled and inconsistent.

It looks like subjectivism leads to contradiction. We can see this by considering its test of truth and falsity:

> A moral judgment is true if it accurately reports one's feelings or commitments, and is false otherwise.

If this test is correct, then people on opposite sides of a moral debate are both saying something true. The pro-choicer is speaking the truth when saying that abortion is morally permitted. And the abortion opponent is also speaking the truth when saying that it is morally impermissible. But abortion can't be both permissible and impermissible. That is a contradiction.

We can summarize the worry in the *Contradiction Problem for Subjectivism*:

1. Any theory that generates contradictions is false.
2. Ethical subjectivism generates contradictions.
3. Therefore, ethical subjectivism is false.

Premise 1 is definitely true. A theory is incoherent if it tells us that the same claim is simultaneously true and false. So subjectivists have to find a way to attack 2.

They have done that. There *is* a subjectivist strategy for avoiding contradiction, but it has its costs. The solution implies that we usually don't mean what we say in our moral debates. What we say are things such as the following:

- The death penalty is immoral.
- Abortion is wrong.
- Eating animals is okay.

But what we *mean* is this:

- The death penalty is wrong, according to me.
- I disapprove of abortion.
- As I see it, eating animals is okay.

And just like that, the contradictions disappear!

Suppose that you and your friend disagree about whether eating animals is wrong. You say it is; she says it isn't. As the subjectivist sees things, you are saying that you disapprove of meat eating; she says that she approves of it. These claims don't contradict each other. This sort of strategy will work across the board, for all moral claims, and so we can save subjectivism from contradiction.

Here are the costs. First, subjectivists have to accuse nearly everyone of misunderstanding their own moral claims. And second, such a view eliminates the possibility of moral disagreement.

To illustrate the first problem, consider this conversation:

ME: Genocide is immoral.
SUBJECTIVIST: What I'm hearing is—you disapprove of genocide.
ME: Yes, I disapprove of genocide. But that's not what I'm saying. I'm not talking about my attitudes. I'm talking about genocide. You're changing the subject.

Subjectivists can't make sense of my reply here. It's not that my reply might be false. Rather, my reply is unintelligible, since it assumes that moral talk is about something other than my own commitments. Most of us assume precisely that. If subjectivism is right, we are badly mistaken.

In order to avoid the problem of contradiction, subjectivists have to say that our moral assertions report facts only about our own commitments. When I say that genocide is wrong, I am not saying that it has a certain feature—wrongness. I am saying that I disapprove of it or that my principles forbid it. I am talking about myself. That's not what most people think they are doing when they make their moral judgments.

The second problem is even more serious. Subjectivism is unable to explain the existence of moral disagreement. In order to avoid generating contradictions, subjectivists have to understand all moral judgments as reports of personal approval or disapproval. The claim that meat eating is wrong becomes the claim that I disapprove of meat eating. The judgment that bravery is a virtue becomes the claim that bravery is something I admire. And so on. But on this line, moral debates that seem to involve intense disagreement become something completely different. In fact, it now becomes *impossible* for people to morally disagree with one another.

To see this, imagine an earlier dispute.

YOU: It's wrong to eat meat.
YOUR FRIEND: It's okay to eat meat.

The subjectivist translates this as follows:

YOU: I disapprove of eating meat.
YOUR FRIEND: I approve of eating meat.

The contradiction has indeed disappeared. But so has the disagreement. If you are both taking this seriously, you'll agree with your friend's claim, and she with yours. If all that moral judgments do is report people's outlooks, then there is no way to morally disagree with anyone who is speaking sincerely. But that seems plainly wrong.

In short, subjectivism faces a dilemma. If we take moral claims at face value, then subjectivism generates contradictions, and so it must be false. If we reinterpret all moral claims to be focused on our attitudes, then the contradictions disappear, but so, too, does moral disagreement.

Cultural Relativism and the Problem of Contradiction

Cultural relativism faces the same dilemma. It says that *a moral judgment is true just because it correctly describes what a society really stands for.* For instance, if different societies disagree about the appropriate political status of women, then members of each society are speaking the truth when they assert (or deny) female moral equality. But they can't all be right. The statement that women are deserving of full political equality cannot be simultaneously true and false.

Relativists can escape this problem in familiar ways. They will claim that moral judgments are true only relative to social agreements. On this line of thinking, moral judgments are just like legal ones. It isn't contradictory to say that smoking marijuana, for instance, is both legal and illegal, so long as we qualify things to note that it is legal in some areas and illegal in others.

Relativists will say that all of our moral claims have to be understood by reference to social agreements. When you say that meat eating is right, and your Hindu friend from Calcutta says that it is wrong, what is really being said is this:

YOU: Meat eating is accepted by my social customs.
YOUR FRIEND: Meat eating is forbidden by my social customs.

And again, both of these claims can be true. The contradiction disappears. There is no single judgment that is said to be both true and false.

But then the existence of cross-cultural moral disagreement also disappears. The same pattern we just saw in the meat-eating case will constantly repeat itself. If all we do when making moral judgments is to issue sociological reports about what our society stands for, then cross-cultural moral disagreement vanishes. We are no longer talking about (say) meat eating, abortion, or drug use. Instead, we are talking about how our society feels about such things.

But it doesn't seem as if that is what serious moral debate is all about. For instance, it appears possible to note that one's society approves of making wives domestic slaves and yet to disagree with the morality of that policy. But that's not so if relativism is to escape the contradiction problem.

So the cultural relativist faces the same dilemma as the subjectivist. If moral claims are taken literally, then relativism generates contradiction. If moral claims are instead veiled reports of cultural commitments, then contradictions disappear, but cross-cultural disagreement becomes impossible.

Indeed, the relativist is in one way more vulnerable than the subjectivist here; the cultural relativist may be unable to escape contradiction after all.

People who are members of subcultures—smaller cultural groups located within larger ones—often face a familiar problem. They are forced to choose between allegiance to the larger society and to their particular subculture. They are members of at least two societies, and when their ethical codes conflict, these unfortunate people are faced with contradictory moral advice.

This isn't some philosopher's fiction. Such cases happen all the time. There are countless examples, but this famous constitutional case should be enough to make the point.

Consider the facts of *Wisconsin v. Yoder*, a case resolved by the U.S. Supreme Court in 1972. Wisconsin then required regular school attendance of all children up to the age of sixteen. The sons of three Old Order Amish families had stopped going to school after the eighth grade, in obedience to their parents' beliefs that continued schooling would conflict with their religious values. The students were found guilty of violating the state law, but the verdict was overturned by the state's Supreme Court. Wisconsin then appealed to the U.S. Supreme Court, which sided with the Amish families.

In its decision, the Court's majority announced the following:

> They [the Amish families] object to the high school, and higher education generally, because the values they teach are in marked variance with Amish values and the Amish way of life; they view secondary school education as an impermissible exposure of their children to a "worldly" influence in conflict with their beliefs. The high school tends to emphasize intellectual and scientific accomplishments, self-distinction, competitiveness, worldly success, and social life with other students.

Amish society emphasizes informal learning-through-doing; a life of "goodness," rather than a life of intellect; wisdom, rather than technical knowledge; community welfare, rather than competition; and separation from, rather than integration with, contemporary worldly society.

The schoolchildren lived in (at least) two societies at once: their Amish community and the larger state of Wisconsin. If relativism is correct, then the morality of your actions depends entirely on whether they are allowed by the standards of the society they are performed in. But if you live in different societies, and their ethical codes clash, then your actions will be both moral and immoral. That is a contradiction.

We could solve this problem if we could figure out which society's code is more important. But relativism doesn't allow us to do that. By its lights, no society's moral code is morally any better than another's. We might be tempted to let the children decide, and say that the social code that takes priority is the one that the children prefer. But this would undermine cultural relativism, since such a move would make the morality of their actions depend on personal choice. They would get to pick the code that is to govern their lives. That is subjectivism, not relativism.

Indeed, critics of cultural relativism often say that the doctrine eventually collapses into subjectivism. When your views and society's views clash, why think that society is always right? If morality is created by humans, then it is hard to justify the claim that moral wisdom always lies with the masses rather than with individuals. The majority may have the power to force the minority to do as it says. But might doesn't make right.

Subjectivists claim that in conflicts between personal and social commitments, the individual is always morally wiser. Cultural relativists take the opposite line. But perhaps things are not so cut and dried. Sometimes individuals have the upper hand; sometimes societies do. And sometimes, perhaps, both individuals and societies are mistaken, even in their deepest commitments. If that is ever so, then we must look elsewhere for an account of morality.

19.4 Ideal Observers

There is a natural way to fix some of these problems for the subjectivist and relativist. We should guarantee that those who create the moral law (whether each individual or whole societies) are not choosing from ignorance, but are equipped with full information. We should also make sure that they are reasoning clearly and avoiding logical errors. In other words, rather than allow us as we actually are (warts and all) to have the final word in morality, we should make the desires and choices of **ideal observers** the ultimate standard of morality. Ideal observers can survey the scene more dispassionately, more knowledgeably, and more rationally. They are better suited to inventing the moral law than we mere mortals are.

According to this new and improved version of subjectivism, an act is morally right just because I *would* favor it were I fully informed and perfectly rational. The relativist version says that an act is morally right just because a society *would* approve of it were its members fully informed and completely rational.

Ideal observers don't really exist—no one, and no culture, knows all there is to know. And no one, and no group, is perfectly rational. But this does not itself undermine the plausibility of the ideal observer view. The familiar idea is to remove the sources of error in our thinking—ignorance of relevant facts, emotional bias, irrational and illogical thinking. Fans of this theory invite us to reflect on what our ideal selves would prefer, not because any of us actually is ideal, but because choices under ideal conditions are supposed to be morally authoritative.

The ideal observer view will surely correct some of the problems that we have noted. (1) Even the core moral beliefs of individuals and societies may now be mistaken, as their views may fail to measure up to those of the ideal observers. (2) The views of individuals and societies will *not* be morally equivalent, since some will better match those of the ideal observers. (3) Sincere endorsements of slavery and genocide will not automatically be morally authoritative, since such endorsements are almost always based on ignorance and irrationality. (4) Moral progress will now be possible, and will occur when the moral views of individuals and societies more closely reflect those of ideal observers. (5) There will be real disagreement between conflicting moral views, since moral judgments will not be reports of personal opinion or cultural consensus, but will rather be claims about what ideal observers will approve of.

These are genuine improvements. But ideal observer views are not problem-free. In fact, there are two serious concerns. The first occurs if there is ever any disagreement among ideal observers. The ideal observer view says that perfectly rational and intelligent people create morality through their choices. If that is so, then if such people make conflicting choices, this will cause contradictions. And contradictions fatally undermine any theory that contains them.

Perhaps perfectly smart and rational people will never disagree about anything. But why the optimism? Those who know all there is to know about embryology, for instance, might still morally disagree about abortion. After all, on the ideal observer views, such geniuses are not trying to understand the morality of the actions they are assessing. Before they make their decisions, there is no morality. Ideal observers don't respond to a world with moral features. Their preferences and choices create morality. But then there doesn't seem to be anything to prevent them from having conflicting attitudes. If they do, contradiction results.

I think that there is a successful solution to this problem. We can borrow a strategy we've seen before,[3] when discussing a similar problem that arose for social contract theories and virtue ethics. The strategy tells us that an action is morally required or forbidden only if *all* ideal observers agree in their attitudes about it. If all ideal observers endorsed an action, then it would be morally required. If they all opposed it, it would be forbidden. And if they disagreed on the matter, then it would be morally permitted—neither required nor forbidden. By making morality depend on the attitudes of all ideal judges, rather than each one individually, this theory can indeed avoid contradiction.

But another problem cannot be handled so easily. The view on the table says this: nothing is intrinsically right; things become right just because an ideal observer would favor it. But what if such people thought that killing off the mentally ill was a great idea? What if they thought that sadism was preferable to compassion? What if they approved of racist policies?

You might think such a thing impossible. But why? Evil people need not be factually ignorant or illogical. Vast knowledge doesn't guarantee a sympathetic nature. Greater logical skills don't automatically translate to greater kindness. Even the most rational among us can be biased, hateful, and cruel. The problem is neatly summarized in a line from Quentin Tarantino's *Kill Bill, Vol. 1*, uttered by The Bride (played by Uma Thurman), telling the victim she's about to kill: "It's mercy, compassion and forgiveness I lack. Not rationality."

Recall how we got here. Subjectivism and cultural relativism allow the basic views of individuals or societies to determine the ultimate moral standards. But such basic views can be the product of ignorance,

---

3. See chapter 14, "Disagreement among the Contractors," and chapter 17, "Conflict and Contradiction."

prejudice, and poor reasoning. We tried to fix this problem by changing the theories so that the authors of morality were ideal versions of us. They would be people with perfect information, and perfect logical skills. And yet, as we've seen, this modified view has troubles of its own, and fails to solve the worry that led to its creation. The very smartest people can also be the coldest and cruelest.

This is a deep problem for ideal observer views. In fact, the problem should be a familiar one, since it is the same one that threatens the divine command theory.[4] The divine command theory says that no acts are intrinsically right or wrong; their morality depends entirely on whether God approves of them. On this view, acts are morally right just because God insists that we do them, and wrong because He loathes them.

The basic problem is that actions don't become right just because someone (even God) happens to favor them. Think back to our earlier discussion of the Euthyphro dilemma.[5] Either God has reasons for His commands or He doesn't. If He doesn't, then the commands are arbitrary, and can't provide the basis for a legitimate morality. But if God does have reasons for His commands, then these reasons, rather than God's say-so, are what explain why various actions are right. God can ratify the moral standards. He can know every one of them. He can convey them to us. But He cannot be their author, on pain of resting morality on arbitrary foundations.

The same line of reasoning works to threaten all of the views we have considered in this chapter. Subjectivism, cultural relativism, and ideal observer theories all share the same basic structure. On these views, nothing is right or wrong in and of itself. Actions have the moral status they do only because I or my society actually approve of them, or would approve of them if we were perfectly intelligent. How can the decisions of any such person or group be so powerful as to transform a valueless activity into something good or right?

These morally all-powerful people either are or aren't basing their decisions on good reasons. If there are no good reasons to support their decisions, then the decisions are arbitrary, and cannot be the basis of a morality worthy of our respect. But if there are good reasons to support the decisions, then the reasons, rather than the decision, determine the morality of the actions in question.

---

4. See chapter 5 for a more detailed discussion of the divine command theory.

5. See chapter 5, "Third Assumption: God Is the Creator of Morality," and the related discussion in chapter 17, "The Priority Problem."

Suppose, for instance, that I (or my society or an ideal observer or God) have reasons that support my disapproval of torture. And these are the reasons: the pain it imposes, its unreliability as a source of valuable information, the disrespect it reveals, and the way it renders its victims utterly powerless. If these really are good reasons, then they are all that's needed to make torture wrong. My disapproval doesn't add anything to these reasons. If I am really wise, then my disapproval can be very good *evidence* of something's immorality. But the approval cannot turn a morally neutral action into a forbidden one.

Socrates's argument against the divine command theory is just as powerful when brought against subjectivism, relativism, and ideal observer theories. If his line of reasoning is correct, then our approval is not enough to make something right. Acts are right because they are supported by excellent reasons, and not because individuals or groups just happen to favor them.

19.5 Conclusion

Both cultural relativism and ethical subjectivism are popular ways of challenging the idea that morality is objective. But as we've seen, both theories face a similar set of problems. They make all moral views or all social codes morally equivalent. They make the deepest commitments of each person or each society morally infallible, even if the commitments are based on ignorance or prejudice. Neither theory offers a way to evaluate our guiding ideals, since these ideals are said to be true by definition. Neither theory allows for fundamental moral progress. Both theories generate contradictions, and can eliminate this worry only by making moral disagreement impossible.

This laundry list of complaints explains why cultural relativism and ethical subjectivism have found little favor among philosophers. For those with doubts about the objectivity of morality, nihilistic alternatives may have more to offer.

19.6 Discussion Questions

1. What is the difference between cultural relativism and ethical subjectivism? Why are both theories inconsistent with ethical objectivism?
2. Why might someone find either form of relativism attractive?
3. In what sense does ethical subjectivism make us morally infallible? Is this an advantage or a disadvantage of the theory?

4. Can ethical relativism make sense of the idea of moral progress? Does moral progress really exist?

5. One might object that ethical subjectivism generates contradictions. How might subjectivists respond to this criticism? Do you find their replies to be adequate?

6. Can actions be performed in more than one society at a time? If so, and if cultural relativism is true, how might this lead to contradiction? Can cultural relativists escape this problem? Why or why not?

7. How does the notion of an "ideal observer" solve some of the problems with relativism and subjectivism? What do you think is the most serious objection to ideal observer theories? Can this objection be overcome?

CHAPTER 20

····· ❧ ·····

Moral Nihilism

Thee are basically three options when it comes to determining the status of morality. Morality might be objective, its rules applying to us independently of our opinions and desires. Or it might be relativistic, and depend for its authority on personal or cultural preferences. Finally, morality may simply be a kind of make-believe, a complex set of rules and recommendations that represents nothing real. This last option is known as *moral nihilism* (from the Latin word *nihil*, meaning "nothing").

Moral nihilists join with relativists in opposing ethical objectivism. Morality is wholly a human creation—in this, nihilists and relativists are united. But nihilists are no fans of ethical relativism. Relativists believe in moral goodness, moral duty, and moral virtue. Nihilists don't. Nihilists deny that there are any moral qualities. There are no moral requirements. Nothing is morally good. Nothing merits praise or blame.

According to nihilists, there is a rigid **fact-value distinction**, which basically says that there is a sharp difference between facts and values. As nihilists see things, values are on the wrong side of the divide. Facts exist; values don't. Of course people do value things, but their attitudes are directed at things that themselves possess no moral value, for nothing possesses any moral value. Value claims cannot be factual, and so cannot be true. Factual claims inform us of things; value claims are not informative, since they describe nothing. You might think that it's a fact that betraying a friend is immoral, or a fact that happily giving to the needy is morally virtuous. But if nihilism is right, there are no such facts. Facts are real; values aren't.

There are two important forms of moral nihilism: the **error theory** and **expressivism**. Error theorists claim that our moral judgments are always mistaken. Expressivists deny this, while also denying that our moral claims can ever offer an accurate take on reality. Expressivism is the more complicated doctrine, so let's ease our way into the nihilist camp by first considering the error theory.

20.1 Error Theory

The Theory and Its Attractions

Did you ever have the feeling, deep down, that morality is a sham? That it's just a set of traditional rules inherited from ancestors who based it on ignorance, superstition, and fear? Perhaps it's only a convenient fiction, with no underlying authority at all.

The error theory of morality is built upon these doubts. It is defined by four essential claims:

1. *There are no moral features in this world.* Nothing is morally good or bad, right or wrong, virtuous or vicious. A careful inventory of the world's contents will reveal all sorts of scientific qualities: being symmetrical, being a liquid, being two feet long, carbon-based, spherical, and so on. But the list will contain no moral features.

2. *No moral judgments are true.* Why not? Simple: there is nothing for them to be true *of*. There are no moral facts. And so no moral claims can be accurate, since there are no moral facts for them to record.

It follows that:

3. *There is no moral knowledge.* Knowledge requires truth. If there is no moral truth, there can be no moral knowledge.

The last defining feature of error theory is

4. *Our sincere moral judgments try, and always fail, to describe the moral features of things.* Thus we always lapse into error when thinking in moral terms. We are trying to describe the moral qualities of things when we make moral judgments. But since nothing has any moral qualities, all of our moral claims are mistaken. Hence the error.

Error theorists are not launching some small-scale attack on morality. They are not criticizing our current views on, say, welfare policy or capital punishment, and trying to replace them with better ones. Rather, as they see it, *all* moral views are equally bankrupt. There is some very deep mistake that everyone committed to morality is making. The error theorist promises to reveal that mistake and to expose the real truth: morality is nothing but a fiction.

For those who are fond of analogies, the following may help. The error theory is to morality as atheism is to religion. Error theorists and atheists deny the truth of a widely accepted worldview. They do this by trying to pinpoint an error that is said to lie at the very heart of the system they oppose.

Atheists are, in effect, error theorists about religion. They believe that there are no religious features of the world, that no religious claims are true, and that religious believers try (and always fail) to speak the truth about God. Atheists deny that there is any religious knowledge. The central explanation for all of this is simple. If atheists are right, then common religious claims (God speaks to me; God created the universe; God knows everything) are all wrong, because they are based on the mistaken assumption that God exists.

Atheists can successfully defend their view only if they can convince us that there is an error at the heart of religious belief. Likewise, moral error theorists can vindicate their view only if they can show that there is some fatal flaw at the heart of morality.

And that depends on what the fundamental error of morality is supposed to be. In principle, we can develop any number of error theories, depending on which basic error morality is supposed to commit. But in practice, there really has been only one candidate.

All error theorists have agreed that the core mistake that undermines morality is its assumption that there are objective moral standards that supply each of us with an excellent reason for obedience, regardless of what we care about. According to error theorists, just as religion crucially depends on the supernatural, morality essentially depends on its being objective and providing us with **categorical reasons**—reasons that apply to us regardless of whether acting on them will get us what we want.[1] If this central assumption is mistaken, then the entire enterprise of morality is bankrupt.

There are two substantial points that error theorists must convince us of. First, they must show that buying into morality really does assume

---

1. For more on categorical reasons, see the discussion in chapter 11, "Morality and Rationality."

a commitment to moral objectivity and categorical reasons. That will be news to many—to subjectivists and relativists, for instance, and to expressivists, whose views we are soon to discuss. If morality does not, in fact, rely on these assumptions, then the error theorist's criticisms will fail.

But suppose that the coherence of our moral thinking and practice does indeed depend on the twin assumptions that morality is objective and that it provides us with categorical reasons. This reveals the second burden that error theorists must shoulder: they must show that at least one of these assumptions is false.

Perhaps they can do that. We have already considered arguments concerning our reasons to be moral,[2] and we will (in the next chapter) look at the most prominent attempts to undermine the objectivity of morality. So, rather than repeat those efforts, let us consider the main attractions of the error theory.

There are two of them. First, the error theory offers us a very simple, pared-down view of reality. It says that the world is as science describes (or would describe, were science perfect). No extras. Assuming that the sciences are not going to ratify the existence of moral values, then such values count as extras. Most scientists and philosophers regard simplicity as a very important theoretical virtue; according to them, if competing theories are otherwise equal, the one that is simpler is likelier to be true. Among metaethical views, the error theory is about as simple as one can get.

Its simplicity explains the other main attraction of the error theory—namely, the fact that it doesn't need to explain either the objectivity of morality or the existence of categorical reasons. Philosophically, offering such explanations is a very big ask, and the explanations that ethical objectivists have offered have always been met with controversy. Error theorists can spare themselves all of that work, precisely because they deny that morality is objective and deny that there are any categorical reasons.

Error theorists do of course have some explaining to do. They need to explain why almost everyone has been duped into thinking that there's something real about morality, that some moral claims are true, and that we have at least some moral knowledge. But these explanations are ready to hand—they are basically the ones offered by ethical relativists, but without any attachment to the relativistic idea that there is moral truth and

---

2. See chapter 8, "Why Be Moral?"; chapter 11, "Morality and Rationality"; and chapter 14, "Why Be Moral?"

knowledge. People invented morality for their own purposes: to coordinate behavior, to strengthen motivations against temptation, to cement power relations, and so forth. But as the error theorist tells it, we largely forgot that morality was an invention, and instead came to regard it, mistakenly, as something objective.

Two Mistaken Objections

Though very few people outside of philosophical circles have ever heard of the error theory, the worry it expresses is familiar enough. And so, too, is the typical response: abandoning morality would have absolutely terrible results. Further, even to seriously consider that morality may be a fiction is to show a corrupt mind, and error theorists are therefore not to be trusted. Once people give up on morality, they will feel free to act in any way they please. It won't be pretty.

There are actually two lines of criticism at work here, and both are mistaken. The first we might call the *Argument from Disastrous Results*:

1. If widespread acceptance of a view would lead to disastrous results, then that view is false.
2. Widespread acceptance of the error theory would lead to disastrous results.
3. Therefore, the error theory is false.

It's an interesting question whether premise 2 is true. I won't venture an opinion here on whether it is. Nor do we need to, since premise 1 is definitely false. The truth of a theory does not depend on the results of everyone's embracing it.

To see this, consider a similar argument against atheism. Some people claim that widespread belief in atheism would generate disaster. I don't know if that's right, but suppose it is. Still, that is no evidence that God exists. After all, if some highly classified state secrets were revealed and became widely accepted, that might cause disaster, too. But that hardly shows that the claims made in those documents are false. So we cannot undermine the error theory by arguing that its popular acceptance would lead to the downfall of civilization—even if it would.

Some have found premise 1 tempting because they have confused it with a close cousin:

1a. If widespread practice of a given action will lead to disastrous results, then that action is immoral.

But this really is a confusion, since premise 1 speaks of theories and their truth, rather than actions and their moral status. And in any event, 1a is false, as we saw in an earlier discussion.[3] If everyone were to practice celibacy, then disaster would ensue. That doesn't show that it is immoral to be celibate.

Others have confused premise 1 with a more specific version:

1b. If widespread acceptance of *a moral theory* would yield disastrous results, then that theory is false.

This cannot be so easily dismissed. Many philosophers have thought that 1b is true, though a number of others—mostly utilitarians—have rejected it.[4] Fortunately, we do not have to settle the matter here, because *the error theory is not a moral theory*. It does not try to tell us where our duty lies, or which character traits are virtues. The error theory rejects *all* moral theories, and says that every single one is mistaken. Since the error theory is not a moral theory, principle 1b simply does not apply to it.

If the error theory isn't a moral theory, then what is it? In fancy terms, it is a **metaphysical** theory—a theory about what the world is truly like, and what really exists. Theism is a metaphysical theory. It says that God exists. Other metaphysical theories try to defend the existence of the soul, or free will, or immortality.

The basic problem with the Argument from Disastrous Results is that metaphysical theories, such as the error theory, cannot be tested in the way that its first premise claims. For instance, we cannot prove that we have free will, just by showing (if we can) that terrible results would occur if we abandoned our belief in it. Metaphysical theories try to tell us what the world is like. Such theories might contain some bitter truths, ones that, if widely accepted, would lead to heartache, or loss of faith, or the breakdown of longstanding customs and social practices. (That's what makes them bitter.) At best, this might give us some reason not to publicize these claims. But that is no reason to suppose that they are false.

Another popular objection to the error theory is really targeted at error theorists themselves. The idea here is that those who reject categorical reasons and the objectivity of morality are bound to be untrustworthy.

---

3. See chapter 11, "Consistency and Fairness."

4. Many utilitarians think that widespread acceptance of the principle of utility might actually have quite bad results, despite firmly believing that the principle is true. See chapter 10, "Motivation," for a discussion of this point.

Conscience serves as an effective check on our antisocial impulses only if we see moral duty as something real, as a set of rules imposed from the outside, ones that have genuine authority over us. Error theorists reject this picture. Critics claim that this rejection will encourage error theorists to let their destructive, selfish impulses take control of their decisions. Anyone who does that is surely untrustworthy.

But this way of thinking is mistaken as well. Error theorists can care deeply about others, and can be strongly opposed to doing the things that we traditionally regard as morally wrong (e.g., killing, stealing, and lying). Of course error theorists, if consistent, will not regard such actions as immoral. But they may still be dead set against such behavior; they might find it distasteful, undesirable, unproductive, or otherwise unappealing.

Still, one might argue that error theorists are not *guaranteed* to have the sorts of goals that we associate with upright behavior. And that is true. But such a guarantee fails to hold for many people who reject the error theory. How many atrocities each year are committed in the name of one morality upon those with different moral beliefs? Far more than those committed by error theorists!

All that aside, this kind of criticism does nothing to address the issue of whether the error theory itself is true. Indeed, it represents a classic kind of fallacy—the **ad hominem attack**. When leveling such a critique, one tries to undermine the truth of a position by criticizing the character of its supporters. Don't like the message? Attack the messenger. Aside from being bad sport, such a strategy entirely misses the mark. We want to know whether morality is all make-believe. We can't answer that question by engaging in character assassination.

The only way to answer it is by doing two things. First, we need to determine whether error theorists are correct in thinking that morality really does depend on two assumptions: (i) that it is objective, and (ii) that it supplies us with reasons to obey it, regardless of our desires. I am not sure whether this is what we really are committed to when thinking morally. Certainly, subjectivists and relativists deny these assumptions. And so they will deny the existence of any error, since they reject the thought that morality depends on claims (i) and (ii).

But suppose that error theorists are right about what we are committed to when we adopt a moral outlook. To assess their view, we must then undertake a second investigation, to determine whether categorical reasons exist and whether morality is objective. Stay tuned: we'll consider these matters at greater length in chapter 21.

20.2 Expressivism

The Theory and Its Attractions

Expressivism is another family of views that deny the objectivity of morality. Indeed, expressivists accept the first three claims that define the error theorist's point of view:

1. There are no moral features in this world.
2. No moral judgments are true.
3. There is no moral knowledge.

Unlike error theorists, however, expressivists think that morality is in pretty good shape. There is no deep error at the heart of our moral thinking. But how can that be, if 1–3 are true?

Simple. Expressivists reject the fourth feature that is essential to error theory:

4. Our sincere moral judgments try (and always fail) to describe the moral features of things.

According to expressivists, we are not trying to speak the truth when making moral judgments. We are not making an effort to describe the way the world is. We are not trying to report the moral features possessed by various actions, motives, or policies. Instead, we are venting our emotions, commanding others to act in certain ways, or revealing a plan of action. When we condemn torture, for instance, we are expressing our opposition to it, indicating our disgust at it, publicizing our reluctance to perform it, and strongly encouraging others not to go in for it. We can do all of these things without trying to say anything that is true.

One of the basic ideas behind expressivism is that moral claims function very differently from straightforward factual claims. Factual claims try to represent the way the world really is. If expressivism is right, moral claims serve quite different purposes.

I know that sounds puzzling. To get a better sense of what is going on here, consider this sentence:

(A) Torture is immoral.

It appears to function just like this sentence:

(B) Water is wet.

Sentence (B) tell us that water has a certain feature—being wet. Sentence (A) looks similar. It appears to tell us that torture has a certain feature— being immoral. And there's nothing special about (A). All moral claims seem to assign a moral quality to something or other. But if there aren't any such qualities, then aren't our moral claims always mistaken?

Not necessarily. If expressivism is true, then the similarity between sentences such as (A) and (B) is only superficial. When we say that torture is immoral, for instance, we are not *describing* torture. We are *not* saying that it has any features at all. We aren't even describing our feelings about it (as subjectivists claim). Rather, it's as if we were saying one of the following:

- Torture—argghhh!
- Don't torture!
- Let me plan a life that doesn't include torturing others.
- Won't everyone please refrain from torture?

These utterances can't be true. But they can't be false, either. And that marks the central difference between expressivism and error theories. The error theorist thinks that our sincere moral claims are always meant to state the truth, but since there isn't any moral truth, such claims are all mistaken. The expressivist, by contrast, thinks that our moral claims are largely alright, since they are doing what they are intended to do.

And what is that? According to expressivists, moral claims are not in the business of holding up a mirror to the world. Their job is to vent our feelings, give orders and commands, and express our commitments. Since they manage to do that just fine, there is no reason to charge them with error.

The basic philosophical motivation behind expressivism is pretty straightforward. Unlike error theorists, who share their rejection of ethical objectivity, expressivists want a way to retain our confidence in morality. In doing so, they also want to avoid the difficulties that hamper cultural relativism and ethical subjectivism.

The biggest problem for relativism and subjectivism (as we saw in the previous chapter) is that these views either generate contradictions or are unable to explain moral disagreement. Expressivism handles both problems with ease; that is its first main attraction.

Contradictions arise when the same claim is said to be true and false at the same time. If expressivists are right, no moral claim is either true *or* false. And so moral contradictions disappear. Expressivists see moral disagreement as a clash of emotions or personal commitments. Debates about abortion, for instance, reveal nothing about its moral features (since there aren't any), but a lot about the feelings of the differing parties. One side feels angered and upset by abortion, and the other doesn't. The emotional investment we see in so many moral debates is just what we should expect, given the expressivist analysis of moral disagreement.

Expressivism's second attraction is its simplicity, a virtue it shares with error theory. Both views regard the world as containing nothing more than what our best sciences tell us. There is no additional layer of reality—moral values—to be added atop the value-free world as recorded by the sciences.

Expressivism's third main attraction is that it neatly explains how our moral judgments so reliably motivate us. Ask yourself this question: if you sincerely judge an action to be your duty, aren't you automatically motivated (at least a little bit) to do it? If you think a plan or a policy is a morally good one, aren't you moved to some extent to help it along? If you answered *yes*, then you share the belief that moral judgments are motivational by their very nature. Their essence is to move people to act. That's exactly what expressivists believe.

If expressivism is true, it's not just a coincidence or some kind of minor miracle that moral judgments are reliable motivators. They play this role because, at their core, what they do is express the very things that cause us to act—our desires, cares, commitments, and emotions. When we judge an action wrong, we are expressing our distaste or hatred of it, our desire that it not be done, our concern for those who might be harmed by it. Our moral judgments express our feelings, and our feelings are our basic motivations. That is why our moral judgments are so easily able to get us to act.

Contrast this picture with another one. Beliefs, unlike moral judgments, are not really in the business of getting us to act in certain ways. They are focused on stating the facts, on reporting the truth, on describing reality. If I believe that there is a computer monitor in front of me and two cats nearby, I am not moved to act in any way at all. If I want to use the Internet or pet my cats, then these beliefs will help to direct my actions. But beliefs can do this only by attaching themselves to my desires. If I didn't want to use the Internet or pet my cats, then neither of these beliefs would have helped at all in guiding my actions.

This contrast between moral judgment, on the one hand, and belief, on the other, inspired David Hume to construct the following *Motivational Argument*:

1. Moral judgments are able, all by themselves, to motivate those who make them.
2. Beliefs are never able, all by themselves, to motivate those who hold them.
3. Therefore, moral judgments are not beliefs.

But if moral judgments are not beliefs, what are they? Ask an expressivist, she'll tell you: they are expressions of our emotions, desires, or plans. Since moral judgments aren't beliefs, they can't be true. But neither can they be false. They are just like the utterances we encountered earlier—neither true nor false.

This is a nice package of attractions. But there are worries, of course. Three seem to be especially serious.

How Is It Possible to Argue Logically about Morality?

If, as expressivists say, moral claims cannot be true, then this makes it very difficult to understand how moral argument is possible. Logical argumentation is *truth preserving*—a logically valid argument is defined as one whose conclusion must be true, provided that its premises are true.[5] If, as expressivists say, moral claims cannot be true, then how could they possibly be used to support other claims?

To see the worry here, consider this argument:

1. All actions that dehumanize people are immoral.
2. Torture dehumanizes people.
3. Therefore, torture is immoral.

The argument appears to be logically perfect. If you accepted both premises, you would have to accept the conclusion. After all, this argument has the very same logical structure as a philosophical classic:

1. All men are mortal.
2. Socrates is a man.
3. Therefore, Socrates is mortal.

---

5. For more on logic and validity, please see the Introduction, "Moral Reasoning."

And everyone admits that *this* argument is logically valid. Given the truth of the two premises, the conclusion can't possibly be false.

From a logical point of view, these two arguments appear to be identical. And there is a natural explanation for this: the first two premises in each argument can be true, and if they are, then the conclusion must be true as well. But expressivists cannot accept this natural explanation, since they deny that moral claims can be true.

Look at the first argument. If premise 1 really means:

1a. Dehumanizing actions—yecchhh!

or

1b. Don't dehumanize people!

then there is no way that this premise can be used to logically support any conclusion. But it seems clear that it is being used in precisely this way. The logic of the first argument is watertight—even if you are suspicious about the merits of the actual premises. Indeed, logical moral argumentation seems like a real possibility—we do it all the time (and have been doing it throughout this book). Expressivism does not seem able to explain this.

Expressivism and Amoralists

An amoralist is someone who sincerely makes moral claims, but is entirely unmoved by them. Such people create a serious problem for expressivism.[6]

Expressivists warn us not to be fooled by the superficial similarity between factual claims (water is wet) and moral ones (torture is immoral). Moral claims assert nothing. They describe nothing. Instead, they express our feelings. Indeed, that is how the expressivist explains why our moral judgments so reliably motivate us. These judgments convey our feelings, and our feelings are what move us to act.

But this makes it impossible for someone, say, to really think that charity is admirable and yet be indifferent when it comes to forking out his own money. It would be impossible for a soldier to think it his duty to face enemy fire while remaining completely unmotivated to do so. Such cases may really be impossible, but the evidence points the other way. Amoralism is unusual, to be sure, but not unheard of.

---

6. For more on the amoralist, see the discussion of Hobbes's Fool in chapter 14, "Why Be Moral"?"

Indeed, expressivism faces the same problem that psychological egoism does.[7] In the face of evidence that supports the existence of altruism, egoists insist that people must be either deceiving themselves or lying to us about their motivations. Expressivists have to say the same thing about the evidence of amoralism. All such evidence must be disqualified. The person who really is lacking in motivation cannot be sincere in his moral claims. Or, if he is sincere, then he really must be motivated, and so his claims to the contrary are either lies or instances of self-deception. Such a diagnosis may be correct. But the burden here weighs heavily on the expressivist's shoulders.

The Nature of Moral Judgment

A final concern has to do with whether expressivists are right to challenge the dominant view of what we do when we make moral judgments. Ethical objectivists, ethical relativists, and error theorists agree on almost nothing. But they have reached consensus on one point: moral judgments are beliefs aimed at describing the moral features that things actually have. Such judgments can be true or false, depending on how well they report the truth about which things have which moral qualities.

Expressivists deny this. They reject the idea that moral judgments are beliefs that aim to represent the way things are. They deny that there are any moral features. They deny that moral judgments could ever offer accurate descriptions of reality. How do we know whether their hypothesis is correct?

Return to our original example, the claim that torture is immoral. If we understand this literally, the sentence says that torture has a certain feature—being immoral. As we saw, expressivists can't read it this way. They have to paraphrase this sentence so that it isn't assigning any specific feature to torture. Perhaps you found the various translations they offered above to be attractive. But what about these claims?

- Nobody but Jeff knows how to behave when the boss is around.
- I'm not sure whether torture is ever acceptable, but I am sure that those who are wiser than I am have the correct answer.
- There is a difference between an action's being required, morally good, virtuous, and deserving of praise.
- Some actions fulfill moral duties and yet lack moral worth.

---

7. See the discussion "Letting the Evidence Decide" in chapter 7.

- The degree of punishment should match the degree of wrongdoing.
- Virtue is its own reward.
- If war is immoral, then military generals are less virtuous than they seem.

Read as objectivists, subjectivists, relativists, or error theorists would do, the sentence structure of these claims is transparent. They are readily understandable. It's not at all clear how expressivists could reword them to turn them into commands, emotional expressions, or plans.

People put their words to various purposes. The best way to tell whether people are joking, questioning, inviting, or trying to state the truth is simply to ask them. People are usually pretty trustworthy on this score. (Not always, of course. When we play to win at poker, or negotiate a business deal, we may be deliberately misleading.) Still, exceptions aside, people are the best judges of their own intentions, and their testimony in such matters is usually reliable.

That's not a thrilling point, but it has a direct bearing on expressivism's plausibility. When we ask people how they think of their moral claims, almost everyone will reject the expressivist analysis. For the most part, we do regard our moral claims as true. We regard our opponents' views as false. We take our moral condemnations to be cases of describing, say, the injustice of insider trading, or reporting the moral corruption of an unprincipled politician. At bottom, we intend our moral judgments to function as something other than emotional outbursts or expressions of commands or plans.

We might all be lying, or deceiving ourselves about what we are actually doing. But by far the more charitable view is that we mean what we say. When making moral judgments, we are trying to speak the truth. We are intending to state the facts. We aim to accurately present the moral details of the situations we are thinking of. If that is so, then expressivism is in serious trouble.

20.3 Conclusion

The vision of morality that so many of us believe in—one that sees morality as a set of objective duties and rules, supplying each of us with strong reasons to do as it says—may be fundamentally mistaken. Subjectivists and relativists certainly think so. And so do error theorists and expressivists. Error theorists are the most pessimistic of the lot, thinking as they do that morality is a bankrupt enterprise. This thought stems from their view that our moral thinking is based on assumptions that turn out to be false. If the foundations of an entire way of thinking are corrupt, then the whole worldview must come tumbling down. That's the way atheists see religious claims. And that is the way error theorists see moral ones.

Expressivists are not so pessimistic. They agree with error theorists in denying that ethics is objective and in denying that moral duties supply us with categorical reasons. But since expressivists do not believe that moral thinking rests on these foundations, they don't feel the need to accuse the rest of us of error. Moral talk does pretty much what it is supposed to do— give vent to our emotions, express our feelings about things, and signal our commitments. And so there is little reason to worry.

But as we have seen, expressivism does give us some cause for concern. True, it offers a picture of morality that frees it of fundamental error. It solves the problem of contradiction. It neatly explains the nature of moral disagreement. It offers a streamlined, simple view of reality. It straightforwardly explains how moral judgments reliably motivate us. And yet it has difficulty making sense of how logical moral argumentation is possible. It fails to make room for amoralism. It clashes with our views about what we are intending to do when we make moral judgments.

Expressivists are hard at work on these problems. There is a very lively conversation about the pros and cons of expressivism going on right now in philosophy departments around the world. In the last decade, this conversation has reached levels of sophistication that would have been unthinkable just a generation ago. It's far too early to tell whether expressivism is down for the count or whether its defenders can identify new solutions to these perennial problems.

Even if, in the end, expressivism turns out to have more costs than benefits, this doesn't leave objectivists in the clear. It may be that morality is all make-believe, as error theorists claim. Most of us (especially we textbook authors!) hope this isn't so. Yet a hope is hardly evidence one way or the other. Whether we should think of morality as bankrupt depends on what the best arguments tell us about the nature of morality. We'll be in a better position to see the force of those arguments after working through the next chapter.

20.4 Discussion Questions

1. What are the two types of moral nihilism, and what is the main difference between them? In what ways does each theory agree with ethical objectivism, and in what ways does each disagree?

2. What do error theorists typically claim is the "error" at the heart of our moral practice? Is the assumption that they identify really essential to our moral thought? If so, do you agree that it is an error?

3. Some critics of the error theory claim that it is false because (i) disaster would result were most people to accept it, and (ii) its defenders are untrustworthy. Why are these criticisms problematic?

4. What does it mean to say that stealing is wrong, according to expressivism? Do you find the expressivist translation to be plausible? Why or why not?

5. Why does the fact that people make logical arguments about moral issues raise a challenge for expressivism? How might an expressivist respond to this challenge?

6. What is an amoralist? Can expressivism make sense of the idea of such a person? If not, is this a problem for the theory?

7. Think carefully about what you are doing when you are forming your own moral judgments. Does the expressivist analysis of moral judgments accurately capture what you are doing? Why or why not?

CHAPTER 21

Ethical Objectivism

21.1 The Theory and Its Attractions

Ethical objectivism is the view that there are some objective moral standards. Given my understanding of objectivity, this amounts to the view that these standards apply to everyone, even if people don't believe that they do, and even if obeying them fails to satisfy a person's desires. Moral claims are objectively true whenever they accurately tell us what these moral standards are, or tell us about what these standards require or allow us to do.

We've considered the leading opponents of ethical objectivism in the last two chapters, and have noted some of the difficulties they face. If these worries cannot be solved, and if objectivism can be defended against criticisms, then objectivism wins by default. Relativism, nihilism, and objectivism are the three options when it comes to the status of ethics. If two of these can be defeated, then the one left standing must be the correct account.

Objectivists, of course, believe that they'll be the ones standing at the end of the day. Whether they are right about that depends on their ability to handle the many criticisms that have been sent their way. We'll turn to those momentarily—there are loads of them, as we'll soon see—but for now, as usual, let's start off by accentuating the positive.

We've foreshadowed the primary attractions of ethical objectivism by noting the difficulties that relativist and nihilist theories face. Objectivism typically shines where they fall short. Relativistic theories have five primary shortcomings[1]: (1) they render individuals or cultures infallible with respect to their fundamental moral commitments; (2) they regard the core ideals of all moral systems as morally equivalent; (3) they deny that it makes sense to question one's own deepest ideals (or those of one's society); (4) they have difficulty accounting for moral progress; and (5) they either generate contradictions or make moral disagreement impossible. Nihilistic theories (6) deny that any moral claims are true and (7) deny the existence of any moral knowledge. Error theories in particular have to defend the claim that (8) we are massively and systematically mistaken in all of our moral views. Expressivism has difficulties (9) making sense of logical moral argument and (10) allowing for the possibility of amoralists. Expressivism also (11) rejects substantial evidence, given by our own sincere reflections, about the nature of our moral judgments.

A theory that can avoid all of these difficulties and addresses these many challenges has a lot going for it; ethical objectivism does the job.

(1) Consider Leo Tolstoy's description of Napoleon: "he had long been convinced that it was impossible for him to make a mistake, and that in his perception whatever he did was right, not because it harmonized with any idea of right and wrong, but just because he did it."[2] Like egotists before and since, Napoleon had several flaws; one of them was his failure to recognize his own fallibility. None of us has perfect moral insight. We are, individually and collectively, able to make moral mistakes—even in our deepest commitments. Ethical objectivism easily explains why that's so: we are not the authors of morality.

(2) According to ethical objectivism, moral systems are not all equivalent; some are better than others, in part because the latter incorporate more moral mistakes, as measured by whatever the objectively correct moral standards are.

(3) Ethical objectivists believe that it can make perfect sense to question one's deepest commitments, or those of one's society, precisely because we are all morally fallible. We can fall into moral error and should recognize that possibility; once we do, it makes sense to ask yourself whether you, or your society, are on target, morally speaking.

(4) Ethical objectivism easily accounts for moral progress: individuals or societies make such progress when their views align more closely with the objective moral standards.

---

1. See chapter 19, "Some Implications of Ethical Subjectivism and Cultural Relativism."
2. *War and Peace*, Book 9, chapter 7.

(5) The fact that different people have deep moral disagreements does not force objectivists to the position that there are moral contradictions. Instead, objectivists say of such disagreements that at least one party holds a false moral belief. There is no problem accounting for moral disagreement: this occurs when one person's moral belief contradicts someone else's.

(6) In line with common sense, objectivists affirm that some moral views are true (and some are false). It is true that genocide is immoral. It's true that justice is a virtue. It's true that bragging about sexually exploiting a vulnerable job applicant is a sign of moral corruption. Objectivists take such talk literally; doing so allows them to preserve the intuitive idea that some moral views are correct and others incorrect.

(7) Objectivists believe that we are sometimes in a good position to grasp moral truths. Often we are not, either because the issue before us is so difficult, or because we are suffering from one or another distorting influence. But sometimes we are well-positioned to appreciate moral truths, and believe them on the basis of the reasons that make them true. When that happens, we can gain moral knowledge.

(8) Though every person is morally fallible, and though some people's moral views are *way* off-base, objectivists deny that everyone is entirely morally ignorant. As just indicated, if objectivism is correct, then we can sometimes light on the moral truth, even if we have some moral blind spots and are sometimes in the dark about what is right or wrong.

(9) Ethical objectivism easily makes sense of how moral arguments can be logically valid. An argument is valid if it is truth-preserving: were all premises true, the conclusion would have to be true as well. If objectivism is correct, then moral claims can be true. So arguments that incorporate moral claims can be truth-preserving.

(10) Ethical objectivists explain the possibility of amoralism (i.e., not being motivated by one of your sincere moral judgments) by means of two claims. First, moral judgments are beliefs. Second, it is possible to be indifferent to your beliefs. Any of your beliefs, moral or nonmoral, can leave you cold on a given occasion.

(11) As just indicated, ethical objectivists regard moral judgments as beliefs—attempts to capture the way things really are. Beliefs can be true or false. Most true beliefs can be known. They can be supported by logically valid arguments. When we reflect on what's going on when we make moral judgments, it certainly seems that they meet these

conditions. That makes perfect sense if those judgments are our efforts to accurately represent a moral reality not of our own making, as ethical objectivists claim.

21.2 Ten Arguments Against Ethical Objectivism

Despite this nice laundry list of attractions, ethical objectivism has been the target of many critiques. As we'll see, some of the most popular ones are also the least plausible. But others represent deep and serious challenges. Let's consider some of the least plausible arguments first, before turning to critiques of objectivism that are more difficult to handle.

Objectivity Requires Absolutism

Many people claim that if morality were objective, then moral rules would have to be absolute. And since they aren't, morality isn't objective after all.

The *Argument from Absolutism* summarizes this line of thought:

1. If moral claims are objectively true, then moral rules are absolute.
2. No moral rule is absolute.
3. Therefore, moral claims are not objectively true.

An absolute moral rule is one that is always wrong to break—no exceptions.

I don't know if there are any absolute moral rules.[3] If there are, good candidates would include the prohibition on rape and on deliberately killing innocent people. Luckily we don't have to settle this issue here, because even if premise 2 is true, and there are no absolute moral rules, premise 1 is false.

That first premise tells us that when it comes to morality, being objective and being absolute go hand in hand. But that isn't so. The moral rule that forbids us from lying is probably not absolute; in some cases, morality would probably allow us to lie. For all we know, though, that rule could be objective. Ross, for instance, thought that the fundamental moral rules are objective.[4] But he denied that they are absolute. Likewise, if God exists, and creates or reveals the moral law, then morality would be objective. But God might allow us to lie in certain circumstances, and might also permit us (in unusual cases) to break other moral rules. There is nothing in the very idea of an objective morality that requires moral rules to be absolute.

---

3. See chapter 15 for much more detailed discussion of this matter.
4. See chapter 16 for a presentation of Ross's views.

There is a general reason for this. The objectivity of moral rules has to do with their *status*: with whether they are correct independently of our opinion of them. The absoluteness of moral rules has to do with their *stringency*: with whether it is ever okay to break them. There is no direct connection between matters of status and stringency. This is clear when it comes to natural laws. Various biological and psychological laws admit of exceptions, and so are not absolute, even though they are objective.

This does not of course show that moral rules are objective. But it does support the view that even if they are, they do not have to be absolute. So premise 1 is false. And since it is, this argument does not threaten ethical objectivism.

All Truth Is Subjective

A popular thought in some circles is that claims can be true only relative to individual perspectives. On this line, there are no objective truths at all. Forget about morality for a moment—claims in logic, chemistry, or history can never be objectively true, either. So it's no surprise that objective morality is an illusion. The *Argument Against Objective Truths* couldn't be simpler:

1. There are no objective truths.
2. Therefore, there are no objective moral truths.

The first thing to note about this argument is that, if it works, there is no special problem for morality. Most opponents of ethical objectivism are trying to show that morality is in some ways second-rate, that it fares poorly in contrast to other disciplines such as mathematics and physics. By embracing premise 1, this argument abandons that strategy.

The problem with this argument is its premise.[5] Premise 1 is either true or false. If it is false, then the argument crumbles right away. So suppose that it is true. But this is impossible. The premise *cannot* be true. If it were, then there would be at least one objective truth—premise 1. And if there is at least one objective truth, then premise 1 is false! No matter how we look at it, then, this premise is false.

---

5. Unlike almost all of the other arguments we've seen in this book, this one has only a single premise: 1. Note that an argument's having just one premise is not by itself any problem. Indeed, the logic of this argument is perfect. If 1 is true, then 2 must be true.

Since that is so, it follows directly that there are at least some objective truths. Perhaps none of them is a moral one. But we can't rely on this argument to support such doubts.

Equal Rights Imply Equal Plausibility

I have heard countless moral disputes end on this conciliatory note: "Well, everyone has a right to their opinion. You have your view, and I have mine. Maybe we're both right."

This familiar refrain is sometimes taken one step further in the following way: since everyone has a right to a moral opinion, no one's moral views are any better than anyone else's. And if everyone's moral opinions are on par with one another, then there is no objective moral truth.

These thoughts can be combined into an *Argument from Equal Rights*:

1. If everyone has an equal right to an opinion, then all opinions are equally plausible.
2. Everyone has an equal right to their moral opinions.
3. Therefore, all moral opinions are equally plausible.
4. If all moral opinions are equally plausible, then ethical objectivism is false.
5. Therefore, ethical objectivism is false.

The fourth premise is true. No question about it. If moral standards are objectively correct, then some people's views are going to be very far from the mark, and others are going to be right on target.

I also believe that the second premise is true. Everyone has a moral right to freedom of conscience. You are morally entitled to decide for yourself what to believe, and not to be brainwashed into thinking what others want you to think. The same goes for everyone else.

If I am wrong about that, then so much the worse for the argument, since it obviously relies on the truth of premise 2. But the argument is a failure even if 2 is true, for premise 1 is false.

From the fact that we each have a right to our opinions, nothing at all follows about their plausibility. I was once walking through a forest with a friend who knows a lot about trees. (I don't.) I suggested that the one I was looking at was an ash. It wasn't. He knew it was a larch. Our views were not equally plausible, even though I had as much a right to my opinion as he did his.

There are countless examples of cases in which people have an equal right to an opinion—that is, an equal right not to be forced to change their mind—even though their views are mistaken. Some historical claims are true and others false, even though we each have an equal right to our historical opinions. The same thing can be said of our opinions concerning economics, trigonometry, basketball strategy, or beer brewing. Most people know more than I do about each of these things, and so my views on these subjects are far less plausible than theirs. And yet my right to hold the views I do is just as strong as anyone else's.

The first premise of the argument confuses two entirely separate matters: whether a person has a right to an opinion, and whether that opinion has any merit. This confusion undermines premise 1, and with it, the argument itself.

Moral Objectivity Supports Dogmatism

Pick any blowhard, tyrant, or political fanatic, and there is one thing they all share. They are all ethical objectivists. These are the folks who believe in moral truth with a capital *T*. Luckily for them, they have managed to discover that Truth. And once you've discovered the Truth, why compromise? Why pretend as if competing views have anything going for them? Once you've landed on the Truth, it's time to shut things down.

Such thoughts support the following *Argument from Dogmatism*:

1. If there are objective moral standards, then this makes **dogmatism** acceptable.
2. Dogmatism is unacceptable.
3. Therefore, there are no objective moral standards.

Dogmatism is the character trait of being closed-minded and unreasonably confident in one's own opinions. Dogmatism is a vice, and if a theory recommends that we always close our minds to competing ideas, then that theory is very implausible. So premise 2 looks good. But ethical objectivism does not encourage a dogmatic attitude. The first premise of this argument is false.

By itself, the claim that there are objective moral standards is perfectly neutral about how broad-minded we should be. Ethical objectivism is a view about the status of moral claims. It does not tell us what is and is not morally acceptable. All it says is that the correct moral code, *whatever it happens to be*, is objectively true.

But we can say more. If moral truth is not of our own making, then it will not always be easy to discover. And that fact should encourage us to be humble, rather than arrogant and closed-minded. The proper outlook of astronomers and geologists and chemists is that of wonder, a recognition of one's intellectual limitations, and an appreciation that no matter how smart you are, you'll never know the entire truth about your subject matter. These are appropriate attitudes precisely because there are objective truths in these subjects. Scientists do not get to have the final word about the nature of reality. They might always be corrected by their peers or by a later generation of thinkers.

If ethics, too, is a subject whose truths are objective, then we should also be open-minded about moral matters. It's perfectly consistent to say that the answers to some questions are objectively true, even though you're not sure what those answers are. If, in ethics, our say-so doesn't make it so, then we should always be open to correction.

It is true that the worst fanatics among us are always ethical objectivists. But that is not a strike against the theory. Rather, it is a strike against the individuals who misapply it.

Ethical objectivism is not committed to saying that moral wisdom is easy to get. In fact, objectivism makes such wisdom harder to come by than its competitors do, precisely because objectivism denies that individuals or societies get to have the final word about what is right and wrong. And so objectivism does not license dogmatism. Thus the first premise of this argument is mistaken. The argument is therefore unsound.

Moral Objectivity Supports Intolerance

A very popular reason for rejecting ethical objectivism is a concern for tolerance. People in open societies rightly value tolerance, but many think that tolerance would be threatened if moral standards were objectively correct. If some moral codes are better than others, then what's to stop those with the upper hand from lording it over those who embrace a faulty code of conduct?

Indeed, these critics say that the best way to support tolerance is to assume that all moral views are as good as any other. If that were so, then no one would be in a position to suppress the lifestyles of those who march to the beat of a different drummer. We would have to agree to disagree, since no one's moral outlook would be better than anyone else's. That is what is needed to support tolerance.

We can trace this line of thinking in the *Argument from Tolerance*:

1. Tolerance is valuable only if the moral views of different people are equally plausible.

2. If ethical objectivism is true, then the moral views of different people are not equally plausible.
3. Therefore, if ethical objectivism is true, then tolerance is not valuable.

That second premise is true. Ethical objectivism rejects the idea of moral equivalence. Some moral views are better than others.

But the first premise is false. In fact, ethical objectivism is much better than its opponents at supporting tolerance. The basic reason is this: *if all moral views are equivalent, then a tolerant outlook is no better than an intolerant one.* The outlook of a committed bigot would be as plausible as yours or mine.

Indeed, we can easily frame a counterargument that shows why the value of tolerance poses a threat to anti-objectivist views, rather than to objectivism:

1. If all moral views are equally plausible, then moral views that support tolerance and those that support repression and intolerance are equally plausible.
2. Moral views that support repression and intolerance are not as plausible as those that support tolerance.
3. Therefore, not all moral views are equally plausible.

The first premise must be correct. And those who value tolerance will want to embrace the second. The conclusion follows directly.

Those who favor tolerance tend to regard its value as universal—good for everyone and every society. This applies especially to areas plagued by intolerance, since tolerance is needed most just where it is least enjoyed. Yet if individuals have the final word on what is morally right, then those who are *fundamentally* intolerant—intolerant at their core, in their deepest beliefs—are making no mistake. The same goes for societies. If social codes, rather than individuals, are the measure of morality, then deeply intolerant societies are no worse than freer ones. Their rejection of tolerance is as plausible as your endorsement of it. That should be little comfort to those who value tolerance.

Those who think of tolerance as very valuable will want to say that tolerance is morally required even for those people and those societies that despise it. Such a view is perfectly compatible with ethical objectivism.

Moral Objectivity Cannot Allow for Legitimate Cultural Variation

If there are objective moral standards, then they will apply to everyone, in every society. If, for instance, it is objectively wrong to slaughter people just for fun, then it is wrong to do this everywhere—not just in my society or yours, but everyone's.

While this seems pretty plausible, other cases raise a worry for objectivism. For it does seem that there can be legitimate cultural variation in what is morally required and forbidden. I never offered my prospective in-laws any cattle before I proposed to my wife. And that was morally okay. But had I failed to make such an offer in certain parts of the Sudan, I would have been acting immorally. Feeding one's children from garbage dumps is immoral in my town but morally acceptable in certain Asian slums. Showing up to school or work naked would be thought a terrible sin in many religious communities, but perfectly fine in a nudist colony.

This sort of variation gives rise to a worry that can be expressed in the *Argument from Cultural Differences*:

1. If ethical objectivism is true, then all moral standards apply universally—to everyone, in every society.
2. Some moral standards do not apply universally, but only in certain cultural or social contexts and not in others.
3. Therefore, ethical objectivism is false.

Ethical objectivists will insist that some moral standards—like the one above that prohibits recreational slaughter—do apply universally. But others—like the one prohibiting public nudity—do not. Thus objectivists will reject the first premise of the Argument from Cultural Differences.

Doing so certainly requires explanation. But objectivists can provide it. The core idea is simple: the *fundamental* moral principles apply to everyone, everywhere. But when we apply these principles to different living situations, they can generate more specific moral advice that can allow for some degree of cultural variation.

For example, it may be that the moral duty to show respect to loved ones is universal. No matter who you are or where you come from, you are morally obligated to show such respect. Fulfilling that duty usually requires also showing respect to the family members of one's beloved. Different societies have developed different ways of doing this; some Sudanese tribes take it as a sign of disrespect if a suitor does not provide a cattle dowry. In our society, we have other ways of conveying such respect.

A natural way to describe this situation is to say that although there is just one basic rule in play here—show respect to others—this rule can generate different moral advice in different circumstances. The rule requiring respect can require men to provide cattle to prospective in-laws in Sudan, even though no such standard governs the behavior of those in the United States. The objectivist explains this moral difference by pointing out that a moral standard that dictates the terms of a dowry is not a basic moral rule. If someone is morally required to provide a dowry in the first place, this must be because of some deeper moral principle that explains why—perhaps, as in our example, by reference to the more general moral rule that counsels us to show respect to loved ones.

The lesson of this example is perfectly general. Customs and traditions can help to shape our specific moral duties. The duties of a Sudanese tribesman will differ to some extent from those of a U.S. citizen. But this difference, and all others that stem from being situated in different cultures or societies, will ultimately be explained by reference to moral principles that apply across the board—to everyone, everywhere. These universal moral rules may well be objectively correct, even if they sometimes support different specific moral duties for those in different cultures or societies.

Moral Disagreement Undermines Moral Objectivity

A classic argument against moral objectivity takes its cue from a simple observation: there is a lot more disagreement in ethics than there is in science. And there is a ready explanation for this. Scientists are trying to understand the nature of objective reality, whereas in ethics, there is no objective reality to be discovered. When it comes to morality, we are merely expressing our personal opinions, ones that have been obviously shaped by the time and place in which we've been raised. Different upbringings, different moral outlooks. But scientists the world over can agree on a wide set of truths, no matter their religious or cultural backgrounds.

The *Argument from Disagreement* nicely summarizes this line of thought:

1. If well-informed, rational people persistently disagree about some claim, then that claim is not objectively true.
2. Well-informed, rational people persistently disagree about all moral claims.
3. Therefore, no moral claim is objectively true.

Perhaps premise 2 is too strong. Maybe there are some moral claims that every smart, rational person accepts. But without a lot more investigation, it would be premature to assume that this is so.

What is clearly true is that for any moral claim—even one you find to be just obvious—there will always be someone else who thinks that it is false. But that doesn't show that premise 2 is true, since such people may not be well informed or rational.

Indeed, moral disagreement is often a product of sloppy reasoning, of not having enough facts under our belt, of having a personal stake in the outcome, or of a general prejudice. What if we were able to correct for these sources of error? Imagine people who were absolutely on top of *all* of the details, say, of affirmative action policies, who were free of personal bias and other prejudices, and who were able to reason flawlessly. Perhaps they'd all agree about whether affirmative action is morally acceptable.

Perhaps. But I am not sure that even perfectly ideal reasoners would agree about every moral issue. So let's accept, at least for the moment, that premise 2 is true. What of premise 1?

That premise must be false. There are counterexamples galore. Brilliant physicists disagree about whether the fundamental elements of matter are subatomic strings; eminent archaeologists disagree about how to interpret the remains discovered at ancient sites; the finest philosophers continue to debate whether God exists. And yet there are objective truths in each area. There are objective truths about the fundamental nature of the physical world, about the nature of various prehistoric tribes, about whether there is or isn't a God. Gaining knowledge of these truths can be hard, and perhaps, in some cases, impossible. But our beliefs on these matters must answer to an objective reality. Our views don't make physical or archaeological or philosophical claims true; the facts are what they are, independently of what we think of them.

There is another reason to doubt premise 1: this premise is itself the subject of deep disagreement. Really smart people still argue about whether it is true. And so, if such disagreement is enough to undermine objective truth, then the premise, by its own lights, can't be objectively true! And it certainly isn't "relatively" true—true just because I, or my society, believe in it. The premise, then, is false.

So deep disagreement, even among the best minds, is not enough to show that there is no objective truth awaiting our discovery. As a result, the many disagreements we see in ethics are perfectly compatible with its objectivity.

Atheism Undermines Moral Objectivity

Recall (from chapter 5) the famous claim of Ivan Karamazov, one of Dostoevsky's finest creations: if God is dead, then everything is permitted. His guiding thought is that true morality can exist only if God underwrites its authority. Morality is a sham if God does not exist, because the only way morality could rest on solid foundations is by being authored by God.

Some atheists have taken up this line of thinking and have used it to justify their rejection of ethical objectivism. If they are right, and God does not exist, then morality can't possibly be objective. The *Argument from Atheism* expresses this outlook:

1. Morality can be objective only if God exists.
2. God does not exist.
3. Therefore, morality cannot be objective.

I'm going to make things much easier on myself by leaving that second premise alone. If it's false, and God exists, then the argument crumbles. But let's just assume for now that there is no God. Then what?

Well, if premise 1 is true, then morality really can't be objective. Many people think that 1 is true. They reason as follows. Moral laws, like other laws, must have an author. But if the laws are objective, then (by definition) no human being can be their author. So who is? Three guesses.

This reasoning has always been very popular.[6] It rests on this key assumption: *laws require lawmakers*. Suppose this assumption is true. It then follows that objective laws need lawmakers, too. But human beings cannot play this role, since objective truths are true independently of human opinion. That leaves only God to do the work.

But if atheism is true, then the key assumption is false. Laws would not require lawmakers. Atheists believe that there are objective laws—of logic, physics, genetics, statistics, and so on. And yet if God does not exist, these laws have no author. We discovered these laws. We invented the words to describe the laws. But they are not true because we believe them to be. Their truth is objective. If atheists are correct, no one authored such laws.

Thus if atheism is true, objective laws do not require lawmakers. So, for all we know, objective moral laws do not require a lawmaker, either.

---

6. For much more on this line of reasoning, see the extended discussion in chapter 5, "Third Assumption: God Is the Creator of Morality."

Atheists might say, though, that *moral* laws require lawmakers, even though other laws do not. But why single out morality like that? Until atheists can provide an explanation for holding moral laws to a different standard from other objective laws, they are best advised to allow that moral laws do not require an author, either.

The Argument from Atheism is thus unpersuasive. It will obviously do nothing to convince religious believers, since it just assumes (in premise 2) that they are wrong. But even if atheists are correct, and God does not exist, premise 1 is highly doubtful, because its best support is flawed. That support comes from the assumption that laws require lawmakers—an assumption that atheists themselves should not accept.

The Absence of Categorical Reasons Undermines Moral Objectivity

Most people think that all moral duties come prepackaged with a special power. They automatically supply people with reasons to obey them. And it doesn't matter what we care about. If it's really your duty to repay that loan or help your aged grandparents, then you've got an excellent reason to do so—even if doing these things fulfills none of your desires.

That's unusual. My reasons for writing this book, using my treadmill, or listening to music, all depend on what matters to me. Most reasons are like this. The reasons that come from morality, however, are categorical. They apply to us regardless of what we care about.[7]

Many philosophers cannot see how categorical reasons are possible. Their puzzlement has given rise to a powerful *Argument from Categorical Reasons* against ethical objectivism:

1. If there are objective moral duties, then there are categorical reasons to obey them.
2. There are no categorical reasons.
3. Therefore, there are no objective moral duties.

This argument has convinced some very smart philosophers. And they may be right to be convinced. But for those with objectivist leanings, there are two lines of response. Since the argument is logically perfect, objectivists have to reject either the first premise or the second.

---

7. For detailed discussion of categorical reasons, see chapter 11, "Morality and Rationality."

Some challenge premise 1. They deny that objective moral duties must supply us with reasons for action. It may be that some people have no reason to do what morality requires of them. Whether there are objective moral standards is one thing; whether they supply us with reasons to obey them is another. The answer to the first question may be *yes*, even if the answer to the second is a disappointing *no*. If this line of thinking is right, then we will have to abandon the age-old hope of showing that everyone has reason to be moral.[8]

The second strategy stands by premise 1, but rejects premise 2. On such a view, objective moral duties really do provide categorical reasons—and these reasons exist. There are reasons to behave in certain ways, even if such behavior doesn't benefit us or satisfy any of our desires.

To make this reply a success, we must reject the most popular view of reasons. This view says that you have a reason to do something only if doing it will promote self-interest or get you what you care about.

The best way to criticize this popular view is by example. (Recall the discussion in chapter 8, "The Best Argument for Ethical Egoism.") Suppose you are hiking along a cliff path and notice a stranger who is absentmindedly walking from the opposite direction. You see that he's about to take a wrong step and plunge to his death. There is a reason to yell to him and alert him of the danger. And that reason applies to you even if you don't care a bit about the man or about the pats on the back you'll receive when the story gets out. There is something to be said on behalf of your warning him, something that favors it, that justifies it, that makes it a legitimate thing to do. These are just different ways of saying the same thing: there is an excellent reason for you to save that stranger's life, even if doing so won't make you any better off or get you anything you care about.

In short, those who believe that morality is objective must show either that its duties do not have to supply categorical reasons, or argue that such reasons exist. Many philosophers nowadays are developing these strategies, though just as many others (surprise!) are working to ensure that they do not succeed.

---

8. If this line can be adequately defended, then we also have a satisfactory reply to error theorists. They claim that moral thinking assumes the existence of categorical reasons, but that no such reasons exist. But if morality does not make that assumption, then it may be in good shape even if there are no categorical reasons.

Values Have No Place in a Scientific World

One of the tools that philosophers use when choosing between competing theories is called **Occam's razor,** after the medieval logician William of Occam (1285–1349). Occam's razor tells us never to multiply entities beyond necessity. What this means in practice is simple. When trying to separate fact from fiction, consider something to be real only if you need to assume its existence in order to explain what happens in the world.

Occam's razor explains why we shouldn't believe in such things as ghosts. Anything they might account for—spooky feelings in graveyards, creaking noises in old houses—can be better explained without assuming that ghosts really exist. Ghosts aren't needed to make sense of what we experience. So Occam's razor tells us that they don't exist.

Many people think that objective values are just like ghosts—creatures of our imagination. These critics deny that we really need to rely on moral features in order to explain the way the world works. Science is our path to understanding the nature of reality. And scientists never have to include moral features in their explanations of molecular structure, biological adaptations, heat transfer—or anything else. Calling something moral or immoral seems like a kind of luxury, one that adds nothing to understanding the ultimate nature of reality.

We can summarize this line of thinking in the *Argument from Science*:

1. We are justified in believing that something exists only if science can verify its existence.
2. Science cannot verify the existence of objective moral values.
3. Therefore, we are not justified in believing that objective values exist.

Note that this argument does not try to refute the existence of objective moral standards. For all it says, there may be some such standards. But that should be cold comfort to the ethical objectivist. For if this argument succeeds, we can never be justified in thinking that any such standards exist.

Ethical objectivists have offered two replies to this argument. The first reply accepts premise 1, but rejects 2. Those who adopt this strategy believe that science is the ultimate test of reality, and also believe that morality can pass the test. Other objectivists are doubtful of that, and so reject premise 1. Let's consider these in turn.

Many objectivists are so impressed with science and its potential for illuminating the nature of our world that they insist that morality be scientifically respectable. Such objectivists must therefore find a place for moral values within a scientific world.

They do this by arguing that moral features are nothing other than ordinary, run-of-the-mill qualities that science can tell us about. We use a different vocabulary to refer to them—we talk of good and evil, right and wrong, rather than neutrinos and quarks and molecules and proteins. But the words we use are not that important. What is important is that, as these thinkers see it, the natural world is the only world there is. So moral features must be part of that world if they are to exist. This kind of view is called **moral naturalism.**

Moral naturalists could claim, for instance, that being morally right is nothing other than maximizing happiness, or that being good is the very same thing as being desired. We can use scientific means to check whether happiness is maximized, or whether people really desire things. On this view, moral features are nothing but a special class of scientific features. There isn't anything mysterious about them. Moral naturalists thus reject premise 2 of the argument, because they think that moral features just are natural (that is, not supernatural) features of our world.

If that is right, then moral values will need to pass the Occam's razor test of reality. Recall that this test tells us that we have reason to believe in things only if they are essential to explaining things. That's why we no longer believe in ghosts (or the tooth fairy or Superman). We have reason to think that physical objects like buildings or apples or planes are real, because their existence best explains why we see and taste and hear what we do.

But are moral features really needed to explain anything? Naturalists say yes. They think, for instance, that Stalin's *evil nature* is what explains his sending millions to their death in prison camps. The *wrongness* of slavery explains why slaves and abolitionists opposed it. The *injustice* of child abuse explains our anger when we learn of it, the child's resentment, and our efforts to protect children from it.

But many are skeptical of such claims. They think, for instance, that we don't need to refer to Stalin's evil nature in order to explain why so many ended up in the Gulag. Instead, we can refer to his beliefs, insecurities, and desires to explain why he undertook such actions. We *could* morally evaluate such things if we like, but that wouldn't be needed to explain why Stalin did what he did. Moral features are wholly optional and unnecessary when trying for the best, most rigorous explanation of why we act as we do and have the experiences we have.

Ethical objectivists who share these doubts about naturalism accept premise 2 of the current argument. They agree that science cannot verify the existence of objective moral values. These thinkers must therefore criticize premise 1, and its claim that science is the ultimate measure of reality.

Their best strategy is to draw our attention to the fact that moral features are **normative features**. Such features are those that tell us how things *ought* to be, or how we *should* behave. They rely on norms: standards of behavior that supply us with ideals or requirements.

The basic idea behind rejecting premise 1 is this. Science tells us the way things really are. Science does not tell us how things ought to be. Science describes; morality prescribes. Science has its limits. It is out of its depth when trying to tell us about our ultimate purpose, the goals we ought to aim for, the standards we should live by. Science can tell us a lot. But it can't tell us everything.

There is some reason to deny that science really does have the final word on *everything*. Consider this:

> (T) A claim is true only if science can verify it.

(T) can't be true. For science cannot verify it. (T) is not a scientific statement. We cannot test its truth by analyzing what we see, hear, taste, feel, or smell. We cannot mathematically test it. There are no lab experiments that will confirm it.

Since (T) is false, it follows that there are some truths that science cannot confirm. Perhaps moral ones are among them.

Now consider this principle, which is very close to premise 1:

> (B) You are justified in believing a claim only if science can verify it.

(B) is also problematic, since science cannot confirm it. Only philosophy can do that. If we take (B) at face value, then by its own lights we cannot be justified in thinking that it is true. So we are not justified in thinking that science is the source of *all* truths.

This line of reply does not prove that objective moral values exist. But if successful, it does show that science cannot have the final say about everything. This means that at least some non-scientific claims are true, and perhaps highly credible. Moral claims may be among them.

21.3 Conclusion

Our discussion of these ten arguments has not revealed a single one that confirms the existence of objective moral values. That was deliberate. I had given over the previous two chapters to the critics of objectivism, and showed how each of the anti-objectivist theories encounters some serious problems.

It's only fair, then, that we devote some time to the many worries that people have about how morality could possibly be objective. I have tried here to outline the ones that are either very popular or very threatening. The most popular ones actually seem easiest to handle. The less well-known arguments strike me as more difficult to rebut.

There is no quick, knockdown argument that will demolish ethical objectivism. Nor is there any short and sweet proof of its truth. I have offered these arguments, and their replies, not in order to create the impression of a victory for either side, but rather to give you a sense of how complicated things can get in this area of philosophy. Those who think that ethical objectivism is obviously false, or just as obviously correct, have simply gotten it wrong. Matters here, as elsewhere in ethics, are too challenging to admit of pat and easy solutions.

21.4 Discussion Questions

1. How might one be an ethical objectivist without being intolerant or dogmatic?
2. What is the best explanation of the existence of widespread disagreement in ethics? Does the existence of disagreement suggest a lack of objective moral truth?
3. How can an ethical objectivist allow for the existence of moral standards that apply only to some cultures but not to others?
4. What are categorical reasons? Do any categorical reasons exist? If not, does this undermine the claim that morality is objective?
5. If ethics is not a science, and moral facts are fundamentally different from scientific ones, would this threaten the objectivity of morality? If so, how?
6. At the end of the day, do you believe that morality is objective? What do you think is the strongest argument in favor of your position?

CHAPTER 22

Is Moral Knowledge Possible?

Five Skeptical Arguments

You're exhausted. I get it. It's been a long haul through a lot of moral philosophy. To send you on your way, I've prepared a short chapter on a central question in metaethics: Can we have any moral knowledge?

To get knowledge in any area is to have, at the least, some beliefs about it that are both true *and* justified. True beliefs aren't enough. They might be the result of guesswork, of relying on untrustworthy sources, or of misinterpreting the evidence. We want beliefs that are not only true, but also well supported (i.e., justified). The problem, says the skeptic, is that we can't have adequate support for our moral beliefs. Even if they are sometimes true—and all the arguments we consider below allow for such a possibility—our moral beliefs are *never* justified. And so moral knowledge is an impossibility.

Here are five influential arguments for **moral skepticism**—the view that we cannot have moral knowledge.

22.1 The Skeptical Argument from Disagreement

For any moral belief you hold, there will be smart and rational people who disagree with you. That seems to spell trouble for the justification of those beliefs, as the *Skeptical Argument from Disagreement* makes clear:

1. If well-informed, rational people persistently disagree about some claim, then we are not justified in believing that claim.
2. Well-informed, rational people persistently disagree about all moral claims.
3. Therefore, we are not justified in believing any moral claims.

This may look like the Argument from Disagreement that we canvased in the previous chapter,[1] but there is a crucial difference. While premise 2 is the same in both arguments, their first premises, and their conclusions, are very different. Last chapter's Argument from Disagreement sought to show that there are no objective moral truths. This argument, by contrast, is silent on that matter. Its purpose is to show that even if there are such truths, we can never be justified in believing them (and so can never know them).

Premise 2 may be too strong—perhaps there are some moral claims that every well-informed and rational person accepts. But let's not make things too easy on ourselves. Let's assume premise 2 is true. (If it's not, then the argument immediately collapses.)

Premise 1, though, is problematic. For if it were true, then we could have no knowledge on any controversial topic. There is disagreement among brilliant, rational people on the question of whether God exists, whether morality is objective, whether we have free will. If premise 1 is true, then none of our views on such subjects is justified.

Perhaps you can live with that. Here's a harder case: some amazingly intelligent and rational thinkers deny that we can know whether there is a world outside of our own thoughts. If the Argument from Disagreement is sound, then you can't know anything about the world outside your thoughts—or even if there is such a world at all.

It's also the case that brilliant people have disagreed about premise 1 itself. Many excellent philosophers have denied that we must give up our beliefs just because other smart and rational people disagree on a given matter. Since that is so, it follows that even if premise 1 is true, we are not justified in believing it! But if we aren't justified in believing it, then we shouldn't be convinced by it, and should *not* accept any argument—including the Skeptical Argument from Disagreement—that includes it.

22.2 Certainty

Many people think that moral knowledge is impossible because we cannot be certain of any moral claim. Their thinking can be expressed by means of the *No Certainty Argument*:

1. You know that a claim is true only if you are certain that it's true.
2. You can't be certain that any moral claim is true.
3. Therefore, moral knowledge is impossible.

---

1. See chapter 21, "Moral Disagreement Undermines Moral Objectivity."

Before assessing this argument, we need to make an important distinction between *feeling* certain and *being* certain. To feel certain is to be extremely confident, very, very sure that your belief is true. But people feel certain of all sorts of claims that turn out to be false. By contrast, to be certain is to have a belief that cannot be false and cannot rationally be doubted. This argument focuses in both premises on *being* certain.

Premise 2 is controversial. If it's false, then the argument is of course unsound. But let's suppose it's true and see what happens. When we shift our focus to premise 1, we can see right away that it sets a very high bar for knowledge. Indeed, the bar is so high that almost no belief can meet it. I feel sure that I know my name and my eye color. I also am very confident that I have two hands, am married, and live in Wisconsin. But I can't *be* certain of any of these things. My belief in each could be false. And I might be able to rationally doubt these claims. I can't decisively refute the possibility that I am floating in the Matrix, for instance, deceived about all of these things. I could also be deceived about whether there is even a world outside of my own thoughts, or a world that has existed for longer than the last five seconds. If knowledge requires certainty, as premise 1 asserts, then we can know almost nothing at all. Importantly, we could not even know that premise 1 is true! After all, we cannot be certain of its truth, and most philosophers have rationally doubted it, precisely because they believe that we can know such things as our own names and those of our family and friends.

Premise 1 might be true, even if we can't know that it is. But lots of things *might* be true. The question is whether we should believe them. If premise 1 is true, then you shouldn't believe it, since you can't be certain of it. And the truth of premise 1 would entail that you can't know (for instance) that you have a nose, that you are capable of reading, and that you have eaten more than one meal in your life. Given these very implausible results, we would need really excellent evidence before being justified in believing premise 1. It's not clear what that evidence could be.

22.3 Who's to Say?

When questioned about the morality of a given action, many people reply with another question: Who's to say? And the answer always seems to be: not me. And not you, either. Really, the idea is that *no one* is in a position to say what's moral or immoral. And if that's so, then no one has moral knowledge.

Those who ask this question—*Who's to say?*—are not always seeking an answer. Sometimes they use the question simply to convey their view that moral knowledge is impossible. When used this way, the question doesn't *support* moral skepticism so much as *express* it; asking the question is just a veiled way of asserting that moral knowledge is out of reach. The question is also sometimes used as a way of signaling to others that you are done with the conversation: you utter the question, shrug your shoulders, and move on. In any event, asking a question is not the same thing as making an argument. Still, some who ask this question do seem to be using it as shorthand for something like the following *Argument from Authority*:

1. We have moral knowledge only if we have the authority to determine what is moral or immoral.
2. No one has that authority.
3. Therefore, no one has moral knowledge.

As I understand things, asking *Who's to say?* is really a way of affirming premise 2. But why think that premise 2 is true, and that everyone lacks the relevant authority? There seem to be two ways of supporting the premise.

First, you get to determine what is moral or immoral only if you are what we might call a *designated authority* whose opinions are, by definition, binding on everyone. To see the idea here, think of Supreme Court justices, who are designated legal authorities. Their decisions are the final word on what the law is, and every citizen must obey their rulings. They clearly get to say what's lawful or unlawful. But when it comes to morality, no one is a designated authority; we're all moral equals. While we do have moral leaders among us, none of them has the authority to decide, once and for all, what counts as moral or immoral. We are free to reject those leaders or their advice if we come to doubt their moral wisdom.

All of this is true. But if we interpret authority as designated authority, and accept premise 2, then premise 1 is false. You can have moral knowledge even if you are not a designated moral authority—indeed, even if *no* authority figure has the standing to tell you what to believe. You can know that genocide is immoral, for instance, even if there's no designated moral authority whose views you absolutely have to obey.

A second way that one might have moral authority is by being the *author* of morality, the one whose feelings or decisions *make* things right or wrong. On this interpretation, a moral legislator is the one who gets to say what's right and wrong. But no one writes the moral law—except, perhaps, God. And we're not God. No human being is the author of morality, so no one has the authority to say what morality requires or allows.

Once again, this line of reasoning, even if correct, would have no skeptical implications. Suppose that we interpret authority to mean authorship, and accept premise 2 of the Argument from Authority. No one has the authority to say what's right or wrong, because no one has authored the moral law. In that case, though, premise 1 would be false. We don't have to be the author of a law in order to have knowledge of what it says. I'm not a political official. I don't write the laws around here. But I know a lot of what's legal and illegal. A biologist doesn't author the laws of genetics—rather, she discovers them. Her opinions about genetics don't make those laws true. Still, biologists have a lot of knowledge about how genes work. Likewise, even if we are not the author of the moral rules, we might still have lots of moral knowledge—about the immorality of slavery and rape, for instance, and the goodness of helping the neediest among us.

22.4 Irrelevant Influences

Another familiar way to try to undercut the chance of gaining moral knowledge is by pointing to the origins of our moral beliefs. Suppose, for instance, that you could show that someone holds his moral beliefs just because he accepts whatever his parents tell him, or because his culture takes that view for granted, or because evolutionary pressures have effectively "programmed" him to believe in that way. Learning about such origins should make us suspicious, since these influences are somehow morally irrelevant. We should form our moral beliefs by being sensitive to the moral facts, rather than by being influenced in ways that may have no bearing on the truth. These suspicions form the basis of the *Irrelevant Influences Argument*:

1. If you hold your moral beliefs just because your parents or culture or evolution have influenced you to do so, then your moral beliefs are not justified.
2. Everyone holds their moral beliefs just because of such influences.
3. Therefore, no one's moral beliefs are justified.

And if no one's moral beliefs are justified, then there is no moral knowledge, since knowledge requires beliefs that are not only true but also justified.

The idea behind premise 1 is subtle, but not too complicated. The basic thought is that you'd be extremely *lucky* if, for instance, your parents or your culture turned out to be morally wise. And such luck is incompatible with knowledge. Consider this comparison. Suppose there is a lottery with 10,000 tickets sold. I buy a ticket. And then I believe—really believe, not just hope—that I have the winning ticket. That's irrational, since I have only a 1-in-10,000 chance of being right. Now suppose that there have been 10,000 different cultural traditions. (I don't know how many there actually have been—maybe more, maybe less. But it doesn't really matter for present purposes.) You were born into one of those cultures. If you hold the moral views you do just because your culture has drummed it into you, then you, too, have only a 1-in-10,000 chance of getting it right. That should undermine any confidence you might have in your moral views.[2]

Now suppose, instead, that your moral beliefs have been formed because of evolutionary pressures. Such pressures work to instill traits, habits, and beliefs that are adaptive, thereby improving our chances of spreading our genes to the next generation. You believe, for instance, that it's morally good for parents to protect their children. Maybe you hold this belief just because your instincts have been shaped by evolution. The belief that it is good to protect your kids is adaptive: those who think this way are much likelier than others to actually offer such protection, and so further their genetic legacy. But why think that adaptive moral beliefs are also true? Mightn't they just be *useful*? Indeed, given all of the possible moral views out there, it seems that it would be sheer luck if evolution, which is directed at promoting adaptive behavior, also steers us in the direction of moral truth.

Here is the deep explanation of premise 1's appeal. If our parents, our culture, or evolution (or some combination of them) fully explain why I have the moral beliefs I do, then I don't form my moral beliefs *because they are true*. I am not being responsive to the moral facts that make my beliefs true, but rather just parroting what my parents or culture tell me to believe, or what evolution programs me to think. But then it would be an amazing coincidence if my moral beliefs happened to be correct. And such a coincidence undermines whatever justification I might have for my moral beliefs.

---

2. Interestingly, if morality is nothing but conventional morality—the traditional standards that happen to be accepted by each culture—then this argument immediately collapses, because premise 1 would be false. If gaining moral knowledge is just a matter of knowing what your culture stands for, then you have loads of moral knowledge. This view of morality is known as cultural relativism; see chapter 19 for a discussion of its strengths and weaknesses.

Now what of premise 2? My own view is that it is true a lot of the time, but not always. Some people really are wholly uncritical, just taking on board whatever their parents or culture tells them. But there are also people whose moral views break with tradition, or with their parents. Many of our moral heroes have done this—they speak truth to power, adopting unpopular moral views in the face of long traditions of oppression. And you don't need to be such a hero in order to take a step back from conventional moral wisdom and think critically for yourself about various moral matters. Further, while evolution has surely influenced us to some extent, there is no good reason to think that all of our moral beliefs are the result of such influences.

It's true, of course, that when we challenge conventional morality, or wonder whether an adaptive moral belief is correct, we do so from the perspective of our *other* moral beliefs. And if these beliefs are nothing more than the product of parental, cultural, or evolutionary influences, then the initial worry just resurfaces. But why think that all of our moral beliefs are like this? This is what the defenders of premise 2 have to *show*—they can't just assume that we are unable to escape from such influences when forming our moral beliefs. It seems that we have many counterexamples to premise 2. Abolitionists, for instance, managed to look past the social prejudices of the day and see slavery for what it truly is—a moral evil. We can readily see that rape is another such evil, even though it might be evolutionarily adaptive, since it might maximize the chance that a man will spread his genes to the next generation.

The bottom line is that if we can show that our moral beliefs are due entirely to parental, cultural, or evolutionary influences, and not at all to attentive reflection, then we do indeed have reason to doubt whether those beliefs amount to knowledge. But so long as many of our moral beliefs have different origins—and, in particular, reveal a sensitivity to the moral facts, such as the evils of slavery and rape—then moral knowledge may be possible after all.

22.5 Hume's Argument

One of the toughest skeptical challenge is centuries old, first offered by David Hume. Let's call it *Hume's Argument*,[3] in his honor:

1. We can know only two sorts of claims: conceptual truths or empirical truths.
2. Moral claims are not conceptual truths.

---

3. The original argument appears in his *Treatise on Human Nature* (1739), Book III, part 1.

3. Moral claims are not empirical truths.
4. Therefore, we can have no moral knowledge.

A **conceptual truth** is one that has four key features. First, it is what philosophers call a **necessary truth**—one that cannot be false. Second, it is true just in virtue of its meaning. Because of this second feature, it also has a third: it can be known just by understanding it. And a fourth: anyone who sincerely denies it doesn't understand it. For if they did understand what the claim meant, they'd see that it is true. Here are some conceptual truths: Squares have four sides; all integers are even or odd; bachelors are unmarried males. There are no scenarios in which these claims turn out to be false. Further, they are true in virtue of the meaning of the concepts they contain. The meanings of the concepts "square," "four," "bachelor," "unmarried," and so forth are what make these claims true. Once you understand those meanings, you can know that the claim is true—you can close your eyes to the world, just think, and know that they are true. And if you sincerely denied these claims, that would show that you don't really know what a square or an integer or a bachelor is.

Empirical truths are not like this. They are known only by relying on evidence from our five senses. Here are some empirical truths: I live in a house that was built in 1940; it was raining in London on June 25, 2007; the Pacific Ocean is larger than the Atlantic; David Hume never married.

Hume thought that every claim we can know must fit into one of these two categories. If, as he thought, moral claims are neither conceptual nor empirical truths, then we can have no moral knowledge.

Why aren't moral claims conceptual truths? Because for any moral claim, we can completely understand it and still wonder whether it is true. That doesn't happen when we ask whether bachelors are unmarried or whether squares have four sides. Anyone who really understands those questions already knows the answer.

Why aren't moral claims empirical truths? Because we don't discover them by means of our senses. No amount of scientific probing in the world will reveal any moral features in it. If you witness a murder or a broken promise you will notice many things. But you can't see its *wrongness*.

Hume had a supporting reason for thinking that moral knowledge could not be empirical. Empirical knowledge tells us how to describe the world. And when we describe the world, we talk about what *is* the case. But morality speaks of what *ought to be* the case. How can we get from descriptions to prescriptions? How does knowing how the world actually works enable us to learn how it ought to work? Hume thought that there was no answer to this question. If he is right, there is a gap between what is and what ought to be, a gap that can never be crossed.

Since there are three premises to Hume's argument, a defender of moral knowledge could take aim at any one of them. Moral naturalists, whom we encountered in the previous chapter, reject premise 3. They think that moral features are just a subset of empirically discoverable features of the world. According to naturalists, we use scientific tools and methods to figure out what's morally right and wrong.

A handful of philosophers have instead taken aim at premise 2, asserting that some moral claims are conceptual truths. But most thinkers have found this puzzling. If something is a conceptual truth, then anyone who sincerely denies it doesn't really understand what they are talking about. For instance, if I sincerely deny that squares have four sides, then I don't really know what a square is. But recall the error theorists we discussed in chapter 20. They sincerely deny all moral claims. And yet they certainly seem to know what morality is about—they appear to understand what it is that they are rejecting, even if, as many hope, their position is mistaken.

The remaining possibility is to reject premise 1, and to argue that there are truths that are neither conceptual nor empirical. There may be such truths. The most promising candidates, I suspect, are philosophical claims, of the sort that we have been considering throughout this book. Think of a philosophical claim you really like, or instead strongly disagree with: that the impossibility of doing something means you aren't obligated to do it; that God doesn't author the moral law; that ethical objectivism supports humility, rather than dogmatism. These don't seem to be claims that are verified by our senses. But neither do they seem to be conceptual truths. And yet it looks like we are able to rationally assess such claims, offering arguments pro and con, coming to considered views that might not only be true but also justified.

Indeed, premise 1 is itself a philosophical claim, and it seems to be neither a conceptual truth nor an empirical one. Unlike a genuine conceptual truth, such as the claim that all squares have four sides, it is not true just in virtue of its meaning. You can fully understand premise 1 while sensibly denying it. Nor is that premise verified by empirical evidence—no amount of scientific testing is going to confirm it. It turns out, then, that if premise 1 is true, we cannot know that it is. That doesn't show that premise 1 is false. But it does make that premise ineligible to serve in any argument designed to establish a skeptical conclusion.

Most moral claims are like (other) philosophical claims in being neither empirical truths nor conceptual ones. The work you've done throughout this book probably has a very different feel from your efforts in science classes and labs. And few, if any, of the hundreds of moral claims that have appeared in this book are likely to be conceptual truths. And yet we've been able to go back and forth in a pretty rigorous way, developing arguments, critically assessing them, and coming to at least some views that seem backed by good reasons. Even if our moral beliefs are not empirical or conceptual truths, then, some of them may be justified after all. If they are, then the first premise of Hume's Argument is mistaken, and the possibility that we do indeed have moral knowledge—perhaps a good deal of it—remains a live one.

22.6 Conclusion

The upshot of this brief chapter is that the skeptical arguments we've considered here are not as powerful as many have thought. But criticizing these arguments is one thing; actually showing how moral knowledge is possible is another. So there's a lot more work that needs to get done. For those who are convinced that we have some moral knowledge, your task is to show how we can acquire it. For the doubters, your task is either to offer adequate replies to the criticisms I've leveled, or to provide a sixth skeptical argument that can withstand scrutiny. Though we can't undertake this further work here, we can draw an important lesson from this discussion—namely, that the skeptical position should not be regarded as the default view. Moral skepticism faces a variety of serious challenges that must be met before it could earn our trust.

GLOSSARY

Absolute: Never permissibly broken; violating an absolute moral rule is always wrong.

Act consequentialism: The normative ethical theory that says that an act is morally right just because it produces the best actual or expected results.

Act utilitarianism: The version of act consequentialism that says that only well-being is intrinsically valuable, and so says that an act is morally right just because it maximizes overall well-being.

Ad hominem attack: An attempt to undermine the position of an opponent by criticizing his motives or character.

Agnostics: Those who suspend judgment on the question of whether God exists.

Altruism: The direct care and concern to improve the well-being of someone other than yourself.

Ambiguous: Having two or more meanings.

Amoralists: Those who do not care about living up to the moral views they sincerely hold.

Argument: Any chain of thought in which premises are enlisted in support of a particular conclusion.

Atheism: The belief that God does not exist.

Autonomy: The capacity to determine for yourself the principles that you will live by. It can also refer to your ability to live according to your own plan of life.

Begging the question: Arguing on the basis of a reason that will appeal only to people who already accept the argument's conclusion.

Categorical imperative: A command of reason that requires a person's obedience regardless of whether such obedience gets him anything he wants.

Categorical reason: A reason to do something that applies to a person regardless of her desires.

Conceptual truth: A true claim that can be known just by understanding it. Such a claim is true just by virtue of the concepts it contains—that's why understanding it enables one to know it. An example: bachelors are unmarried men.

Consent, tacit: See *tacit consent*.

Consequentialism: A family of normative ethical theories that share the idea that the morality of actions, policies, motives, or rules depends on their producing the best actual or expected results. See also: *act consequentialism, rule consequentialism, act utilitarianism*.

Continent: Doing the right thing while suppressing desires that tempt one away from doing one's duty.

Contractarianism: See *social contract theory*.

Cultural relativism: The view that an act is morally right just because it is allowed by the guiding ideals of the society in which it is performed, and immoral just because it is forbidden by those ideals.

Decision procedure: Any method designed to guide us in successfully deliberating about what to do.

Deist: One who believes that God exists, created the universe, and then refrained from becoming involved in human affairs.

Desire satisfaction theory: A theory of human well-being that claims that the satisfaction of your actual or informed desires is necessary and sufficient to improve your welfare.

Divine command theory: The view that an act is morally required just because it is commanded by God, and immoral just because God forbids it.

Doctrine of Doing and Allowing (DDA): The view that it is always morally worse to do harm than to allow that same harm to occur.

Doctrine of Double Effect (DDE): The view that if your goal is worthwhile, you are sometimes permitted to act in ways that foreseeably cause certain harms, though you must never intend to cause those harms.

Dogmatism: The trait of being closed-minded and unreasonably confident of the truth of one's views.

Empathy-altruism hypothesis: The hypothesis that the existence of empathy can prompt altruistic motivation. A corollary is that the greater one's empathic response to someone else, the likelier it is that one will be altruistically motivated to offer help.

Empirical truth: A true claim that can be known only by means of evidence gained through the senses. Understanding what such a claim says is not enough to know whether it is true—you have to check the claim "against the world" to test it. An example: the Empire State Building is 1,453 feet tall.

Error theory: The metaethical view that there are no moral features in this world; no moral judgments are true; our sincere moral judgments try, and always fail, to describe the moral features of things; and there is no moral knowledge.

Ethical egoism: The normative ethical theory that says that actions are morally right just because they maximize self-interest.

Ethical objectivism: The view that there is at least one objective moral standard.

Ethical particularism: The view that there are neither any absolute nor any prima facie moral rules. According to ethical particularism, no feature of the world is always morally relevant, and none is always morally decisive.

Ethical pluralism: The view that there are at least two, and possibly more, fundamental moral rules.

Ethical relativism: The view that correct moral standards are relative to individual or cultural commitments. Ethical relativism can take two forms: cultural relativism or ethical subjectivism.

Ethical subjectivism: The view that an act is morally right just because (a) I approve of it or (b) my commitments allow it, and that an action is wrong just because (a) I disapprove of it or (b) my commitments forbid it.

Eudaimonia: The state of living well; happiness, or flourishing.

Evaluative beliefs: Beliefs that evaluate something, and so assess it as good or bad, virtuous or vicious, and so on.

Exemplar, moral: See *moral exemplar*.

Exemplary punishment: Punishment designed to make an example of the one who is punished.

Expressivism: The version of moral nihilism that denies that there are any moral features in this world; claims that there is nothing for moral judgments to be true of; and analyzes moral judgments as expressions of emotions, orders, or commitments, none of which are the sorts of things that can be true or false.

Fact-value distinction: The view that there is a sharp difference between facts and values; value claims are not factual, and so cannot be true.

Feminist ethics: A family of theories that emphasize the moral equality of women, and the importance of attending to women's experience in the development of moral ideas and ideals.

Fidelity: Being faithful to one's word; keeping one's promises.

Fitness: The level of an organism's ability to survive and reproduce.

Free-rider problem: A situation in which people are able to obtain a share of some common good without contributing to it. In such situations, it appears to be rational (if your withholding can go unnoticed) to refrain from contributing, thus enjoying the good at no expense to yourself. The problem is that if enough people act rationally, then there will not be enough resources to produce the relevant good, thus harming everyone.

Free will: To have a will that is free is to be capable of making decisions that are genuinely your own, decisions that you author, ones that you originate and are responsible for.

Fundamental: A moral rule is fundamental just in case its justification does not depend on any more general or more basic moral rule.

Golden rule: The normative ethical principle that says that your treatment of others is morally acceptable if and only if you would be willing to be treated in exactly the same way.

Good will: The ability to reliably determine what your duty is, and a steady commitment to do your duty for its own sake.

Hedonism: The view that pleasure is the only thing that is intrinsically valuable, and pain (or unhappiness) is the only thing that is intrinsically bad.

Hypothetical imperative: A command of reason that requires a person to take the needed means to getting what she wants.

Iconoclasts: People whose views differ radically from the conventional wisdom of their society.

Ideal observers: Those (probably imaginary) people who are fully informed, perfectly rational, and otherwise perfectly suited to determine the content of morality.

Imperative, categorical: See *categorical imperative.*

Imperative, hypothetical: See *hypothetical imperative.*

Individual relativism: See *ethical subjectivism.*

Innate: Congenital. Innate traits are inborn traits, as opposed to traits that are acquired after birth.

Instrumental goods: Those things whose value consists in the fact that they help to bring about other good things. Examples include vaccinations, mothballs, and money.

Intrinsic values: Those things that are good in and of themselves, considered entirely apart from any good results they may cause. It is controversial which things are intrinsically valuable, but happiness, desire satisfaction, virtue, and knowledge are frequently mentioned candidates.

Lex talionis: The law of retaliation, the principle that says that a wrongdoer deserves to be treated just as he treated his victim.

Logical validity: The feature of an argument that indicates that its premises logically support its conclusion. Specifically, an argument is logically valid just because its conclusion must be true if its premises are all true. Another way to put this: logically valid arguments are those in which it is impossible for all premises to be true while the conclusion is false.

Maxim: A principle of action that you give to yourself. It contains your intended action and the reason you are doing it.

Metaethics: The area of ethical theory that asks about the status of normative ethical claims. It asks, for instance, about whether such claims can be true and, if so, whether personal, cultural, or divine opinion makes them true (or none of the above). It also considers issues about how to gain moral knowledge (if we can), and whether moral requirements give us reasons to obey them.

Metaphysics: The branch of philosophy that discusses the nature of reality, what exists, and what does not exist.

Moral absolutism: The view that absolute moral rules exist.

Moral agent: One who can guide his or her behavior by means of moral reasoning, and so someone who is fit for praise or blame.

Moral community: The set of those beings whose interests are intrinsically important. Membership signifies that you are owed respect, that you have moral rights, and that others owe you moral duties for your own sake.

Moral exemplar: Someone of outstanding moral character; someone who can serve as a proper moral role model.

Moral luck: A case in which the morality of an action or a decision depends on factors outside of our control.

Moral naturalism: The view that moral features are natural (i.e., not supernatural) features, whose existence can be confirmed by means of the natural sciences.

Moral nihilism: The form of moral skepticism that says that the world contains no moral features, and so there is nothing for moral claims to be true of. Its two major forms are the error theory and expressivism.

Moral skepticism: The view that there are no objective moral standards. Moral skepticism is also sometimes taken to refer to the view that we can have no moral knowledge.

Moral worth: The praiseworthy feature of an action that fulfills one's moral duty.

Natural law theory: The normative ethical view that says that actions are right if and only if they are natural, and wrong if and only if they are unnatural; people are good to the extent that they fulfill their true nature, bad insofar as they do not.

Necessary truth: A claim that cannot be false.

Non-maleficence: Not harming others.

Norm: A standard of evaluation. Norms tell us how we should or ought to behave. They represent a measure that we are to live up to.

Normative ethics: The area of ethical theory focused on identifying which kinds of actions are right and wrong, examining the plausibility of various moral rules, and determining which character traits qualify as virtues and which as vices.

Normative features: Those features that tell us how things ought to be, or how we should behave. They rely on norms to do this.

Objective moral standards: Those moral requirements that apply to people regardless of their opinions about such duties, and independently of whether fulfilling such duties will satisfy any of their desires.

Objective theory of human welfare: There are many such theories, all sharing a common feature—they claim that certain things are good for people whether or not they believe them to be and whether or not such things satisfy a person's actual or informed desires.

Occam's razor: The instruction never to multiply entities beyond necessity. In the context of selecting from among competing theories, it tells us to choose that theory that can explain as much as any other, while making the fewest assumptions.

Omniscient: All-knowing.

Optimific: Producing the best possible results.

Optimific social rule: A rule whose general acceptance within a society would yield better results than any other such rule.

Paternalism: The policy of treating mature people as if they were children. More specifically, it is a policy of limiting someone's liberty, against his will, for his own good.

Premise: Any reason that is used within an argument to support a conclusion.

Prima facie duty: A permanent, excellent, but non-absolute reason to do (or refrain from) a certain type of action.

Principle of humanity: Kant's thesis that one must always treat a human being (oneself included) as an end, and never as a mere means.

Principle of universalizability: Kant's thesis that an act is morally acceptable if, and only if, its maxim is universalizable.

Principle of utility: The ultimate utilitarian moral standard, which says that an action is morally right if and only if it does more to improve overall well-being than any other action you could have performed in the circumstances.

Prisoner's dilemma: A situation in which everyone involved would be better off by reducing his or her pursuit of self-interest.

Proceduralism: The view that says that we must follow a certain procedure in order to determine which actions are morally right, or which moral claims are true.

Psychological egoism: The view that all human actions are motivated by self-interest and that altruism is impossible.

Punishment, exemplary: See *exemplary punishment*.

Punishment, vicarious: See *vicarious punishment*.

Relativism, cultural: See *cultural relativism*.

Relativism, individual: See *ethical subjectivism*.

Rule consequentialism: The normative ethical theory that says that actions are morally right just because they would be required by an optimific social rule.

Self-evident: A claim is self-evident just in case (1) it is true and (2) adequately understanding it is enough to make you justified in believing it. The best candidates for self-evident claims are conceptual truths.

Self-regarding actions: Actions that affect only oneself.

Slippery slope argument: A utilitarian line of reasoning that advises against certain social innovations by predicting that allowing them will have very bad results whose badness will go unnoticed in the future.

Social contract theory: A view in political philosophy that says that governmental power is legitimate if and only if it would be accepted by free, equal, and rational people intent on selecting principles of cooperative living. Also, a view in normative ethical theory that says that actions are morally right if and only if they are permitted by rules that free, equal, and rational people would agree to live by, on the condition that others obey these rules as well.

Soundness: A special feature of some arguments. Sound arguments are ones that (1) are logically valid, and (2) contain only true premises. This guarantees the truth of their conclusions.

Standard of rightness: A rule that gives conditions that are both necessary and sufficient for determining whether actions (or other things) are morally right.

State of nature: A situation in which there is no central authority with the exclusive power to enforce its will on others.

Strictly conscientious action: Action motivated by the thought or the desire to do one's duty for its own sake, rather than from any ulterior motive.

Supererogation: Praiseworthy actions that are above and beyond the call of duty.

Tacit consent: Agreement that is expressed through silence or inaction.

Theist: One who believes that God exists.

Universalizability: The feature of a maxim that indicates that every rational person can consistently act on it. Here is the three-part test for a maxim's universalizability: (1) carefully frame the maxim; (2) imagine a world in which everyone shares and acts on that maxim; (3) determine whether the goal within the maxim can be achieved in such a world. If so, the maxim is universalizable. If not, it isn't.

Validity: See *logical validity*.

Value theory: The area of ethics concerned with identifying what is valuable in its own right, and explaining the nature of well-being.

Veil of ignorance: An imaginary device that removes all knowledge of one's social, economic, and religious positions; one's personality traits; and other distinguishing features. It is designed to ensure that the important choices of social contractors are made fairly.

Vicarious punishment: The deliberate punishment of innocent victims, designed to deter third parties.

Virtue ethics: A normative ethical theory that says that an action is morally right just because it would be done by a virtuous person acting in character.

REFERENCES

.... ❧ ....

Aquinas, Thomas. *Summa Theologica*. Available in many translations.

Aristotle. *Nicomachean Ethics*. Available in many translations.

Aristotle. *Politics*. Available in many translations.

Batson, C. Daniel. *The Altruism Question: Toward a Social-Psychological Answer* (Hillsdale, N.J.: Erlbaum Publishers, 1991).

Batson, C. Daniel. *Altruism in Humans* (New York: Oxford University Press, 2011).

Bellow, Saul. *Humboldt's Gift* (New York: Viking, 1975).

Bentham, Jeremy. *Introduction to the Principles of Morals and Legislation* (1781). Available from many publishers.

Colfax, Richard. *Evidence Against the Views of the Abolitionists, Consisting of Physical and Moral Proofs, of the Natural Inferiority of the Negroes* (New York: James T. M. Bleakley, 1833).

Dershowitz, Alan. *Why Terrorism Works: Understanding the Threat, Responding to the Challenge* (New Haven, Conn.: Yale University Press, 2003).

Doctorow, E. L. *The March* (New York: Random House, 2004).

Dostoevsky, Fyodor. *The Brothers Karamazov* (1880). Available in many translations.

Feinberg, Joel. "What Is So Special about Mental Illness?" in Joel Feinberg, *Doing and Deserving* (Princeton, N.J.: Princeton University Press, 1970), pp. 272–292.

Fireside, Harvey. *Soviet Psychoprisons* (New York: W. W. Norton, 1982).

Foot, Philippa. *Natural Goodness* (New York: Oxford University Press, 2001).

Fraser, Flora. *Pauline Bonaparte: Venus of Empire* (New York: Alfred A. Knopf, 2009).

Fraser, Suzan. "Turk Kills 14 Year Old Daughter," AP newswire, April 29, 2004.

Gilligan, Carol. *In a Different Voice* (Cambridge, Mass.: Harvard University Press, 1982).

Golding, William. *The Lord of the Flies* (1954). Available from many publishers.

Grayson, William John. *The Hireling and the Slave* (Charleston, S.C.: John Russell, 1855).

Hare, R. M. "What Is Wrong with Slavery," *Philosophy and Public Affairs* 8 (1979): 103–121.

Hari, Johann. "The Two Churchills," *New York Times Book Review* (August 15, 2010), p. 11.

Hobbes, Thomas. *Leviathan* (1651). Available from many publishers.

Hooker, Brad. *Ideal Code, Real World* (New York: Oxford University Press, 2000).

Hornby, Nick. *How to Be Good* (New York: Riverhead Books, 2001).

Hume, David. *A Treatise of Human Nature* (1739). Available from many publishers.

Huxley, Aldous. *Brave New World* (1932). Available from many publishers.

Kant, Immanuel. *Groundwork of the Metaphysics of Morals* (1785). Available in many translations.

Kant, Immanuel. *Observations on the Feeling of the Beautiful and the Sublime* (1764). Available in many translations.

Karr, Mary. *The Liars' Club* (New York: Penguin, 1995).

Kennedy, Kelly. *They Fought for Each Other: The Triumph and Tragedy of the Hardest Hit Unit in Iraq* (New York: St. Martin's Press, 2010).

Kesey, Ken. *One Flew over the Cuckoo's Nest* (New York: Viking Press, 1962).

Kidder, Tracy. *Mountains Beyond Mountains: The Quest of Dr. Paul Farmer, a Man Who Would Cure the World* (New York: Random House, 2003).

Levi, Primo. *The Drowned and the Saved* (New York: Knopf, 1986).

Mill, John Stuart. *On the Subjection of Women* (1869). Available from many publishers.

Mill, John Stuart. *Utilitarianism* (1861). Available from many publishers.

Moore, G. E. *Principia Ethica* (Cambridge, U.K.: Cambridge University Press, 1903).

Nozick, Robert. *Anarchy, State, and Utopia* (New York: Basic Books, 1974).

Plato. *Euthyphro*. Available in many translations.

Plato. *Republic*. Available in many translations.

Rawls, John. *A Theory of Justice* (Cambridge, Mass.: Harvard University Press, 1971).

Reddaway, Peter, and Sidney Bloch. *Soviet Psychiatric Abuse: The Shadow over World Psychiatry* (Boulder, Colo.: Westview Press, 1984).

Ross, W. D. *The Right and the Good* (Oxford, U.K.: Oxford University Press, 1930).

Rousseau, Jean-Jacques. *Emile: On Education* (1762). Available in many translations.

Smart, J. J. C. "Extreme and Restricted Utilitarianism," *Philosophical Quarterly* 6 (1956): 344–354.

Styron, William. *Sophie's Choice* (New York: Random House, 1979).

Toi, Miho, and C. Daniel Batson. "More Evidence that Empathy Is a Source of Altruistic Motivation," *Journal of Personality and Social Psychology* 43 (1982): 281–292.

Waugh, Alexander. *Fathers and Sons* (New York: Doubleday, 2007).

Wisconsin v. *Yoder*, 406 U.S. 205 (1972).

SUGGESTIONS FOR FURTHER READING

············ ❧ ············

Where to Start

Most of the topics covered in these pages are also represented in the companion volume to this book, *The Ethical Life: Fundamental Readings in Ethics and Moral Problems*, 6th ed. (Oxford University Press). That book provides selections of original work by other philosophers. If you want a relatively short collection that ranges over the main issues discussed here, plus a lot of coverage of specific moral problems, such as abortion, the death penalty, and animal rights, then that might be a good place to start.*

An excellent source for the entire range of philosophical issues, not just those in ethics, is the *Stanford Encyclopedia of Philosophy*, a free online resource containing articles written by experts in the field: http://plato.stanford.edu/. The articles are usually pitched to those with little prior knowledge of the topic under discussion.

Three very good anthologies provide fairly accessible survey articles of the major theories in and about ethics. One of these is *A Companion to Ethics* (Blackwell, 1991), edited by Peter Singer. Another is *The Blackwell Guide to Ethical Theory* (Blackwell, 2000), edited by Hugh LaFollette. The last is *The Oxford Handbook of Ethical Theory* (Oxford University Press, 2007), edited by David Copp. *The International Encyclopedia of Ethics* (Wiley, 2013), edited by Hugh LaFollette, is available in most college and university libraries and offers entries on all of the topics covered in this book.

---

* All sources that appear in **boldface** in this section are included in *The Ethical Life*.

Hedonism

Epicurus's works are available in many editions. A reliable and well-priced version is *The Epicurus Reader*, edited by L. Gerson and B. Inwood (Hackett, 1994). His *Letter to Menoeceus*, included in that collection, summarizes the main doctrines of his philosophy. **Robert Nozick's experience machine discussion** can be found in his *Anarchy, State, and Utopia* (Basic Books, 1974), pp. 42–45. **John Stuart Mill's version of hedonism** is presented in chapters 2 and 4 of *Utilitarianism* (many publishers). Jeremy Bentham's version of hedonism can be found in his *Introduction to the Principles of Morals and Legislation* (1781), available from many publishers. Perhaps the most sophisticated contemporary defense of hedonism is offered by Fred Feldman in his very clearly written *Pleasure and the Good Life* (Oxford University Press, 2006). A defense of the view that informed and autonomous happiness is the key to a good life is given by L. W. Sumner in his *Welfare, Happiness, and Ethics* (Oxford University Press, 1995). His book also provides a nice overview of the issues surrounding the nature of the good life.

Getting What You Want

Very few philosophers have defended the view that satisfaction of our actual desires, based as they often are on ignorance, prejudice, and faulty reasoning, serve as the key to a good life. Contemporary philosophers who come close are Mark Murphy, "The Simple Desire-Fulfillment Theory," *Nous* 33 (1999): 247–272, and Simon Keller's accessible and enjoyable "Welfare and the Achievement of Goals," *Philosophical Studies* 121 (2004): 27–41. **Chris Heathwood's "Faring Well and Getting What You Want"** is a very accessible defense of the idea that desire-satisfaction is the key to a good life for human beings.

James Griffin's *Well-Being* (Oxford University Press, 1985), part 1, provides a good discussion of the various difficulties surrounding the desire satisfaction theory, but also offers a qualified defense of the view. The view that the satisfaction of our filtered, more informed desires is the basis of personal welfare is defended by John Rawls, *A Theory of Justice* (Harvard University Press, 1971), pp. 417ff. A lovely critical discussion of the desire view, with lots of examples meant to damage it and to provide indirect support for the author's own more Aristotelian view, can be found in Richard Kraut's *What Is Good and Why?* (Harvard University Press, 2007), chapter 2. An absolutely delightful book, chock full of real-life stories and interesting examples, is Jean Kazez's *The Weight of Things* (Blackwell, 2006). She defends an objective view about well-being in chapters 5 and 6.

Morality and Religion

Plato's *Euthyphro* is available in many translations. At about eleven pages, it's an enjoyable introduction to Plato's early work. Defenses of the divine command theory tend to be fairly complex and difficult. A pretty accessible version is by the late Philip Quinn, in his article on the theory in Hugh LaFollette, ed., *The Blackwell Guide to Ethical Theory* (2000). Robert Adams is another notable defender of the theory. His work is not easy for the beginner, but "A New Divine Command Theory," *Journal of Religious Ethics* 7 (1979): 66–79, might not be a bad place to start. Though it focuses on many other issues as well, *God? A Debate Between a Christian and an Atheist* (Oxford University Press, 2004), written by William Lane Craig (the Christian) and Walter Sinnott-Armstrong (the atheist), also contains some common lines of defense and criticism surrounding the divine command theory. It is written in a very lively style. A critical discussion of the divine command theory that is quite easy to read can be found in Erik Wielenberg's *Value and Virtue in a Godless Universe* (Cambridge University Press, 2005), chapter 2.

Natural Law

The attempt to base morality on human nature can be traced in the West all the way to **Aristotle. His** *Nicomachean Ethics*, especially Books I and II, are the place to start. Medieval philosopher Thomas Aquinas, whose work continues to exercise the largest influence on Roman Catholic moral theology, is the essential source for thinking about developments of natural law over the past 700 years. Aquinas isn't that approachable; you could dip a toe into the water by having a look at **Questions 90–94 of the Prima Secundae of his** *Summa Theologica*. A good book for beginners is *Aquinas: Selected Writings* (Penguin, 1999), edited by Ralph McInerny.

Important contemporary natural lawyers include John Finnis, whose *Natural Law and Natural Rights* (Oxford University Press, 1980) did much to revive this ethical tradition within secular academic circles. A good scholarly history can be found in Knud Haakonssen's *Natural Law and Moral Philosophy: From Grotius to the Scottish Enlightenment* (Cambridge University Press, 1996). Philippa Foot's *Natural Goodness* (Oxford University Press, 2001) is a delightfully written book by a very important moral philosopher.

Psychological Egoism

Though it is nowadays the subject of some debate among scholars, it seems that Thomas Hobbes committed himself to psychological egoism in several passages of his masterpiece, *Leviathan*, available from many publishers. Joseph Butler, an eighteenth-century bishop, produced criticisms of psychological egoism that many still regard as decisive. See his *Fifteen Sermons Preached at the Rolls Chapel*, the relevant portions of which are presented in *Five Sermons* (Hackett, 1983), edited by Stephen Darwall. David Hume, a master stylist himself, also criticized psychological egoism in appendix 2 of his *Enquiry Concerning the Principles of Morals*, available from many publishers.

A very clear, approachable article that explains the motivations and problems of psychological egoism is Joel Feinberg's "Psychological Egoism," in Feinberg and Shafer-Landau, eds., *Reason and Responsibility* (Cengage, many editions). Empirical work on psychological egoism is given a careful review by C. D. Batson, *The Altruism Question: Toward a Social-Psychological Answer* (Erlbaum, 1991). Elliot Sober and David Sloan Wilson provide a scientifically well informed and philosophically sophisticated approach to the merits of psychological egoism in their *Unto Others: The Evolution and Psychology of Unselfish Behavior* (Harvard University Press, 1999).

Ethical Egoism

What I have called "The Best Argument for Ethical Egoism" can be pieced together from claims made by **Thomas Hobbes in his *Leviathan***. The claim that we have reason to do only what will serve self-interest is defended by David Gauthier in his important (but difficult) book *Morals by Agreement* (Oxford University Press, 1986), chapter 2. A crystal-clear historical survey of this thesis about reasons is given in Robert Shaver's *Rational Egoism* (Cambridge University Press, 1999).

Ayn Rand has defended ethical egoism in many of her books. An accessible and short version of her influential views can be found in her article "The Ethics of Emergencies," reprinted in her collection *The Virtue of Selfishness* (Penguin, 1963).

Lester Hunt defends the view that ethical egoism will not require us to violate the rules of conventional morality in his "Flourishing Egoism," *Social Philosophy and Policy* 16 (1999): 72–95. Gregory Kavka's "The Reconciliation Project" is a terrific exploration of how far self-interest and conventional morality can be reconciled. His view is a bit less optimistic than Hunt's, but only a bit. It can be found in David Zimmerman and David Copp, *Morality, Reason, and Truth* (Rowman and Allanheld, 1984), pp. 279–319.

Consequentialism

John Stuart Mill's *Utilitarianism* is the place to start. It is short and elegant; many editions are available. Perhaps the greatest utilitarian treatise ever written is Henry Sidgwick's *The Methods of Ethics* (1907; available from many publishers). Sidgwick's writing style does not endear him to the reader, however—especially the introductory reader. R. M. Hare's writing style, by contrast, is clean and elegant; his sophisticated defense of utilitarianism can be found in his *Moral Thinking* (Oxford University Press, 1981).

A very influential defense of act utilitarianism and critique of rule utilitarianism is given in J. J. C. Smart, "Extreme and Restricted Utilitarianism," *Philosophical Quarterly* 6 (1956): 344–354. A terrific book that set the terms of the debate for the next generation of moral philosophers is one that Smart wrote with Bernard Williams, *Utilitarianism: For and Against* (Cambridge University Press, 1973). Brad Hooker defends rule consequentialism in a clear and accessible way in his contribution to Hugh LaFollette's *The Blackwell Guide to Ethical Theory* (Blackwell, 2000), and in his book *Ideal Code, Real World* (Oxford University Press, 2000).

Kantian Ethics

Kant's writing is not at all easy to work through. The most accessible (or rather, least inaccessible) of his works is also the shortest: *The Ground-work of the Metaphysics of Morals*. It comes in at a bit under sixty pages; parts 1 and 2 (there are three parts in all) can occasionally be read with pleasure and ready comprehension. Paul Guyer's *Kant's Groundwork of the Metaphysics of Morals: A Reader's Guide* (Continuum, 2007) is a helpful book to have by one's side when reading this classic text.

A number of fine philosophers have written engaging essays that interpret and apply Kant's moral philosophy and demonstrate its contemporary relevance. You might try Barbara Herman's *The Practice of Moral Judgment* (Harvard University Press, 1993) and *Moral Literacy* (Harvard University Press, 2008), Thomas E. Hill Jr.'s *Autonomy and Self-Respect* (Cambridge University Press, 1991) and *Dignity and Practical Reason* (Cambridge University Press, 1992), Christine Korsgaard's *Creating the*

Kingdom of Ends (Cambridge, 1996), or Onora O'Neill's *Constructions of Reason* (Cambridge University Press, 1990).

Social Contract Theory

Thomas Hobbes's *Leviathan* is the place to start. For those with only a relatively short amount of time on their hands, go directly to **chapters 13–15**, and then keep reading as time permits. John Locke's *Second Treatise of Government* and Jean-Jacques Rousseau's *The Social Contract* (both available in many editions) are also important classics in this tradition.

The Hobbesian approach to morality is given an important and sophisticated update by David Gauthier, in his *Morals by Agreement* (Oxford University Press, 1986). Gregory Kavka's *Hobbesian Moral and Political Theory* (Princeton University Press, 1986) is wonderful both as commentary and as good, clear-headed philosophy.

John Rawls's *A Theory of Justice* (Harvard University Press, 1971; rev. ed. 1999) was recognized as a masterpiece upon its publication. A shorter presentation of his central ideas can be found in *Justice as Fairness: A Restatement* (Harvard University Press, 2001, 2nd ed.). Rawls's theory is, as its title suggests, a theory of justice rather than a theory about the whole of morality. Still, its influence in ethics, as well as in social and political philosophy, would be difficult to overstate.

A nice collection of excerpts and essays from social contract theorists is offered by Stephen Darwall, ed., *Contractarianism/Contractualism* (Blackwell, 2002).

Ethical Pluralism

A nice collection of articles, some in defense of absolutism and others critical of it, can be found in Joram Haber, ed., *Absolutism and Its Critics* (Rowman and Littlefield, 1994). An unusual introduction to ethics, one that contains a number of pieces that focus on the Doctrine of Double Effect and the Doctrine of Doing and Allowing, is *Ethics: Problems and Principles* (Wadsworth, 1992), edited by John Martin Fischer and Mark Ravizza.

A fascinating piece that renewed interest in the DDE and DDA is **Philippa Foot's "The Problem of Abortion and the Doctrine of the Double Effect,"** *Oxford Review* 5 (1967): 5–15. Foot introduced the now-famous trolley problem to the philosophy literature, as well as numerous other examples that have stimulated philosophical discussion for the past several decades. See also Judith Jarvis Thomson's articles "The Trolley Problem" and "Killing,

Letting Die, and the Trolley Problem," both reprinted in her marvelous collection *Rights, Restitution, and Risk* (Harvard University Press, 1986).

W. D. Ross presents his ethic of prima facie duties in **chapter 2 of *The Right and the Good*** (Oxford University Press, 1930). Jonathan Dancy put particularism on the map with a series of articles in the 1980s; his book *Ethics Without Principles* (Oxford University Press, 2004) offers his latest views on the matter.

Virtue Ethics

Study of virtue ethics must begin with **Aristotle's *Nicomachean Ethics***. Many good translations are available. *The Blackwell Guide to Aristotle's* Nicomachean Ethics (Blackwell, 2006), edited by Richard Kraut, is highly recommended. It includes instructive articles on many important aspects of Aristotle's ethical thought by a who's who of leading scholars.

The best short overview of virtue ethics that I have read is by Julia Annas, in her contribution to David Copp's *The Oxford Handbook of Ethical Theory* (Oxford University Press, 2007). Two excellent collections on virtue ethics are Stephen Darwall, ed., *Virtue Ethics* (Blackwell, 2002), and Michael Slote and Roger Crisp, eds., *Virtue Ethics* (Oxford University Press, 1997).

Alasdair MacIntyre's much-discussed *After Virtue* (University of Notre Dame Press, 1981) rekindled interest in this tradition after a long period of dormancy in the United States and Britain. Other important recent works in virtue ethics include Rosalind Hursthouse's *On Virtue Ethics* (Oxford University Press, 2000), Michael Slote's *Morals from Motives* (Oxford University Press, 2003), and Christine Swanton's *Virtue Ethics: A Pluralistic View* (Oxford University Press, 2005). Martha Nussbaum is a wonderful writer and has done a lot of work on Aristotle and ethics. One of her most important papers defends Aristotle, and virtue ethics, from the charge of relativism. See her "Non-Relative Virtues: An Aristotelian Approach," *Midwest Studies in Philosophy* 13 (1988): 32–53.

The Ethics of Feminism

A good place to start is **Hilde Lindemann's *An Invitation to Feminist Ethics*** (McGraw-Hill, 2006), written with non-philosophers and beginning students in mind. Its **first chapter** provides a nice, brief overview of feminist ethics, while chapter 4 offers a succinct review of feminist criticisms of utilitarianism, Kantianism, and contractarianism. But the entire book is worth a read.

Those with an interest in the ethics of care should start with Carol Gilligan's fascinating *In a Different Voice* (Harvard University Press, 1982) and proceed to Nel Nodding's *Caring: A Feminine Approach to Ethics and Moral Education* (University of California Press, 1984). Two recent studies by important philosophers are Michael Slote's *The Ethics of Care and Empathy* (Routledge, 2007) and Virginia Held's *The Ethics of Care: Personal, Political, Global* (Oxford University Press, 2007). Those who want a much briefer, but still substantial treatment of the subject, would do well to have a look at Held's "The Ethics of Care," in *The Oxford Handbook of Ethical Theory* (Oxford University Press, 2007), edited by David Copp.

Helpful overviews of the huge range of work in feminist ethics include Alison Jaggar's "Feminist Ethics: Projects, Problems, Prospects," in Claudia Card's collection *Feminist Ethics* (University Press of Kansas, 1991), pp. 78–103. Another nice overview, titled "Feminist Ethics," written by Rosemarie Tong and Nancy Williams, appears online in the *Stanford Encyclopedia of Philosophy*.

For a taste of the many moral issues that receive fresh light when seen from a feminist perspective, you might try *Feminist Philosophies* (Prentice Hall, 1992), edited by Janet Kourany, James Sterba, and Rosemary Tong. Cheshire Calhoun's collection, *Setting the Moral Compass: Essays by Women Philosophers* (Oxford University Press, 2004) includes essays by a roster of outstanding philosophers writing on issues in and around feminist philosophy.

The Status of Morality

Most of the work done in metaethics is not that accessible for beginning students. I have written a very elementary introduction to metaethics, titled *Whatever Happened to Good and Evil?* (Oxford University Press, 2004), designed for those with no prior philosophy knowledge. Robert Audi's *Moral Value and Human Diversity* (Oxford University Press, 2007) is also pitched to an introductory audience. For a more advanced treatment, Mark van Roojen's *Metaethics: A Contemporary Introduction* (Routledge, 2015) is a valuable resource.

For a wide-ranging collection containing many classic and contemporary writings on the subject, along with a dozen substantial introductory essays designed with the student reader in mind, see Terence Cuneo and Russ Shafer-Landau, eds., *Foundations of Ethics: An Anthology* (Blackwell, 2006).

INDEX

.... 🐀 ....

I–1